BEYOND DEATH AND EXILE

BEYOND DEATH AND EXILE

THE SPANISH REPUBLICANS IN FRANCE, 1939–1955

LOUIS STEIN

HARVARD UNIVERSITY PRESS
Cambridge, Massachusetts
and
London, England
1979

Library of Congress Cataloging in Publication Data

Stein, Louis, 1917–
  Beyond death and exile.

  Bibliography: p.
  Includes index.
  1. Spain—History—Civil War, 1936–1939—Refugees.
2. Refugees, Political—Spain. 3. Refugees, Political
—France. 4. Spain—Politics and government—1939–
1975. 5. France—History—20th century. I. Title.
DP269.8.R3S73   325′.21′0946   79–12797
ISBN 0–674–06888–2

To Mariano Puzo

ACKNOWLEDGMENTS

I wish to acknowledge my great debt to William R. Keylor and Nancy L. Roelker of the Department of History of Boston University for their inspiration, advice, and criticism in the writing of this book. My thanks go also to Sidney A. Burrell, Thomas Glick, and Fred M. Leventhal of Boston University for their discerning reading of the manuscript.

During my work on this book, I received tremendous assistance and encouragement from many people in the United States and France. In particular, I am indebted to Jeanne Place, director of the Social Service Bureau for Refugees in Perpignan, for providing background on and contact with Spanish refugees, and to Nancy Macdonald, director of the Spanish Refugee Aid, for sharing her incomparable knowledge of the Spanish exiles and for her support throughout the project. Jordi Planes, director of the Foundation for the Study of the Causes and Consequences of the Spanish Civil War, was lavish with his advice and counsel and generous with the use of the great resources of his institution. David Wingeate Pike of the American College in Paris gave unstintingly of his profound knowledge of the era. At the departmental archives in Perpignan I had the good fortune to work closely with two extraordinary *fonctionnaires,* Jules Lagarde and Claudine Delos. I am grateful to many friends who helped in numerous ways: Silvie Larrimore, Antony Esposito, Marie Thérèse Le Normand, Margaret Thompson, Lawrence Metzger, Roni Grad, David Eberly, and Leslie Ortiz. Peter McPhee deserves special mention for his careful and perceptive reading of the manuscript, as does Robert G. Colodny.

I would like to thank Editorial Planeta, Barcelona, for permission to reprint illustrations from Eduardo Pons Prades, *Repúblicanos españoles en la Segunda Guerra Mundial;* Ruedo Ibérico, Paris, for permission to reprint illustrations from Antonio Vilanova, *Los olvidados: Los exilados españoles en la Segunda Guerra Mundial;* Pierre Izard, of Argelès-sur-mer, for permission to use his photographs of the Spanish exodus into France; and Ediciones Era, Mexico City, for allowing me to quote from Leon Felipe's poem "Alli no hay nadie ya," published originally in Dario Puccini, ed., *Romancero de la resistencia española.*

This book has been dedicated to the late Mariano Puzo, who fought for the Spanish republic, for the French Resistance, and in the postwar guerrilla campaign in Spain. I would like to express my deep gratitude to all the Spanish exiles I met and interviewed in Perpignan and Toulouse. And to my wife, Edith, I say: you have lived it all with me, seen it all happen. I am grateful.

CONTENTS

BEYOND DEATH AND EXILE

INTRODUCTION

I N 1936 the Second Spanish Republic was suddenly confronted with a powerful counter-revolutionary attack from an Iberian variant of fascism. The Spanish people chose to resist and the country became the battleground for a savage civil war. Spain became the focus of international attention for two and one-half years until the nationalist forces of General Francisco Franco triumphed over the republic.[1] The events leading to this crisis were rooted in the long struggle of the Spanish people for freedom, but the immediate cause was the creation of the Second Spanish Republic on April 14, 1931. This republic was intended to carry out "not a Socialist Revolution, but a long overdue Jacobin one," which would transfer power from the landowners to the middle classes, who would be supported by a satisfied peasantry.[2] The aims of the new republic were to hold the powerful political church within bounds, to democratize the structure of the army, to laicize the educational system, and to effect a modest redistribution of the land.[3] The election of a tremendous majority of republicans and their socialist allies to the constituent Cortes in June 1931 indicated popular support for these announced goals.

However, besides threatening the entrenched interests of the church, the army, and the landowners, the government's program, particularly its religious and educational reforms, alienated a large number of Catholics and middle-class people who might otherwise have supported it. In September 1933 the government resigned and in the ensuing elections the parties of the Left suffered a smashing defeat. The new ruling coalition of center, right republican, and Catholic groups repealed or allowed to lapse almost the entire body of legislation enacted by its predecessor. During the next two years violence was widespread, with brutal repression of protests, strikes, and a revolt of the miners in Asturias. The escalating conflict finally resulted in the fall of the government on October 29, 1935. The socialists had been radicalized during this period and the Spanish anarchists had issued a call for social revolution. The polarization of forces within Spain and the manner in which the Asturian revolution was quelled made civil war inevitable.[4]

Two short-lived governments failed to ease the crisis, and new elections were called in January 1936. A popular-front coalition of left republicans and socialists won a narrow popular victory but gained a sizable majority in the Cortes. The communists received sixteen seats, and the parties of the center collapsed. A new government, composed of left and moderate republicans, with left socialist and communist support in the Cortes, attempted a minimal reform program. Manuel Azaña, the prime minister, declared that "we want no dangerous innovations. We want peace and order. We are moderate."[5] But his protestations fell on deaf ears. The country was ranging itself behind Largo Caballero, the left socialist leader, and the Falange, a new right-wing party led by José Antonio Primo de Rivera. Strikes, assassinations, and street-fighting punctuated the spring of 1936 while General Francisco Franco and his military cohorts prepared a pronunciamiento.

The slow-burning fuse finally reached the powder keg in July 1936. The military garrisons revolted simultaneously in almost every city in Spain on July 17–19. By the end of July Franco and his co-conspirators were in control of areas of the southwest, west and northwest—roughly a third of the country. For the next two and one-half years war was to devastate Spain, with the nationalist forces slowly winning the upper hand.

International involvement came immediately and Germany and Italy supported the nationalists with troops and materiel. The Soviet Union dispatched military equipment to the republicans. An abortive attempt by the French popular-front government of Léon Blum to aid the republic was quashed by outcry in his own country and by the hostile attitude of Great Britain. The device of the nonintervention agreement was then put forward by Blum, which pledged signatories not to become involved in the Spanish situation. The democracies complied, the Axis powers and the Soviet Union did not. Henceforth, the Spanish republicans were to claim that nonintervention constituted a betrayal of their cause and was directly responsible for Franco's victory.

In April 1938, the nationalists split the republic in two when they reached the Mediterranean at Tarragona and isolated Catalonia from the rest of republican Spain. The January 1939 campaign in Catalonia triggered the mass flight of a half-million republican refugees into France and set the stage for the events described in this book.

In the view of the Spanish refugees, not only had the democratic world betrayed them in their struggle against fascism, but it had compounded this callous attitude by turning its back on them once the struggle was concluded. The French government received them with suspicion, the other great democracies ignored their very existence. The Soviet Union, which had been the only Great Power to assist them during the civil war, also abandoned them when the outcome of that struggle became clear. What happened to the Spaniards who took refuge in France—from their entry in February 1939 through the German victory, their participation in the Resistance and liberation, and the final failure of their efforts to reinstate the Spanish republic—is the subject of this book.

The saga of the Spanish republican refugees in France spanned five epochs. The first, from February to September 1939, encompassed their exodus from Spain and their incarceration in the beach concentration camps of southern France. The second extended from the outbreak of the Second World War in September 1939 to the French defeat and the armistice of July 1940. During this period Spanish republicans fought in the ranks of the French army, or were assigned to labor battalions fortifying northern and eastern France, or worked in French agriculture and industry. Thousands suffered the agonies of the German onslaught; some escaped to the unoccupied zone of France or to England, but many were captured and sent to Mauthausen concentration camp.

In the third epoch, July 1940 to May 1945, Spanish republicans were again organized into labor battalions by the Vichy government and forced to work for the Germans in France or in Germany itself. Thousands joined the Resistance movement or the Free French military forces and were active in the battles of liberation. The fourth period—May 1945 to December 1955—found the Spaniards clamoring for Allied assistance in reclaiming their homeland from Franco, but again their hopes were dashed. The Allies refused to oust Franco themselves or to arm a resurgent Spanish republican army, the United Nations contended itself with a temporary ostracism of the Spanish Caudillo, and the Spanish republican guerrilla movement in Spain was blunted because of the lack of support. Cold War pressures dictated an American and British reversal in the United Nations. In 1953 the Americans signed a military and economic aid agreement with Franco. Two years later nationalist Spain was admitted to the United Nations.

These failures gave rise for the first time to an exile mentality among the Spaniards, in which they were forced to accept the probability of living out their lives in France. The fifth epoch extended from 1955 to 1975, when Franco died. It was a period of intense, albeit fruitless, activity, in which political organization continued, newspapers were published, and clandestine missions were carried on in Spain. The flame of anti-Franco sentiment was kept alive, but that was about all. The exiles were dying at a rapid rate, victims of their years of hardship, combat, and frustration.[6]

Although there have been a number of Spanish memoirs and accounts of the World War II years, written from partisan political points of view, there has been no attempt to synthesize the available information into a comprehensive story. French accounts, with the exception of a few writers who lived and fought with the Spaniards, have either ignored or minimized the latter's role in the French Resistance and in the armed forces. The English-speaking world is largely unaware of the sufferings and the struggles of those whom they had idealized and romanticized during what was for the Western world "a most passionate war."[7] French archival sources, which throw light on French attitudes and actions, were closed to research until very recently; many still are. There is a great deal of truth in the assertion of the Spanish republicans that they are "the forgotten ones" of the war years.

The story of the Spanish republican refugees in France is one of suffering, neglect, heroism, and a continuation of their battle against fascism. Throughout the Second World War they nurtured the belief that when Hitler and Mussolini had been destroyed, the vast armies of the Allies would turn southward with them and destroy the fascist regime of Francisco Franco, the last of the dictators. A French Resistance leader, watching the victory parade after the liberation of Toulouse, saw the Spanish Maquis march past the reviewing stand. He asked himself: "What will France and the other democracies do for the Spaniards, who had given so generously of their blood and fire in the Resistance?" The answer has now been recorded: nothing.

CHAPTER ONE

RISING TIDE

THE FIRST REFUGEES, 1936–1938

But while the refugee may be a hunted and wounded creature who must be helped, he is at the same time an alien with no ties to his Government, an alien with no rights, an isolated human being.

Jacques Vernant, The Refugee in the Postwar World

SPANIARDS SEEKING REFUGE following political upheavals at home have long been familiar sights to residents of the border towns and provinces of southwestern France. For hundreds of years French Catalans and Basques have watched long lines of their Spanish counterparts coming through Cerbère on the Mediterranean Sea, through the narrow passes of the Pyrenees, or across the bridge at Hendaye on the Atlantic coast.

The political exiles have always been perceived as a different sort from those Spaniards entering France in search of work, either seasonal or permanent. The political exiles have been people driven from their native land by fear of prison or death, rather than by the inexorable need to earn a daily pittance. Although many have settled permanently in France, new turns in the wheel of political fortune have inevitably sent others back over the border to enjoy victory. Indeed, political refugees returning to Spain have at times crossed paths with their defeated enemies at the French border. In 1868, when Isabella II entered France after her abdication from the Spanish throne, her train passed a group of homecoming exiles who taunted her with cries of "Down with the Bourbons!" "Long live liberty!" and "Long live the republic!"[1]

In the nineteenth century and the first third of the twentieth, Spanish emigration to France was accelerated, and exiles poured regularly across the border.[2] No accurate figures are available on the nineteenth-century migrations,[3] but it is possible to trace the broad outlines of these movements, which culminated in the gigantic flight of Spanish republicans after the fall of Catalonia during the penultimate stage of the Spanish Civil War in January 1939.

There were five great political emigrations of Spaniards into France during the first half of the nineteenth century.[4] The twentieth century saw a further increase of Spaniards in France, up to the advent of the Second Spanish Republic in 1931.[5] The advent of the Spanish Civil War in July 1936 altered the picture radically. The military advance of the nationalists spun off increasingly larger numbers of hapless Spanish republicans. Between July 1936 and December 1938, France, the chief haven of refugees from both warring sides, witnessed the scrambled comings and goings of hundreds of thousands of Spaniards. Just how many refugees crossed and recrossed the border is unknown, with estimates ranging from 200,000 to 340,000.[6] But this early experience with Spanish refugees did not prepare the French government or people, either psychologically or materially, for the mass of Spanish humanity that was to sweep across the border with the crumbling of the Catalonian front in late January 1939. The 1936–1939 influx altered the volume and composition of the Spanish colony in fundamental ways. The trickle of agricultural and unskilled migrants in the first half of the decade had become a cross-section of Spanish society, a tidal wave of political emigrés and soldiers retreating before the insurgent troops.[7]

Between July 1936 and April 1939 the civil war produced five distinct waves of emigration from Spain. Each was tied to specific military campaigns in which the nationalists extended their domination over formerly republican territory, and with each new conquest, large groups of republicans felt compelled to flee to the neutral soil of France. The first three phases of exit came with the end of the battle of Irún, August-September 1936; during the final phase of the war in Asturias, May-October 1937; and following the occupation of Alto Aragón, April-June 1938. Between June 1938 and January 1939, the French border was officially closed to refugees, although this did not completely stem the flow of Spaniards. The fall of Catalonia in January 1939 gave rise to the fourth and most massive phase of republican flight. The fifth and final outpouring of refugees came with the surrender of Madrid and the end of the civil war in April 1939, although the clandestine movement of refugees across the border continued even up to the time of Franco's death.[8]

The harbingers of migration were aristocratic families and members of the upper middle class, who, even before the outbreak of war, had sought to avoid the tribulations associated with the new regime, which was stigmatized as revolutionary and Red. The women, children, and young men (*señoritos*) of the grandee families were no strangers to the magnificent beaches of the French Basque coast, and they soon filled all the best hotels. Living luxuriously, they were certain that their country would be rescued from the Marxists, and when Irún fell in September 1936, many of them returned to Spain with the assurance that the old order had been reimposed.[9] Those who remained in France aroused the ire of the Left. *Le Populaire* railed at the "arrogant behavior" of the nationalist refugees in the St. Jean de Luz area. It accused them of roaming the streets like conquistadores, and it estimated that fully 70 percent of the Spaniards inhabiting the Hendaye and Bayonne areas were pro-Franco. Moreover, and perhaps even more infuriating to the socialist newspaper, the overwhelming majority of the refugees openly supported the French rightists Colonel de la Rocque and Jacques Doriot.[10]

But with the passage of Irún into nationalist hands, the first large-scale flight of republican supporters took place. On the night of August 30, two thousand people presented themselves at Hendaye. They were followed by thousands of Basques after the taking of San Sebastian. Javier Rubio says that at the end of 1936, allowing for an undetermined number of repatriations, there were some 10,000 refugees in France.[11] Scenes that were to become familiar to the French as the war progressed, and especially after the collapse of Catalonia, were first enacted at the International Bridge at Hendaye during those first frantic days: "On foot, by wheelchair, by motor car, by coach, by horse, with domestic and farm animals, with babies, with a few precious articles of cheap furniture or pictures, the refugees fled to the frontier impelled by a blind panic, many in tears and penniless."[12] The French government put into practice what was to become its standard policy, the dispersal of Spanish refugees to a number of departments. Some were sent to the Basses-Pyrénées and the Haute-Garonne, others to the Gard and the Ardèche.[13] The Government also allowed 800 republican militiamen to proceed from Bordeaux via Perpignan to Catalonia, where they rejoined the combat.[14]

A second and larger group of refugees surged across the border in May-October 1937, during the final phase of the northern campaign. *L'Humanité* reported that Basque authorities had requested French and English protection for merchant ships evacuating refugees by sea. The Communist newspaper feared that England would refuse to do so and that France would follow her example. Despite Franco's statement that aerial bombardment of the port area would continue during evacuation of the refugees, the two nations did afford assistance in the rescue venture. By June 19, 1937, when the nationalists captured Bilbao,

30,000 Spanish refugees had been safely received in French ports. The evacuees were mainly women, children, and old people. When Santander became endangered in July, the French government realized that it faced a growing problem. A policy was devised to permit the debarkation of noncombatants, who would be given the choice of returnign to Spanish republican control or to the side of General Franco. There were, however, two conditions: the French consul at Santander would be furnished with lists of prospective refugees, and no man of arms-bearing age would be accepted by France. The fall of Santander at the end of August produced an additional 29,000 refugees;[15] among them were 8,000 combatants, an augury of what was to follow.[16] By the beginning of October 1937, in spite of the efforts of the French authorities to encourage repatriation, there were some 60,000 refugees remaining in France, still not a large figure compared to the numbers of Russians and Armenians, the two largest refugee groups in France.[17] The fall of Gijón on October 21, and the end of the Asturias campaign three days later, added some 9,500 refugees to the total.[18]

In April 1938, a third wave of Spanish refugees swept across the border as a result of the campaign in Aragon—Rubio has estimated the number at 15,000–17,000, based upon daily reports in *La Dépêche de Toulouse,* the leading radical socialist newspaper of southwestern France. Another 8,000 entered France in June. The Aragon refugees included 12,000 to 14,000 soldiers from the Thirty-first and Forty-third divisions of the republican army.[19] Given the choice of repatriation to either the nationalist or republican side, the Spanish soldiers opted decisively for the republic. A dispatch by G. R. Cals in *La Dépêche* reported that only 254 of the 5,000 or 6,000 soldiers of the Thirty-first Division selected the nationalists. Similarly, only 646 soldiers of the Forty-third Division, less than 10 percent, elected to go to the nationalists. Perhaps their choices were influenced by the way some French officers put the question: "Do some of you wish to return to fascist Spain?" The journalistic ire of Gabriel Péri, correspondent for *L'Humanité,* the Communist newspaper, was aroused by a variation of this question, which, on the face of it, seemed to be favorable to the Republican side. The Spanish soldiers were asked: "Do you wish to continue to defend the republic or to gain the rebel zone?" He commented that "this outrageous procedure [is] an invitation to treason" and added that the French government would be better advised to find and expel members of the Franco fifth column who proliferated throughout the Pyrenees.[20] By June 18, only several hundred wounded soldiers remained in France awaiting repatriation. Thus, in mid-June 1938, according to the conservative estimate of Rubio, there were 40,000–45,000 refugees in France, of whom about 25 percent were children.[21]

The steady increase in the flow of Spanish refugees caused increasing restlessness among the French. The government's participation in the nonintervention pact produced embarrassment and guilt within the popular front, hostility and clamor for aid to the refugees among the groups of the Left, and antirefugee manifestations from the Right. The thousands of Spaniards on French soil provided a visible focus for the acting-out of these feelings. French concern about the growing Nazi menace and fears of internal strife generated by the right-wing groups caused the government to act with caution. France in 1936–1938 was a nation torn between its traditional role as haven to the politically dispossessed and the awful expediency demanded by its own political circumstances.

French governments during the period July 1936–January 1939 sought to limit entry to Spanish civilians. They were skittish about the presence of military combatants in their country and made every effort to repatriate any who sought refuge. They were vulnerable to charges by the French Right that they were incurring heavy expenses for the maintenance of the refugees. They were sensitive to the vehemence of rightist accusations that the Spanish republic was communist-controlled, and they were generally concerned about actions that might be construed as violating French neutrality.

The tone for the discussion was set by rightists such as Léon Daudet in *L'Action française,* and Henri Beraud in *Gringoire,* who expressed anxiety at the thought that France might be converting itself into "the dungheap of the world." They also deprecated the laws that required France to welcome the refugees. In March 1937, the minister of the interior instructed police commissioners to prepare lists of all foreigners between 18 and 48 years of age. General Menard, commander of the Seventeenth Army Corps (Toulouse), informed his superiors in April of the same year of the "constant and massive" penetration of French territory by refugees from Lérida and Huesca.[22] An article in *La Liberté* raised the possibility of a communist plot against France; the resulting reaction of the French army foreshadowed the large-scale panic that was to strike the host nation when the huge flow of Spanish refugees entered in January and February 1939. The newspaper expressed the fear that Spanish republican troops, aided by the French Communist Party, would extend the Red revolution into France. Arsenals would be seized and efforts made to bring the French army over to the revolutionary side. Four days after the article appeared, the French minister of war issued a secret order, authorizing the equipping of the Garde Républicaine Mobile with machine guns, to be used only on authorization from the ministry.[23]

The popular-front government attempted to ameliorate the conditions of the refugees, but their efforts were criticized both on financial grounds and out of fear that they might jeopardize French neutrality. As increasing numbers of Spanish military retreated behind the French frontier, they aroused hatred and fear among many segments of the population, and the government policy of offering repatriation to either side drew fire: some held that since France had not granted belligerency rights to either contender, it was not obliged to adhere to Article 14 of the Hague Convention of 1907 requiring aid to the wounded and their removal from future combat.[24] A suggestion by Deputy Daher (Bouches-du-Rhone) that France could save money by sending all republican refugees to Valencia and all nationalists to Salamanca was supported by *L'Epoque*. But this notion that France should rid itself of all refugees was at odds with the policy of the popular front, which had permitted the repatriation of soldiers while providing refuge for civilians. The second Blum cabinet considered disarming and returning to Spain all able-bodied men, while guaranteeing the right of asylum to women, children, the old, and the sick.[25] But this hot-potato approach disturbed the men of the Right. Frédéric Delebecque, in *L'Action française*, maintained that many republican refugees might not wish to return to the loyalist zone. Moreover, a policy of forcible return would reinforce the republican army and constitute a deliberate act of hostility toward General Franco. *Le Journal de Toulouse* denied that there were any bona-fide refugees: "Those who are called refugees," it wrote, "have been evacuated by the compulsion of the Reds, and who hope only for the victory of Franco."[26]

Resentment against the Western democracies and the Soviet Union manifested itself in barbed articles suggesting that all Spanish refugees ought to be sent to the USSR. "The whole world ought to participate," the conservative *Le Matin* declared, "It is not good that only one country be burdened with the whole load." The refugee problem could have been solved at one stroke if the Spanish interlopers had been delivered to the Soviet Union where they would have found "an immense brotherhood" of compatible souls. "France will take charge of the organization; the United States the money; Great Britain the ships; Russia the hospitality, and Geneva the operations."[27] Financial aid given to Spanish refugees formed a focal point of dissent by rightists and radical socialists. France was in an economic depression, and the French resented having to support Spanish refugees. Jean Montigny, a radical deputy (Sarthe), pointed out that while French elderly were continuing to receive pensions of 50 francs per month, the Spanish refugees were receiving between 210 and 240 francs per month. Furthermore, he alleged, there was an additional monthly subsidy of between 105 and 150 francs for each Spanish child. The feelings aroused by this charge were not changed when Louis Guilloux, a novelist identified with the communist group in France and secretary of the First World Congress of Anti-Fascist Writers, asserted that the subsidies applied only to Spanish children under two years of age.[28] The result, at the beginning of October 1937, was a decree that all Spaniards "who are not able to assure themselves of their sustenance would be returned to their country."[29] The French position was based on the alarming and progressive rise in expenditures for Spanish refugees, which, between mid-July 1936 and December 1938, amounted to 88 million francs.[30] It must also be noted that official expenditures were supplemented by an unknown but considerable amount of financial aid from other governmental and private sources. Members of the French General Confederation of Labor, for example, had given 12,283,639 francs by the end of 1938 for aid to Spanish refugees.[31]

Hostility—overt and covert—increased with the advent of the Daladier government in April 1938. The groundwork for a change in attitude and policy toward the Spanish refugees was laid by demands for the tightening of conditions under which they would be allowed to remain in France. But in fact, despite all the decrees issued by governments, the refugees held their French foothold with great tenacity and with the active help of many Frenchmen. The radical journalist Dominique called for the repatriation of those Spaniards who fell into several categories: invalids, the mentally ill, those with venereal disease or tuberculosis, sexual perverts, alcoholics, the elderly, political propagandists, and criminals. For good measure, and quite possibly this was the point of it all, he included those who lacked the means to live without public or private assistance.[32] The Daladier government in its first decrees refused entry to the military and forced stringent controls upon civilian refugees. Minister of Interior Albert Sarraut prepared the way in a report to the Council of Ministers, in which he asserted that a decree authorizing surveillance and repatriation of undersirables would soon be issued.[33] Soldiers presenting themselves at frontier posts were simply requested to choose between returning to loyalist or nationalist territory. An act of May 2, 1938, required all Spaniards to secure identity cards from the police. A fine of 50 to 1,000 francs was to be levied on those lacking such cards, plus a possible prison sentence of one month to one year. For Frenchmen who might be tempted to help illegal

Spanish refugees the same punishments were mandated. Foreigners were given one month to clear up their passport situations; after that they would be expelled. Control points on the frontiers were to be strengthened. The widespread traffic in false passports and papers was to be vigorously repressed. In certain cases forced detention was mandated.[34]

These laws were attacked by the Left, which held that asylum was not a privilege but a right. *L'Humanité* asserted that they would injure only "the little people" and called for restrictions on the activities of the agents of foreign and French fascism. For the more conservative Frenchmen, however, the laws were not strong enough. Leon Bailby, for example, called for doubling or tripling of penalties for foreigners.[35]

If the 1936–1938 migration prefigured the great exodus of January–February 1939, the treatment accorded the refugees during the earlier period foreshadowed the attitudes that were later to be expressed by the French and their Spanish guests. Many Spaniards believed that the French were inherently xenophobic and, specifically, held Spaniards in contempt. They believed that their unwilling hosts were callous to their plight, indifferent to their welfare, and hostile to the cause for which they fought. Many French people, on the other hand, felt that they had shouldered the major burden of succoring Spanish refugees, that the Spaniards were ungrateful, that much more had been done for the refugees than was acknowledged, and that differences in national cultures had made for basic misunderstandings. Exceptions were noted by both camps, but generally the atmosphere was heavy with recriminations.

The policy of dispersing the refugees had done much to reduce large concentrations of them, but nevertheless there were disproportionate numbers of Spaniards in the southwest, and some cities contained more than they could care for efficiently.[36] Many republican refugees, while unable to emulate the grandiose style of the Franco sympathizers were still able to avoid the refugee camps and to find employment.[37]

Louis Guilloux, who in 1937 was working on a novel in a French town he calls X, kept a diary of his experiences with Spanish refugees assigned to a camp in X and of his tribulations with the local prefectorial administrations. Some 1,200 refugees had been allocated to the entire department, which, he declared, was a comparatively small number, other departments having been allotted as many as 3,000. The town of X, with a population of 30,000, was required to accommodate 300 women, children, and old men. The French government had designated eight francs per day for the support of adults and five francs for children. Responsibility for the refugees was split between the municipality and the prefecture. Guilloux kept his diary from September 8 to October 30, 1937, and he was thoroughly angered and frustrated by the treatment given to the refugees. X, he said, was "a hard-hearted little town," which alternated between neglecting the refugees and profiting from their needs. The refugees were installed in an abandoned factory that had at one time made agricultural machinery. They slept in a huge shed 200 feet long and 35 feet high. There was no heat or fire, and no possibility of getting either. Even in early autumn the shed was "exceedingly cold . . . straw mattresses have been thrown at random on the bare floor." Beds had been ordered, but as of October 30 they had not yet arrived. Nothing had been done to remove old machinery and industrial debris, but the Spaniards were blamed for not keeping the shed clean and for attracting numerous rats and spiders. Refugees were still wearing the clothes in which they had left Spain, and many were barefoot. Most of the children were suffering from the itch, measles, and whooping cough, and despite this, he noted on September 8, twenty-one additional children had been introduced into the camp. He concluded that "this place is the height of misery."[38]

Secours Populaire, a local group, attempted to alleviate the poor conditions by working with the municipal and prefectorial authorities, but it met with guile, evasions, or reluctant acquiescence. Guilloux and a committee that had visited the camp were told by the prefect that further visits would be denied because of the danger of epidemic and a suspicion that the group "wished to carry on a political agitation" in the camp. Later, the prefect relented and granted the group a one-month visiting privilege. When told that a sum of 1,500 francs belonging to the refugee fund was being withheld, the prefect professed indignation and ordered that it be made available immediately, for the purchase of such necessities as shoes, clothing, and soap.

At a meeting of the municipal council, a councilor sympathetic to the needs of the refugees declared that the unused factory was uninhabitable and asked where the Spaniards would be moved when winter came. The mayor disclaimed responsibility for the refugees—the question must be asked of the prefect. Both authorities admitted that the onset of winter would create an intolerable situation for the refugees, but neither official had any solution to the problem. On September 14, Guilloux noted that the weather had turned colder, that rain had been soaking the area for several days, and that the refugee shed leaked. Although one franc per day from the eight-franc allowance had been set aside for rent, no repair work had been undertaken: "It is reported that one of the people who have been benefiting [from the rental money] has been heard to boast publicly that he had made a good thing of it."

A week-old baby was discovered to be living in the shed. The mother had given birth in the town maternity clinic, but had been sent back to the camp after a few days. Guilloux described the scene: "In this filthy, icy place . . . the mother and child are lying on a straw mattress under a heap of old clothes that serve them as bed coverings. It is raining on them. And the mother smiled! She smiled as she showed us the baby's little pink face." The effort to transfer the mother and newborn illustrated the subtleties and confusions of the French bureaucracy in dealing with refugee problems. Guilloux complained to the prefecture secretary, who in turn telephoned the *commissaire* and insisted that an inquiry be made. The *commissaire* investigated and reported that the woman had herself requested return to the camp. The secretary smiled as he repeated this to Guilloux. The next day the mother and child were removed to the Bureau de Bienfaisance.[39]

In the kindness of some of the tradespeople and in the financial support of the workers in the town, Guilloux found the redemption of France. On September 15 he reported that many shopkeepers had shown great goodwill. Most of them were ignorant of the miseries experienced by the refugees in the camp. Prices were reduced for the aid committee, and many gifts of cash were made, both of which represented real sacrifices on the part of the givers. Parcels of clothes and shoes were also delivered by private individuals to the Maison du Peuple. By September 18, shoes had been provided for 111 refugee women and children. From the 1,500 francs on deposit in the prefecture —of which 500 had already been deducted for the cost of postage— only 295 francs were made available. The balance had come from Secours Populaire and individual contributions.

To rally the support of the townspeople, Guilloux and his committee staged a meeting on September 25. Only fifty people attended, mostly workers. Guilloux concluded that "this lack of curiosity, of sensibility, in the face of distress—whatever the reasons, and they must necessarily be bad—seems . . . a most disastrous sign." Guilloux hoped that the attitude displayed in X did not represent that of the rest of France.

France, however, was not prepared to cope with the problems of the refugees in the approaching winter. Interior Minister Marx Dormoy declared that the cost of caring for the 45,000 refugees supported entirely by the French government had risen to a million francs a day. Therefore, the refugees would be given the choice of returning to either the republican or nationalist zone of Spain. Those refugees who lived with private families or earned their own livings would be permitted to remain. Children supported privately or through trade-union efforts would also remain in France.[40]

The experiences of the town of X—both good and bad—were to be repeated in the early months of 1939 on a scale magnified almost beyond comprehension. Instead of forty to fifty thousand refugees there would be more than half a million. In addition to unused factory sheds there would be vast sandy beaches and hastily constructed shelters, and instead of relatively few departments and municipalities, almost all of France would be immersed in the tidal wave of Spaniards seeking refuge. If there were any lessons to be learned from the experience of X and similar towns, they were ignored. For when the dam broke and the human flood from the south engulfed France, the country was still in a state of unreadiness, still squabbling internally, as unwilling to face the implications of the refugee situation as it was to confront the greater danger from Germany.

In June 1938, in fact, the border with Spain had been "hermetically sealed" by the French government, a move that Gabriel Péri charged was dictated by Pierre Laval and Neville Chamberlain. Daladier and Foreign Minister Bonnet hoped thereby to slow the immigration.[41] In official terms they succeeded, but there was no way in which clandestine crossings could be controlled. An undetermined number of Spaniards continued to enter France.

The splitting of Catalonia from the rest of republican Spain in April 1938 precipitated a cabinet crisis. President Manuel Azaña and Minister of Defense Indalecio Prieto foresaw an inevitable Franco victory, while Prime Minister Juan Negrín and his communist supporters were determined to continue the struggle. The growth of peace sentiment within the Spanish republican government produced a warning to the French government of the possibility of a massive influx of Spaniards to French soil in the event of a republican collapse.

On April 23, 1938, Joaquín Camps Arboix, consul of republican Spain in Perpignan, sent a curious letter and memorandum to Raoul Didkowski, prefect of the Pyrénées-Orientales department, which abutted Spain from the Mediterranean Sea to Andorra. This department was destined to take the major shock of the incoming refugees. The consul asked Didkowski "to consider this memorandum as purely personal, entirely independent of consular direction." The Camps Arboix memorandum declared that "it is not outlandish at the present time to foresee the possible victory of Franco. This victory would create political problems in France which are not mine to analyze. Other problems of a humanitarian nature would also result, and I permit myself to point out and formulate some suggestions regarding these." Specifically, Camps Arboix was concerned about "the convulsions, both deep and contradictory," which a massive flight to the French border might produce. But he backed away from any criticism of actual French policy or actions. He then proceeded to make it clear that he was concerned about the situation because of Spanish characteristics: "Spanish passion, inherent in the character of the race, is what easily leads to extremes which range from an unlimited cruelty to the most chivalric generosity"; with the exception of Catalans, all Spaniards carried within themselves an unpredictable mixture of Torquemada and of Don Quixote, and all civil wars in Spanish history had been no-quarter affairs. This knowledge, he felt, should have alerted everyone to the possibility of catastrophe.[42]

Camps Arboix then described two stages of potential "horror and ignominy" that might take place in Catalonia as the war there ground to its final phases. In the first stage the despair and anger of the conquered might translate itself into reprisals against presumed fascists and a scorched-earth policy to hamper the conqueror. In the second stage he saw the all-powerful and uncompromising victors arriving, filled with hate and imposing their despotism in inquisitorial fashion. France, with its great humanitarian tradition, could not refuse asylum to the afflicted Spanish republicans.

The exodus promised to be massive and potentially disruptive to France. How could conflict be avoided? Here, Camps Arboix broached his plan. England, France, and the Spanish Nationalists would agree to set up a neutral zone in the province of Gerona, where right of temporary asylum or provisional extraterritoriality would be recognized. France and England would insure order and guarantee the lives of the refugees. Well aware of French and English fears of German and Italian troops remaining on Spanish soil after the war, Camps Arboix declared that the project would give the democracies "a trump card" in case the Axis nations broke their promise to evacuate.

Obviously, Camps Arboix intended that the document be passed to the Foreign Ministry for consideration. There is no evidence in the files of the departmental archives at Perpignan that Didkowski did in fact transmit the memorandum. Yet, on January 25, 1939, Foreign Minister Georges Bonnet proposed a plan for a neutral zone that was so faithful to the one Camps Arboix suggested that there is little doubt that the Spaniard's memorandum had found its way to the Quai d'Orsay. There was still some question whether armed combatants should be included, and the area mentioned in the Foreign Ministry's version was smaller than what Camps Arboix had envisaged. But the major outlines of the original proposal, including British participation, were intact.[43] What had prompted its sudden release after almost nine months of silence? It would seem that the imminent fall of Barcelona and the oncoming collapse of the entire Catalonian front had brought to ugly reality the mass exodus so carefully and vividly projected by Camps Arboix.

Thousands of civilian refugees had already begun their flight to the border. France had been forced to accept large numbers of women, children, the elderly, and wounded soldiers, all of whom waited patiently and hungrily outside the frontier posts, drenched by a persistent rain. And at last the specter of those hundreds of thousands of Spanish troops, now fighting a desperate rearguard action but soon to have nowhere to retreat except into France, became manifest to the government in Paris. The catalyst came in the form of a request by Julio Alvarez del Vayo, foreign minister of the Spanish republic, that France accept 150,000 refugees. The request was rejected but the neutral-zone plan was advanced in its stead.[44] Reaction to the plan in France and in Britain was generally favorable. *L'Action française* reported that the British appeared to welcome it, but it complained that everyone was ignoring the views of the Burgos government, whose approval was necessary for adoption of the plan. *L'Oeuvre* called it a "humanitarian solution," and urged that the nonintervention committee be given a role in its implementation. *Le Midi socialiste* agreed with *L'Oeuvre* and reported that the English Red Cross supported the idea. *La Dépêche de Toulouse* said it was "the best solution." *L'Indépendant* (Pau), stressing that France could accept only a limited number of refugees, endorsed the idea of a neutral zone. It added that the food supply for refugees ought to be undertaken by an international aid organization.[45]

But the plan failed to win the approval of General Franco. On January 28 it was learned that he was opposed to the idea of the creation of a neutral zone in Spanish territory.[46] With the rejection of the neutral zone plan, France was faced squarely with the burgeoning problem of what would happen to the Spanish refugees as the nationalist troops continued to roll toward the frontier. According to David Wingeate Pike, "the French Government had left to it no alternative but to put a cheerful face on the matter."[47] *La Dépêche* saw the situation as one of extreme urgency in which France had a "double duty . . . to reconcile its security obligations and its imperative humanitarian duties."[48] The military was still not to be allowed into France, although Prefect Didkowski, in a press interview four days before the opening of the border, said that the entry of civilian refugees had "never been in doubt." He reiterated that the plan of the ministry to receive, classify, and evacuate refugees to designated departments was still operative and would be carried out as smoothly as possible.[49]

This insistence on denying entry to the military demonstrated anew French reluctance or refusal to see the problem in its true dimensions. Very shortly it would become evident that the sheer volume of Spanish refugees made it impossible for them to be dispersed in a controlled way, and this, in turn, was to lead to chaos on a grand scale. And as the defeated Spanish republican army of Catalonia turned at last from its native soil and looked to France for haven, it was to prove impossible for the French government to deny the Spanish soldiers their last opportunity to escape from Nationalist firing-squads or prisons. The French tradition of asylum was to triumph over internal dissension. Yet, because very little had been done to prepare for this eventuality, the price was to come very high—for France and for those whom it received.

THE LONGEST MONTH

I salute you my sun. I salute my land. I salute you Spain. Will I
again see your sky in the silver moon of enchanted nights?

My heart is heavy and tired. I leave you my country! O soil blessed
by the gods, where the men are wolves.

Jean Olíbo, *Parcours*

ALONG THE MEDITERRANEAN littoral of the Côte Vermeille,
which follows the shore in a gentle arc from the Spanish border
to Séte, the month of January 1939 was, as usual, "cold and sunny, with
damp mornings which the sun soon chased away."[1] A string of pearl-
like villages punctuates the coast, of which Argelès-sur-mer (Pyrénées-
Orientales), roughly equidistant between the Spanish border and Perpignan, is distinguished by a fine sand beach that attracts vacationers
during the summer. But the soul of the village is in the land. In 1939
most of its 2,945 people were agricultural, in occupation and in spirit.
They worried about their vines, their fruit orchards, and their truck
farming.

To the south of Argelès lie the port and fishing villages of Colliourc
(3,018 population in 1939) and Port Vendrcs (3,515). On the north
are the sandy beaches of St. Cyprien (1,172) and Barcarès (508). Together they form the eastern limit of the Département des Pyrénées-
Orientales.[2] The most southerly department in France, it has an area of
4,122 square kilometers, and it measures 50 kilometers from north to
south and 120 kilometers from east to west. Although it contains six
regions, the department is most generally known by the ancient name
of one of them—Roussillon. Under the kings of Mallorca and of
Aragón, it received an indelible imprint of Catalan culture, becoming
French in 1659 under the terms of the Treaty of the Pyrenees.

The department stretches westward from the Mediterranean plain
through the hills into the high peaks of the Pyrenees. On the south it

borders Spain from the Sea to Andorra. Sleepy villages such as Cerbère,
Le Perthus, Bourg-Madame, and La Tour-de-Carol are dotted along
this border. To the north the department is contiguous with the departments of L'Aude and L'Ariège. Strongly agricultural in character,
Pyrénées-Orientales is an area of small farms. Viticulture, fruits, grains,
and vegetables form the bulk of its agricultural production. Animal
husbandry has declined somewhat, but lumber and wood products remain important. Iron and marble are mined. The ancient fishing industry still graces the coast. Tourism was a minor industry in 1939
but has grown steadily since the end of World War II. The market
center of the department is Perpignan, prefectoral headquarters and
today the forty-ninth largest city in France. In 1936 it had a population of 72,207. The department is blessed with a warm, pleasant climate
for most of the year, but January, with an average temperature of
8.2° C, and February, 11.6° C, are cold, wet, and snowy.

This geographically varied land, with 233,347 people in 1936,[3] most
of whom lived in the densely populated lowlands and river valleys,
was to become the storm center of the Spanish republican exodus,
and Argelès-sur-mer was to become the locale for the first great concentration camp organized to immobilize the refugees. At the beginning of January 1939, the ancient calm of French Catalonia seemed
to prevail in Argelès, but it was "a calm full of menaces." Pierre Izard,
who was the young first deputy mayor of Argelès at the time, recalled
that the people were more concerned about threats from the exterior
than about the domestic infighting then wrecking France. The looming
menace of Hitler, the fear that Italian troops might remain in Spain
or even invade France, and, above all, the Spanish Civil War itself,
"contributed to thicken the atmosphere, to create a climate of anguish
. . . [to sound] the knell of the joy of life in our fields." Sentiment was
overwhelmingly in favor of the Spanish republic, but fear of the possible escalation of the war into a general conflagration that would surely
engulf France made people cautious. And they were confused by the
hesitations and oratory of the Daladier government.[4]

Not that the Argelèsiens were of one political mind. There were
"reds" and "whites," but these old political distinctions were muted
in the face of the Spanish war. "Each pitied the neighboring country
and friend, victim of indignities, of ideas expressed by modern armament." There was an air of unreality, a feeling of suspended time, an
unease that pervaded the fields, the cafés, the homes of the people.
"Everyone feels himself watching a stunning event, something grave,
never seen, imprecise, but unpleasant, sad, distressing . . ." January
1939, Izard wrote, was to become "the longest month."[5]

Agony was to be January's hallmark: the fall of Barcelona, proudest city of Catalonia; the suffering of the defeated Spanish republicans as they took the road to exile, and the ambivalence of the French people as they succored the incoming hordes at the same time as they succumbed to a wild fear for the safety of their fields and possessions. In this process, the destinies of the defeated Spanish republicans and the soon-to-be defeated French were to be entwined. Together they were to endure the humiliation of the conquered, persecution from the Nazis, and repression from the authoritarian men of Vichy. Later, thousands from both sides were to join in resistance to the tyrants.

The push on Catalonia began on December 23, 1938, when Navarrese and Italian troops crossed the river Segre and met with little opposition. Further north, nationalist troops also crossed the river, causing a general pullback along the Segre front. On January 14 a swift nationalist advance south along the Ebro River succeeded in reaching the sea at Tarragona, thus cutting Catalonia in two. The insurgents then tried to continue to the French border while also moving along the sea to Barcelona. By January 22 they were only 34 kilometers from the Catalan capital. Resistance on that front had slackened, but heavy fighting was in progress to the northwest as the republicans tried to keep the fascists from closing their French escape route.[6]

These developments inspired a surge of last-ditch activity in France. In an impassioned series of articles Léon Blum, eloquent spokesman of the Left, though fallen from his former position as premier of the popular-front government, demanded that the frontier be reopened for the passage of arms to the beleaguered republicans.[7] A debate in the National Assembly produced statements from Daladier and Bonnet that Spain was finished, while Blum and other elements of the French Left argued to the contrary. The frontier was opened briefly, and an undetermined quantity of arms was shipped to Catalonia.[8] On January 20 and 21 a *Le Midi socialiste* headline cried: "Open the Franco-Spanish Border," and, in response to the general unease about Italian troops driving closer to French territory, the paper exhorted: "Aid Spain to Save France!" It declared that the exodus was taking place because "we have allowed this heroic people to starve . . . To aid the refugee is good. To aid Republican Spain . . . would be better."[9] But *L'Action française,* the voice of the French monarchists and ultra-rightists, if still indulging its appetite for pro-Franco propaganda, nevertheless had a truer perspective on the outcome of the struggle when it reported the imminent "liberation of Spain." Nationalist forces, it said, were a mere 22 kilometers from Barcelona and "Red resistance is weak."[10]

As the enemy approached Barcelona, "the inquietude of the city grew, foreshadowing the disaster." To Dr. Pedro Vallina, an army doctor working in the Hospital Medico de la Bonanora, great changes were apparent. In the streets and stores, he wrote, one could already see the signs of the approaching death of the city. "It is time to end the war, whatever may happen," was a refrain increasingly heard. In the bookstores, he observed, volumes that might be politically dangerous when the fascist army entered Barcelona had already been removed from the shelves.[11] The restlessness in the city had permeated the wards of the hospital and was reflected in the faces and actions of the wounded soldiers, the majority of whom were unable to leave their beds. The sudden abandonment of the hospital by a group of civilian doctors precipitated a panic. Arriving there to help calm the soldiers, Captain Vallina noted that "the place looked crazy, with everyone screaming and gesticulating wildly at the same time."[12] The evacuation of the city accelerated and Dr. Vallina, a known anarchist, was urged to move northward. Making his last ward rounds, he encouraged ambulatory patients to depart and said farewell to the others. He observed some of the wounded crying, "not for what was happening to them, but for the death of our liberties." Military doctors, still under orders, remained with the patients.[13]

On January 23 the republican Council of Ministers appointed a commission "to preside over the orderly and methodical evacuation of the civilian population."[14] The exodus from Barcelona and, successively, the towns between it and the French border, which had begun slowly during the early days of the month, gained volume as the conqueror approached, until it became a "river of humanity."[15] When the victorious nationalist troops entered Barcelona on January 26, 1939, much of the civilian population was strung out on the roads leading to France, or waiting silently outside its gates for admission; the huge military influx was to come later. The loss of Barcelona, while not decisive in a military sense, affected profoundly the morale of the people throughout the republic. In the view of Pierre Broué and Émile Témime, "the death throes of the republic began that day."[16]

Symbolizing and perhaps contributing to the drop in morale was the flight of members of the Spanish republican government. As the seat of political action in the north moved first to Gerona and then to Figueras, the unrest of the people grew. When the fall of the latter city appeared imminent, many members of the government fled to France. Some later made their way to Valencia. The government also organized several offices in Perpignan, mainly to assist refugees with passport and other problems. The difficulty of maintaining communications, both with the vast exodus of frightened people and among government agencies, quickly created a political vacuum. Foreign Minister del Vayo announced that the republican government would not engage in politics while on French soil. Although some government officials were interned in the concentration camps, the important leaders were allowed to go free.[17] President Manuel Azaña crossed into France on February 5, and later established himself in Montpellier. Foreign Minister del Vayo and Luís Companys, president of the Catalan autonomous government, arrived the same day.[18]

Prime Minister Juan Negrín and Education Minister Marcelino Domingo arrived at Toulouse on March 1. The former prime minister, Francisco Largo Caballero, took up residence near Albi. His manner of flight was strongly criticized. Constancia de la Mora, Spanish republican press officer assigned to work with foreign correspondents, related how Julien Cruzel, mayor of Cerbère, showed her several Spanish ambulances parked in the rear of the mairie. When she insisted that they be sent immediately to Spain for use in evacuating wounded soldiers, he told her that they had arrived on January 27, "filled with the files and household goods" of Largo and Luís Araquistáin. They were still fully loaded and he had orders to keep them safe for the officials.[19] The communist leaders General Lister and Dolores Ibarruri (La Pasionaria) lived secretly in the Paris home of the communist deputy Prosper Moquet. Later, they and other communist leaders went to live in the Soviet Union.[20] *Gringoire* took advantage of the situation to strike at two of its favorite targets, the Spanish republic and French Minister of Interior Sarraut. In a cartoon it depicted Azaña leading the flight to the border, where Sarraut greets him eagerly. The caption says: "The Example Comes From the Top—A Leader Ought Always To Give the Example."[21]

Whether or not the actions of the top leadership were exemplary, many of them appear to have suffered very little during their flight from Spain. There were notable exceptions, but in the main it would seem that "the masses, the rank and file who had fought for the republic, suffered more in defeat and subsequent reprisals than the bourgeoisie who had governed."[22]

The mood and immensity of the dolorous evacuation that clogged the roads to France were best expressed by a headline in *Le Midi socialiste*: "Martyred Spain on the Road to Exile."[23] There was an overriding feeling of tragedy, of mourning, a sense of loss coupled with inchoate frustration. The *New York Herald-Tribune* gave a vivid word picture of the retreat: "All day Sunday and yesterday the wreck of the Spanish republic was streaming northward through the passes of the

Pyrenees—the weary crowds of peasants and workpeople, the escaping officials, the hungry women, the lost and orphaned children, and the broken fragments of a valiant army—in one vast tide of disorganization and defeat." The newspaper compared this withdrawal with those of the Greek army through Anatolia in 1922, the Belgian troops abandoning Liège in 1914, and the rout of the Grande Armée at Waterloo. It found that "none [of these] is quite a parallel for this mass fear and flight, this simultaneous dissolution of an army, a government, a people, and an idea under the merciless blows of modern warfare."[24] Participants and observers from one end of the political spectrum to the other, grappling to capture the meaning of the flight, could find parallels only in religious symbols: "martyrdom," "Calvary," "crucifixion," "exodus," "Golgotha." Even Eberhard von Stohrer, German ambassador to General Franco's government, called it "this road of suffering."[25]

Within the rapidly diminishing arc of safety, hundreds of thousands of Spaniards milled about, pushing blindly toward refuge as nationalist airplanes bombed and strafed them almost constantly, food became scarce, and barriers and unremitting rain greeted them at the French frontier.[26] From the air a German or Italian pilot might see all the roads "absolutely jammed with people in cars, in trucks, on donkeys, on foot. Peasant women holding a child or a goat or a chicken to their breasts. Young women trailing their children behind them."[27] And as he dived towards this mass, individual shapes would become clearer: a file of blind soldiers, bandages over their eyes, holding each other's hands and groping along the road; a woman giving birth to a baby in an open cart, a group of children scattering from a bus to escape the pilot's bombs.[28]

To Federica Montseny, anarchist leader and sometime minister of health in the Spanish republican government, the worst aspect of the retreat was "collective panic, this beastlike terror that debases human beings at such times, usurping all rational faculties, all capacity of reflection, and limiting all measure of order and prudence." Fleeing with her mother, two young children and others, she was struck particularly by the plight of sick and wounded people. "The hospitals were evacuated, those wounded fled who were able to do so with their arms in slings or legs in casts, the sick consumed with fever. Those who were not able to escape remained, being the first prizes of the fascist barbarians."[29]

Isabel de Palencia noted that the trains could go no further than Gerona and it was almost impossible to make one's way through the crowds jamming the road. Many people were forced to abandon the few precious belongings they had taken with them. Food became scarce and "ravenous hunger was added to the other trials."[30] In sheer desperation thousands of Spaniards left the roads and began the difficult climb over sinuous pathways in the icy mountains. Dr. Vallina, who had been ordered to effect the evacuation of a hospital at Massanet de Cabrenys, decided to avoid the roads and take his people—including the wounded—directly over the mountain to France. Moving with great difficulty his party arrived at a plateau near the peak in late afternoon and he decided to camp there for the night, not far from another group of refugees. A local farmer approached Vallina and pleaded with him to continue the climb. "I fear that the advancing fascists will assassinate me on the pretext that I furnished aid to you," he told the doctor. Not wishing to endanger the peasant's life they made their way to the peak, where Vallina beheld "a heart-rending scene. It was a true anthill of human beings, among them women, children, and old people." The anguish was heightened when a hard rain began to fall and very few could find shelter. In the morning, the more than one thousand persons who had endured the night continued their walk to France.[31]

From the French side of the border the approaching tidal wave of Spanish humanity was watched with deepening apprehension. If this huge mass of people represented only the civilian population, what would happen when the hundreds of thousands of Spanish republican troops at last abandoned the struggle and became refugees? Montseny later declared that "nothing had been foreseen nor prepared" for the influx.[32] If that were true, it was certainly not for lack of discussion, for the refugee question had been very much on the minds of the French government and people. The policy then in force, which had been developed through experience with the 1936–1938 refugees, was still thought to be adequate. An inkling of the escalation of the problem had been gained from del Vayo's request that France accept 150,000 refugees, but it served merely to demonstrate that if on January 24 the French government was unaware of the magnitude of the problem, so was the Spanish republican government. It still seemed feasible to receive women, children, older people, and wounded, while turning back soldiers and able-bodied civilian males. The truth of the matter was that the French simply refused to think in realistic terms. To do so would have been to admit an involvement and an obligation that most of them were reluctant or unwilling to assume.

The dissonance of French political life, which had intruded into the reception of the earlier refugees, was now magnified in the face of the oncoming horde. Left and Right expanded on the themes they had sounded in the previous period. The difference now lay in the growing desperation and anger with which they were expressed. Pierre Rouzard, correspondent for the extreme right-wing *La Garonne,* wrote from the border post of La Tour-de-Carol (Pyrénées-Orientales) on January 30 that he had "come to understand with as much terror as piety the indescribable horrors of a civil war." But his perception was influenced by his politics: "Why have the Reds ordered or permitted this lamentable exodus? The women, the old ones, are innocent. It is impossible that soldiers, however proud they may be of their victory, would take vengeance on them."[33] The obvious answer, at least to the ultra-rightist press, was that the Spaniards had been forced to flee by the communists and anarchists. *Gringoire* accounted for the large number of refugees by charging that the communists and anarchists had spread rumors that Franco would kill all who remained.[34] Constancia de la Mora thought, on the other hand, that the Franco fifth column was trying to spread confusion and chaos, thus clogging the roads. At Figueras she had seen an officer of the Carabiñeros standing on a platform in the main square, shouting that the nationalists were about to enter the town. He exhorted the population to flee. She believed him to be a secret supporter of Franco, for the nationalists were not at that moment threatening the city.[35] At Olot, *Gringoire* said, Marxist soldiers had forced people to flee at gunpoint. Teachers had been made to take their pupils on the march, and the parents had followed their children.[36] P. J. Sautes, in *L'Action française,* also wondered why innocent people would wish to flee the liberating nationalist army. "Does not General Franco bring forgiveness, along with bread and justice?" he asked.[37]

La Dépêche de Toulouse, the most important paper in the southwest of France, was in a particularly difficult situation. Owned by the family of Interior Minister Albert Sarraut and with a strong radical socialist bias, it was constrained to defend the actions of the Daladier government. With the breakup of the popular front it had moved from a position of sympathy and welcome for the refugees to an attitude similar to that of the extreme rightist journals in its emphasis on fear of refugee vandalism, dangerous political possibilities, and insistence on severe military control of the Spanish republicans. It condemned the loyalists for ordering a sudden evacuation of the population. It drew attention to the large numbers of sick women and children among the refugees and warned of the danger of epidemic, but it praised the government for performing efficiently in the face of great obstacles. The paper warned that France would not tolerate any disorder and lauded the government's decision to send the Twenty-fourth Regiment of Senegalese tirailleurs from Perpignan to the border. Jean Vidal, correspondent for the newspaper, chided the refugees for their "ancestral habits" of dirtiness, cheekiness, and laziness, and he decried their "scandalous attitudes." Venting its frustration in still another direction, the newspaper called upon Great Britain and the Soviet Union to assume a share of the expense involved in supporting the refugees.[38] Despite these attacks and misgivings, *Le Populaire* insisted that sanctuary should still be provided for the Spanish refugees. Otherwise France stood to lose whatever remained of its dignity.[39]

Under the impact of the growing numbers of refugees clamoring for admission, the Sarraut policy had virtually no prospect of success. Sarraut and Prefect Didkowski had outlined a series of orderly steps to process the refugees. They would be received at the border, disarmed, and given a meal of coffee and milk, a quarter pound of bread, an egg, a piece of cheese. They would be washed and vaccinated and then entrained in consecutive waves and carried to departments in the interior.[40] This plan remained an objective for Sarraut and a mirage for the refugees.

On the night of January 27–28 the border was opened to women, children, and the elderly. Refugees were supposed to enter at the rate of 2,000 per day.[41] Well before that date the river of humans had begun to trickle through and around the French net. They had come through the narrow mountain passes and in small ships that deposited them at numerous Mediterranean ports. Toulouse reported the arrival by air of twenty-eight women and children, dependents of Spanish airmen.[42] Joseph Rous, a deputy from Pyrénées-Orientales, pointed out that asylum for civilians was an act of humanity that international custom had made a right.[43] As more refugees swarmed into the steadily narrowing north-south corridor that was still under republican domination, the French authorities lost control of the situation. The target of 2,000 refugees per day became ludicrous. It was impossible to keep the pipeline flowing in the manner envisaged by Sarraut. Encarnación Avilés Rodríguez, who was nine years old at the time, recalled that she and her mother waited eight days at the border before being admitted.[44] On January 30 the French authorities decided to intern all able-bodied men who were already in France in a camp being constructed at Argelès-sur-mer, with the thought that they would be repatriated to Spain in a short time.[45] On January 31 it was decided to permit the entry of wounded men.[46] The evacuation of Figueras, twenty kilometers from the frontier, was begun on a large scale, and the crowds pressed into the border area. Herbert L. Matthews, a correspondent for the *New York Times,* described the scene at La Junquera, only five kilometers from the French frontier: "There are not ten square yards anywhere near roads that have not their refugees. Every side road, every field, and even the hills are swarming with unhappy thousands who are gradually finding their way to La Junquera. There by the thousands they wait patiently or stand in lines to get food that the international commission is sending from France."[47] The scene was, as *Le Midi socialiste* said, "a tragic spectacle; and in fact unimaginable for those who are far from the drama."[48]

By February 2 the disarray had become so great that the French government decided on the immediate admission of all but able-bodied men; it would house the refugees in whatever makeshift shelters could be arranged. The steady buildup of French security forces continued. To the Twenty-fourth Regiment was added the 107th Regiment from Limoges, infantry battalions from the Sixteenth Military Region, detachments from the Eighty-first Regiment, the Seventh Regiment of Spahis, motorized dragoons from Mont-Louis, an unknown number of Gardes Mobiles companies, and numerous gendarmerie. *Le Midi socialiste* noted that the Pyrénées-Orientales was rapidly becoming a vast fortified camp. The troops were used to herd the refugees into shelter areas and to sweep the fields and forests for "uncontrolled" Spaniards.[49] The patent absurdity of transferring such great troop strength to the Pyrenees was apparent; they would have filled a greater need on the Meuse.

At this point two major problems remained. What to do with the huge influx of civilians, which Sarraut put at 130,000 by February 5, and which gave no evidence of diminution,[50] and whether eventually to admit the republican armed forces. Sports stadia and large open meadows were used as temporary shelters until concentration camps could be organized to contain the enormous numbers of refugees. The first of these was staked out on the beach of Argelès-sur-mer. It was soon necessary to build others at St. Cyprien and Barcarès. In addition, large open camps were organized in the western, more mountainous area of the department, but these were soon abandoned in the face of freezing weather conditions.

Pierre Izard, who had earlier noted the deepening crisis in and around Argelès, now became directly involved in French moves to avoid a complete breakdown of order. At 11:00 A.M. on January 25 he was summoned by Mayor Frédéric Trescases. With the mayor was Commandant Boutillon, a black commander of the gardes mobiles. Boutillon wasted no time. "We await the Spaniards who are fleeing before Franco's troops," he told Izard. "We must establish a camp of welcome at the beach. It must be enclosed and some barracks must be built. You are a wood merchant, first deputy mayor, army reserve officer. Therefore you are my man. To work!" Surveying the beach, they selected a lonely ten-kilometer stretch between Argelès and St. Cyprien. The commandant lacked precise orders or plans. He had been told simply to "Faites un camp, d'urgence!" This command symbolized the improvised, haphazard nature of the French attempt to cope with what had become an unbearable, seemingly insoluble, problem. Boutillon ordered Izard to commence the building of barracks with the only available labor, some wounded and even amputee Spanish refugees who were already huddled on the beach. Several days later he summoned Izard and canceled the construction of barracks. Instead he ordered wooden stakes driven in the sand to form rectangles of one hectare each. The rectangles were each to be enclosed with barbed wire. "I dared not ask why this was being done," Izard wrote.[51]

The reason became clear on February 1, when Boutillon informed Izard that Minister of Interior Sarraut and Health Minister Marc Rucart were touring the frontier area and were due at Argelès to monitor progress in building the concentration camp. Izard now knew why Boutillon had opted for stakes and barbed-wire instead of barracks; the minister would be more impressed with security than shelter. But thus far only the outer perimeter and some of the nearby rectangles had been enclosed with wire, for Izard had been unable to procure enough for the entire camp. The vast reaches of the beach, therefore, offered a panorama of naked stakes against the backdrop of the Mediterranean sea and sky. It was a scene, Izard mused, that would appeal to Bernard Buffet.[52] Sarraut was a favorite target of the extreme right, and the well-publicized inspection tour was designed to reassure the nation that its government was not going to leave it at the mercy of the Spanish hordes. Izard, obviously not an admirer of the interior minister, described his visit to the camp:

[Sarraut] arrives in a prefectoral auto which stops where the paved road ends, the entrance to the camp. He walks on a boardwalk fixed on the sand. Short, heavy, stiff-legged, he halts at the end of the planks, he touches the ground with his cane and makes some cautious steps on the sand. His shoes, low and polished, were not designed to test this uncertain ground. He tips his hat, closes his hands, and does not go any further. He sees the few barracks and the stakes further toward the north, indicating the enclosures. He does not see the details . . . Disarmed, because he is incapable of walking on the sand, the minister of interior returns to his auto, shakes hands and leaves. Later, no doubt, when he was alone, he unlaced his shoes to get rid of the insidious grains of sand which hurt his ministerial toes.[53]

Sarraut and Rucart completed their inspection tour by viewing the refugees and installations at Le Perthus, Bellegarde, Prats-de-Mollo, Arles, and Cerbère. The minister then held a private meeting with the prefect, from which he barred the socialist deputies Parayre and Noguères, who represented the Pyrénées-Orientales in the chamber. Later, he granted a press conference, at which he declared that he was impressed by what he had seen. "I expected visions of horror, haunting things. I have seen that order was perfect, and that actions have been taken to meet any eventuality; I am satisfied." He reiterated that barbed wire would enclose the Argelès camp; 500 Spanish soldiers were completing the construction of the camp. He affirmed that camp discipline would be strict, and that military and police reinforcements would be sent to the endangered area. He said that hospitals would be organized to care for the 3,000–4,000 Spanish wounded already admitted to France and that additional medical personnel would be assigned. The minister also announced preventive health measures "against the danger of possible contamination" of the French population."[54] When Health Minister Rucart reported to the chamber's Committee on Public Health a week later, he was not as optimistic as Sarraut had been on the question of health measures. He spoke with great emotion about the "serious and cruel" situation of the refugees and admitted that the medical actions in progress were "insufficient." There were difficulties in securing the use of the army's war reserve of supplies. He had appealed to the army and the Red Cross to send doctors and nurses. A number of beds had been assigned to local hospitals. The National Society of Railroad Workers and the Ministry of Public Works were equipping a medical train. But all these measures did not begin to fill the needs.[55]

La Dépêche extolled the actions of the ministers,[56] but *Gringoire* spoke for the Right when it accused Sarraut of incompetence. Despite two years of warning signals, the paper said, "nothing has been done . . . The health and security services are practically nonexistent. The surprise has been complete."[57] *Gringoire* was not entirely correct. Something had been done, but the achievement was miniscule. The Ministry of Public Works boasted that between January 28 and February 2, forty-five special trains had evacuated 45,000 refugees to the interior.[58] But 100,000 soldiers had entered France by February 7, swelling the total of refugees to between 240,000 and 260,000.[59] The vast majority who were not transported to the interior either awaited assignment in one of the open-air triage areas, camped in the forests and fields, gravitated to the towns, or were herded into the concentration camps at Argelès, St. Cyprien, or Barcarès.

For one group of refugees the long wait on both sides of the border was a particularly grueling experience. By February 6 more than 8,000 wounded soldiers and civilians had been received at frontier posts, and their number was eventually to swell to 10,000.[00] Despite Minister Rucart's intention of providing increased medical service, little or nothing had been done to alleviate the situation since his visit to the frontier. Wounded men were still lying in the open or in railroad stations, with minimal or no care. At Cerbère (Pyrénées-Orientales), for example, two hospital trains bearing 1,700 patients arrived in tandem on February 6. This raised the total of seriously wounded to 3,500 at Cerbère.[61] Hospitals in Perpignan and other towns had made a certain number of beds available in existing facilities and had rehabilitated others that had been abandoned, such as the Hôpital St. Louis in Perpignan. Two hospital ships were anchored at Port Vendres. At Argelès and other camps there were still no hospital units of any kind. The result was suffering on an unimaginable scale. A reporter for *Le Midi socialiste* overheard a French doctor, who had been working for ten consecutive days in the old Fort Bellegarde, which had been converted into a hospital, say: "I helped 1,000 wounded. Tonight, there are 300 new ones, all with fresh wounds. I have not closed an eye. We have operated and amputated without rest, until now."[62] A nurse who in 1939 cared for wounded Spanish soldiers at the Hôpital St. Louis in Perpignan, could recall years later the horror of that time:

> How can I begin to tell of what happened? They came walking, all the way from Argelès, some of them, with all kinds of terrible wounds. And some of them had been walking from Barcelona or Figueras before that with these same wounds. Others came in by train or ambulance. They had cut branches off the trees and improvised splints. Their plaster casts were black with mud. They tried to keep their filthy dressings from unravelling by tying rope around them because they thought that even a dirty dressing was better than nothing at all. Many of them were gangrenous, all of them were emaciated, hungry, and exhausted. I wondered how men could endure such much and still keep coming on in the hope that at last somebody might help them. When we got our first patients I worked for thirty-six hours, then rested for six and came back for another thirty-six-hour duty. And I could have worked that way for weeks and not have made much impact. There were too many of them.[63]

An anonymous soldier told Federica Montseny that he arrived in France in the first week of February as part of a group of fifteen hundred wounded from the military hospital at Camprodón. It was intensely cold, but no clothing, blankets, or medical attention were provided. The soldiers slept in the open. When some ambulatory patients set small fires the guards extinguished them immediately on the grounds that "your imprudence will start a fire." Some townspeople invited a few wounded soldiers into their homes for coffee, but the guards discouraged it: "It is not necessary to have pity for them. They are Reds."[64]

Francisco Finestres, who was born in Lérida and left school at eleven years of age to work in the fields, had fought through the entire war, becoming a sergeant and finally a lieutenant. Wounded on December 31, 1938, when a shell shattered his upper right arm, he was recuperating in the hospital at Figueras when the exodus began. "Franco's airplanes and German airplanes bombed the city of Figueras," he said, "and three bombs fell on the hospital, killing and wounding many soldiers and hospital workers. They told us that anyone who was able to walk should leave and take the road to France." Arriving at Cerbère on February 6, the hungry wounded had to wait three days before being admitted and sent to Argelès. "Nobody came to look at us, no medicine was given to us," Finestres said.[65]

In a clinic that had been set up hastily in Le Perthus, Montseny saw many women who implored the lone doctor there to help their infants. The children, after sleeping in the rain and in the open for a week or more, were coughing and feverish. The doctor told Montseny: "Most of them will die—they all have pneumonia. If they had been able to get attention some would have been saved. But we are unable to do anything, nor is it possible to hospitalize them."[66]

How many Spanish refugees died during this early period? Nobody knows. Spanish cemeteries exist near most of the concentration camps and Perpignan has a large one, but it is impossible to know which graves represent deaths during the first weeks of February 1939 and which hold the remains of refugees who died afterward. Nor is it possible to trace the gravesites of Spaniards who died in other parts of France at this time. The situation is further complicated by the fact that the figure of 4,700 deaths that is generally accepted includes refugees who escaped from the camps and are listed as having "disappeared."[67]

However, even the abundant evidence of refugee suffering elicited barbs from the rightist press. A Doctor Cousin, in *Petit Bleu,* raised the specter of an epidemic among Frenchmen because the refugees were not being given preventive vaccinations before being dispersed throughout France. "If France avoids multiple epidemics she will be incredibly lucky," he declared.[68] *L'Action française* also managed to connect the Red menace with the sick and wounded. It claimed that in the old Hôpital St. Louis in Perpignan, Russian doctors were taking care of the wounded. Further, the monarchist newspaper said, Spanish wounded were not only refusing to allow nursing nuns to help them but were insulting the sisters.[69] Spanish chicanery was also alleged by the *Gazette de la Haute-Loire.* It reported that when three "wounded" soldiers in the Hôpital Emile-Roux were forced to take off their bandages, they were found not to have any wounds.[70]

If January was the longest month, February was the shortest, for with events breaking ever more rapidly the French government was forced to take stands on a number of major problems. February 5 was a day of momentous decision for France and for the Spanish republicans. Figueras, barely 20 kilometers from the French border, was on the verge of falling to Franco. There was now no room for maneuver and the republican army, "not being able to fight anymore, and not wishing to surrender," retreated to the frontier.[71] Having enabled hundreds of thousands of civilians to cross to France in safety, the army now left the anarchist Durruti Division (the Twenty-sixth) and troops of the Army of the Ebro commanded by the Communist colonels Juan Modesto and Enrique Lister to fight a rearguard action covering the evacuation of the other troops and those civilians still on the Spanish side of the border.

For the French this was the critical moment, dreaded beyond all other possibilities in this infuriating war. Only the invasion of Southern France by Italian and Spanish nationalist troops could have been more dangerous in French eyes, and in that instance, at least, there would have been no hesitation in the response. _La Dépêche,_ which reflected government policy, was haunted by the fear of a mass exodus of the "terrorist hordes" of republican Spain.[72] It agonized over the terrible complications that would ensue if the _Franquistes_ succeeded in pinning the republican troops against the border. Yes, the French could "install a line of machine guns to stop [the republicans] and deliver them to the bullets of their adversaries. But if we welcome them charitably, would not their enemies seek to decimate them on our soil?"[73] And what would happen then? Never was the question of French humanitarian tradition versus the imperative of security posed so poignantly and with such overwhelming import. The humanitarian tradition triumphed. The order to allow passage to the Spanish republican army was given at Cerbère at 8:00 P.M. on February 5 and at Le Perthus at 4:30 P.M. on February 6. Thus began the final march of the Spanish republican soldiers who had tried to hold Catalonia against odds that proved to be overwhelming. With them came the last civilians. Though they were "unenthusiastic and even ill-mannered," the French authorities had nevertheless admitted the Spanish republicans.[74]

Gustave Regler, German novelist, former communist, and wounded veteran of the International Brigades, was with Herbert L. Matthews at the frontier when the afflux began. To him it appeared "like a medieval picture of the Crucifixion." At first, civilians came down the narrow hill paths, advancing with dignity and trust toward the guarded plain teeming with soldiers.[75] Later, the republican troops arrived. "They were received as though they were tramps. We saw them in the distance marching towards us, with their rifles over their shoulders, still with a mile or more of Spanish soil between them and the frontier which represented the death of all their hopes." One of the conditions of sanctuary was the surrender of arms, and the troops complied, some with relief, others with bewilderment, most with reluctance. But then followed a search of personal possessions. With Prefect Didkowski and several French generals observing the scene, the contents of haversacks were dumped into a roadside ditch. Whatever feelings of solidarity the Spaniards believed they shared with the French were dissolved at that instant. "The dirty road on which the disarmed men stood was not merely the frontier between two countries, it was an abyss between two worlds." When Matthews objected, Didkowski instructed the guards to "show a little more courtesy."[76]

Constancia de la Mora, a member of the press department of the republican government, was trying to reach Perpignan to establish contact with newspaper correspondents there. Her husband, General Ignacio Hidalgo de Cisneros, was commander of the air force, and his chauffeur had driven her to the French border. With a woman friend and the friend's child she walked across the dividing line and found herself on a country road in France. A French farmer and his wife spoke Catalan to her and offered assistance. Suddenly a French garde mobile appeared. "Are you armed?" he asked, and took a revolver from de la Mora's friend. He ordered them to continue on the road until they should meet a group of Spaniards who had been rounded up a short time ago. Something about the man's "harsh voice and his peremptory commands" troubled de la Mora. Her worst fears were confirmed when the same garde mobile reappeared and began to separate women and children from their men. She was rescued from the garde mobile by the couple she had met a short time before. As they drove away the farmer "swore a black oath against the French government which welcomed the Spanish refugees with terror instead of kindness."[77]

At Cerbère, Le Perthus, and Bourg-Madame (Pyrénées-Orientales) the Spanish army moved into France in "an unending stream." In one random five-minute period Matthews counted 455 men, thirteen vehicles, two mules, and a bicycle crossing the bridge at Le Perthus. "When the moment so dreaded by France came," he wrote, "and the troops that the local press calls 'the Marxist horde' started to pass the frontier, it was discovered that the huge French military forces had very little to do. A few dozen New York traffic policemen were all that was needed . . . The men wanted to know what to do and where to go and that was all. It was a disciplined army." He noted that the French civilians were in the main kind and considerate to the refugees and said that even with the best of intentions the French government could not have hoped to cope efficiently with the situation.[78]

Jean-Maurice Herrmann, correspondent for *Le Populaire* and *Le Midi socialiste,* was awed by the scene: "It is night. The stars are brilliant, the cold pinches the fingers. The rumble of motors makes the earth vibrate. The exodus of Catalans seems to continue indefinitely . . . an entire people, preferring exile to slavery, marches past without stop, without haste, without complaint, since the dawn." By midday of February 6 more than 50,000 had entered France. Herrmann was amazed at the diversity of their uniforms, their armament. Carabiñeros coolly directed traffic on the Spanish side of the border. A group of 200 guards trotted past on their horses, resplendent in their "too-long beards," their blue and orange cloaks. On the serpentine Maureillas–Las Illas road marched a long column of troops with blue helmets and red bands—the Guard of Honor of the Generalitat: "they have yielded the last bit of soil to the invader." Some soldiers carry their rifles in one hand, guitars in the other. Members of the International Brigades cross the bridge, singing. The sound of rifles clattering to the ground, stacks of them growing higher and higher on either side of the road. A soldier is determined to keep his trophy—an Italian Bersaglieri helmet— but is forced to relinquish it. Herrmann is aware that the passage of these troops and civilians is even at this moment being "paid for with blood" in rearguard actions. All have but a single hope: to reach the tricolor sentry-box. And he wonders whether Frenchmen will understand that "the cannons of international Fascism . . . that have broken their [Spanish] flesh without touching their faith—will menace Perpignan [tomorrow]."[79]

For many soldiers it was difficult to grasp the reality: for them the war was ended; they were no longer soldiers, but refugees. Miguel Gómez, a twenty-seven-year-old cobbler, crossed into France with the idea that the army would stay there only long enough to regroup and be shipped to the Madrid front. He was surprised when his rifle was taken from him. Only in 1945, after the Allied victory, would he assess the international situation and come to the conclusion that the victors did not intend to dislodge Franco. Then he realized that his stay in France would be a long one.[80]

Another soldier who was convinced that the French government would allow the Spanish troops to rejoin the fighting on the Madrid front was Mariano Constante. On February 7 he was promoted to lieutenant and ordered to protect the retreat of the army to Puigcerdá, the last Spanish town before the French frontier post of Bourg-Madame. He commanded thirty men, and his heavy weapons comprised two French machine-guns that had been allowed across the Franco-Spanish border during a brief period when it had been reopened. But he had insufficient ammunition, and it was all soon expended against Moorish and Italian troops. Constante and his men were ordered to retreat into France. At Puigcerdá the next morning German planes attacked them for the last time. He was astonished by the silence of the Spaniards, "not a single cry, no moaning, no complaints." Under a gray-black sky they all waited for the line of men and trucks to move forward. His sergeant said: "The sky is in mourning to see our defeat. God has hidden his face behind his snows in order not to see so many crimes."[81] Constante was to see many such skies, in occupied France and, later, in the German concentration camp of Mauthausen.

When Luís Bazal and his fellow artillerymen first saw the French frontier, they turned their backs on it because they could not face the fact it represented. They were told that the French government had conceded the right of asylum and this angered him: "Criminals ask for asylum, the afflicted ask for refuge." A comrade said: "We have lost the war. Do you know what this means? It is the greatest misfortune." Another soldier suddenly took out his pistol, and, without a word, killed himself. Bazal, unthinking, started to do the same, but was stopped by a sergeant who shouted: "No, no you will not do this . . . we are of a race that must not die . . . We are an accusation and a living protest against the world."[82] Other groups showed their reluctance to acknowledge defeat by delaying the act of submission to French control. José Gros and his unit passed into France on February 10. They had already learned that they were destined for a concentration camp. They returned to the Spanish town La Agullana where they foraged for warm clothing and destroyed abandoned military equipment. They spent that night in Spain. The next morning, still concealed in the hills on the Spanish side of the border, they watched the arrival of the nationalists. The men of Franco began to haul down the republican flag and this act set off a booby-trap explosion of dynamite under the flagpole. Then Gros and his comrades crossed into France and presented themselves at the control point.[83]

Finally, the rearguard troops abandoned the struggle and entered France. At 3:00 A.M., February 9, Colonel Modesto, Commander of the Fifteenth Army Corps, crossed into Cerbère from Port-Bou. His arrival was preceded by tremendous explosions in which the Port-Bou railroad station and quantities of war materiel were destroyed. He announced that the only republican troops left in that area were the headquarters section of a machine-gun battalion and a battalion of dynamiters. "The *Franquistas* will have absolutely nothing remaining," he declared, "We prefer to destroy everything that would give them any satisfaction."[84] At Bourg-Madame the anarchist Twenty-sixth Division (the Durruti) retreated into France on February 10, while a suicide unit of 150 men delayed the taking of Puigcerdá until the following day. The slogan of the last-ditch resisters was "in death let us take ten Fascists for every one of us." Those who entered France cried, "Vive la France, vive la République!" Antonio Herrero, member of the Twenty-Sixth Division, related that "as soon as we arrived, reinforcements were sent for. We were considered the most dangerous of the refugees." Many of the Durruti-men were sent to the Castle of Mont Louis and later to the punishment camp of Le Vernet (Ariège), which was largely reserved for prisoners considered to be politically questionable or dangerous.[85]

On February 11, a remnant of a rearguard unit approached the border near Prats-de-Mollo (Pyrénées-Orientales). Pascual carried a broken machine-gun on his shoulders: "He accepts all loss but this machine, even though broken, is sacred; the others will not be able to repair it." Enrique carried a wounded comrade. Silently they traversed the snowy summits and ravines. "When will this Calvary be finished?" they asked silently. Then they saw the French gardes mobiles. "At last! To fall down, to stretch out on this soil where peace reigns . . . To sink, to die, then to revive and believe it to be a resurrection. To become another." Then the deliverance turned into another ordeal. "Jetez vos armes!" (throw down your arms) a garde shouted. The Spaniards kicked their rifles "into the void." Pascual, pushed to the extreme limit, threw his machine-gun violently. Enrique deposited the wounded one gently on the ground and discovered that he was dead. Olibo reflected that those who fought the republican battle had become "prisoners of a destiny without equal."[86] These scattered and broken units of the rear guard would be, it was thought, the last to enter France. But on February 14 some 12,000 to 15,000 troops emerged from the mountains near the Col d'Ares (Pyrénées-Orientales) after having evaded pursuing Navarrese soldiers. They were indeed the last organized troops to pass the frontier.[87] Catalonia now belonged to Francisco Franco, and *La Dépêche* reported that his forces had captured 35,000 republican soldiers.[88]

Despite some isolated incidents, the Spanish republican army had made its final retreat in good order, notwithstanding the fact that its adversary was only a thirty-minute automobile ride from Le Perthus.

Most French journalists agreed that it "did not have the look of a routed army."[89] But the perception of *L'Action française* was different. "Quel cohue! Quel desordre!" ("What a mob! What disorder!"), the newspaper fumed. The fleeing soldiers, it declared, were nothing more than "the debris of the Red army."[90]

During the "longest month" of January and the first fortnight of February, France had absorbed between 350,000 and 500,000 Spanish refugees.[91] This immense outpouring of humanity, in the direst of circumstance, had, with the exception of some 50,000 previously distributed refugees, been deposited willy-nilly in the department of Pyrénées-Orientales. Refugees outnumbered inhabitants by two to one. Under these circumstances, and with the best of intentions, it was almost inevitable that strains would develop, even given the cultural kinship of the French and Spanish Catalans and the largely favorable attitude of the Roussillonais toward the Spanish republic.

THE GREAT FEAR
OF 1939

Thousands [of Spaniards] are prowling all over the Southwest. The
danger of moral and physical contagion, without speaking of
risk of armed aggression, becomes pressing.

M. Pagés, Patriote des Pyrénées

ESET BY PROBLEMS, both internal and external, the French
nation was ill equipped to cope with the massive influx of Spanish
refugees. The unsettled mood of the country was reflected in the op-
portunistic policies of the Daladier government. The final slide to the
Second World War had begun, and an unnamed but no less potent feeling of drift pervaded the country. In this ambivalent atmosphere the
nation fell prey to the insidious attacks launched by the French right
wing against the Spanish republicans. Fear of galloping epidemic,
hordes of dangerous radicals unloosed upon France, robbery, rape,
pillage, destruction of homes and fields, and even of armed Spanish
and French communist insurrection, abounded in the rightist newspapers. The resulting panic escalated into waves of raw anxiety and
brought on the "Great Fear" of 1939. The Spanish refugees became the
twentieth-century "brigands." The communists and anarchists became
the sinister agents for the organization of destruction and take-over.
French nationalism transmuted the Black Legend into the Red Legend.
And, as in *La Grande Peur de 1789*, frenzied preparations were made
for defense against an ominipresent, ephemeral enemy. The Roussillon,
it was believed, could become tranquil again only when all Spaniards
were penned behind barbed-wire and security troops saturated the
infected area.

The purveyors of fear were doubtless motivated by their phobic
obsession with Marxism. They were seeking to promote the restruc-
turing of French-Spanish relations in a manner favorable to the new

nationalist regime, and in their view only the forcible repatriation of Spanish refugees would both aid this process and cleanse French soil of the undesirables. Thus they proclaimed the perfidy of an entire people and equated the Spanish republic with communism. This position influenced the Daladier government, which found the republicans an embarrassment in its just-begun negotiations with Francisco Franco.

The French Left and the vast mass of Frenchmen who had entertained a general sympathy for the Spanish republic were left with feelings of guilt at French failure to intervene in the civil war. They countered rightist attacks on the Spaniards, opposed forced repatriation, and fought against early recognition of the Franco government. Later, their exposures of inhumane conditions in the concentration camps and the unwarranted brutality of French security personnel were to be instrumental in securing changes in governmental policy.

One can understand why the farmers and townspeople of the Pyrénées-Orientales were swayed by suggestions that the refugees were dangerous to French well-being. In the first maddening days of the exodus it seemed as if the local people and their possessions would be stomped into the ground under the primeval force of an uprooted nation sweeping all before it. Under this pressure the desire to assist the Spaniards gave way to apprehension and fear. Pierre Izard experienced the influx as "an onslaught, abrupt as an inundation, sudden as a cataclysm."[1] Argelèsiens, "sad at heart . . . were speechless with stupor in watching this army of misery boiling through the smallest streets of the town . . . One did not know whether to remain in his house or to venture out to familiar places."[2] The immensity of the phenomenon awed Izard—the flight of entire villages and cities, complete with as much of their worldly goods as the fugitives could carry. "One was astonished that the earth did not follow [after them] . . . It was grandiose enormous, frightening!" Argelèsiens were swept aside by this tidal wave and could only "offer drink, food, a shelter for the night to mothers and children on the road to the camp."[3] For fifty hours after the opening of the border, Argelès "disappeared under the flood." Security forces seemed sparse and were unable to maintain a steady flow of refugees to the concentration camp. A nascent vigilante spirit emerged when a number of citizens suggested to Mayor Trescases that former French soldiers form a militia to channel the arrivals toward the camp and thus protecting their houses. Izard notes that the suggestion, which was not accepted, was ill-founded because "the Spaniards manifested no hostility toward the French."[4]

Citizen involvement proved unnecessary, however. By February 3 the build-up of security forces was gaining momentum and Senegalese units of the Twenty-fourth Infantry Regiment arrived in Argelès. Izard was with the mayor when the commanding captain appeared. "In a half-hour I shall unleash my Senegalese! They will not make any distinctions." The Senegalese had no trouble with the Spaniards. In response to the words "al campo" the refugees went willingly, even gratefully, for the word "camp" meant shelter, warmth, rest. Their anger when they first saw the "camp" was matched by their bitterness about the harsh and cruel treatment they claimed to have suffered at the hands of black and "Moorish" troops. Continued contact with these soldiers infuriated the Spanish refugees, who never forgave France for emulating Francisco Franco by the use of African troops. *L'Humanité* however, alert to the delicate issue of racial bias, carefully credited the Senegalese troops with being very sensitive to the needs of the refugees. Many dug into their own pockets to buy delicacies for the Spanish children.[5]

The Spaniards, despite their grievances, took full account of the colonial exploitation suffered by the Africans and interpreted the brutal actions of some as stemming from explicit approval from one white group to practice aggression upon another. The irony of the situation lay in the cynical act of General Franco, representative of the traditional Christian order that had expelled the Moslems from Spain, of reinserting Moroccan troops into Spanish life as defenders of the Roman Church. Therefore, the French employment of Moorish and black troops as guardians of the defeated Spanish republicans seemed to demonstrate underlying French sympathy with the nationalists and a desire to degrade the republicans.

No doubt, some Spaniards were guilty of robbery and of despoliation of French farms, of carrying small firearms and even grenades. But these incidents were magnified by the rightist press in its attempt to create mass hysteria. Izard, a man of moderation, conceded that a number of Spaniards had behaved poorly, but how, he asked, could one "separate the good from the bad?"[6] This question was brushed aside by the rightist newspapers and *La Dépêche de Toulouse*. All Spaniards were depicted as bloodthirsty revolutionaries who, having been thwarted in their Marxist aims on their own soil, were now determined, in collaboration with the French Communist Party and the Soviet Union, to work their evil designs on France. In this endeavor Spanish communists, socialists, anarchists, and even the Marxist Workers Party of Unification (POUM) were put into the same basket, despite the fact that the communists and socialists, while disliking each other, shared a positive hatred for the POUM, which was cordially reciprocated. Moreover, the refugees were depicted as dirty, smelly, inherently lar-

cenous, and, worst of all, callously ungrateful to the French who had welcomed them and provided sanctuary.
The tone was set by the use of scare headlines:

"The Army of Crime Is in France: What Are You Going to Do about It?"[7]

"Close Our Frontier to the Armed Bands of the F.A.I. and the P.O.U.M."[8]

"France Is Invaded"[9]

"Will the Army of Riot Reorganize Itself in France?"[10]

Even before the entry of the republican army *La Dépêche* warned darkly that communist, anarchist, and extremist elements were only a few kilometers from the border, and it called for military reinforcements. *Le Figaro* drew attention to the presence of "the famous division composed entirely of anarchists" (the Twenty-sixth, or Durruti, Division) and declared that France was becoming the depository for all the Spanish "undesirables and subversives." Vladimir d'Ormesson blamed popular-front policies for the influx and predicted "a wave of xenophobia such as had never before been seen in France!" It would penetrate the entire country and might become "savage and irresistable."[11] The theme of massive infiltration by communist and anarchist soldiers was further developed in articles and cartoons. A drawing by A. R. Charlet in *Gringoire* depicted a burly, leering Spanish soldier with a red star on his helmet walking along a road. A sign points to "Francia." The Red, armed with rifle and pistol, carries a huge sack on his back. It is filled with loot and one can see protruding from it a jeweled cross, silver goblet, and other jewels. The caption says: "And now I come to 'work' in France."[12] The same newspaper sounded alarms about native communist conspiracy. It asserted that fifty French communist deputies, led by André Marty, had infiltrated the concentration camps and were trying to incite riots. They were also seeking to reassemble the International Brigades and to whisk them to Paris for later use. In Paris itself, the paper said, the police had arrested forty-five Spanish Reds and anarchists who had demonstrated on the Montmartre butte and in Vintimille Square on February 10 and 11. The Red suburbs were hiding their Spanish brothers to protect them from police roundups.[13] Georges Ravon, in *Le Figaro* for February 3, reported the fears of the mayor of Perpignan that those refugees already in France were not being properly supervised, and he wondered what would happen when Gerona and Figueras were captured. Perpignan would be overrun by "numerous suspects of a particularly dangerous nature," the paper said, and lauded the system of searches of hotels and furnished rooms that had been instituted by the mayor.[14] Ravon also discussed the situation with the mayor of Banyuls-sur-mer, who said he had had quite enough of Spanish depredations. They had stolen chickens, wine, and other foodstuffs. They had molested the women of the town, and had been boisterous and aggressive in the cafés. Ravon also reported that the French Communist Party was distributing subversive literature among the refugees. *Le Figaro* joined the cry for massive reinforcement of existing security units, demanding that at least 40,000 regular troops and police be assigned to the frontier area.[15]

Theo Ripoll in *L'Action française* added to the tension with his assertion that Spanish arms were being stockpiled in Le Perthus, which straddled the French-Spanish border, and that agents of the French Communist Party were arranging to transport them to the interior. "How many anarchists have been able to enter our country with impunity? How many arms have the International Brigades been able to hide?" asked Ripoll.[16] *La Garonne* declared that if French tradition imposed a duty to welcome the unfortunate it did not oblige them to receive the despoilers of nuns or "to tame shrews of the Pasionaria type."[17] The same newspaper added a new dimension when it charged that among the refugees were an unknown number of common criminals who had escaped from Spanish prisons during the exodus.[18] On the basis of such information the French government moved to the panic-laden calculation that there were some ten thousand Spanish common criminals at large in France.[19] It ordered the detention and repatriation of any Spaniard who was found "uncontrolled" on the roads or who was deemed capable of having committed crimes in Catalonia.[20]

The catalogue of Spanish misdeeds compiled by the conservative and extremist press ran the gamut from plots to subjugate France to the commission of crimes against property and, perhaps worst of all, criticism of French cuisine. What could one do with women, supposedly starving, who refused French rice because it was not prepared "a la Valenciana"? Or men who rejected potato purée?[21] Moreover, the "intolerable attitudes" of the Spaniards ill-befitted their roles as guests of France. Their mien was "arrogant"; the officers were "proud and insolent"—they displayed unashamedly their hatred of the black and Moslem soldiers who guarded them, and they even cursed the white French soldiers who enforced a "strict discipline."[22] French and Spanish communists were also holding street demonstrations.[23] All of which inspired a feeling of "immense disgust" in Jean Taillemagre, correspondent of *La Garonne*.[24]

The situation had so corroded the sense of news values that *L'Action française* printed an eyewitness account by its special correspondent that found sinister implications in the fact that certain Spanish refugees carried the French communist newspaper *L'Humanité* in their hands.[25] *L'Indépendant* of Perpignan, a Radical newspaper, recounted the story of a Spanish child who was sheltered by nuns. The next morning, when a nun went to see if the child slept well, the young ingrate greeted her by singing the "Internationale," the communist hymn.[26] *La Dépêche* decried the "vulgar manner" in which some refugees asked for cigarettes and tobacco, heaping insults on those who failed to accommodate them. The Radical newspaper concluded that these incidents demonstrated the lack of feeling and the bad manners of Spaniards. It was no wonder, then, that Frenchmen were "unable to contain their indignation at being treated in this way."[27] Izard, however, felt that the broad coverage given the exodus by the press represented only "imperfect renditions" of the "deep disarray" of the area. He deplored the one-sidedness of the reportage, which did not take sufficient account of the plight of the Spaniards, who were "hungry and cold."[28]

Less fanciful were the claims made against Spaniards for property damage and destruction of crops. On February 9, Minister of Health Rucart returned for another look at the Argelès camp. Mayor Trescases protested against the continued lack of medical facilities and supplies. He also drew attention to damages sustained by buildings near the beach and the virtual destruction of the beach itself. Rucart promised solution of the problems but warned that it was not possible to do it better or more quickly. Medical personnel would be sent to the area, but it was difficult to do so because the army refused the services of its people or equipment.[29] Izard noted a paradox in the behavior of the Spaniards. Although "they cut the trees, break into the fruit store rooms, burn the roofs of barns," they are "bewildered, tired, pushed forward by the instinct of self-preservation and the attraction of free France."[30] One evening, he recounted, a shipment of beams and boards was received at the camp, amounting to about four hectares of young pines. Early the next morning, when Izard returned to the camp, there was no trace of the building materials. During the night the refugees had burned every scrap of wood or used it to shore up the holes they had dug in the sand for shelter. "They preferred the immediate warmth of a consumed rafter," he said, "to the future shelter which had been promised them . . . They were hungry, they were cold."[31] The extent of the gulf between the French and the Spanish is illustrated by the different interpretation given this same event by a Spaniard who participated in it. The refugees jumped to the conclusion that the lumber was not for them, but for the French guards. "They had no wood for us, but they did have wood enough to construct buildings for the French soldiers," he said. "We saw it, stole through the barbed wire, took the wood and used it for shelter and warmth."[32]

La Garonne proclaimed that "our farms are in danger."[33] It predicted that the forthcoming crop in Roussillon was doomed, and it bemoaned the tremendous losses that would be suffered by the tourist industry.[34] Large quantities of Spanish livestock, which had been brought by the refugees, were unaccountably not slaughtered for food. Instead the animals roamed the fields and ate the truck crops and anything else they could find. Many died of cold or sickness and their corpses abounded everywhere. On February 13 the mayor complained to the prefect about the abandoned animals.[35]

Upon the shoulders of Minister of Interior Albert Sarraut fell the lash of right-wing disapproval of the situation in the Pyrénées-Orientales. He was accused of failing to develop adequate plans for meeting the crisis. Didkowski, prefect of the Pyrénées-Orientales, after consultation with the military authorities, had asked Sarraut for 50,000 troops, but only 15,000 were on station by February 9, at which time the Spanish republican soldiers were still arriving in great numbers. Thus the mayor of Argelès, in fear of a refugee revolt at any moment, had advised the people of the village to remain indoors after nightfall.[36] The interior minister was also charged by Vladimir d'Ormesson in *Le Figaro* with exposing the entire French nation to "a variety of microbes" allegedly carried by the refugees.[37] *Gringoire* combined the medical threat with the political danger in a biting cartoon. It shows Spanish soldiers being inoculated by a French doctor at the border. Sarraut stands nearby, reassuring a French citizen. "Have no fear," the minister says, "I am protecting you against typhus, smallpox, scabies . . ." The citizen replies: "And what about the red pest?"[38]

On February 2 Senator Léon Bérard (Basses-Pyrénées) departed for Burgos to begin negotiations for the recognition of the new Franco government. This brought a public sigh of relief from Dr. D. L. Baudru, mayor of Perpignan, who envisaged the quick repatriation of the Spaniards as a result of any agreement that might be concluded. He was dismayed, he said, that Sarraut and Rucart had failed to note the critical condition of Perpignan during their recent inspection trip and had been too optimistic in their appraisal of the situation. The town was congested with refugees, he declared, and the health and security of the inhabitants was thus imperiled. He had told the minister to desist from making Perpignan a garbage dump.[39]

The heavy expense of sustaining the refugees was widely criticized, and other nations were castigated for not participating in their support.

The cost of maintaining a single refugee was put at eight francs per day, which was more expensive than the maintenance of a French soldier.[40] This would bring the total daily cost to three, four, or five million francs per day, depending upon the ultimate number of refugees. *La Dépêche* defended the admission of the Spaniards but added that it was "unthinkable for other nations not to share costs.[41] At a meeting of the Senate Committee on Foreign Affairs on February 2, additional aid of fifteen million francs was made available. Another fifteen million francs were appropriated later in the month. The Soviet Union provided twenty-eight thousand pounds for refugee assistance and Great Britain contributed fifty thousand pounds to the Red Cross for work in the camps.[42] French authorities confiscated a number of Spanish trucks that were transporting millions of dollars worth of Spanish jewels and precious metals. The French government also withheld 41,-850,000 francs that the Bank of Spain had on deposit with the Bank of France. These assets were used to defray refugee expenses.[43]

As much to reassure his own countrymen as to intimidate the Spaniards, the minister of the interior instituted a regime of strict discipline, harsh treatment of refugees, police sweeps in town and country, and an increasing military presence in the affected areas. Although there was a general recognition of the difficulty of providing essential food, housing, and medical care for the refugees, their continued lack gave rise to grave doubts about the government's intentions. "It is certain," Hugh Thomas said, "that the French government hoped, by neglect, to force as many as possible of the refugees to throw themselves on General Franco's mercy."[44] This policy of not-so-benign-neglect was construed by much of the French press as a tribute to the efficiency and devotion of their troops and gendarmes, who acted with "firmness, tact, and humanity."[45] However, Herbert L. Matthews, correspondent of the *New York Times,* wrote of the "inexcusably hardhearted treatment of the refugees by the French officials." For this he was admonished by his editors not to send "emotional reports" about camp conditions. The London *Times,* however, reported in great detail on living conditions in the camps, including the lack of housing, poor and insufficient water supplies, absence of medical attention, inadequate food, and dangerously unsanitary environment.[46]

Much of the Spanish bitterness about this period can be traced to their feeling of being humiliated by Senegalese, Moorish, and Algerian soldiers, although the white French troops and gendarmes also receive a goodly share of the blame. Mariano Constante was racked with fever when he and a group of fellow officers arrived at Septfonds (Tarn et Garonne) camp. Senegalese soldiers, commanded by white French officers, podded the Spaniards with rifles and sticks along the road to the camp. Unable to keep up with the group, Constante fell slightly behind and was pushed by a rifle butt. Immediately, his captain, "with a terrible blow, sent the Senegalese to the ground, unconscious." When the young French captain arrived on the scene his Spanish counterpart told him in French: "Treat us like human beings. We are used to battle and we will not permit anyone to maltreat us." The *Times* reported from French sources criticism of the behavior of Senegalese and gardes mobiles.[47] Dr. José Pujol wondered who had originated the idea of dispatching Senegalese troops to the scene. It was, he said, "an act of moral cruelty . . . The accumulated odium in the hearts of the blacks against the despotism and cruelty of the whites, the instinctive feeling of revenge," was allowed to play itself out against the hapless Spaniards.[48] Actually, the Twenty-fourth Regiment, which contained a sizable number of Senegalese, was traditionally stationed in Perpignan and was assigned because it was readily available. Antonio Vilanova, while concurring in accusations of harsh treatment by the Senegalese, indicated that at least in part their actions were dictated by official French expectations. He said that "when they were not watched by the French officials, they were very tolerant with us."[49] The Algerians, mounted on their small, wiry horses, were used to "scour the fields and round up the scattered refugees."[50]

The Pyrénées-Orientales department had been divided into five sectors by the minister of the interior after his initial visit: Perpignan, Cerbère, Le Perthus, Prats-de Mollo, and Bourg-Madame. Prefect Didkowski was given extended police powers over Perpignan and the other sectors were in command of subprefects of secretaries-general. A special force of sixty gendarmes and three companies of gardes mobiles were assigned to Perpignan, and they conducted continual street forays and searches of hotels, restaurants and other public places to corral stray Spaniards who had either escaped being sent to the concentration camps or who had escaped from them.[51] Constancia de la Mora, who had established herself in an office near the Spanish consulate in Perpignan, wrote that the consulate was a dangerous place for refugees to visit because the special police squards raided its environs regularly, carrying off any Spaniard who did not have proper papers.[52] Isabel de Palencia, reunited with her husband and three sons in Perpignan, saw them all seized and sent away. Her husband, the former Spanish republican minister to Finland, was sent to Paris. Two sons were sent to the camp at Prats-de-Mollo and were caught in an escape attempt. The third son, an artillery officer, was transferred to Haras, a reception center in Perpignan that housed several generals and members of the

Cortes. In Paris itself, where most refugees had no identification papers, a constant manhunt was conducted. The police ordered all hotel managers and concierges to report Spanish guests and their visitors.[53] Jordi Arquer, political commissar of the second division of the POUM, arrived in France on February 3 or 4 and was hunted by both the communists and the French police. He was smuggled into Perpignan where he was assisted by friendly socialists and members of his own group. Then he was hidden in a truck and taken to Paris. His friends there hated Minister of Interior Sarraut, who "made the lives of the Spaniards very miserable" and pressed a sustained effort to unearth all "uncontrolled" Spaniards. Without papers or money, Arquer was able to exist only because of the aid proffered by French sympathizers. He moved constantly from one house to another. His position was such that if the police apprehended him he would most assuredly have been sent to a prison camp. If the communists had caught him his life would have been in danger.[54]

The extent of French zeal in seizing Spanish refugees is illustrated by a report from a security inspector in Toulouse. On February 7, 1939, his men conducted a sweep of furnished rooms and hotels in that city. They questioned ninety individuals of diverse nationality and detained twelve for further interrogation. Nine of the latter group were Spanish, two were Italian, and one was Polish.[55] At Poitiers the prefect refused to allow French socialists to visit or to bring food to a group of five hundred Spanish arrivals and even refused access to representatives of the Spanish republican government.[56] At Flers de l'Orne a speaker for the Parti social français (the former Croix de Feu) declared that the Spaniards should have been greeted by gunshot and warned that if "dictatorship of the left" came to power in France, the PSF would use its stockpile of arms to "do what Franco did."[57]

There were those in France, particularly among leftist groups, who did not succumb to the hysteria and attempted to mitigate the police state mentality toward the refugees. Men like Pierre Izard understood the collective trauma of the Spanish republicans and, although insisting on punishment for malefactors, refused to indict and condemn the entire group. There were thousands of examples of kindliness and concern shown by Frenchmen for the unfortunate fugitives. By March 1939, there were 102,000 internees (equal to the present-day population of Perpignan) filling every bit of beach at Argelès.[58] The camps at St. Cyprien, Barcarès, and elsewhere were growing rapidly. The primitive conditions under which this mass of humanity was formed to live aroused sympathy and understanding in Izard. A tent had finally been set up as an infirmary and it gave off an overpowering smell of ether while the air was punctuated by "cries, groans, and howls." A rumor that political groups were attempting to hold meetings brought swift mobilization of security troops and patrols throughout the camp. Once every day a military truck arrived in the camp and loaves of bread were thrown into the air. Immediately, "there is a rush! The truck becomes a human cluster. One listens to cries, blows, men falling, striking, fleeing with bread."[59]

Far from being a marauding horde, the Spaniards appeared to some observers to display "extreme lassitude" and "the passivity of a herd." Invariably, at least during the influx of early February, they demonstrated their gratitude with the cry, "vive la France."[60] They may have been restless and may have complained about the shortcomings of the camp, but one correspondent, at least, understood their feelings: "They have marched days to get to the frontier and then thirty kilometers more to get to Argelès, where one offers them the beach to lie on and the cold of the night . . . Yesterday they were in battle. It is unheard of that today they should be docile, also resigned."[61] Jean-Maurice Herrmann, viewing the scene at Le Boulou where refugees roamed the hillsides, noted that hundreds of children had slept in the open for a week or more. To the comment of a French guard that this was very bad for the children, he replied: "It is more than bad. It is a crime." He criticized government inaction and asked, "Is it so difficult . . . to erect tents to shelter women and children at night? The national defense would not suffer." And he asked a question that was troubling the French Left: "Is this [being done] because [Foreign Minister] M. Bonnet seeks to merit the friendship of Franco?"[62]

A different kind of pressure was brought on the government by prominent Catholics, who, however they might disagree politically and morally with the Spanish republicans, nevertheless felt that France should answer the call of humanitarian assistance. A manifesto signed by a number of prominent clergymen, politicians, and intellectuals declared that "France ought to accept the honor of relieving the horrible misery of Spaniards who direct themselves toward its frontiers." The manifesto was signed by Cardinal Verdier, Henri Bergson, Justin Godard, Isely, Léon Jouhaux, the Marquess of Lillers, Jacques Maritain, François Mauriac, Jean Perrin, Henri Pichot, and Paul Valéry.[63] A week later, another manifesto appealed for assistance to Spanish artists, writers, and intellectuals. The list of signers, in addition to Mauriac and Maritain, included Benjamin Cremieux, André Gide, and Jules Romains. Georges Bidault in *L'Aube,* a Catholic newspaper, condemned those who pinned the label of coward on the Spanish republican army. He recalled their courageous actions in thirty months of combat.[64]

Above all, the French Left was concerned with an apparent switch in attitude displayed by such newspapers as *La Dépêche,* which seemed to echo a corresponding change in the policy of the Daladier government. In an editorial on February 7, *Le Midi socialiste* asked: "Is *La Dépêche* becoming franquiste?" It criticized *La Dépêche* for presenting the Spaniards in such a light that readers "will see in every contingent of the refugees a band of brigands." Although *Le Midi socialiste* agreed with the Radical newspaper's stricture that "we want neither anarchy nor anarchists in our house," it resented the intimation that anarchy already reigned among the Spaniards in France because of the alleged dominance of that persuasion among the Spanish refugees. Furthermore, *La Dépêche,* by urging the repatriation of all able-bodied men, was charged with adopting the position of *La Garonne* and the French franquistes. *La Dépêche,* for its part, accused certain "Soviet apostles" of mounting an injurious campaign against the efforts of the French government.[65]

By mid-February the situation seemed to be stabilizing, in some eyes, at least. In contrast to more fanatical newspapers, *L'Indépendant* (Perpignan) felt that "the disarray provoked by the massive and unexpected arrival of the Spanish refugees is now in regression. Order is reestablished thanks to the military, provisioning is assured, the uninvited guests who fled the camps are now corralled."[66]

If the Great Fear of 1939 was losing some of its intensity among the French, those Spaniards who remained surrounded by barbed wire or who were hunted in the cities and in the countryside nursed a great resentment at what they saw as a continuing betrayal of their cause by France and the other democracies. They felt that the use of African troops to police them was a visible symbol of French cynicism and cruelty, that the French sought to debase them morally, and that they were holding them as repatriation pawns in the negotiations with Franco. They resented not having been treated with the respect shown to other defeated armies that had sought sanctuary in friendly countries. In their feverish postdefeat state of acrimony they believed that the French fascists were dictating national policy to a spineless government, that French contempt for Spaniards was rampant, and that the unbridled French bureaucracy was demonstrating its hatred of liberty by its treatment of the symbols of that liberty. Above all they hated the loss of their freedom of movement and the badge of inferiority that this loss pinned on them. A few voices of moderation professed to understand that the French were trying to help, but that time and circumstance had conspired against them. But the mass of Spaniards concluded that the sacrifices they had made for democracy in their struggle against international fascism were brutally disregarded and unappreciated. They had expected that "France would open her arms to receive the defeated people of Spain,"[67] but instead were "treated like dogs, robbed, whipped," and shunned as "undesirable elements."[68]

"It was truly a Calvary," Federica Montseny declared in an interview in April 1974. "We were victims of an unqualified discrimination, treated as prisoners of war, in spite of the fact that France was not at war with Spain, nor with the Spanish republic above all. We suffered horribly . . . many elderly and children and wounded lost their lives, and every time we remember this, it opens wounds that will never heal [*abre llagas que no se cicatrizarán nunca*]."[69] Because of the later Spanish republican role in the Resistance, she added, postwar French governments "have done all that is possible to stanch the wounds opened in the hearts of thousands of Spaniards. Nevertheless, the treatment given to those who came then was bad because France—perhaps the same occurs in every country—has a very developed nationalistic sentiment and a reserve, not to say hostility, toward all foreigners."[70] Resentment and bewilderment boiled furiously in the hearts of many Spaniards almost four decades later. In July 1975, Mariano Puzo, a former Spanish republican soldier, vacationed in the village of Enveigt (Pyrénées-Orientales), which is near La Tour de Carol, an entry point for thousands of Spanish refugees in February 1939. From the porch of his friend's home he could see the water-logged meadow where the refugees—soldiers and civilians alike—spent their first nights in France, without blankets or food and soaked by snow and rain. Still obsessed with the exodus, he asked many of the older residents why the French had behaved as they had. "The people of these mountains are habitually unpolished and uncommunicative," he wrote, "and in this particular instance they refused absolutely to discuss the matter." In 1939 many of them had been pro-Franco, he believed, and had been happy to see the republicans suffer in defeat. They "also robbed us of whatever possessions we still retained." Later, under the German occupation of that territory, many of the French fled across the Spanish border and sought refuge. "In the camp of Miranda de Ebro," he said, "the French refugees had barracks, sanitary facilities, and aid from the Red Cross. But in 1939 all they gave us was disdain and humiliation."[71]

The "most galling" aspect of the Spanish experience was "the loss of liberty." "All the rest, physical discomforts of every kind, were nothing compared to the lack of freedom," Palencia declared.[72] Vila-nova was of the opinion that the French government "literally lost its head under the impact of the human avalanche. Its myopic perspective of the situation left it totally exposed, and its only preoccupation was to contain that human tide, to enclose, not to allow free movement to those dangerous beings . . . The French repressive apparatus was mobilized to control what the authorities estimated was . . . an invasion by a horde of savages and assassins, and they treated them as such."[73]

Equally maddening to the Spanish was the feeling that behind the cruel treatment lay a French desire to break their spirits and to encourage repatriation. Miguel Angel reported that Spanish military officers and government officials "were humiliated before their soldiers."[74] Montseny observed that "in this deliberate manner, almost scientifically, they debased us morally, diminishing us in our own eyes . . . making of the human person . . . a hungry beast, dirty, obsessed with the vilest necessities."[75] The Spanish republicans, she added, despite the attitudes of some French men and women of goodwill, were in general viewed "with disgust and with hostility. We carried on ourselves the weight of all the crimes that had been attributed to us by nationalist propaganda, and we were marked by the eternal stigma of all revoluitonaries."[76]

Who was to blame? Or was there any blame to assign? Sentiment among Spaniards was that, despite the presence in France of "true and honest democrats," the fascists and conservatives were the stronger elements in the politics of the nation.[77] The weakness and apparent impotence of the French Left in ameliorating the lot of the refugees was a source of bitterness among Spanish republicans. "There were socialist ministers in power, there was a great strength of the Left in France," Montseny wrote, "All, without distinction, are responsible for what was done to us . . . We were treated worse than German prisoners of war."[78]

Despite the profound sense of disillusionment displayed by so many Spaniards, there were those among them who had kind—or at least understanding—words for their hosts. The harsh political measures taken by France should not obscure the fact that republican Spain owed a great debt to France for its basic humanitarianism, according to Alvarez del Vayo.[79] Some among the soldiers, while viewing the treatment of refugees as an extension of the neglect shown by the democracies during the civil war, at least understood the impossibility of building enough barracks in such a short period of time.[80] And if Montseny apportioned guilt equally among the groups of the French Left, the communist Miguel Angel felt that the official French attitude had been defied by "the people, the democratic organs, and particularly the Communist Party [who] did all they could to help the refugees in

1   *Le Perthus: children and wounded soldiers await evacuation.*

2   *Spanish republicans on the road to exile in France.*

3   *Le Perthus: the exodus of the Spanish civilian population.*

4 *Le Perthus: the nationalist forces arrive at the frontier.*

5 *Le Perthus: arms confiscated from the republicans.*

6   *On the road from Banyuls: republican soldiers heading for Argelès.*

7   *The camp at Argelès: Spanish republican refugees behind barbed wire.*

the concentration camps, and to house and aid those that were able to escape."[81]

Albert Sarraut, target of numerous attacks for his apparent unpreparedness, even found a defender in del Vayo. The foreign minister of the Spanish republic declared that it would be unjust not to recognize the personal effort made by the French minister of the interior on behalf of the refugees. He pictured Sarraut as making desperate efforts "to counteract the pressure of those groups who insisted that the best way to solve the problem of the Spanish refugees was to send them back en masse to Franco."[82] Sarraut defended his policy in a General Assembly debate in mid-March. "If the preparations [for building barracks and other facilities] had become known, they would have raised a multitude of protests. I would have been accused of predicting the collapse of the Catalan front, and of contributing to it with my prediction: I would have been accused of attracting to France an exodus that, until the last minute, I tried to prevent."[83] In fact, the war was still in progress in Spain in March 1939, although it was to end two weeks after Sarraut's speech.

There is no doubt that in early 1939 the Spanish republican exiles continued to be trapped in the deadly cross currents of French and world politics. The hue and cry raised by the conservative, monarchist, and fascist elements within France influenced the policy of an ambivalent coalition government, which at this late date in the development of the Spanish Civil War had neither the will nor the desire to antagonize its English allies or its potential adversaries, unless its direct interests were threatened, as by sinkings of French ships or the threat of a continuing Italian presence in Spain after the war. The main thrust of its policy was to come to quick agreement with the new Franco government in Spain. In this light the republican refugees hung like albatrosses around the neck of the Daladier government. But while this would explain in part the political basis for the treatment of the refugees, it does not account fully for the panic and hostility that swept France, and particularly the Pyrenees border areas, which allowed almost free rein to repressive measures by the police, the military, and the bureaucracy. For this we must look to the ancient French suspicion of foreigners. Aided by the acceleration of ideological and racial enmity, the old feelings surfaced, sweeping away the cultural affinity of French Catalans with their Spanish brothers and substituting a wild fear for the security of person and property. It must also be said, however, that the Spaniards fell back upon their own particularist prejudices under the lash of misfortune. "If the French people are anti-foreigner," Jordi

Arquer said, "It must always be remembered that the Spaniards have similiar feelings for the foreigner."[84] Having fought what they considered to be the common battle of democracy against fascism, the Spanish republicans expected to be greeted as brothers and heroes. When the reverse occurred, they reasserted their own ancient hostility toward the French. At a time when extreme emotion dictated the course of events, perhaps no other outcome could have been expected. For, despite the veracity of French claims that the Spanish were ungrateful, had stolen, and had committed radical political acts on French soil, none of these causes, by themselves or in totality, could realistically have been called an immediate and powerful threat to the French nation. The interaction of reactionary doctrine with ancient prejudice had called into being the Great Fear of 1939. With the bulk of the Spaniards safely locked up, the worst of the panic passed by mid-March. The French were now to become preoccupied with such matters as Czechoslovakia, Poland, and the Nazi-Soviet nonaggression pact. The concentration camps became institutionalized and their inhabitants waited with apprehension for the beginning of that war which they, better than most others, knew was inevitable.

IN THE EYE OF
THE HURRICANE

THE BEACH PARTY

Spaniard of the exodus of yesterday and Spaniard of the exodus of
today . . . There, nothing remains.

Dig a hole in the soil of your exile, plant a tree. Water it with
your tears and wait.

There, there is nothing any more, remain here and wait.

León Felipe, in Romancero de la resistencia española

FINALLY, THE RIVER OF HUMANITY was dammed. Cascading
over the Franco-Spanish border it had inundated the Roussillonais
coastal plain, boiled through the mountain passes, and lapped at the
peaks of the Pyrenees. Slowly, it had been contained and channeled
into the immense reservoirs of the concentration camps. Some thousands of the Spanish mass had been directed toward the north, but the
bulk of the refugees had been led, pushed, cajoled, and driven onto the
beaches of the Côte Vermeille. The defeated ones seethed within their
barbed-wire enclosures. Many of them could and did slip through the
barriers to find extra food or shelter in the homes of friendly Frenchmen. But by mid-February the period of mass movement had ended.
Civilians and soldiers were now to become preoccupied with the problems of living under virtually prison conditions, of the threat of forced
repatriation to Spain, and, later, of deciding whether to remain in
France or to seek to emigrate to other countries.

Argelès, the first camp, had been quickly saturated with refugees. By
February 7 another beach camp had been opened at St. Cyprien, a few
kilometers to the north, and two days later a third camp was activated
at Barcarès, a sandy spit of land lying between the sea and a broad
lagoon, 15 kilometers north of St. Cyprien. With this redistribution the
refugee population at Argelès dropped to 65,000–75,000. St. Cyprien
filled up so rapidly that within one week of its opening it had between
72,000 and 95,000 inhabitants. Barcarès, which received its first contingents on February 11, contained some 300 barracks that accommo-

dated approximately 13,000 refugees. Some 50,000–60,000 Spaniards there were nevertheless forced to seek shelter on the beach.[1] A number of camps that had been set up in the Pyrenees Mountains, notably the installation at Bourg-Madame, were evacuated because of the intense cold, but at the end of February *Le Midi socialiste* noted that 75,000 Spanish republican soldiers still remained without shelter in the mountains.[2]

The volatile mass of humanity that stirred restlessly within the barbed-wire cages was unlike any previous Spanish political or economic migration. The key difference, in addition to sheer volume, was the presence of a large number of skilled workers and professionals among the traditional farm laborers and unskilled workers.[3] A partial census of refugees taken in July 1939 revealed that 16,578 refugees, comprising 10.5 percent of the sample of 159,149 male Spaniards surveyed, were white-collar workers or professionals. Industrial workers also passed into France in greater numbers than in former migrations, comprising 45.4 percent of the total sample. The agricultural group constituted 30.4 percent of the total:[4]

Occupational group		Number of refugees	Percentage
Agricultural sector			
Agricultural laborers		45,918	28.9
Specialized workers		2,451	1.5
	Total	48,369	30.4
Industrial sector			
Mines		3,645	2.3
Wood industry		5,922	3.7
Metallurgical, mechanical, electricial industries		18,894	11.9
Construction and public works		15,628	9.8
Food industry		4,926	3.1
Transport		9,558	6.0
Other industries		13,729	8.6
	Total	72,302	45.4
Service sector			
Commercial employees		6,325	4.0
Administrative employees		3,616	2.3
Liberal professions		4,265	2.7
Professional military		2,372	1.5
	Total	16,578	10.5
Doubtful classification		21,900	13.7
	Grand total	159,149	100.00

Catalans, comprising 36.5 percent of Spanish refugees, were the largest single group to enter France, according to a sample of refugees living in southwestern France after the liberation in August 1944. However, other Spanish regions were also well represented, many of their natives having fled to Catalonia in earlier stages of the war: 18.0 percent were from Aragon; 14.1 percent from the Levante; 10.5 percent from Andalusia; 5.9 percent from Castilla la Nueva; and 15.0 percent from other regions.[5] (See Appendix B).

The new camps at St. Cyprien and Barcarès, while alleviating the inhuman overcrowding at Argelès, were not intended to lift the spirits of the Spanish republicans. Anger, despair, and depression were the dominant moods among the refugees. Jean Olibo noted that the only activities among the camp inmates were card-playing, woodcarving, dominoes, smoking, and sleeping, all designed to kill boredom. "The ennui, our enemy! It is anguish, anger, and ugly thoughts."[6] Some improvement in physical and emotional camp conditions took place later in the month, "but with what slowness," Jean-Maurice Herrmann lamented. He decried the French policy of neglect of the refugees and the tendency to badger them with excessive discipline. But he noted that despite their miseries the refugees maintained excellent morale. "If one hopes to drive them to gestures of revolt, one is wasting one's time."[7] The press corps and representatives of aid organizations were discouraged from visiting the camps, especially Argelès, for several weeks. *La Dépêche de Toulouse* declared that the camp officials had begged the journalists not to enter, and Salvador de Madariaga observed that "the recruiting sergeant and the merchant penetrated [the camps] more easily than the sister of charity, the social worker, or the doctor." The cellist and composer Pablo Casals, who did visit the camps, likened them to Dante's Inferno.[8]

Spanish refugees are unanimous in their recollections of the mind-deadening and body-destroying bleakness of their early days in the camps. The first sight of St. Cyprien was of "an immensity of sand, and, on the sand, some beings . . . They appeared miniscule, diminished, and almost unreal . . . A mass of mingled shadows, squeezed together, compact. A fantastic troop of prisoners in an enclosure." The apparent hopelessness of his position brought a deep despair to one refugee: "I am torn: in this hard universe, this inhuman spectacle, I remember and I cry out that all, all, was in vain . . . I know, exiled, the hollow destiny." But he revived himself with the thought of his commander's injunction, whispered as he was dying in the retreat to France: he had told the survivors that they did not have the right to renounce the struggle; all must conduct themselves with dignity to the very end.[9]

Antonio Herrero, a member of the Durruti Division, recalled the arrival of wounded men at Septfonds, himself included: "The men flung there like rags were no longer men. They were no more than *piltrajas* (skinny pieces of human flesh), abandoned by the whole world."[10] Septfonds, which was later to serve as an assembly point for skilled industrial workers scheduled for work in French and German industry, was called Camp Judas by its inmates.[11] Antonio Vilanova, commenting upon the lack of latrines at St. Cyprien, noted that the Spaniards sarcastically named the beach "Avenida Daladier," in honor of the "fraternal reception" the French premier had given the exiles. Barcarès, according to Vilanova, was the best camp, boasting 300 barracks, disinfection equipment, and a paved road. At the beginning of World War II it was transferred to the French army. Similarly, the camp at Amelie-les-Bains (Pyrénées-Orientales), a resort area that catered to British tourists, had an abundance of firewood and other amenities. It also had for a neighbor an elderly British woman who came daily with baskets of raw mutton chops for the soldiers and complained bitterly that she was unable to cook properly on a slab of sheet iron balanced on boulders.[12]

Excessive French discipline and measures to insulate the refugees from the outside world angered the Spaniards and their French sympathizers. Distribution of left-wing newspapers was prohibited but that of right-wing papers was authorized. To the socialist press this was proof that the Spanish republicans were being treated as prisoners of war. In Perpignan, by order of the prefect, street collections of funds to assist the refugees and the issuance of pamphlets and posters were forbidden. Meeting halls refused to rent their facilities to socialist and communist groups, and the offices of these parties were searched.[13] The refusal of some internees to answer a call for a formation was treated as a potential revolt, the men being immediately surrounded by troops and marched off. Herrmann reported that a garde mobile beat some Spanish republicans with a stick because they crowded around a bread truck.[14] Unrest was further manifested by frequent escapes from camp and by the assassination of several Spanish communists who had been involved in anti-anarchist police work.[15] French control was further enhanced by the installation of loudspeakers that transmitted orders from headquarters and broadcast nationalist propaganda urging the refugees to volunteer for repatriation. The latter tactic heightened refugee fears of forced repatriation and added to their general restlessness. Between announcements the loudspeakers blared rumbas and tangos.[16]

The collective misery of the camps was quickly exposed by parliamentary delegations from the communist and socialist parties. Their activities, combined with continued complaints from municipal officials in the Pyrénées-Orientales and articles in the world press, propelled the issue onto the national stage and forced important changes. An informal group of communist deputies toured the camp areas and declared that the Spanish republicans were being treated worse than German prisoners in the First World War. They compiled a list of cruel acts to which the Spaniards had been subjected and condemned the "odious brutalization" of refugees. They called for Spanish control of the camps, absolute neutrality of French officials in any choice by refugees between going to Madrid or Burgos if they opted for repatriation, transportation of Spanish soldiers to the central zone, permission for French liberal and leftist newspapers to circulate in the camps, and free access to the camps by parliamentary and trade union representatives. The group also demanded the immediate dismissal of Prefect Raoul Didkowski and the constitution of an all-party parliamentary committee to launch a full-scale investigation of the camps. Among the signers of the letter were André Marty (Seine) and Charles Tillon (Seine). Both men had been members of the International Brigades; Tillon was later to lead the Francs Tireurs et Partisans Francais (FTPF) in the Resistance.[17]

Less political and more analytical in its approach, the Socialist Party delegation focused its efforts on securing better living conditions for the Spanish refugees. From February 9 to 14 it toured refugee installations in the Pyrénées-Orientales, spoke at great length with camp inmates, and met with Didkowski and General Falgade, the commander of the Sixteenth Military Region, and with local mayors. In addition, it held sessions with Spanish republican officials and members of the Spanish Catalan, Basque, communist, socialist, and bourgeois parties. The tone of the document that the committee produced under the chairmanship of Vincent Auriol was reasoned rather than bombastic, logical rather than emotional, and, while it spoke frankly about French shortcomings, was geared to practical change within the camps. The delegation said it had limited its purpose to the exposure of facts, without any prejudice: "We have suppressed our feelings of sadness and shame at such a scandalous and atrocious situation." It recognized that the rapidity with which the refugee situation had developed, and its unexpected breadth, had placed undue strains on the French capacity to receive the Spanish republicans in proper fashion. Even so, the report declared, many French officials and citizens "had done everything humanly possible." That is, all but the French Red Cross, which was accused of being "reserved . . . and perhaps hostile." The Red Cross had made an appeal for volunteers but had never put its resources at the service of the sick and wounded. In contrast, the Aide Centrale Sanitaire Internationale and other private service organizations had worked with the wounded under extremely difficult conditions. However, the report contended, the longer the emergency continued the less pardonable became "the slowness and incompetence" of the responsible government agencies, particularly the army, in eliminating such camp abuses as neglect of the wounded and sick, absence of hygiene, poor food, and lack of organization. Immediate changes in administration and services were required if France were not "to run the risk of dangerous epidemics and of grave incidents provoked by suffering and despair."[18]

The underlying cause of mismanagement, according to the socialist delegation, was failure to place the direction of the camps under a single authority. The separation of functions between military and civil officials had resulted in a dangerous lack of coordination.[19]

In a detailed, factual exposure of the situation as it existed at the time of their inspection, the socialist deputies focused national attention on the shortcomings of the camps and the need for far-reaching changes. It cited the plight of refugees who were forced to "live in the open air, in a whirlwind of sand, and under the glacial cold of the nights." Although such a situation was excusable from January 27 to February 5, it was inexcusable by February 14, the report said. From the hygienic point of view the situation was even worse: "The filth is dreadful." There was insufficient water for drinking, even less for washing, and no latrine facilities. All of which had created apprehension about the possibility of epidemic. The delegation visited an infirmary: "Simple and ugly, on the sand, without floor, without chair or bench for the wounded." Supplies were in pitifully short supply: old dressings were frequently reused and there was not a single container of aspirin. Administrative disorder extended to the provisioning of the camps, the delegation found. The standard menu was bread and water, with occasional bits of vegetables. The army had failed to provide field kitchens, thus the first meat apportioned to refugees had been raw. Only in the past few days had the army begun to use the livestock that had been brought by the Spaniards, as well as Spanish republican army field kitchens.[20]

The socialist parliamentarians commended the work of many officers and men of the army, gardes mobiles, and gendarmerie, but it commented harshly on the widespread abuses practiced by other men of these units. The report found an overriding perception of the refugees as prisoners of war or criminals, leading to an attitude that excused excessive physical beatings, pressure on refugees to return to nationalist

Spain, and theft of personal belongings of Spaniards. It called for severe punishment of French personnel guilty of engaging in these practices.[21]

Spanish resentment at being guarded by Senegalese and Moroccan troops was held by the socialist group to be valid. It was a "regrettable psychological error" to place these troops in direct contact with the refugees, even granting the fact that the Sixteenth Military Region garrisoned a strong proportion of African troops. The Spanish republicans had too recent and bitter a memory of Franco's use of such soldiers to accept easily the black guards.[22]

To avoid a catastrophe the report urged the adoption of several major reforms. They included unity of command, dissolution of large camps that enclosed hundreds of thousands of men and women, and closer cooperation between French and Spanish officials. It was too late to attempt to build an adequate number of barracks in the present camps. The report noted that wood sufficient for sixty barracks had arrived at Argelès, but at such a pace, many refugees would still lack shelter in September. Only the army and the centralized organizations of the national state could furnish the wherewithal for rectification of the situation. To effect a rapid evacuation, beginning with Argelès, it was suggested that Spanish military personnel be transferred to a number of large French military installations that were then empty. The huge camp at Larzac was cited as an example. The French army had steadfastly refused to entertain this notion, on the grounds that the camps and their supplies might be needed—on an instant's notice—to house French reservists reponding to a sudden mobilization. The socialist report contended that even if the wooden barracks at such camps could not be utilized it was entirely feasible to erect tents in other areas of the camps to house the Spaniards and to make available the necessary sanitary and culinary facilities.[23]

Unity of command, deemed indispensable for the erasure of the inefficiency and chaos, should extend to cooperation with the Spanish civil and military authorities within the camps, the report asserted. Spanish soldiers should be placed under the discipline of their own officers and assigned responsible tasks in the camps, including cooking, postal services, health, and maintenance of sanitary facilities. The French role should be limited to surveillance of the camp perimeter and provision of central supply and other services. Spanish medical and technical personnel should be identified and utilized to the fullest extent. The report also urged a reclassification of Spaniards that would lead to the release of all who had regular passports; placement of the elderly, women, and children in special facilities; reunion of camp inmates with relatives residing in France; detection and isolation of common criminals; and the housing of elderly Spanish officers and civil officials in special hotels.[24]

Along with purely administrative matters, the socialist report concerned itself with what it called the "moral conditions of existence" among the refugees. Of paramount importance was the need to assist the refugees to reestablish connections with their dispersed families. Several French newspapers had already begun to print refugee inquiries concerning the whereabouts of their families,[25] and the report urged official cooperation in this venture. It also called for the issuance of free postage, paper, and pencils, and the distribution of tobacco. Visits between different sections of the camp were to be encouraged. All major newspapers were to be permitted to circulate inside the camps. The report also suggested that the Spaniards be authorized to print a refugee bulletin, which would be submitted to prefectorial censorship.[26]

Above all, the report declared, the actions of all French personnel should be guided by the knowledge that the Spanish soldiers "are neither prisoners nor deserters . . . One ought to regard them [with] the generosity which one accords to soldiers stricken with adversity while defending the independence of their country." On the contrary, the report noted, many French officers and civilians had been guilty of complicity in advancing the repatriation drive of the victorious nationalists. "Too many *franquiste* officers and soldiers come into France and hobnob regularly with the French fascists or royalists," it added.[27]

Léon Blum noted that Edouard Daladier was deeply impressed with the findings and appeared to share the socialist delegation's convictions. Daladier had been "astonished" that tents had not been placed at the disposal of the refugees. But Blum wondered why the premier hesitated to translate this sympathy into acts.[28] The refusal of the army to house the refugees was attributed to a Daladier-Bonnet plan to deliver them to Franco. The premier was accused of harboring the thought that it was "better that these refugees do not recover too soon."[29] A newly formed group of 300 deputies, known as the Group of French-Spanish Friendship, decried the actions of those Frenchmen who "sought to create in France an animosity toward the Spanish soldiers and civilians," and asked the government to take necessary actions to alleviate camp conditions, "compatible with the human dignity" of the Spaniards.[30] *Le Midi socialiste* criticized the "absurd obstinacy of the minister of war in refusing to give up even one blanket of his stocks" because of the possibility of French mobilization. If this dire step became necessary, the paper said, the Spanish republican army could be reconstituted under the command of its own officers: "armed with material, in 48 hours they would be at the frontier, at the side of our own troops." However, radical supporters of the government ridiculed the socialists for suggesting that the refugees lacked necessary comforts and approved the decision against opening the army camps.[81]

When the cabinet council finally discussed the crisis on February 18 the socialists felt that it was in agreement with the basic premise of the report—namely, that the situation prevalent in the camps could not be maintained. But the ministers did not change their stand on army camp utilization. Similarly, the stress of the official communique was on "accelerating the voluntary repatriation to Spain" of civilians and the military. Minister of Interior Albert Sarraut, who was praised by the socialists for the humane tone of his presentation, maintained that although repatriation was desirable, the French government would insist on voluntary decisions by the refugees and, further, would seek guarantees from the Spanish nationalists that there would not be reprisals against the republicans. He was supported in this stand by Bonnet. The council also decided to assure greater coordination in the management of the camps and to ameliorate poor conditions, but it was silent on the socialist proposal to place the refugees under the discipline of their own officers. The only firm decision taken at the meeting was to send General Menard, commandant of the Toulouse Military Region, to Perpignan with the mission of unifying the administration of the camps. *Le Populaire* remarked that for the moment the question was apparently not one of emptying Argelès and St. Cyprien, but of "decongesting" them.[32] Even before this meeting the minister of war had sent General Besson, of the Conseil Superieure de la Guerre, to Argelès to study conditions regarding food, shelter, and hygiene.[33]

Pressure for changes in the camps was also generated by the mayors and deputies of the Pyrénées-Orientales. Under the initiative of the socialist deputy Louis Noguères, these officials met with Prefect Didkowski on February 19 and presented numerous complaints and suggestions for reforms. The prefect, perhaps stretching the truth somewhat, told the group that the hygienic state of the camps was "excellent." The sole source of potential danger, he added, was the presence of fifty-six typhoid victims in the old military hospital at Perpignan. Dr. D. L. Baudru, mayor of Perpignan, seized upon this disclosure to demand the dispersal of refugees to other departments as a means of avoiding epidemics. Frédéric Trescases, mayor of Argelès, protested against the continuing existence of the concentration camp in his commune. The mayors of the mountain communities of Prats-de-Mollo and Arles-sur-Tech (Pyrénées-Orientales) declared that there were still many uncontrolled Spaniards hiding in the mountains. The officials feared that, "pushed by hunger or bad instincts, [they] might become dangerous." Trescases also informed the prefect that the cemetary at Argelès would not be able to receive more than twenty new bodies and urged the creation of a new burial ground for refugees on the property of one Thomas Deprade. The mayors also suggested that Spaniards who had resided in France before enlisting in the Spanish republican army be allowed to leave the camps. Didkowski announced that Spanish livestock would be reserved for use in the camps and urged the mayors to draw up lists of property damage for possible repayment by the government. The proposal made by Noguères to reconstitute the Spanish republican army was rejected. The demands of the officials were presented to Premier Daladier on February 22.[34]

Largely as a result of the vigorous complaints of the socialist and communist deputies and the local mayors, General Menard announced a new governmental policy for the refugee camps on February 25. Barcarès, which had become the most overcrowded camp, was to be reduced to a total of 40,000–50,000 people by March 10. Argelès was to be similarly diminished in number and the installation at Prats-de-Mollo was to be closed. A number of new camps, dispersed among the departments of Tarn, Garonne, and L'Ariège, were to be organized, each with no more than 15,000 to 20,000 inmates. The program of barrack-building was to be accelerated.[35] But the notion of utilizing army camps and supplies was completely ignored by the government. In the minds of the ministers of foreign affairs, war, and interior, any type of arrangement was temporary, for the keystone of their refugee policy was still the eventual repatriation of all able-bodied men as part of a general understanding with the new Spanish regime.

The apogee of the first, hectic stage of French relations with the Spanish refugees was reached in a violent debate on the floor of the Chamber of Deputies on March 10. Right-wing virulence and hate insured that the discussion would be acrimonious and devoted less to the refugee problem than to political charge and countercharge. Deputies Ybarnegaray (Basses-Pyrénées) and Philippe Henriot, adherents of the Croix de Feu, vented their hatred of the Spanish republic and the French left-wing parties in a fashion that made the debate "ugly, disgusting, depressing," to the socialists. Joseph Rous, a socialist from the Pyrénées-Orientales, opened the session with a long defense of the rectitude of the French action in receiving the refugees. Ybarnegaray countered with a bitter charge of Spanish republican cowardice in the Catalan campaign and the reiteration of earlier allegations that bands of Spanish *pillards* (thieves) and assassins had entered France along with the military. Then he derailed the rational process by accusing André Marty (Seine) of having murdered a French member of the International Brigades and declared that the communist deputy was not worthy of sitting in the chamber. Marty denied the charges, but Ybarnegaray and Henriot further confused the situation by quoting Marx Dormoy, who was not in the chamber at the time, as having said that during his time in Spain Marty had "bathed in a sea of blood." Subsequently Dormoy denied having made such a statement. The debate continued on March 14 but remained in the realm of political vituperation.[36]

It is quite clear that the inquiries of the left-wing parliamentarians and their physical presence in Roussillon furnished an effective counterpoint to the anger and hate that had been generated by the right-wing press. After several weeks of the Great Fear, the situation seemed to be stabilizing and the need for ameliorative action concerning the Spanish refugees had been made abundantly clear. Although the socialists failed to win acceptance of their key army camp proposal, they did cause a visible shift in governmental policy regarding centralization of authority, overcrowding, housing, food, health, and sanitary conditions. The overriding issue of repatriation remained to be settled.

In the matter of housing the Spanish republicans quite literally were in a prehistoric situation during the first days of February. Francisco Fenestres and five comrades dug a large hole in the sand and pooled their Spanish army blankets to provide a roof. Another, more substantial type of housing was devised by J. Plazas. With several comrades he commandeered some army autos that had sunk into the sand and converted them into shelters; the men had to enter by crawling on all fours. Vilanova added a modern touch when he dug under the barbed-wire perimeter and entered a parking area for sequestered Spanish military trucks. In one of these he found a mattress, which he dragged back to camp and placed in one of the "auto hotels" on the beach; five refugees shared this prize—in rotation. He also found a supply of tinned food and stole two quarts of oil from the Senegalese. These feats made him a hero. Jean Taillemagre, correspondent of *La Garonne,* in an uncharacteristic bit of reportage, noted the wide variety of living quarters created by the Spaniards: oilskins, stolen planks, crude thatching with tree branches. Even so, he added, many men were without shelter of any kind: like neanderthal hunters they huddled around small fires, squatting on their haunches and draped with ragtag bits of blankets.[37] Housing conditions improved somewhat when the French authorities began construction of the first barracks. Izard, who was in charge of this venture, designed an extremely simple shelter. On three sides of a light framework of rafters he mounted horizontal lathes covered by tar-paper. The fourth side was built of reeds cut from nearby marshes. A thin sheet of metal served as a roof. The first barracks of this type were assigned to the wounded,[38] but a doctor from the municipal council of Argelès complained that there was a notable lack of barracks to quarantine patients suffering from contagious diseases.[39] Thus, although Lucien Castan, correspondent for *La Dépêche,* asserted on February 16 that he had not seen anyone forced to the extremes of drinking urine or eating reeds, he acknowledged a serious lack of barracks.[40]

With the shift in government policy came an end to the "febrile improvisations"[41] that had marked the first weeks. Orders for building materials were issued in mid-February, and the construction of more substantial barracks and utilities was begun by February 19.[42]

French authorities now began to utilize Spanish labor and military vehicles. On February 18 Cazes informed Colonel Gauthier, commandant of camps in the Pyrénées-Orientales, that "in the next few days it will be necessary to increase the work force [at Barcarès] to about 1,200 Spanish workers, from the current levels of 450–500." He requested authority to recruit qualified workers from other camps.[43] The official reports show that the number of Spaniards employed at Barcarès did increase from 500 on February 17 to 1,300 on February 24.[44] In addition to the regular fare, each "worthy laborer" was to receive 200 grams of bread and 50 grams of conserves or chocolate; these extras were of course independent of the wine ration. The official note did not define the criteria used to determine who was a worthy worker. Free tobacco, in the form of a pack of cigarettes every other day, was also authorized. However, local commanders were warned that these benefits were to be extended only to those who were *"really employees"* (Colonel Gauthier's italics). Lieutenant Colonel Bois, commandant at Barcarès, emphasized that the extra rations were considered a reward to be given only to those who performed satisfactorily, and requested his subordinates to furnish lists of worthy Spaniards. The Bridges and Roads Department at Barcarès certified that eighty of its one hundred employees merited the extras.[45]

However, the effort to provide better refugee housing was beset by numerous difficulties. There were gaps in the procurement of materials, time lost because of the rain and cold, and squabbles among officials. On March 1, 1939, the *New York Times* reported that wooden barracks were being erected at a rate of twenty per day.[46] On the same date the socialist deputy Louis Noguères (Pyrénées-Orientales), was complaining to Prefect Didkowski that 50,000 former Spanish republican soldiers were still camped outdoors on the road between

Arles-sur-Tech and Prats-de-Mollo, and a larger number were still without shelter in the camps along the Côte Vermeille. "Days, weeks have passed," the deputy said. "Construction continues at Barcarès but [the Spanish soldiers] continue to wallow in filth . . . Is it not possible to accelerate the pace of construction?"[47]

The lack of coordination of construction efforts between the civil and military arms of the government finally drove Lieutenant Colonel Moufflet, commandant of camps of the Sixteenth Military Region, to lodge a sharp complaint with Prefect Didkowski. He noted that an agreed-upon plan of procurement was three weeks behind schedule and insisted strongly on immediate action to remedy the situation.[48]

If the building of barracks proceeded slowly, the provision of medical and sanitary facilities seemed scarcely to progress at all. To the grim picture painted by the communist and socialist parliamentary delegations and Mayor Baudru's fears of a major typhoid epedemic were added other diseases that were prevalent among the refugees. *Time* magazine estimated that 60 percent of the Spaniards suffered from dysentery and pneumonia.[49] Other common illnesses were tuberculosis, leprosy, conjunctivitis, and scalp ringworm.[50] Lice, "in an unbelievable quantity," infested the camps.[51] Dr. Joaquín D'Harcourt, a medical colonel of the Spanish republican army, declared that mental and neurotic manifestations among the refugees were potentially a greater problem than physical ailments. The Spanish doctor was particularly critical of the treatment given his compatriots by French physicians. He asserted that many Spanish soldiers had suffered needless amputations because the French surgeons were ignorant of methods for preventing wound infections that had been developed by the Spanish medical service.[52] John Stevens reported in the *New Republic* that in an unspecified camp one French doctor cared for 400 Spanish patients: "Wounds are not dressed and gangrene has set in in many cases. On several occasions the refugees have been fed donkey meat of such a quality that everyone got sick."[53] Even when the population of the camp at St. Cyprien was reduced to 30,000 in April 1939, half of this number was registered as ill with one disease or another.[54] In this same camp, despite the erection of primitive wooden infirmary barracks and tents, the wounded still lay on straw pallets placed directly on the sandy floor and shared the available space with white wooden coffins that were delivered every evening. It was estimated that during a two-week period in February there was an average of twenty-five to thirty deaths daily. Refugees lining up for daily sick call saw the coffins carried past them on the way to the cemetery.[55]

The total number of deaths in the camps between February 15, 1939, and the outbreak of the Second World War is impossible to tabulate. The French government announced on February 24 that since the beginning of the exodus there had been 124 deaths, including 12 children,[56] but this was palpably false. The death of the great Spanish poet Antonio Machado in Collioure on February 23, 1939, because of exhaustion and illness,[57] captured headlines in the world press, and his tragedy served as the visible symbol of the fate that befell many of his countrymen. In Perpignan alone the interment of 112 adults and 11 children by February 25 necessitated the opening of a new section in the municipal cemetary.[58] At St. Cyprien and Argelès, as previously noted, new burial grounds had already been opened. That Spanish republicans continued to succumb in large numbers long after the initial period of exodus is shown also by the records of the city of Perpignan, which paid 200 francs per funeral. In the first quarter of 1940, after large masses of refugees had been moved out of the camps and into the Foreign Legion, labor battalions, or work groups on farms, sixty-seven deaths were reported by two Perpignan hospitals. Among the deceased were forty-eight men and nineteen women; other than the listing of a sixteen-month-old infant, ages of the deceased were not given.[59] Additional deaths were incurred in the concentration camps and other places of domicile for Spaniards, to say nothing of fatalities caused by the massive German attack launched in May 1940.

Perhaps the most trenchant observations on the state of medical care and sanitation in the camps were made by Dr. Peloquin, a retired French army doctor, who visited St. Cyprien, Argelès, and Prats-de-Mollo from February 17 to 19 and reported to the Parliamentary Group of French-Spanish Friendship on February 23. The situation, he declared, was "repugnant." The refugees were being given equal treatment with the livestock they had brought with them—that is to say, left to fend for themselves most of the time. Food was distributed once per day at Argelès, with no order or system. He decried the lack of the most elementary sanitary precautions to prevent contamination of underground wells. This raised serious problems of transmission of contagious diseases to the camp population and the French inhabitants of the area. He inveighed against the French authorities for hoarding Army medical and sanitary equipment. "The affirmation that the employment of these supplies would in some way compromise the national defense is ridiculous and false," he declared. Above all he criticized the slowness and apathy of French authorities in meeting health and sanitation needs.[60]

A chart drawn up by an engineer at Barcarès underscored the slow pace of constructing sanitary facilities. On April 10 there were 980 latrine-containers in use, while 1,870 were needed. On April 22 the

number was down to 946 because of loss and breakage. By May 10 the
number of containers rose to 1,516, still some 354 less than the amount
that had been declared necessary a month earlier.[61]

With such thorough exposure of French shortcomings—and they
proved to be extensive—the encomiums for the performance of French
personnel sounded routine and defensive when expressed in newspapers such as *La Dépêche de Toulouse,* which supported the government's policies. While commending French officials involved with the
refugees the newspapers of the Right continued to attack Sarraut and
Rucart as incompetent. The left-wing press was careful to praise both
the ministers and the rank-and-file French operatives, but also criticized
governmental policies from their own perspective. However, there is no
doubt that many French doctors gave their skills and time almost without limit. The example previously cited by John Stevens was doubtless
repeated in many other instances. An unpublished journal of Señora
García-Bastide (first name unknown), contains an emotional entry concerning two such French physicians. "Drs. Simon and Pagés . . . have
much good will and understanding of the Spanish tragedy. They work
with the Spanish doctors and even got some vegetables and milk for us.
For us, Pagés and Simon will remain two great names."[62] In truth, the
avoidance of dangerous epidemics in such terrible conditions must be
counted a minor miracle.

The plight of the French government, which continued its near-soli-
tary role in shouldering the financial burden of the Spanish refugees,
also earned sympathy from some quarters of the world press. *Commonweal,* a liberal lay American Catholic journal, declared that the French
answer to its critics was "Well, they are here! The other countries are
certainly slow to help out."[63] The *Nation,* a liberal American weekly,
identified with the average Frenchman's resentment of criticism and
pointed out that at a time when the threat of war placed an intolerable
strain on French finances, France had succored the refugees "as well as
could be expected of any government." It reserved its condemnation for
the French Right, which "had seized upon a few isolated incidents in
the camps . . . to prove that Spaniards are not worthy of French 'hospitality!' " Viscount Lord Halifax, in a House of Lords exchange,
lauded the French for the manner in which they had dealt with this "un-
precedented . . . problem of enormous dimensions."[64]

The budgetary problem was, in fact, growing worse. The Finance
Committee of the Chamber of Deputies approved a government request
for 150 million francs on March 8. It was brought out that expenditures
for refugee support had escalated from 5,250,000 francs in 1936 to the
requested 150 million. No end was in sight, and foreign countries and

private aid organizations were providing minimum assistance.[65] By June 1939 the government was dispensing between six and seven million francs daily for Spanish refugee purposes.[66]

Despite financial difficulties and delays in alleviating camp conditions, it appeared as if the French government was facing up to the obligations that fate had imposed upon it. That it was seeking to rid itself of the larger part of the burden through the device of repatriation was a notion suspected by the Left and encouraged by most other political groups. But if the manifestations of the Great Fear seemed in regression, they were still very much alive in the nether world of the police and the military security forces. Panic dominated their activities as they searched relentlessly for real or suspected anarchists and communists; in their eyes there was really no difference between the two. A severe discipline was maintained in the camps, suspect refugees were transferred to prison camps, and many Spaniards were summarily expelled from the country. The entire police network cooperated regionally and nationally in attempts to flush out the dangerous ones and their French confederates.

Strict military discipline was exercised through frequent roll-calls, patrols, constant surveillance, and confinement to camp. Infractions were punished by placing the perpetrator in what the refugees dubbed the "hippodrome," a space of some ten square meters on an exposed portion of the beach. In the center of the space was a single pillar. The culprit was forced to remain within the open square for a period of not less than twenty-four hours, and many times for longer periods, without blanket or other means of protection against cold and rain. If the man being punished was considered an habitual recalcitrant he was tied to the pillar and thus forfeited the opportunity of keeping warm during the night by running around the enclosure. The Spaniards learned soon enough to protect themselves from this and other punishments. When loudspeakers were installed in the camps they quickly became the vehicles for warning particular refugees that they were in trouble with the authorities. One of the methods employed was for the Spanish refugee who announced the name of a person wanted at headquarters to misspell it and to add, "The spelling is not clear." This would trigger either the escape or the disappearance of the person somewhere inside the camp. In any case, the object of French punishment would simply not respond to the summons.[67]

Behind the scenes, intelligence was being exchanged and a constant search conducted for "suspect or dangerous Spanish refugees to keep under surveillance or to find for internment in a camp." The extent of the problem may be gauged from the fact that in Perpignan alone lived more than 24,000 people of Spanish extraction and that in the month of February 1939 there were 20,000 arrests of Spanish refugees in the Pyrénées-Orientales.[68] Didkowski received a list of suspects and was requested to make inquiries concerning their whereabouts and their connections with French radicals: F. P., an alleged assassin, was believed to be hiding in a French sympathizer's house; at Saint Marsault (Deux-Sèvres) three Frenchmen, one a former communist mayor, were reported to be sheltering members of the Federación Anarquista Ibérica (FAI); "Frederica Monseny [*sic*], very dangerous," was said to be living with a Frenchwoman in Banyuls-sur-mer (Pyrénées-Orientales); E., who had escaped from a concentration camp, was also believed to be in the same town; a certain house in Perpignan was named as a well-known FAI headquarters; between Saleilles and St. Cyprien a small house was alleged to serve as a gathering point where camp escapees were directed by communists to safe places in the interior.[69]

The prefect of L'Herault informed Didkowski that a prisoner in the concentration camp at Lodève had received a copy of the *Bulletin d'Information du P.O.U.M.* from a certain J.S., living in the house of J.M. at Pia. Information was requested on J.S.[70] The police believed that they had uncovered an FAI escape ring operating under the guise of an aid organization that visited the camps regularly: a truck that brought oranges and other foods into the camps actually contained clothing, money, and other supplies for potential escapees; on occasion fugitives were hidden in the truck and escaped in it. A certain J.J.B. was named as the master-mind of the operation; in the view of the police agent, "it has never been a question of oranges." Later, the police revoked permission for the truck to enter the camps and gave J.J.B. 48 hours to leave the department.[71]

Toulouse was seen as another center of Spanish intrigue. The Confederación Nacional del Trabajo (CNT), the anarcho-syndicalist labor organization, was accused of setting up its new headquarters in Toulouse and of planning to publish a clandestine newspaper. The alleged leaders of the group were banned from the city. In Toulouse, too, a police sweep of hotels and houses yielded 1,200 refugees without proper papers; they were sent to the camps. The arrest at Sigean (L'Aude) of fourteen alleged FAI members who had escaped from an unnamed camp was announced on February 18. They had maps showing how to avoid main roads.[72] Suspicious citizens of Port Vendres reported that some Spanish refugees living in a villa on the heights above the town were operating a clandestine radio and also giving searchlight signals to a ship at sea. Following an extensive inquiry the police reported that they had found nothing.[73]

Those Spaniards or International Brigaders who were identified as communists, anarchists, general troublemakers in the camps, or common criminals were sent to one of the many prison camps or forts situated in the Pyrénées-Orientales, l'Ariège, and other departments.[74] The punishment centers at Collioure (Pyrénées-Orientales) and Le Vernet (l'Ariège) came to be hated by the Spaniards with the greatest intensity. Even in 1974 the mention of Collioure and its thirteenth-century castle, a stronghold of the Knights Templar, could bring shudders of horror to the Spanish exiles. Federica Montseny said: "Its smiling beaches, its golden coast, its marvelous steepness can never be dissociated from the sinister and evil silhouette of the castle."[75] Housed in underground cells, the prisoners endured a harsh regimen that lasted from 6:00 A.M. to 7:00 P.M. Their work was breaking stones, and their meals were calculated on a subsistence level. There were usually 350–400 men in the prison, plus ten to twenty youngsters between the ages of fourteen and eighteen. They were organized into nineteen sections, plus a special unit for those considered most dangerous. A trough five meters long served as a bath, and the entire prison population was given a total of ten minutes per day to use it. The latrine was a single compartment of two by four meters, and Vilanova noted the "sad and loathsome spectacle" provided by almost 400 men fighting with each other every morning to use this facility in the brief time allotted to them. He noted that "whipping, forced labor, caning, excessive cruelty, and tortures" made Collioure "a castle of horrors."[76] Men were driven to desperate actions in attempts to escape from Collioure: Peidró, a leader of the Socialist United Youth, crawled through a sewage pipe only to find his exit blocked by an iron barrier. He was found some hours later by a French patrol and rescued from his slimy prison. He was punished with one month in solitary confinement.[77]

Conditions at Collioure were exposed in May 1939 by Pierre Brandon, a lawyer who was active on behalf of refugees appearing before the Perpignan courts; by Paul Bourgeois, of the International Committee for Aid to Republican Spain; by the League for the Rights of Man; and by the Parliamentary Group for French-Spanish Friendship. Prefect Didkowski and the departmental courts were accused of imposing indefinite sentences on alleged law violators without proper charges or trial. At a meeting of the parliamentary group, Brandon declared that French magistrates dealing with Spanish refugees were "filled with a kind of panic." The courts of Perpignan, Ceret (Pyrénées-Orientales), and Montpellier (l'Herault), were said to be especially repressive. Bourgeois charged that the prison commander at Collioure, Captain Rollet, had "an innate dislike for the Spaniards." Agustin

Villela Freixa, a republican army officer, testified that whenever French government officials visited the fort, eight sections of prisoners were locked into subterranean cells, so that they would not be seen. Accordingly, the inspecting authorities were convinced that the prison inmates received better treatment than that afforded in the camps. A garde mobile stationed at Collioure admitted: "I am ashamed of being French." The League for the Rights of Man sent a letter to Prefect Didkowski seeking answers to questions involving violations of legal rights, but failed to receive an answer. It demanded to know whether, in 1939, on the 150th anniversary of the French Revolution, public opinion was "ready to tolerate the reestablishment of *lettres de cachet.*"[78]

The resulting furor caused the transfer of Captain Rollet and the diminution of some of the more flagrant abuses. However, the prison continued to exist. Montseny later pointed out that the policy of establishing punishment camps and prisons for the Spaniards was initiated by Daladier, followed by Reynaud, and continued by Pétain.[79]

Le Vernet, a fifty-acre punishment camp in the mountains of l'Ariège, at various times held between 2,000 and 5,000 men of thirty nationalities, mostly Spaniards and International Brigaders who had been sent there from other centers because they were "political undesirables" or were "unruly."

Arthur Koestler, Hungarian novelist and ex-communist, who had fought in the Spanish Civil War and been incarcerated in a Franco jail for a time, was interned in Le Vernet during the winter of 1939–40 and has furnished a compelling description of life in that French camp. The camp contained 2,000 prisoners at that time. From the moment a prisoner's head was cropped, subjecting him to "the extraordinary psychological effect of imposing the convict skull on a man," he was subjected to a rigorous discipline that Koestler characterized as worse than that in Franco's prisons. The camp was divided into three sections. Section A was composed of aliens with criminal records, B of aliens with radical political backgrounds, and C of men who had no definite charge against them but were "suspect" either politically or as criminals. Koestler was assigned to the latter group. The hutments, thirty yards long and five yards wide, each contained 200 men. Built of wooden planks and insulated with waterproof paper, they provided no defense against the bitter mountain cold. The men slept at right angles to the long walls, in compartments that gave each man twenty-one inches of sleeping space. They slept on their sides and when one man turned the others had to do likewise. There were no stoves, lighting, or blankets. Nor was there a single table or stool in any of the huts. No eating implements were provided, nor any soap. Food consisted of a daily ration of eleven ounces of bread, with black coffee in the morning and a pint of soup at midday and in the evening the soup was "a pale liquid containing no fat and only a few grains of chickpeas, lentils, or vermicelli." Three ounces of boiled beef were served at the midday meal, but it was "so smelly that only the hungriest would eat it."[80]

In winter the prisoners worked from 8:00 to 11:00 A.M. and from 1:00 to 4:00 P.M., the hours limited only by the available light and the physical debility of the men. Koestler wrote that the rate of sickness was always over 25 percent. The prisoners, who were not paid, performed road-building tasks and were responsible for camp maintenance. No working clothes were provided, he added, and "as the majority of prisoners possessed only what they stood up in—they had long ago sold the last spare shirt or undergarment for a packet of cigarettes—they worked in rags and soleless shoes in 20 degrees Fahrenheit." The slightest offense fetched a punch or blow of a leather crop from the gardes mobiles. More serious offenses resulted in a minimum eight-day sentence of imprisonment, "the first day without food or drink, and the next three days bread and water only." Koestler condemned the gardes mobiles as "the most reactionary and brutal force in France." Understandably, Koestler labelled Le Vernet as the worst French camp, but he went further. In a grim comparison he recounted the evaluation of thirty men of Section C who had previously spent time in Nazi concentration camps, including Dachau, Oranienburg, and Wolfsbuttel, which qualified them as experts. They were in agreement that with regard to food, accommodation, and hygiene, Vernet was even below the level of the German camps. Koestler was writing in 1940, before the Nazi camps had acquired their function of mass extermination. But he insisted that even in the concentration camps of Franco the food had been "far more substantial and nourishing" than the fare offered at Le Vernet. Perhaps the most interesting comparison was that between the life of German prisoners of war captured by the French in 1939 and that of the Spanish republicans and other aliens in Le Vernet. The prisoners of Le Vernet saw a series of photographs depicting the routine of the German POW's: "We saw them having a meal in a tidy refectory, and there were tables and chairs and dishes and knives and forks. And we saw them in their dormitory, and they had real beds and mattresses and blankets." To the defeated Spanish republicans and the men of the International Brigades these pictures confirmed their isolation and sense of betrayal: "If you were a Nazi, you were treated decently; but if you were an anti-Nazi, you were treated as mud."[81]

To the tattered Spanish republicans, then, as they wandered restlessly about their barbed-wire *cabañas* or rotted in punishment camps, the world appeared to be a schizophrenic nightmare. For being the first to take up arms against fascism they were imprisoned and punished by those who should have been their comrades-in-arms. While the stricken Spanish republic still fought the enemy, those who had preached nonintervention were making indecent haste to intervene and recognize the fascist conqueror. And their reluctant hosts were making plain their desire for the defeated ones to return to Spain and throw themselves upon the mercies of he who had sworn to kill them.

CHAPTER FIVE

REQUIEM FOR A REPUBLIC

RECOGNITION, REPATRIATION, RESETTLEMENT

After the fall of Catalonia, the world concluded that the Spanish war was over.

Hugh Thomas

The structure of the second Spanish Republic had collapsed. The vast majority . . . believed that there was nothing more to be done than to end the shooting and hope that the Nationalists would be merciful to the population.

Gabriel Jackson

THE GOVERNMENT for which the imprisoned Spanish republicans had fought and endured great privation was in disarray and could do nothing to alleviate their suffering. The rout in Catalonia had shorn it of its last pretense to power. Although a government existed in name, as Broué and Témime observed, "the state had already ceased to exist."[1] Whatever energies the government possessed were dissolving in a struggle between those who recognized defeat and sought to make peace on almost any terms, and those who were intent on continuing the struggle in the central zone. The power to act was almost totally interdicted the moment the ministers entered French territory. They could live there only as simple Spanish refugees, and under no circumstances could they exercise their accustomed prerogatives.[2] Spanish Foreign Minister Alvarez Del Vayo acknowledged this reality at a press conference on February 9, 1939, when he announced that Prime Minister Juan Negrín would abstain from all political activity on French soil.[3]

From the beginning of February until the war ended on March 31, a grim internal battle dominated the republican scene.[4] Prime Minister Negrín was determined to wrest concessions from General Franco as the price for ending the war. Failing that, he was insistent on continuing the struggle. He was supported by some republican elements, in addition to communist officials and military officers, including Dolores Ibarruri (la Pasionaria); General Ignacio Hidalgo de Cisneros, chief of the republican air force and husband of Constancia de la Mora; colonels Juan Modesto and Enrique Lister; and Major Francisco Galan. However, a substantial number of important officials and military officers were convinced that negotiations would be fruitless and wished to end the war as soon as possible. President Manuel Azaña led this group, which also comprised Indalecio Prieto, former war minister; Diego Martínez Barrio, president of the Cortes; José Antonio Aguirre, president of the Basque republic; Luís Companys, president of the Catalan republic; generals José Miaja, Vicente Rojo, and Cipriano Mera; and Colonel Segismundo Casado. They were resolved not "to preside over another disaster on the scale of the Catalan defeat." General Rojo asked: "What shall we resist with? Why are we going to resist?"[5]

At a meeting of the pitifully depleted Cortes in Figueras on February 1, the sixty-two deputies in attendance had approved Negrín's three conditions for peace: guarantees of independence and national integrity, freedom for the Spanish people to choose their own destiny, and no reprisals against republicans.[6] Of the three, only the last was considered to be a viable negotiating point, but Franco told the British and French representatives that the war was finished and he would settle for nothing less than unconditional surrender.[7]

Despite rumors concerning peace efforts, the republican government maintained an official attitude that "there is no question of mediation and never has been."[8] At a press conference Constancia de la Mora told the foreign correspondents that the government would return to Madrid and the central zone would be defended. But after acknowledging that President Azaña would not return to Spain with the cabinet, she concealed the reason by saying that he was remaining in France to carry on important talks with the French and British governments.[9] Negrín and del Vayo attempted to convince Azaña to return to Spain, but the President was firm: "My duty is to make peace. I refuse to help, by my presence, to prolong a senseless battle. We must secure the best possible guarantees, and then conclude as soon as we can."[10] Surveying the situation after reaching the central zone, Negrín was convinced that the republic had no choice but to resist and he so informed the commanding officers of the remaining republican armies on February 26. His announcement produced dissents from several commanders who took the position that further military resistance was impossible.[11]

The joint French-British recognition of the Franco government on February 27, 1939, deepened the republican governmental crisis and precipitated outright revolt against the Negrín policy. The next day Azaña resigned his presidency and Martínez Barrio refused to succeed him. The burgeoning peace movement only spurred Negrín to greater efforts. On March 2 he moved to retain control of the central zone by promoting key communist officers to major military commands, including control of the remaining evacuation ports. His offer to make Colonel Casado a general and put him in command of the Madrid front was refused. Casado had been working steadily to solidify peace sentiment and had already formed a Consejo Nacional de Defensa which included almost all of the noncommunist elements of the popular front. On March 5 the Casado junta seized power in the central zone, with General José Miaja, the defender of Madrid, as president and Julián Besteiro, a much respected socialist, making the key radio address to the people. He accused Negrín of attempting to maintain power illegally and charged him with raising false hopes as to the reception of new arms and the imminence of a world war that would make Spain an ally of the democracies. The newly appointed communist military chiefs rose against Casado, and civil war resulted in Madrid and Ciudad Real. Generals Mera and Escobar suppressed the rebellions by March 13 and Negrín returned to France.[12] There followed a series of frustrating attempts at negotiations with General Franco as the republican troops began to surrender. Madrid was occupied on March 28, 1939, and on April 1 the Caudillo declared that the civil war had ended with the complete and unconditional victory of the nationalist forces.[13]

Of the half-million troops and unknown thousands of civilians who might have wished to abandon Spain during the second half of March, relatively few succeeded. The fifth—and final—wave of mass emigration consisted of approximately 15,000 to 20,000 people, although the exact total will never be known.[14] Several large ports were available for evacuation, but the French and British responded with marked reticence to the republican government's appeal for ships. Thousands of republicans thronged the docks at Alicante, Almería and Cartagena, but very few were taken off in any organized manner. Many of those who did manage to escape did so on small fishing and merchant vessels. Only a few hundred refugees managed to reach Marseilles, among them Colonel Casado, who was given passage on the British hospital ship *Maine*.[15] The cloudy political and military situations also militated against large-scale departures. Unlike the Catalan campaign, where the republican army had been driven against the French frontier by an aggressive offensive, the military lines in the central zone remained fairly static for much of the final month. Only during the last week did the republican lines yield, and then they melted away. Groups of soldiers or individuals either made their way to the ports or simply went home. The final nationalist drive, which had been in preparation for months, was largely unnecessary; the Franco forces simply moved into the vacuums created by the disintegrating republican army. In other cases, entire divisions surrendered. Many of those who attempted to reach the ports were cut down by advancing Francoists, those who made it joined the milling throngs that clogged the water fronts. Joaquín Raluy, a soldier with General Mera, was one of those who tried to reach Alicante. A few miles from the city his group was engaged by pursuing fascists and he was cut down on the road. Suffering serious chest wounds he was carried to hospital at Alicante. When he awoke from surgery the next day he found that the entire staff had evacuated the hospital. Shortly afterward a nationalist officer appeared and announced that all the patients were prisoners of the new regime. Later, Raluy escaped from the hospital and made his way to France.[16]

French North Africa received the bulk of the final migration, one wave arriving at the beginning of March and the other at the end. On March 7 a number of ships of the Spanish republican navy sailed to Bizerte, Tunisia, where they were surrendered to French officials. The ships carried 4,132 officers and sailors, as well as some 300 civilians. All were promptly interned in a concentration camp at Maknassy. The last frantic scramble from the Mediterranean ports produced somewhat more than 10,000 refugees, who were taken to Algeria and imprisoned in concentration camps in Boghari, Beni-Hindel, Carnot, and Cherchell.[17]

The last act of the Spanish tragedy had been played on the still vast stage of the central zone, but it was more epilogue than finale. The real action had taken place off-stage, in Paris, London, and Burgos, where, during the month of February, the French and British governments had negotiated with General Franco. When, on February 27, 1939, these negotiations culminated in formal recognition of the nationalist government, the March maneuverings of Negrín and Casado lost significance except to those killed during their course.

Even as the forlorn meeting of the Cortes was taking place in Figueras on February 1, its last-ditch three-point program to end the war on decent terms was being undercut by the French and British diplomats. On February 2, Senator Léon Bérard, a radical from Basses-Pyrénées, met with General Gómez Jordana y Sousa in Burgos to discuss the terms of French recognition of the victorious government. Sir Robert Hodgson carried on negotiations for Great Britain. The tight-lipped, smiling Bérard refused to divulge any of the details of his conversations with Jordana and others, as he made three separate trips to Spain during the month. In each instance he merely commented upon the warmth of the reception he had received from the nationalists and upon the continuing success of his mission.[18] Hugh Thomas, however, contends that Bérard was received coldly.[19] But government secrecy was unable to stem a rising and vigorous debate in political and press quarters. The Left was concerned with the fate of the Spanish refugees, the total abandonment of the republican government by France, and the danger of a continued Italian presence at the French-Spanish border and in the Balearic Islands. The center and the Right felt that the republicans had been defeated and French national interest demanded that an accommodation be reached with the victor. The Right, moreover, was pleased with the outcome and wished to empty French soil of the refugees.

"What frenzy drives [the governments] of Paris and London, who appear singularly impatient to obtain the capitulation of republican Spain?" asked Pierre Brossolette. Léon Blum pointed out that the Spanish republican government continued as a legal and viable entity. Any talk of recognizing Franco, he added, represented treason. Rhetorically, this was consistent with Blum's position of support for the republic during the civil war, but it also pointed up his consistent failure to act positively in 1936–37.[20] Several cabinet ministers, among them Albert Sarraut, Jean Zay, and Cesar Campinchi, agreed with Blum's contention and decried Foreign Minister Bonnet's plan to give de jure recognition to Franco "immediately and without reserve."[21] The threat of an Italian force permanently implanted in the Pyrenees and in the Balearic Islands frightened the socialists and radicals. *La Dépêche* accused Bonnet of going even further than Great Britain in appeasing the Spanish nationalists. At least, it said, the British insisted on the withdrawal of foreign troops before granting recognition. The French-Spanish Friendship Group, composed chiefly of communist and socialist members of the Chamber of Deputies, declared itself against recognition of the nationalists and pointed out that Italian occupation of the Balearics menaced France's North African routes. *Le Populaire* expressed disbelief at the alleged promises by General Franco that Italian troops would leave Spain. "Only Mussolini will decide" that question, it said.[22]

There was general agreement within the Left that the Spanish republican refugees were in grave danger of mass repatriation as part of any overall bargain that might be struck by the negotiators. Apprehension was fueled by Bérard's statement—the only substantive comment he permitted himself—on the fate of the exiles. Yes, he said, he would have occasion to raise the question of the unhappy refugees. It was necessary that the problem be resolved quickly, but it was inseparable from many others. *L'Humanité* asserted that recognition meant the delivery of the refugees to "torture and execution." *Le Midi socialiste* agreed and accused Bonnet of sanctioning a Spanish White Terror.[23]

The policy of the Daladier government had been clear from the beginning. In order to keep Spain neutral in case of a French-German war, amicable relations with the new Burgos government had to be established as quickly as possible. As part of this settlement Spanish exiles would be returned to nationalist control, along with all war materials and Spanish national treasure.[24] To this end the French government had created the concentration camps, neglected the basic needs of their inhabitants, depressed the morale and health of what had been a disciplined army, and exerted strong pressure upon the exiles to choose repatriation as a "voluntary" action. These moves were made at the precise time when Bérard was engaged in negotiating with the Burgos government.

Left-wing newspapers were caustic in denunciation of French tactics. They charged that "shameful Francoist propaganda," promising beneficial treatment for repatriates, was permitted to circulate within the camps. The choice for republicans was narrow: either return to Franco or remain in the camps.[25] An Associated Press dispatch reported candidly: "French authorities make no secret of their hope that as many as possible would choose the Insurgents, for otherwise the French may have to keep them for an indefinite time." And John Stevens reported that the refugees were "harried night and day by a barrage of Franco propaganda from loudspeaker automobiles. They are told of the joys of life in Franco Spain and urged to return there immediately. . . . The French policy seems to be to make things so hard for them that they will be glad to go." But Stevens thought that the highly visible suffering of the sick and wounded, added to the hunger of women and children, were more effective than the propagandists in convincing many refugees to leave the camps.[26] Perhaps the most flagrant example of French complicity in Spanish nationalist repatriation attempts was the visit of General José Solchaga Zala to the Republican camp at Gurs (Basses-Pyrénées). Solchaga, who had earned a reputation as the executioner of thousands of republican soldiers and civilians, was permitted to tour the camp area in an effort to convince a thousand Spanish republican aviators to return to Franco's Spain.[27]

Displaying obvious pleasure at the continuing victories of the nationalists, the right-wing press hailed Bérard's efforts to negotiate a pact with Franco as necessary and even overdue. The return of the Spanish exiles to their homeland was seen as beneficial to relations between the two countries and as the removal of a blight on the French landscape. For the French Right the situation represented a fortuitous confluence of political preference and diplomatic necessity. A forceful argument was advanced which held that French-Spanish diplomatic relations rested not upon principle or type of regime, but on the French presence in Madrid to safeguard France's interests. France would gain nothing from continued tension.[28] Wladimir d'Ormesson declared that the art of diplomacy required one to know the opportune moment for action, and that that moment had come. He regretted that the process of recognition was proceeding by stages instead of being consummated in one stroke. From the simple humanitarian point of view, he maintained, enough blood had been shed and continuation of the civil war was insupportable.[29] *Le Matin* was no less vigorous in greeting the decision to negotiate. "At last," it exclaimed, "France is going to talk with Franco. French interest . . . material and moral, requires it."[30] *L'Action Française* warned Daladier not to pay attention to the negative attack launched against negotiations by the "socialo-communistes" and to bear in mind the paramount interest of France: to keep its territory safe from foreign invasion, in this case Italian.[31] And *République,* agreeing with the necessity for French diplomatic relations with Spain, said that ideology should not be a factor in the negotiations: "L'idéologie nous a toujours joué de mauvais tours" ("Ideology has always played nasty tricks on us").[32]

It was widely assumed that Bérard would discuss repatriation of refugees as a priority issue, and this was a source of great satisfaction, particularly to conservative newspapers in the southwest of France. That the refugee issue struck a resonant chord with the Right was evident when Robert Brasillach, a French fascist, wrote that the Spanish refugees remained *la pierre d'achoppement* (the stumbling block) to French-Spanish relations, even after recognition of the Franco government. It would have been better, he added, if the frontier had never been opened to the Spanish republicans.[33]

The secrecy surrounding French-British negotiations with the Nationalists was broken when a group of fifty French leftist deputies petitioned for a debate on the matter. Premier Daladier rejected the demand and thus precipitated a vote of confidence in his administration. The ensuing debate on this question, on February 24, enabled the Left to interrogate the government on the possibility of a continuing Nazi-Fascist presence in Spain and the fate of the Spanish refugees. Both sides presented the arguments that had been previously advanced in the press. Daladier offered a further insight into the problem when he revealed that Great Britain had already decided on recognition after receiving assurances from General Franco that German and Italian troops would leave the Iberian peninsula immediately upon conclusion of hostilities. The premier did not deal directly with a question raised by Georges Izard, a socialist deputy, concerning repression of republican Spaniards, but the press had previously reported nationalist acquiescence to British-French requests that all Spanish refugees returning to Spain, as well as those still in arms in the central zone, would receive amnesty. However, Franco had made it clear that forgiveness would not extend to "those who are open to criminal prosecution for criminal offenses." The Chamber gave the government a strong vote of confidence, 323 to 261, and on February 27, 1939, the French and British governments jointly announced the unconditional recognition of the nationalist Spanish government. The terms of the agreement in effect gave the nationalists all they had demanded. The French and Spanish people were to live in amity as good neighbors, to cooperate in Morocco, and to prevent all activities directed against one another's security. France undertook to return to Spain all Spanish property, whether frozen assets or property taken to France by the republicans. This included all materials of war, documents, art treasures, physical property, and financial resources. In return the nationalists agreed only to receive a French ambassador at Burgos. That ambassador turned out to be Marshal Philippe Pétain, who had fought with Franco against the Riff insurgents in Morocco in the mid-twenties and was a staunch friend and admirer of the Caudillo. Wladimir d'Ormesson called it a "victory for common sense," but *Le Midi socialiste* was unreconciled; it was convinced that the agreement was a one-sided victory for Franco and that he was still "a prisoner of the Italians."[34]

Several important factors contributed to a slowing and eventual breakdown of the repatriation project. The French government had never said officially that it required all refugees to depart, although its actions and propaganda sometimes seemed to point in that direction. The Spanish republicans themselves and their cohorts of the French Left fought for the principle of voluntary repatriation. Franco further impeded the process by promulgating a tough "Law of Political Responsibilities" and the organization of political courts to try returned Spaniards. Because of delays in processing repatriates, their number was held to 200 to 300 per day. Despite an eventual increase in the rate, the flow of returnees never attained the level desired by the French authorities.[35]

Under the provisions of the Law of Political Responsibilities the nationalists declared that anyone found guilty of crimes or treason against the rebellion was liable to heavy punishment. The law set the period October 1, 1934, to July 18, 1936, as one during which it was a crime to have participated in the Asturian and Andalusian revolts against the center-right administration that ruled the republic for part of that time. For the period after July 18, the law presented a long list of criminal offenses: taking up arms against the "movement," holding office in political parties of the popular front, membership in regional separatist or autonomist parties, candidacy in the popular front in the February 1936 elections, membership in the Cortes of 1936–1939, being an official of the republican government on any level, adherence to free-masonry, and passive resistance to the nationalist movement and military forces. Common soldiers who could prove that they were simple conscripts would be dealt with lightly. Sentences for the guilty included loss of rights and possessions, in addition to fines. Cases involving murder or treason would be heard by military tribunals or criminal courts.[36] With such a prospect it was not likely that a reverse mass exodus of Spanish refugees would clog the southward roads and mountain passes of France. The Spanish head of state also invoked the Convention of 1877, which provided for the return of common criminals as distinct from political refugees, but he included "war criminals" under the former heading.[37] Another deterrent to mass repatriation was the reports of excessive harshness and punishment meted out to repatriates. According to *Le Midi socialiste*, the moment the exiles set foot on Spanish soil they were conducted to the commandant and asked in which unit they had fought. If the reply was the Lister Division (communist) or the Durruti Division (anarchist) they were taken out and shot without trial. As of February 20, the paper said, at least 200 returned militiamen had been executed in this manner.[38] True or not, such reports circulated freely in the camps and undercut the French program of encouraging large numbers of Spaniards to leave the country.

Repatriation was also slowed by the Spanish authorities' refusal to process more than 200 to 300 returnees a day in the early stages. Thousands were stacked up on the French side of the border after spending long hours in trains from Perpignan to Hendaye, which was the only entry point opened by the nationalists. Even after admission to Spain the republicans were sent to camps where, if they were not immediately punished or tried, they were forced to secure two recommendations from nationalists in good standing before they were released.[39]

For the French, the principal problem was how best to achieve "the massive return to Spain" of the exiles.[40] The government had given repeated assurances that the refugees' decision to return must be voluntary. In the assembly debate of March 14, 1939, Interior Minister

Sarraut had declared that "we do not have the right to deliver them by force," and a ministry circular had ordered prefects "not to exercise any compulsion on a decision which ought to be free." But Sarraut demonstrated the true direction of his thought when he stipulated that all but possibly 50,000 Spanish refugees should be persuaded to leave France. The frontier was open for them to go at any time. Deputy Pinelli indicated in the same discussion that if asylum was a right it was an individual right and not a collective one.[41] There were other disturbing signs that the French government was not only encouraging and aiding Spanish nationalist proselytizing in the camps but was itself making ominous moves toward forced repatriation. Certainly there was no planning for the future absorption of the Spanish republicans. The Comité de Solidarité Internationale de Paris reported cases of forced repatriation; in some instances, children had been taken involuntarily, thus forcing their parents to accompany them to Spain. In other cases, republican exiles had been told that they were going to Valencia and then delivered to the nationalist authorities at Port Bou.[42] Jesús Abenza testified that at Argelès camp there were periodic raids for the purpose of sending refugees back to Spain despite their protests.[43] Léon Jouhaux, leader of the Confédération Générale du Travail, expressed concern over many reported examples of direct pressure on refugees, but he was concerned also about the indirect pressures exerted on Spanish republicans: low wages in the camps and on contract farms, and "intolerable living conditions." These practices, he said, were enough to cause the exiles to risk return to Spain to escape them.[44]

Perhaps the most serious evidence of the intention, if not the execution, of forced repatriation came in early April. From many parts of France came reports that sent waves of apprehension through the refugee camps and French left-wing circles. *Le Midi socialiste* published the text of a circular being distributed by departmental prefects to mayors of towns that had refugee installations. The particular circular printed by the newspaper emanated from the Basses-Alpes and was dated March 25, 1939. It noted that the opening of additional exit points along the French-Spanish frontier now permitted rapid repatriation of refugees. The prefect requested the preparation of refugee lists that indicated birthplaces. This process called for the listing first of Basques and Catalans, and then of people from other regions. Objections from exiles were not to be entertained: "The order for repatriation is general and no exception will be allowed," because when the order became effective the government would no longer support the refugee centers. Jean-Maurice Herrmann, author of the article containing the text of the circular, declared that the multiplicity of concurring information proved that it was not a matter of an overzealous *fonctionnaire*. The orders came directly from Paris. He called upon Sarraut to issue a countermanding order, in view of his previous statements.[45]

Whatever plans might be germinating in the Quai d'Orsay, the French were increasingly resentful of a certain stiffness exhibited by the Franco government in approaching the question of repatriation. The Generalissimo appeared to be more interested in the return of Spanish arms, ships, and gold than of Spanish nationals, although he was aware of the implications of allowing hundreds of thousands of enemies to remain outside of his control. The amicable relations expected by the French as a result of the one-sided recognition agreement had not materialized, except for the now-evident intention of Franco to send the Germans and Italians home after the fall of the republic. The agonizingly slow rate of repatriation complicated French plans and resulted in a request that the rate be speeded up to 5,000 to 10,000 per day. A *New York Times* dispatch declared that, if the situation did not improve, France would change its attitude toward repatriation. It reported that several Paris newspapers urged independent action: give the refugees enough food for several days and send them across the frontier.[46]

It is difficult to determine exactly how many Spaniards were repatriated in 1939. The highest estimate is that 340,000 had returned to Spain by mid-December 1939. The lowest estimate is 100,000. The actual number probably lies somewhere between these projections; it is likely that between 150,000 and 200,000 were repatriated.[47] In considering these estimates one must take into account an increased rate of return at the outbreak of World War II. Thousands of Spaniards had no desire to fight for France, especially in view of the less-than-hospitable welcome they had received; these returned to Spain to take their chances with the Franco brand of justice. On balance it is not too much to say that the French program of ridding itself of its Spanish guests failed by a wide margin. Resistance to the project by the Spanish republicans, support of their stance by the French Left, and the contrariness of Francisco Franco were too much to overcome. Nevertheless, between 15 and 20 percent of those Spanirds who had entered France during the exodus were eventually repatriated. Later, the French Resistance against its own Vichy government and the occupying Nazis was to have good reason to welcome this failure.

If the Spanish republicans and their French supporters fought the policy of repatriation to Francoist Spain, many of them were not averse to—and indeed welcomed—the possibility of emigrating to other countries. Predictably, the French government approved heartily of this alternative. Foremost among these havens was Mexico. President Lázaro Cárdenas had been unstinting in his support of the republic and continued to show a lively concern for the welfare of the refugees after the conclusion of hostilities. Another country of refuge was the Soviet Union, which, however, took only 4,000 Spanish communists. Various other Latin American nations admitted smaller numbers. Great Britain and the United States lagged far behind the others in offering sanctuary to the defeated ones.

But even in matters of relief and resettlement the republicans were unable to escape the complexities and rivalries of Spanish politics. The split between Prime Minister Juan Negrín and his minister of defense, Indalecio Prieto, had begun as early as April 1938, when Prieto felt that the war was lost and Negrín continued to believe that it could be won. The two moderate socialists had been friends and collaborators in their dislike of Francisco Largo Caballero, but Negrín had dismissed Prieto because of his peace stand and his alleged indecisiveness, and thus increased his own reliance on the communists. This sequence of events resulted in an unhealthy postdefeat rivalry between the two for control of the republican government-in-exile and whatever funds were still available. The Prieto followers, in conjunction with republican parties, formed the Junta Española de la Liberación. It repudiated what it called the "communist-tainted" Negrín government and argued its own legitimacy on the grounds that it represented the major political parties of the republic of 1931. Outside of the Junta, in addition to the Negrín socialists, were the communists, Basque nationalists, and anarchists. In 1945, the Junta called a meeting of the Permanent Committee of the Cortes in Mexico City, set up a government headed by José Giral, and located its headquarters in Paris.[48]

Because of the split, no central agency was established to coordinate selection of emigrants and furnish aid to the camps. Characteristically, each faction organized its own association and labeled it the sole legitimate entity for relief and resettlement functions. First in the field was Negrín's group, Servicio de Emigración para Republicanos Españoles (SERE), founded in March 1939. It plunged immediately into cooperation with Narciso Bassols, Mexican ambassador to France, who had received instructions from President Cárdenas to arrange for the transportation of an unlimited number of Spanish exiles to Mexico.[49] Negrín was initially in control of the funds available to the defeated republic and decided to send part of them to Mexico for safekeeping. The yacht *Vita* was selected for this task and dispatched with a cargo of jewels, art objects, and negotiable securities. When it arrived in

Tampico on March 28 it was appropriated by Prieto instead of by Dr. José Puche, former rector of the University of Valencia, who was the authorized recipient. Why President Cárdenas allowed Prieto to accomplish the coup, how Prieto learned of the voyage of the *Vita,* and how much money the ship's cargo yielded, were and are the subject of controversy.[50] The result of course was that Prieto acquired the financial muscle to challenge Negrín's position within the Spanish republican government and the refugee community. Prieto placed the money at the disposal of the Permanent Committee of the Spanish Cortes and was appointed to head a new aid organization, the Junta de Auxilio a los Refugiados Españoles (JARE).[51] In 1940 SERE was abolished and JARE assumed sole responsibility for the transportation of refugees, but the initial selection of emigrés for Mexico in 1939 was made by SERE in conjunction with the Mexican government. In July 1939 the Prieto socialist group refused to recognize the Negrín government and ousted the communists from the Cortes and from representation in SERE.[52]

In theory, SERE gave representation to the entire spectrum of Spanish political and anarchist organizations. Anarchists Federica Montseny and Mariano Rodríguez Vázquez sat with communist leaders Juan Comorera and Mariano Rojo and the moderate socialist Ramón Lamoneda on the committee that was responsible for selecting emigrants to Mexico and providing relief for the concentration camps. Some 100 million francs were expended between March and December 1939 on these efforts. The cost of transporting a refugee to Mexico was sixty dollars, plus forty dollars for clothing.[53] Each group was given a quota and requested to prepare a list of emigrants. The information included occupation, number of family members, war service, political affiliation, and country of choice. SERE refined these lists and gave them to the Mexican officials for final decisions.[54] But here the inevitable political infighting entered the picture. In order to obtain a visa, it was charged, the applicant had to praise Negrín and condemn the Casado-Prieto group as traitors. The anarchists claimed that SERE always gave priority to communist applicants and other Negrín supporters. Further, Mexican ambassador Bassols and his assistants, Federico and Susana Gamboa, were all communists and weighted the scales in favor of their Spanish cohorts. According to Silvia Mistral, an anarchist who emigrated to Mexico, the official percentages apportioned to the exiles by the Mexican officials were: Marxists, 38 percent; republicans, 33 percent; anarchists (CNT-FAI), 24 percent; and independents, 5 percent.[55] In practice, however, anarcho-syndicalists and supporters of the Prieto-Casado coup were given a disproportionately small share of the available places. In the first two unofficial sailings, 600 refugees left France on April 3, and 1,700 on May 24. It was alleged that the overwhelming majority of these passengers were communists.[56] In the first official sailing, June 2, 1939, the *Sinaia* departed with 1,599 people; its arrival date is not known. The *Ipanema,* whose departure date is unknown, arrived in Mexico on July 7 with 994 emigrants, and *Mexique* on July 27, with 2,091 Spaniards. The *De Grasse* carried 207 passengers to New York, whence they were sent by train to Mexico.[57]

Later, it was charged, the proportion of anarchists in the Mexican emigration was reduced to 2 or 3 percent.[58] Fernando Solano Palacio asserted that on his own voyage to Chile on the *Winnipeg,* only 9 percent of the passengers were anarchists. He claimed that they constituted only 7 or 8 percent of the voyagers aboard the *Ipanema* on its first trip to Mexico.[59] The anarchist Antonio Vilanova, on the other hand, experienced no discrimination when he answered the first call for Mexico at St. Cyprien in May 1939. The 180 selectees at St. Cyprien were immediately transferred to Barcarès, where they were placed with other prospective emigrants in "Camp Mexico." Life there was far different from what it was in the beach concentration camps. The people slept on cots, were issued blankets and clothing, and ate decent food. Vilanova was in the group that left on the *Sinaia* on June 2.[60] But for many exiles, particularly those who had no affiliation with a political party or syndicate, the idea of going to Mexico was an unattainable dream. Typical was Francisco Fenestres, who subscribed to no political doctrine but wanted desperately to go to Mexico or some other Latin American country. The "political complications" involved in securing sponsorship frustrated his desire.[61]

The complaints regarding the communist bias of Bassols and the Gamboas soured the emigration effort. Although many Mexican officials then working in France denied the political bias of their chiefs, and a substantial number of Spanish refugees refuted allegations that SERE was "a tool of the dominant communist elements in Negrín's government," the charges have persisted to this date.[62] Bassols and the Gamboas were later dismissed by President Cárdenas, proving to Lois Smith that he was aware of and disapproved of their preference for the communists.[63] Pablo Neruda, the poet, who served as Chilean consul in Paris, was also recalled by his government, ostensibly for displaying a procommunist bias in the selection of emigrants for that country.[64] Fagen has declared that although there is sound evidence of the procommunist bias, nevertheless refugees running the gamut of Spanish political ideologies did in fact come to Mexico so that it is "unlikely that the selection procedures were effectively exclusive."[65] Be that as it may, there is very little doubt that the selection procedures were biased and effectively excluded large numbers of anarchists and independents. The situation changed when JARE took control of emigration, but the rate of emigration decreased sharply because of the international situation. Almost no ships were chartered in 1940 but many exiles made their way to Mexico through arrangements made by families, friends, and aid organizations. In 1941 and 1942, under the aegis of JARE, several ships were able to reach Mexico. The German occupation of all France in December 1942 put an end to further emigration.[66]

As with other statistics concerning the Spanish refugees, estimates on the number who reached Mexico are inconclusive. Ship counts were inaccurate, many exiles entered unofficially, and records were not uniform. The Dirección General de Estadística listed 6,234 Spaniards entering the country in 1939, 1,746 in 1940, 1,611 in 1941, and 2,534 in 1942. This adds up to a total of 12,125, but a more accurate reckoning would be 15,000 to 20,000.[67] Despite Mexico's expressed desire to receive skilled agricultural workers and fishermen, a large number of intellectuals and professionals were included in the immigration. Fagen notes that "Mexico received by far the greatest number of educated and trained individuals."[68] José R. Marra-López, commenting upon the drain of the "well-educated sectors" of Spanish society, declared that it "nearly destroyed intellectual life in Spain for a generation thereafter."[69] He might have added that the drain also deprived those Spaniards who remained in France of much-needed leadership.

Smaller numbers of Spanish exiles were admitted by other Latin American countries, including Chile, Cuba, the Dominican Republic, Argentina, and Venezuela. But it was Mexico, as solicitous for the welfare of the Spanish republicans in defeat as it had been for their success in war, which opened the door widest and gave the refugees citizenship if they wanted it, and almost unlimited economic opportunity. In total, the emigration to countries other than France was approximately 25,000 to 40,000.

Thus, a good proportion of the Spanish republicans who had sought refuge in France had now seized the opportunity to escape the vengeance of their conqueror and the indifference, if not outright hostility, of their hosts to seek new lives in Hispanic America. Mistral noted that when her ship weighed anchor from Bordeaux for Mexico the refugees were jubilant. There were shouts of "Viva Mexico!" and Viva Cárdenas!"[70] But there was not a single "Viva Francia!" or "Viva Daladier!", cheers that had been loudly voiced a scant four months before.

Yet, in a way, the experience of Arturo Barea was more prophetic. Crossing the Channel to England he conversed with two French sailors and delivered himself of a long list of grievances against the French. He asked whether France was blind to the German menace or whether it had given up on its own liberty. One of the sailors assured him that the French workers would fight. "Look, comrade," he said, "don't go away from France in bitterness. We'll fight together yet."[71]

CHAPTER SIX

FATHER DON QUIXOTE, DELIVER US . . .

Father Don Quixote
Who is in Heaven,
Deliver us from odium and abandonment.

Father Don Quixote,
Deliver us, Señor,
From cowardice
And from dishonor.

Father Don Quixote,
Most high and perfect,
Deliver us from life
Without an ideal.

Juan de Pena

THE ISSUES that had exacerbated relations between the Spanish refugees and their French hosts in the early days of the exodus seemed to fade somewhat after April 1939. The clamor for mass repatriation ceased, and the Spaniards reluctantly began to accept camp life as an alternative, albeit disagreeable, to freedom. In the face of the deteriorating European political scene the French government now became acutely aware of the immense reservoir of industrial, agricultural, and military skills among the Spanish republicans. Discussion of repatriation virtually ceased and Spanish nationalist pressures were resisted. Increasingly, French efforts were directed toward the mobilization of refugee skills to supplement the nation's war resources.[1]

Two important developments served to stabilize the situation of the Spanish refugees. A number of new camps were opened, relieving the tensions and overcrowding in the older camps. And the camps themselves were being improved and organized on a paramilitary basis. Although Spaniards still found much to criticize, most of them grudgingly accepted the relative stability of the new situation. There were, according to an American relief worker on the scene, more than 2,000 places throughout France in which Spaniards were lodged. The overwhelming number of those in areas other than the South were small, housing anywhere from a half-dozen to two thousand refugees.[2] Additional thousands were contracted out to farmers. In the larger camps there were at least 220,000 Spanish republicans and probably many more:[3]

Concentration camps	Department	Number of refugees
Barcarès	Pyrénées-Orientales	70,000
Argelès	Pyrénées-Orientales	43,000
St. Cyprien	Pyrénées-Orientales	30,000
Vernet-les-Bains	Pyrénées-Orientales	500
Gurs	Basses-Pyrénées	16,000
Bram	l'Aude	16,000
Agde	l'Herault	16,000
Septfonds	Tarn-et-Garonne	16,000
Mazères	l'Ariège	5,000
Montoliou	l'Ariège	Indeterminate
Other Camps		4,000
Prison camps		
Ft. Collioure	Pyrénées-Orientales	400
Le Vernet	l'Ariège	Indeterminate
Ricucros (Women's Prison)	l'Ariège	Indeterminate
	Total	216,500

The decentralizing reforms signaled by the governmental policy statement of February 25 were being put into effect.[4] Concurrently, the camps were assuming permanent form through the erection of barracks and service buildings and the initiation of more efficient administrative procedures. The structure of administration was broadened to include Spanish participation in command and service functions. Each camp was commanded by a senior French officer who exercised control of the central administration and of supply and security services. The camps were generally divided into sections (Barcarès, for example, had thirty) with varying numbers of barracks and internees. Usually, the sections were divided by branch of military service, with separate sections for civilians.[5] A Spanish chief was appointed for each section and for each barrack. The refugees maintained their own internal discipline and administered their kitchen, sanitation, and similar services. French guards patrolled the outer and section perimeters. The resulting distance between the Spanish internees and their guards helped damp the explosive atmosphere that had prevailed during the first stages of the exodus.[6] The degree of improvement varied greatly from camp to camp, as did the responses of the internees.

Perhaps the relative improvement in camp conditions is best illustrated by the experience of Mariano Puzo. When the war ended he was captured in the central zone and imprisoned to await trial. He succeeded in escaping and made his way to France with false papers, assuming the name of Riús de la Puerta. Happy at finding safety in France, he was assigned to St. Cyprien in early May and was somewhat at a loss to understand the protests of his comrades. "I felt satisfied and content, because we had something to eat, which was not the case in Spain," he said.[7]

The Spanish *Jefe* (Chief) of the civilian section in Argelès also demonstrated the relativity of the situation in an interview with a correspondent from the *Manchester Guardian*. With some 16,000 people in his section, he was proud of what had already been achieved and was full of plans for the future. A lawyer and former high official of the Spanish republican government, the Jefe was now obsessed with the desire to better the lot of his charges. From a little office in a wooden barrack, equipped with table and typewriter, he supervised a corps of barracks chiefs and a working brigade of 900 refugees who were building wooden barracks and keeping the section area clean. The correspondent noted that one could walk on the beach without finding so much as a potato peel, but he also saw groups of half-naked men boiling their rags and blankets to free them from the ever-present lice. Although many people were still sleeping in holes scooped in the sand, the jefe showed scale models for the construction of what could only be called a comfortable town. There were to be married quarters for the 200 families in which the women and children had refused to leave the men. One barrack was to be converted into a studio for the twenty-three artists among the refugees. Another would become the Centro de Cultura, where resident professors would give lectures and conduct classes. There would be barber shops, canteens, and other stores. Most importantly, one barrack would serve as a theater. The jefe appealed to the British public for contributions: musical instruments, lesson books, paper, envelopes, pencils, barber tools. When informed that the English might rather wish to concentrate on such basic materials as medical supplies or clothing, the Jefe remonstrated that "spiritual needs are as great as physical . . . Men die when they have lost all hope in living." The correspondent, although doubtful of the eventual success of the project, was favorably impressed with "that resilience which is characteristic of Spaniards."[8]

In at least one camp the French succeeded in evoking warm and enthusiastic responses from the inmates. Bram (l'Aude) was widely regarded as a model camp. Valentín Torras, former chairman of the Socialist Party in Manresa, Spain, and a historian of World War I, wrote to *Le Midi socialiste* expressing the gratitude of the inmates for the rapid construction of barracks and the efforts of the French authorities to furnish essential services and conveniences. Similarly, the French were proud of the camp at Gurs (Basses-Pyrénées), with its comprehensive health and sanitation services.[9] General Menard, inspector general of refugee camps, visited Bram on March 28 and was welcomed by the exiles with shouts of "Vive la France!"[10] Further, the refugees at Montoliou and Bram provided rousing welcomes for Minister of Interior Albert M. Sarraut when he visited them on May 5. The minister, who had been battered from both sides, had finally emerged as a hero to many Spaniards after his vehement defense of their rights in a Chamber of Deputies debate on March 11. At Montoliou (l'Ariège) he was greeted with a speech by a refugee extolling the virtues of France and its estimable minister of the interior, and he toured an exhibit of refugee arts and crafts. At Bram he heard a concert by Spanish musicians.[11]

Francis G. Smith, an American observer, presented an optimistic view of the situation. Construction of barracks and sanitation facilities had been accelerated. Medical attention was now provided for the sick. With few exceptions, he added, the Senegalese soldiers had been removed from guard duty. Food rations, while still not substantial, had been upgraded in quantity and nourishment value. He described a camp at Morlaas (Basses-Pyrénées), one of the numerous small units established throughout France, where eight women and fifty children were quartered in the Chateau de Terres Horas, donated by its owner to the government. They slept in beds with straw mattresses and had adequate blankets. The food consisted of bread, potatoes, meat, beans and peas, sugar and salt. Thirty liters of milk were distributed daily. The children attended school for three hours per day and had adequate play periods in the outdoors. Most of the youngsters appeared healthy and vigorous.[12]

The practice of publishing lists of inquiries from Spaniards seeking information on the whereabouts of family, relatives, and friends was widespread in French newspapers. On May 6, 1939, for example, *La Dépêche de Toulouse* printed an entire column of such material. In all, there were forty-eight separate inquiries involving hundreds of names.[13]

The Spanish yearning to transcend camp surveillance and restrictions sometimes found expression. On a hot July day, Juan Olibo recounted, two refugees were sent from Argelès camp to deliver a package to the mairie in town. Suddenly, they were beyond the gates, free, cavorting along the road like schoolboys. In the village, people were friendly. An old man bought them a drink; the wine was delicious, the chat simple and earthy. They delivered the package as a thunderstorm broke. A man invited them into his house, fed them a real dinner, talked to them a long time, offered them a comfortable bed for the night. In the morning, the woman of the house gave them a food package. As they were leaving, they remembered that the words "camp" and "exile" had not even been mentioned. Their host escorted them to the camp and explained the situation to the guards. Then the camp gates closed on them again, and they were back to reality. They had had an interlude between sojourns in hell, but they had reaffirmed their identities and learned something new: "Liberty! It is beautiful and rare and precious. [And] ghettos are not eternal."[14]

Not even the accolades for the long-suffering Sarraut could, however, eliminate Spanish ambivalence about camp conditions. Opinion was fairly widespread that much in the camps had changed for the better. In some aspects, notably housing, there were dramatic advances. But many Spaniards could and did find much to criticize, even in a place as highly touted as the model camp at Bram. The evident desire of Frenchmen to conclude that the nasty phase of the immigration was finished and that France had regained its traditional laurels of humanitarianism was blunted by complaints concerning insufficient services and the rigidity of the bureaucracy.[15]

Health and sanitation, as well as the quantity and quality of food, were the main sources of dissatisfaction. The general secretary of a major international refugee aid organization took exception to Smith's laudatory report. She characterized the situation at Bram as one of "slight improvement," but maintained that lodgings were still unsatisfactory, food insufficient, and hygiene impossible. At Collioure, harsh treatment of prisoners continued despite previous exposure of wrongdoing.[16] Dr. Pujol, who was an internee in the camps at Argelès, St. Cyprien, and Bram, from February 1939 to the armistice, corroborated these complaints and added details. He noted that SERE, the Spanish government-in-exile aid organization, had contributed funds to construct a hospital at Argelès and had sent food supplies to many camps. He claimed that French personnel appropriated much of the food for personal use and that the hospital, provisioned with Spanish republican army supplies and equipment, was built on a marshy plot next to the Tech River where it emptied into the Mediterranean.[17] In August 1939, the French camp engineer warned of the danger of flooding during rainy seasons and urged the construction of a protective dike. The project was approved but never begun. In October of 1940 the river rose and inundated the hospital and a number of nearby barracks, destroying great quantities of electrical, medical, and sanitation equipment.[18]

Initially denied the privilege of practicing medicine in the camps, Dr. Pujol finally received permission to do so under the supervision of French doctors. He was appalled at their laxity, which risked the spread of epidemic. In St. Cyprien, in July 1939, he found several cases of malaria but the French authorities refused to recognize any danger. They were finally forced to do so when Dr. Pujol and another Spanish doctor verified the presence of the anopheles mosquito (the carrier of malaria) in the swampy area surrounding the camp.[19] As late as May 1940, Dr. Pujol found the medical service to be ineffective at the model camp of Bram. Medical supplies were scarce, the menu consisted largely of sweet potatoes, and the French medical chief, Dr. Lebof, was notoriously hostile to the Spaniards and unprofessional in his dealings with them, according to Dr. Pujol. He recounted the appearance of two typhus cases that prompted Dr. Lebof to order mass vaccination. He overrode the objections of the Spanish doctors that it would be dangerous to administer the vaccine to anyone already harboring the disease—that a rapid, usually fatal, case might then result. Pujol asserted that Dr. Lebof's action subsequently produced forty deaths in a few days. In another instance Lebof distributed powdered milk to infants suffering from gastroenteritis, instead of condensed milk, which, although available, was given instead to Alsatian refugee children. More than thirty Spanish infant deaths resulted from this action, Pujol said.[20] Another indignity suffered by the Spaniards was the French regulation requiring Spanish doctors to be accompanied by a guard or nurse when examining female patients. The Spanish doctors refused to permit males past the door to the ward: "Spanish women are like other women, able to show their bodies to their husbands or to their doctors. But no law obliges them to do so for a policeman."[21]

In one aspect of camp life there was no amelioration. Pervasive suspicion of the Spaniards as Reds continued on every level of French administration, drawing charges that the republicans were still seen as "suspects and traitors."[22] There was no cessation of surveillance, searches, and imprisonment at Collioure or Le Vernet for those considered dangerous to French security. With the signing of the Nazi-Soviet pact, the outlawing of the French Communist Party, and the beginning of the war, this activity escalated to the scale of the earlier Great Fear of 1939.

A new danger presented itself to the anxious French authorities, the suspicion that among the Spanish refugees were a number of Axis infiltrators, allowed over the border by the Spanish nationalist government. Two weeks after the outbreak of war the Ministry of Interior received information that two high officials of the German espionage service had arrived at Pamplona to coordinate sabotage plans against the Dewoitine aircraft factory in Toulouse and the huge electric station at Marignac (Haute-Garonne).[23] Later reports said that nationalist Spaniards had been sent to France on sabotage missions, including a project to make and float small time-bombs down the rivers and canals that fed various hydroelectric stations. As a result of the fears aroused by these exotic reports the minister of interior instructed the prefect of Haute-Garonne to send all recent Spanish arrivals to Le Vernet. It was indicated, however, that the new Spanish government was doing all it could to impede this traffic, although that notion contradicted the earlier information to the effect that Franco officials had connived at infiltration.[24]

The near-hysteria produced in France by the Hitler-Stalin agreement resulted also in the apprehension and jailing of many French and Spanish communists. For the Spaniards these actions resulted from an identification of the Spanish republic with the Soviet Union, owing to the strong Soviet support of the republic during the civil war and the prominent role played by Spanish Communists in the republican government. In October 1939, the Ministry of Interior alerted security officials to the imminent arrival of four Soviet agents who were proceeding from Belgium with the mission of planting bombs in French trading places.[25] The offices of SERE were registered and its commercial fleet requisitioned. *Ce Soir,* a left-wing newspaper partially funded by Juan Negrín, was suppressed, along with *L'Humanité.* Deportation was threatened for anyone distributing political publications in the camps. If they had endured harassment previously, the Hitler-Stalin agreement put the Spanish communists to the supreme test, according to Miguel Angel, communist official and writer. He was convinced that their "traditions of battle and of international proletarianism" were the real reasons for the persecution. He accused the "aggressive bloc of the capitalist countries" of fomenting the destruction of the land of socialism. Further, he asserted, the French police had created a network of "rogues" and "miserables" within the camps to find and denounce the communists. Anarchists, too, continued to be hunted and imprisoned. Many had been isolated and placed in Fort Collioure, Mt. Louis (Pyrénées-Orientales), and Le Vernet, but the French police sought the others relentlessly. On April 9, 1939, the Sureté published a list of two hundred anarchists and distributed it nationally, calling for their arrest. Most of the wanted ones evaded the net because they had been provided with false papers. Nevertheless, at the outbreak of war, hundreds of alleged anarchists were seized and detained.[26]

Apart from the red scare, there were very few news stories concerning the exiles in the conservative French press. From July 1939 to July 1940, *Le Figaro,* for example, virtually ignored them. The Spanish news in *Figaro* consisted largely of the contacts between the new nationalist government and the Quai d'Orsay. Space was given to the sentencing of various republican leaders in Spain. Marshal Pétain's visit to a refugee camp, where he reviewed the guards but had no contact with the internees, rated a two-column picture. Only the arrival of a ship bearing twenty-seven new refugees who had hidden in the Galician hills for two years merited publication.[27] When war came the same newspaper noted that many foreigners—Czechs, Poles, Austrians, Jews—thronged French recruiting stations, but failed to mention that Spaniards had already enlisted by the thousands and that additional thousands were enrolled in labor companies erecting new fortifications in the north. Later, it was to ignore the significant contributions of Spanish soldiers in the Norwegian campaign and in resisting the German breakthrough.[28] *L'Indépendant* (Pau) a radical paper serving the Basses-Pyrénées, devoted more space to the exiles than *Figaro* did—the article on health and sanitation services at Gurs, for example—but it too was more concerned with relations between the French and the Spanish nationalists than with what transpired in the camps. It reported the departure of sixty Spanish communist officials for the Soviet Union and an incident in which Spanish carabiñeros had violated French soil to shoot a shepherd believed to have aided two escapees to cross the border. *Le Midi socialiste* was somewhat more generous, with a salute to the third anniversary of the outbreak of the Spanish Civil War.[29]

Security measures were increased in the camps with the outbreak of war. The occasional escapes of inmates had always distressed the French authorities but now stricter measures were taken. At St. Cyprien, three Spaniards escaped shortly after the war began. Immediately, the camp was put in a state of alert. Everyone was confined to barracks. Constant roll-calls were made. The prisoners, for their part, "laughed and prayed"—laughed at the discomfiture of their French captors, and prayed for the success of the escapees. But Olibo felt that escape served no purpose. If the escapees regained Spain it was tantamount to suicide. If they went to the center or north of France they would be caught and returned. If they remained in the camp they might gain work contracts and permission to leave the camp. Nevertheless, all wished success to the escapees because of the embarrassment it would cause their unpopular hosts.[30] Another reason, not given in this instance, but omnipresent, was the pride taken by Spaniards in their ability to escape almost at will, to pass through the barbed wire with impunity, and thus to demonstrate their superiority over the French.

In this desperate, tragicomic, and sometimes deadly French-Spanish refugee confrontation, politics were the touchstone. Many Frenchmen, including officials in the security services, believed that all the Spaniards were Reds and therefore needed to be strictly controlled. Painfully aware of intensive political activity inside and outside the camps, they carried on an unceasing campaign to apprehend the leaders. With the signing of the Nazi-Soviet pact this search became part of the war hysteria. Although the Spanish communists did not actively attempt to sabotage the war effort, their association with the French communists made them highly suspect in French eyes. Actually, nothing demonstrated the fragmentation of the Spanish republic more than the political infighting that abounded in the camps and among the leaders of the impotent government-in-exile. The shattering defeat had sundered the frayed bonds of Spanish republican unity. The pretense of solidarity in the face of a common enemy was no longer necessary, and the surviving Spaniards were faced with a two fold task: to explain the disaster and to reorganize the remnants of their political organizations for effective action inside the camps and when the inevitable return to Spain occurred.

With exile came what Broué and Témime called the age of controversy.[31] The antagonisms of communists and their leftist and socialist allies against the anarchists, the POUM, and the republican parties were no longer muted by the need to display outward harmony. Bitter argument, plot and counterplot, and struggles for domination within the camps became the rule. The center parties had disintegrated. A meeting of republican leaders in Toulouse, under the leadership of Paulino Gómez Sainz, who had been Juan Negrín's minister of interior, was routed by the French police. Later, these men were driven from the Haute-Garonne and forced to scatter among several departments.[32] Although a provisional government was formed in London after the French defeat, it lacked authenticity, had minimal contact with the Spaniards in France, and was largely ignored by the British.[33] The anarchists had suffered the imprisonment of many key militants and, despite strong representation in some camps, were unable to organize on a large scale until late in 1941.[34]

Communist organizing ability was most in evidence during this period. Despite the fact that four thousand of their leaders and many militant workers had emigrated to the Soviet Union they possessed many strengths, even in the unpromising milieu of the camps. Greater in number than their adversaries, they were distributed plentifully in all the camps. Party discipline was called into play. Most importantly, they possessed an invaluable ally in the French Communist Party, which provided them with shelter, false papers, liaison with the Third International, and necessary funds for supplies and other party work.[35] The key to communist success lay in the rapidity and thoroughness with which they organized cells in every echelon of Spanish command and service personnel, down to the numerous barracks chiefs. Wherever they preempted these positions they exercised control over many aspects of camp life. They censored and many times destroyed mail, excluded all except communist newspapers, harassed and withheld food from their rivals, dominated the official refugee newspapers, and boldly pushed their slogan, "Unity and Popular Front." None of these measures went without opposition from members of other parties and the anarchists. When the camp bulletin at St. Cyprien, *La Voz de los Españoles,* declared that unity "ought to be manifested by clearing out the bandits, saboteurs, traitors: anarchists and Trotskyites, old and new allies of the renegade Franco,"[36] the anarchists formed a Committee of Agitation and Propaganda which issued its own bulletin and asserted: "The unity proclaimed by the Communist Party was not, is not, and never will be possible because it is an unreal unity, sectarian, adjusted to the advantage and supremacy of the Communist Party, which is detrimental to the sentiments and ideals of the workers who fought for the emancipation of their class, without distinction of creeds."[37] Physical violence was pervasive and there were a number of murders. In several camps noncommunist prisoners asked to be separated from the influence of the communists.[38]

Mariano Constante described how the scattered elements of the Communist Party reorganized themselves at Septfonds, beginning on the day of their arrival. As soon as a new barrack was occupied, responsible comrades would be named to organize a committee or cell there. Manpower was plentiful because many officers and political commissars from the former communist Forty-Third Division were interned at Septfonds. Constante was chosen to be secretary of Barracks 37 and carried out multiple tasks: to "cut short all provocation from some uncontrollable elements, maintain the dignity of the prisoners as combatants of the Spanish republican army, prevent unjust acts by the French authorities, ameliorate the material hardships of the internees, and carry on a campaign of political information." He shed light on the system of political education initiated by the com-

munists. A network of comrades translated articles and editorials from
L'Humanité, which was smuggled into the camp by a gendarme who
was a member of the French Communist Party. Constante than supervised the making of fifty or sixty copies by hand and distributed them
to the various barracks.[39] The work was often disrupted by the French
authorities, however, whose resentment grew when the communists
led a campaign against the recruitment of volunteers for the labor companies and the Foreign Legion. So thorough was communist preparation
at Septfonds that a standby team of leaders was organized and ready
to assume responsibility in case of need. When the gardes mobiles arrested twelve communist leaders and sent them to Fort Collioure, their
replacements stepped immediately into the breach.[40]

The determination, speed, and efficiency of the Spanish Communist
Party in setting up contacts with the outside world was recounted by
José Gros. At St. Cyprien in February 1939, 90 to 100 of the 225 members of the Spanish Fourteenth Corps of Guerrillas were communists.
The French showed great interest in interviewing them but they shunned
calls from the loudspeaker. In March 1939, Gros was asked to establish contact with a top party leader being sheltered in the Elne
home of a French communist. Exit from and reentry into St. Cyprien
was not difficult. The route lay through a swamp that skirted the
Spanish refugee cemetery, and it was easy to avoid the patrols of
mounted Moroccans. The greatest discomfort came from the hard
tramontane winds and the rain. Once established, this liaison provided
a means for the transmission of information and commands. The communists inside the camp felt bolstered by their connection with the
Spanish party organization and the aid of the powerful French Communist Party.[41] According to Miguel Angel, the bold activity of the
Spanish communists was instrumental not only in restoring their own
dignity and purpose but in leading the way for later resistance against
the Nazis.[42]

If the communists seemed to enjoy some success in their organizing
efforts, other parties were not as fortunate. We have seen how the
attempts of the republican parties failed. The socialists fared no better.
As for the anarchists, despite strong organizations in some camps and
continued contact with comrades outside the camp, they were unable
to produce large-scale activity until late in 1941. Antonio Vilanova
recounted the half-hearted circulation of names of the Spanish Socialist
Workers Party (Partido Socialista Obrero de España) in the camps. The
project was abandoned by the party executive because the French government had ruled against Spanish political activity in exile. The executive saw its main task as the deliverance of the refugees from the

camps and their absorption into French life. Vilanova listed the difficulties faced by those who sought to engage in political work: communication with the outside world was too difficult; the French penalized those who were caught, with arrest and dispatch to prison camps; and Spanish political leaders were prohibited from living in Paris and were instead dispersed throughout the country. The emigration of actual and potential leaders left a huge gap.[43]

The departure of large numbers of intellectuals, professionals, and artists had indeed left a void in the political arena, but it had done more. The cultural exuberance and experimentation that had marked the interwar period was now moribund, like that other great adventure, the Second Spanish Republic. Penned into concentration camps, the remnants of this movement turned inward, contemplating a world shrunken to a few meters of sand and a future that extended only to the next roll-call. The splendid literary garments spun by Federico García Lorca, Antonio Machado, and many others hung in tatters on the barbed wire. Despair was the dominant mood, but it was mingled with rage at the destruction of their dreams, reconciliation with the savagery that flawed Spain, persistent hope for reconquest of their soil, and reassertion of the life spirit over defeat and degradation.

The tragedy of the nightmare retreat, when the roads drank the blood of the defeated ones, had ended in the all-embracing blankness of sand, wind, and barbed wire. "All is sand," lamented Juan de Pena, "I am sand, you are sand, he is sand, the gardes mobiles are sand . . . my soul no longer exists."[44] And the aftermath is death, always death:

> This is a small boy,
> And this is the body of his father,
> Enclosed in four pine planks.
> They are coming to bury him.
>
> Man of Spain, more than a man,
> My promise accompanies you.[45]

And the bittersweet memories of Spain, that "soil blessed by the gods, where the men are wolves," are tempered by memories of its severe beauty:

> I salute my sun and I salute my land.
> I salute you Spain.
> Will I again see your sky in the silver moon
> Of enchanted nights?
>
> My heart is heavy and tired.
> I leave you my country.[46]

In the "dark February afternoon" of Argelès the poet recalled this anguished farewell and reflected that

> . . . I never believed
> That I would suffer such
> Great unhappiness.[47]

But the will to survive and to reconquer was stronger than galling defeat and world betrayal:

> Spaniard of the exodus of yesterday,
> And Spaniard of the exodus of today,
> There, nothing remains.
>
> Dig a hole in the soil of your exile,
> Plant a tree,
> Water it with your tears and wait.
>
> There, there is nothing any more.
> Remain here and wait.[48]

As they suffered the sand and the wind of the open beaches, an insistent question haunted them: amid the wreckage of their lives, what did they want now? And the poet hurled the answer: "We wish to be!"[49] To survive, to feel their humanity and retain their dignity was all that remained of their struggle.

Efforts to organize cultural activity on a national level failed because the very organizations that were created looked away from France and toward Mexico. The Junta de Cultura Española was founded in Paris early in 1939 with the objective of establishing artists and intellectuals in other countries. The headquarters was removed to Mexico at the end of 1939.[50] One Spanish cultural giant did remain in France and dedicated himself to aiding his countrymen in the camps. Pablo Casals, the great cellist, established himself in Prades and mobilized a number of people to aid in this work. Casals raised funds to buy gifts, food, garments, and other necessities. Visiting the camps frequently, he performed for the internees and wrote letters to them, but the emotional and physical deterioration he saw in the camps saddened him.[51]

Hopes for a Spanish cultural renaissance amid the chaos of defeat and exile were impossible to realize, but the determination of the refugees did bring into existence many grass-roots cultural and educational programs. A newspaper, written entirely in Catalan, printed items of interest from many camps. At Barcarès, the issue of May 1939 reported, volunteer teachers were conducting classes in Catalan grammar and the history of Catalonia, "to conserve the enthusiasm and patriotic fervor of our youth." At Agde, a famous tenor had organized a choir whose concerts "make our people vibrate with enthusiasm." An exposition of Spanish art by Basques and Catalans was being prepared. A festival in St. Cyprien featured music by a military band, the "Liberty Chorus," and poetry readings.[52] Similar activities were carried on in other camps. Drama was a major activity at Septfonds, where a Spanish actor formed a repertory group. Berruezo noted that an orchestra had been created "out of nothing." And an anarchist exhibition on "The Progress of the Spanish Revolution" contained ten sections detailing progressive phases of the anarchist collectives during the civil war.[53]

It must not be imagined that funding and art materials were made available on a massive scale for these projects. A trickle of supplies, including musical instruments and writing materials, were made available by SERE and other aid organizations. But the Spaniards performed miracles in creating their own supplies: driftwood was used in carving; broken tools were employed in sculpting in stone; a low-grade clay was found at Argelès and used and reused in shaping objects; tattered rectangles of brown army canvas were stretched and painted with pigments stolen from the French; barracks walls were filled with murals; and squares of wood—cut from the interiors of barracks—were polished with sand and carved into woodcuts. All of these activities, carried out on the most basic level, satisfied "the needs of the spirit, the necessities of the soul," and helped the refugees to defend themselves against the dreaded enemies of desperation and tedium.[54]

While the political-military time bomb ticked on, in the spring and summer of 1939, the French could at least try to convince themselves that the problem of the Spanish refugees had been solved. True, there were many annoyances, but the situation had been stabilized. The hordes of Spaniards no longer merited attention in the newspapers. Threats of mass breakouts, looting, and anarchist-communist conspiracies against the security of the French state were under control. It was worth the heavy financial burden to achieve this equilibrium, which allowed the government to turn its full attention to diplomacy. In the face of intensified Nazi pressure on Poland, French emissaries moved about the Continent, cementing Anglo-French understanding, engaging in will-o-the-wisp negotiations with the Soviet Union, worrying about Belgian and Dutch neutrality. Reassuring statements of French military strength and readiness filled the newspapers. Photographs of the impregnable Maginot Line, modern fighter aircraft, invincible French tanks, the tough sons of the *poilus* of 1914–1918 manning the improved and feared 75-mm cannon, recollections of the glories of French arms, all inundated the consciousness of the citizenry and bolstered its morale. If the madman Hitler persisted in ignoring reality the French would this time go all the way to Berlin. But the reassurances lacked credibility. The people were not ready for war, craved a way out. If there were any image to describe the feeling of the French people, it was that of the stricken fly awaiting the spider's pounce.[55]

To the Spaniards enmeshed in their web of barbed wire, senses sharpened by two and one-half years of combat against fascism and finely tuned to the nuances of politics, the situation seemed to be deteriorating in alarming fashion. They might think that the oncoming war was six months too late to have an immediate bearing on their own cause, but they were antifascist to the core. They understood clearly that their survival and hope of eventual victory rested on joint opposition to the Nazi power. Despite implacable resentment of French callousness, the Iberians were ready to follow their host's lead.

They too waited.

CHAPTER SEVEN

DÉJÀ VU

WAR AND DEFEAT AGAIN

What will France do? We wait, ready to contribute in fullest
measure to its action. We owe much to France and, despite
certain rancors, we have become its children.

Jean Olibo, Parcours

The gardes mobiles strike the flag in the melancholy afternoon.
Today they do not make fun of us, ex-soldiers of Spain,

"inferiors" and "defeated ones."

Today they do not subject us to kicks. With empty stomachs, with
fevered brains, with distressed hearts, with dry eyes, the

internees of Argelès are silent.

The flag ripping in the day-long tramontane, Lamentable lowering
to the ground. Many Guards are crying. A friend at my side says:
"They are crying at last. They have a soul."

José María Alvarez Posado, "Armistice Day"

TRIAL BY FIRE, military defeat, and flight from their native land
was the fate of the Spanish republicans. Now it was the turn of
their French hosts. Day by day, in the deepening twilight of spring-
summer 1939, the probability of war grew greater. When war arrived,
a curiously misshapen stepson of the war of 1914–1918, the French
nation moved through the motions of warrior ritual without conviction,
anger, or resolve. The stunning German triumph of May–June 1940
was seen in retrospect as foreordained. Now French and Belgian soldiers and civilians clogged the roads, streaming southward; a new class
of refugees had come of age. The Third French Republic joined the
Second Spanish Republic in the trophy room of the Fascist conquerors.

The defenders of Catalonia were destined, in this first phase of the
Second World War, to fight and die far from their accustomed bat-
tlegrounds. From September 1939 to June 1940, they would see combat
with the French Foreign Legion and the French army, or be enrolled
in workers' companies to aid the war effort. They would fight on the
northern and eastern fronts and in Norway. They would be thrown
into the fateful gap between the Maginot Line and the English Channel

107

to erect stopgap fortifications. They would man French defense in-
dustries and tend French crops. Six thousand of them would die in
battle before the armistice. A handful would reach England from
Dunkirk, but 14,000 trapped in the inferno of Belgium and northern
France would be taken prisoner. Segregated by the Nazis, they would
be denied the comparative honor of a prisoner-of-war camp and be
sent instead to concentration camps or factories in Germany. Of the
12,000 who entered Mauthausen camp, only 2,000 would emerge alive
at war's end. Others would die in the camps of Oranienburg, Dachau,
Buchenwald, and Auschwitz. The involvement of France in the war
against fascism, so strongly desired by the Spanish republicans, came
at last, but with dismal consequences.[1]

In the fever of preparations for the oncoming crisis, France had, as
previously noted, become sharply aware of the potential of the Spanish
republicans as experienced soldiers, skilled industrial workers, and valuable agricultural laborers. There was never any doubt about the
massive utilization of the latter two categories, but there was considerable nervousness exhibited at the possibility of placing former
Spanish "Reds" in the French army.

From April 1939 to the onset of war in September, the French permitted the Spaniards to leave the camps by several routes: individual
contracts with industrialists or farmers, enlistment in the Foreign
Legion, enrollment in a workers' company, and, lastly, by joining—
if approved—the regular French army. For the refugees the only desirable avenue was the contract system, which provided an opportunity
to leave a camp as an individual and to reside, even with one's family
if it could be reunited, in quarters provided by the employer. The pay
of fifty centimes a day for farm work was minimal, but no value could
be placed on the freedom from camp restrictions. Employers visited
the camps, searching first of all for Spaniards who might have worked
in their fields as seasonal laborers before the civil war, and after that
for any healthy, experienced hands. The selection process included the
appraisal of an applicant's physical state. "They examined the mouth,
the teeth, and the muscles to see if we were strong, if we were young,"
according to Mariano Puzo, who went to work as a miner.[2] Women
were "inspected with an eye for work and lovemaking." Growing demands for war-related factory work led the French government to
prepare inventories of the industrial skills of the refugees in the camps.
Craft workers in metals, masonry, carpentry, and other fields were
transferred to special camps, such as Septfonds, where they signed
contracts for work in industrial centers throughout France. By August

21, 1939, for example, fifty Spaniards had gone to work at a metal factory in Lille.[3]

French authorities encouraged enlistment in the Foreign Legion, using the carrot of regular pay and allowances, plus liberation of legionnaire families from the camps, or the stick of forcible repatriation to Spain in case of refusal. There was widespread resistance to joining the legion, especially before the war, but several thousands enrolled. The American journalist Janet Flanner, visiting the camp at Amelie-les-bains (Pyrénées-Orientales), saw three contingents "of the younger and bolder men march off, singing and shouting," to join the legion. The reasons for this decision were varied. Some sensed adventure and freedom from camp miseries. Others made the move because of a feeling of hopelessness. The threat of forced repatriation was used frequently in the early days of the exodus, surprisingly, according to Vilanova, against the anarchists who entered France with the Twenty-Sixth (Durruti) Division. This accounts for the strong representation of anarcho-syndicalists among Spaniards in the legion, where they were under strict control. Ultimately, 15,000 Spanish refugees saw action on many fronts with the legion. General Auguste Noguès, addressing the Spanish legionnaires at Barcarès, acknowledged them to be "young soldiers but old combatants. I know them in battle and I know of their valor and combativeness."[4]

Whether Spaniards should be permitted to enlist in the regular French army was a thorny question. In the early months of 1939 the policy was to accept a limited number of exceptionally healthy, combat-hardened veterans. These were assigned to the First Regiment of Foreign Volunteers. As war became probable, the French general staff considered enrolling large numbers of Spaniards in volunteer units under the command of French officers. General Georges, chief of the high command, recalled the meritorious service of 14,000 Spaniards in World War I and favored such a program. But when General Maurice Gamelin, chief of the general staff, visited the camp at Gurs in August 1939, he registered a negative opinion because of the poor physical condition of the Spaniards. Nevertheless, it was still possible for *L'Indé-pendant* (Pau) to wax indignant over the sight of Spaniards playing volleyball at Gurs when, in the view of the newspaper, they should have been in uniform.

The signing of the Nazi-Soviet pact blasted all hopes for a Spanish military organization. Prejudice against the politics of the Spaniards, always high, now exceeded all limits. Despite the fact that Spanish communists did not hew to the Stalinist line on resistance to the war,

they were mistrusted by the French government. When war came, therefore, an estimated ten thousand Spaniards who enlisted in the French
army were dispersed in battalion or company strength among French
units. Only after the French defeat would the Spaniards fight again
in their own military and guerrilla formations. In contrast to Poles,
Norwegians, Czechs, and other nationalities, the Spaniards lost their
national identity, were ignored by the military and political establishments, and were forgotten by the world. But those who donned French
uniforms relished the pleasure of seeing themselves converted instantly
from "anarcho-communists, the scum of society, to glorious soldiers
of the French army."[5]

The idea of establishing workers' companies from the remaining
mass of Spanish manpower recommended itself highly to the French.
In militarized formations the refugees would be under control and
available for any necessary work. In pressing this objective the authorities brushed aside other plans that would have achieved similar ends
but given the Spaniards full civilian status. The Conference d'aide aux
refugiés espagnols, under the presidency of Professor Victor Basch, met
in July 1939 and developed a proposal. Senator Maurice Viollette suggested replacing 50,000 to 70,000 foreign agricultural workers with
Spaniards. Albert Forcinal emphasized the plenitude of Catalan technicians and urged their full utilization in war-related factories. As for
the International Brigaders, they would be trained in French military
tactics and incorporated into the army. The balance of the refugees
could be used to repopulate many abandoned French towns. The cost
of these projects would be shared by France and other friendly governments and through private contributions, which already totalled
800 million francs. Meanwhile, a committee consisting of François
Mauriac, Georges Duhamel and Mme. Montbrisson approved a plan
put forward by the Confederación Nacional de Trabajo (CNT) for
the creation of great cooperatives to work in the fields and forests of
France. Both of these plans were rejected in favor of a huge buildup of
workers' companies.[6]

As early as April 1939, pressure mounted on the refugees to enroll
in several newly formed workers companies. This was stubbornly
resisted by the Spaniards, who had no love for France at this point
and saw the move as one designed to convert them into forced laborers.
Mariano Constante reported that a scant two hundred volunteers answered the call at Septfonds. But the French persisted, often constituting
companies by edict and banishing recalcitrants to the punishment
centers.[7] As the months passed, however, and war came closer, Spanish
attitudes changed. Despite the fact that they considered their own de-

feat largely due to Anglo-French policy, they recognized that the struggle against Hitlerian domination of Europe was the chief priority. They realized that the exigencies of the hour had made them the children of France. The question became not "should we fight?" but "will we triumph?" Still, their burning desire for the reconquest of Spain made them look beyond this question. They had abiding faith in the ultimate victory of the democracies, but some asked: "And after their victory, will we not again be the dupes? The eternal dupes?" Pedro Alba, an anarchist, put it this way: "We were antimilitarists, but we decided to take arms again, preferring to fall in battle against Nazism than to die of hunger, misery, and cold in the concentration camps."[8]

It is impossible to determine the exact number of Spaniards who served in the workers' companies, because available French records are untrustworthy and in many cases have been refused to researchers. Eduardo Pons Prades, republican veteran and resistance fighter, who undertook a study of the workers' companies, was able to verify the existence of forty-two units. However, he believed that after commencement of the war the number may have grown to more than two hundred. The number of men in the companies ranged from 250 to 400. Most of the workers' companies were assigned to the northern and northeastern areas, which were to become the battlefields of the first stage of World War II.[9] French reserve officers were in command of the workers' companies, with Spanish captains serving as coordinators. The French staff for each company consisted of a chief sergeant, a detachment of soldiers, and several gendarmes. The Spanish captain had a subchief, secretary, and several interpreters. The pay for workers was fifty centimes per day. Promises to reunite families at places of work were made but not often kept. Living conditions and food, which were supposed to be the same as for the French army, were almost as poor as in the camps. Continued regimentation under the paramilitary structure of the companies grated on the refugees.[10] Nevertheless, the system seemed to work to the satisfaction of the French. In a Chamber of Deputies exchange with Deputy Ybarnegaray, that inveterate detractor of the Spanish republicans, Albert Sarraut, the minister of interior, noted that all branches of the French economy were competing for the services of the Spaniards. He added that all reports from commanders of military regions "express satisfaction with the work of the Spaniards, in the districts near the front, in the industrial establishments, and in agriculture."[11]

By February 1940, most of the Spaniards were working under contract or in the workers' companies or were fighting in the armed forces. Those still in the camps were usually old, sick, women, or children. A sizable number of "undesirables" were still incarcerated in the punishment camps. An inmate of Le Vernet later said that two-thirds of the prisoners volunteered for military service in September 1939 but were rejected.[12]

When the war began many Spaniards were already in forward positions, either as soldiers manning positions from the Italian border to the English Channel, or as members of workers' companies. From September 1939, to May 10, 1940, they participated in the *drôle de guerre*. When the massive German attack broke on the latter date they were caught up in its furies, sharing in the humiliation and destruction of the French army, swirling in the human currents that led to Dunkirk or southward to what remained of France. Many of those who escaped the German net found themselves back in the same concentration camps they had left such a short time ago.

In this phase of the war, as in the later stages, the Spanish exiles fought heroically in battles from Strasbourg to Dunkirk to Narvik. Despite this record their participation has been noted marginally or wiped entirely from the slate. In very few instances has proper recognition been afforded to the Spaniards who fought with the French army.

One of the most glaring examples of this neglect was the Norwegian campaign of April-May 1940. In response to the German attack on Norway on April 9, 1940, the French-British command decided to send an expeditionary force to make amphibious landings at Narvik and Trondheim. Of the 3,600 French troops initially involved, at least 1,200 were Spanish members of the French Foreign Legion. The legion's 13th Semi-brigade was exclusively Spanish. Their casualty rate was unbelievable, with 900 killed and an unknown number wounded. They formed a large part of the first assault wave that landed north and south of Narvik on April 14, 1940, taking several towns in hand-to-hand bayonet fighting. In a subsequent action in the hills around Narvik, a French lieutenant who watched the Spaniards pick their way through snow and rocks marvelled that they were "as agile as goats." The final assault on a stubborn machine-gun emplacement on the peak of the hill was made by three Spaniards, two of whom lost their lives in the attempt. The attack on Narvik was successful, following the repulse of a severe German counterattack. One Spanish company lost seventy men in the action. Pursuing the Germans, the expeditionary force was fourteen kilometers from the Swedish border when the order to halt and reembark for England arrived on June 4, 1940. They were needed to help stem the German onslaught in France. On June 29, General Charles de Gaulle visited the legionnaire camp and gave the men the choice of remaining with him in England or going to Morocco. Most of the surviving Spaniards elected to fight with de Gaulle. At the end of July 1940, General de Gaulle had 7,000 men at his disposal; almost 1,000 of this nucleus of the French resurrection were Spaniards.[13]

Contemporary accounts of the fighting in Norway either ignored the Spanish contribution or were unaware of it. *Le Figaro,* lauding the "brilliant improvisation" of the Narvik landing, noted only the participation of British, French, and Canadian troops; between April 23 and June 11 there was no mention of the Spaniards in the extensive coverage given the battle. The only French unit identified was the Chasseurs Alpins. An article by Lucien Romier on the campaign stressed British-French cooperation. A long piece by A. Thomazi went into great detail on the Allied landing in Norway, with kudos for French and British valor, but without a word concerning the Spanish republicans, who numbered half the French force.[14] Accounts written in the immediate postwar period, although lauding Spanish participation in the Narvik campaign, were also curiously involved with the "Red Legend" surrounding the exiles. Georges Blond described them as being "disciplined, hardened, accepting the hard regimen . . . and united in an exceptional solidarity." Many officials, suspicious of the alleged communism of the Spanish legionnaires—and therefore their willingness to defy the Stalinist line of opposition to the war—complained about their inclusion in the Norwegian campaign. "Now," Blond said, "inheritors of the military virtues of their race, these Reds, or ex-Reds, fought like lions in the snowy mountains of Norway." There would be no more jokes at their expense or gratuitous insults thrown at them.[15] M. J. Torris, historian of the expedition, revealed still another facet of the morbid French obsession with the crevices of Spanish politics and character. Four machine-guns had been wiped out by the Spaniards in a particular action; several Germans were killed and eight wounded. The French lieutenant observed that the Spanish legionnaires were still agitated by the combat. He recalled their prebattle bloodthirsty threats of vengeance on the Germans and now he wished "to know the depths of the souls of the men he commands, the depths of their secret and tormented souls." He secretly withdrew the bullets from his revolver, offered it to a Spaniard, and invited him to kill the wounded. The Spaniard growled, "I am not an assassin," and turned his back. The lieutenant then offered the firearm to Montane, who was known as a "hard one." His entire family had been killed in Spain by Nazi bombs. Montane took the revolver, hesitated a long time. Then he threw it to the ground. "No, I cannot do it," he said. "It is stronger than me. I have never assassinated anyone." He turned to his chief. "Truly, lieutenant," he asked, "have you taken us for assassins?"

Even today, Spaniards feel bitterness at the lack of recognition given to their role in the Norwegian campaign. Vilanova pointed out that at postwar commemorations, representatives of all governments involved in the battle participated, with the sole exception of the Spanish Republicans. A monument in the Narvik cemetary says: "France—to its sons and their brothers-in-arms who fell gloriously in Norway . . . Narvik 1940."[16]

Spanish soldiers were also heavily involved in combat against the massive German attacks launched on May 10, 1940, against the northern and eastern fronts of France. In later accounts of those Spaniards who experienced the desperation of flight from an omnipresent enemy, the common denominator words were "salíamos," "escapamos," and "nos hizo prisoneros" ("we departed," "we escaped," "we were made prisoners").

The Eleventh Foreign Regiment, with heavy Spanish representation, was part of the French Second Army in Lorraine. It formed the pivot for other units retreating on its left flank. The regiment defended the forest of Inor between the Meuse and the Chiers, near Stenay. There, the legionnaires suffered daily coordinated artillery and Stuka dive-bomb attacks, as well as infantry thrusts. Orders to retreat arrived too late and the regiment was surrounded at St. Germain-sur-Meuse. The Second Battalion attempted to open a gap through the German lines and, although it succeeded, suffered 75 percent casualties. The Twelfth Regiment, involved in the defense of Soissons, was also charged with protecting the retreat of other units. Completing this mission it continued to fight its way through the German lines and arrived at Limoges shortly before the armistice. When it regrouped there, the regiment's battalions each had an average of two hundred men, evidence of the punishment it had taken.[17] Arriving at the front just as the German attack began, the Twenty-first, Twenty-second, and Twenty-third regiments were mauled in combat. The Twenty-first was decimated by Stuka attacks, tactics that the Germans had perfected during the Spanish Civil War. As for the Twenty-second Regiment, the last communication it sent from its position near Villiers-Carbonnes reported that it was being crushed by tanks.[18]

Antonio Soler enlisted in the French army on January 12, 1940. After brief training at Barcarès his unit was sent to Alsace and then to the Somme. He observed that if the Germans had a significant material superiority over the French, they had a devastating advantage over the Spaniards. Their armament dated from the war of 1914–1918, including rifles that were charged by a string. Under such disadvantages, and with German automatic weapons dominating the action, the Spaniards surrendered on June 6, 1940. They destroyed all letters and photographs that could compromise them, but the language barrier remained. They declared themselves as Spaniards to the Germans. Six days later they found themselves in Stalag IB, in East Prussia, and, almost immediately, they were put to work in nearby factories. Soler was liberated by the Russians in January 1945.[19]

For Pedro Alba of the Twenty-second Regiment, a different kind of odyssey began on the Somme, on June 6, 1940. The enemy opened a tremendous artillery barrage, "so intense that at times we doubted whether it was artillery. The atmosphere was so thick that we could not see ourselves more than ten paces away. The noise was deafening, apocalyptic. The howitzers opened up in their turn, sowing death among our comrades. We believed that the end of the world had really come." For the thirty minutes their ammunition lasted, they held off the Germans. They surveyed the situation. Only eleven men of the company remained. A French sergeant, the only commissioned or noncommissioned officer still able to give commands, although one of his arms was nearly severed and he had lost a foot, gave the order to retreat. Then he begged Alba to kill him. The Spaniard refused and fled with the survivors through heavy German fire. Alba and a young Asturian were the only ones to escape. Fleeing always southward, they passed through a countryside almost completely devoid of human beings. Farmhouses had been abandoned, livestock wandered untended. The fugitives slept in farmhouses and scrounged for food. They encountered a young Spaniard who had obviously lost his mind; he scratched at them and howled when they approached. They left some food for him and continued their flight. At last, they met a group of French artillerymen. But the lieutenant accused them of being German parachutists and locked them in a cellar. Shortly afterward, a German unit approached and opened fire. Alba and his companion begged for their arms, which were finally returned, and they joined in a brief skirmish with the Nazis. Judging that the outcome was certain death or capture, the French unit tried to escape, but only the two Spaniards succeeded. Once more they took a southerly direction, but now the roads and fields were alive with Germans. Two days later they ran head-on into an enemy contingent and were made prisoners. Placed in a farmhouse room with a number of French soldiers, they understood that the entire group would very soon be transferred to a prison camp. At dawn of the following day they squeezed through a narrow window, the only one in the room, and escaped.

Now Alba and the Asturian exchanged their uniforms for peasants' garb and found two abandoned bicycles. With these, they moved more freely along the roads, rarely being challenged by the Germans. On one occasion a Nazi sergeant stopped them and commandeered a bicycle. But he only wanted it for a brief pleasure ride and returned it to them. At last they reached the point of furthest German penetration. Lacking safe-conducts or other papers they could not cross the bridge. Moving down the river bank they found a rowboat, piled the bicycles and themselves into it, and crossed into territory still held by the French. Finding a unit that was gathering stray soldiers and forming a new combat group, Alba and his friend were once more clothed in French uniforms and received new equipment. But within two days they were again attacked by the Germans and once more the Spaniards narrowly eluded encirclement and escaped. Later that night they encountered a company of Senegalese troops and joined them, thinking of the exquisite irony involved in the act. Later, Alba was to comment most favorably on his experience with the black troops: "I have an excellent memory of them . . . Many whites would wish to be as decent and comradely as those blacks."

They were now near Paris and the roads were clogged with fleeing soldiers and civilians. When they entered the city they found it in the grip of a growing panic. There was no evidence of an organized defense, people ran about aimlessly in the streets. The Spaniards decided that they would simply cross Paris and continue to the south, joining the motley caravan of vehicles and frightened citizens. But here, tragedy struck. They were detained by two gendarmes. An argument ensued and a policeman shot the young Asturian to death. "Here was the reward France gave us for all the suffering we endured for her," Alba said. He was taken to police headquarters where he was subjected to a brief interrogation and released. He continued his journey, found two Spaniards of the Twenty-third Regiment, and, together, they finally reached Nontron, in Dordogne, on June 24, 1940.[20]

The military disaster that enveloped the French army also caught the workers' companies in its furious denouement. Most of them were stationed on the front between Switzerland and the English Channel, working on military-related projects. The belated effort to construct fortifications from the end of the Maginot Line to the Channel fell heavily on the Spaniards. The concentration of Spanish republicans in that area doomed them to embroilment in the German attack, the retreat to Dunkirk, and subsequent capture by the invaders. Many survivors of the campaign condemned the French officers who led them during that period, although other Spaniards enjoyed comradely relations with their officers. The complaints against French officers were that they were inept in carrying out their responsibilities and tardy with orders to retreat, or that they abandoned their Spanish charges altogether in the face of the German onslaught. "From the first, we could see the disorder of the French army . . . In the war against an enemy like Nazism, one saw more clearly the defects and failings of the French army," Mariano Constante of the Thirty-second Workers' Company observed. His unit labeled its commanding officer *La Foca* ("the seal").[21] Manuel Razola Romo of the Thirty-first Company agreed with Constante that commanders of Workers' Companies, who were drawn largely from the reserves, in many cases retained anti–Spanish-republican attitudes. "Our Captain was a real blabbermouth," he said, "without the least sense of authority."[22] Joan Pagés noted that the commander of the Sixty-third Company failed to order a retreat from a dangerous position because he had not received instructions from a higher headquarters and was afraid to use his own discretion. The Spaniards took the initiative but it was too late; the company was decimated.[23] Juan López López said that when his company, the 118th, came under Nazi pressure, the French officers suddenly became "meek as lambs."

As the German assault developed strength and ferocity, thousands of workers' companies' personnel were forced to take arms and combat the enemy. Approximately 20,000 Spaniards were in the endangered sectors of Belgium and northern France, but only 8,000 or 9,000 succeeded in reaching the Dunkirk redoubt. Of this number, between 1,000 and 2,000 reached England.[24] Others were trapped further east and either escaped or were taken prisoner.

The story of the 117th and 118th workers' companies, which retreated into the Dunkirk pocket, illustrates the experience of other Spanish republicans. Approximately ninety members of the companies succeeded in reaching Dunkirk. Once there, they wandered about, seeking to join one of the lines of men awaiting embarkation. But the British waved them off at gunpoint and the French also refused them. They went then to Bray-les-Dunes, six kilometers north of Dunkirk, but were also unsuccessful. They then split into smaller groups, hoping in that manner to gain places on available ships. José Cercos Redon, who was with a group of sixteen Spaniards, cocked an ear and listened to the gunfire. "We have twenty-four hours or less before the Nazis arrive," He told his companions. Almost that whole day was devoted to shuttling back and forth among the possible embarkation sites, without result. Finally, at Bray, an Italian member of the International Brigades found a vessel so old and decrepit that it had been abandoned.

A Galician sailor among the group thought it could be repaired and they scrounged up and down the entrenched area searching for the necessary materials. The Galician was as good as his word, at least for the present, and the men embarked. They went first to Dunkirk, hoping to secure water and food, but were unable to enter the harbor. Pointing the old ship into the Channel the Spaniards chugged slowly away from the Continent. The boat leaked badly, requiring constant bailing. As night fell they held to a course which they hoped would lead to England, but they had no real notion of where they were going. At 5:00 A.M. they encountered a ship carrying French soldiers, but couldn't keep up with it. Finally, in the early morning light, they were challenged by a British destroyer. To the Spaniards' identification: "We are Spanish republican soldiers with the French army," the British vessel signaled passage and shortly afterward they were in Dover.[25] A ship commandeered by another group sank in midchannel, but the men were rescued by a British craft. The Belgian ship *Leopold Anna,* last to leave Dunkirk, carried twenty-six Spaniards.[26] Those who remained in Dunkirk were taken prisoner and sent to Mauthausen concentration camp.[27]

To the east of Dunkirk the Germans had broken through, encircled, and sent spearheads of troops ranging in all directions. The fragmented French army, including the Spanish workers' companies, was corraled piecemeal, its massive substance melting under the rain of German shells. Five workers' companies were encircled at Bar-sur-Seine, including the Sixty-third, of which Joan Pagés was a member. In his opinion the French military hierarchy, with rare exceptions, was never in control of the situation.[28] Everywhere on the northern and eastern fronts, members of the workers' companies were forced to take up arms again as French resistance disintegrated and almost all official contact was broken. They were, in most cases, left to fend for themselves as the disorderly retreat accelerated. For the Spaniards it was still the same war against the fascist invaders, but this time they were fighting far from home and against odds greater than had ever obtained during the civil war.

The Thirty-second Workers' Company was formed in April-May 1939 at Le Barcarès. It was sent first to the region of Sarralbe-Sarreguemines, near the Maginot Line, then to Longwy, at the juncture of the French, Belgian, and Luxembourgian borders. There, the company constructed antitank traps. Constante related how, at Sarre-Union, the French people hid themselves from the Spaniards. "The Red Legend had followed us even here," he said. Under the impact of the Nazi thrust, the Thirty-second and Thirty-first companies retreated in uneven spurts to the vicinity of Rambervilliers, where, on June 21, 1940, the four hundred Spaniards still in motion were captured. Shipped to Austria, they languished in Stalag XVII A, near Kaisersteimbruck. Finally, on April 7, 1941, they were delivered to the concentration camp at Mauthausen. Placed inside a football stadium at Rambervilliers, Constante noted the demoralized condition of the French prisoners: They walked around like phantoms." As for the Spaniards, they felt themselves to be under a death sentence, but they rallied the next morning. Marcelino, a former political commissar, encouraged them: "Men of our tempering have not the right to whimper. It is certain that the Germans will do everything to liquidate us; but if they do it, let them exterminate men, and not weaklings *[non de mauviettes]*."[29]

In November 1939, the Thirty-third and Thirty-fourth Workers' companies left St. Cyprien to work on additional defenses for the Maginot Line. José Ortuño López, a member of the Thirty-third, related that in April 1940, the two companies were joined by the Twenty-fifth, Twenty-sixth, and Twenty-eighth companies in a move to Clermont-en-Argonne (Meuse), where they cut wood and constructed antitank traps. When the German attack began they were sent to Remiremont (Vosges), where they again built antitank defenses. But the German advance unrolled so swiftly that the cement never had a chance to dry. The Spaniards were captured and directed toward Alsace in a long column of prisoners. A small number of Spaniards, including Ortuño, managed to escape during this march and reached the unoccupied zone. Ortuño learned later that his less fortunate companions had been deported to Mauthausen.[30]

Amadeo Cinca Vendrell joined the 103rd Workers' Company in November 1939 and was sent to the extreme western portion of the Maginot Line. Later, the unit was transferred to a point twenty kilometers south of the Franco-Belgian border, where it constructed fortifications with the 101st and 102nd companies. During the German assault the Spaniards were ordered to retreat in the direction of Amiens, where they were captured. They were trundled to Stalags at Triers, Mobsburg, and Nuremberg. Separated from the French prisoners, they were told that they would be sent to a special work camp, which turned out to be Mauthausen.[31]

Another Spanish experience illustrates the widespread dissemination of the Red Legend, even in Switzerland. Organized at Septfonds in September 1939, the Thirty-first Workers' Company was assigned to the eastern end of the Maginot Line and escaped the early blows of the Germans. However, on June 6 it was ordered to retreat and a decision was made to move toward Switzerland. At the border the

Spaniards were allowed to enter with minimal checks. The following day, however, they were separated from the French troops and told that they would be returned to a safe part of France. They were taken to Basel, and, much to their surprise, placed in a prison. The fifty Spaniards stifled their suspicions and waited. After several days they were transported in closed prison vans to what the Swiss said was French territory. Shortly afterward, Nazi troops arrived and took the Spaniards into custody. It was June 21, 1940. The Spaniards were placed in a prison in Belfort and in January 1941 they were transferred to Stalag XI A in Germany. On April 26, 1941, they were conducted to Mauthausen with three hundred other Spaniards. Of this group, Razola said, only one in ten emerged alive at the end of the war.[32]

Only once during the early days of the war did the Spaniards fight under their own Republican flag. It was near Tourcoing, where Manuel López, a former teacher in Estremadura, was assigned to a workers' company that dug fortifications near a small chateau, under constant German artillery fire. Abandoned by their French officers, one hundred surviving Spaniards entered the chateau and found a French sergeant and several wounded soldiers. A German infantry unit opened fire on the besieged men. The Spaniards seized four machine guns and distributed rifles. With these weapons and a moderate supply of ammunition they offered a stubborn resistance to the Nazis. One of the Spaniards suddenly disrobed and unwrapped a large Spanish republican flag from around his body. The flag was quickly secured to a pole and hung from a balcony. By night fall three of the machine guns had jammed and ammunition was in short supply. A mere thirty men were still able-bodied, the other seventy being either dead or wounded. The young captain who had been elected commander, a former medical student in Madrid, had wounds in an arm and a thigh. Before the Spaniards could hold a council the Germans made a desperate assault and penetrated the chateau. The Spaniards surrendered. The German commander inquired as to the identity of the flag and was incredulous when informed. A short time later the Spaniards were transported to a prisoner-of-war camp near Yser. The following night, five of them, including López, escaped. Perhaps the strangest commentary on this bizarre episode came on May 31, 1940, when the nationalist radio station in Barcelona broadcast a German bulletin. It recounted the day-long resistance of a unit that had held up the advance on Dunkirk, and it identified the fighters as Spanish refugees. The Barcelona newsman added that although the exiles were, of course, Reds, the story was deemed newsworthy because they were, after all, Spaniards who knew how to fight and shed their blood with Spanish honor. "The Spanish

race is the same, no matter where it finds itself," the broadcast concluded.[33]

One who almost got away was Casimiro Climent Sarrió, of the
Thirtieth Workers' Company. This group left Barcarès on November
1, 1939, and was engaged in building fortifications in Lorraine. In June,
the company was ordered to retreat and Sarrió was captured on June
20, 1940. He escaped from a prison at Château-Thierry but fractured
his right hand when he dropped from the wall. Three days later, unable to endure the pain any longer, he approached several peasants in
a barn who secured medical treatment for him. But Climent felt that
his benefactors also denounced him to the Nazis because several hours
later a German motorcycle squad arrived and made him a prisoner
again. He was taken to Stalag XI B where he stayed until November 23,
1940. On that date he was transferred to Mauthausen, with a group of
forty-seven Spaniards.[34]

Many members of workers' companies succeeded in eluding the Nazi
net. Typical of these was José Luís Fernández Albert, of the Tenth
Workers' Company. Created in Argelès at the end of April 1939, the
unit was assigned first to an area east of Grenoble and then to the
Maginot Line. Under the full fury of the German attack, the unit fled
southward but was finally surrounded at Bourguignon-les-Conflens.
The men were transported to a nearby stockade and put to work for
the Germans. The next evening, finding themselves still working outside the barbed wire at nightfall, Fernández's group made a spur-of-the-
moment decision to flee. They made their way to Mâcon where they
learned that the armistice had been signed, whereupon they continued
their movement toward the south and eventually reached Toulouse.[35]

Mauthausen concentration camp, as the foregoing makes clear, was
the destination of most Spanish soldiers and workers who fell into
the hands of the Nazis. The camp sat atop a huge granite quarry near
the tranquil Austrian village of Wienergraben, situated near the confluence of the Enns and Danube Rivers. According to Jacques Vernant,
the Spaniards were separated from their French comrades and directed
to Mauthausen because of pressure from the Spanish Ministry for
Foreign Affairs.[36] It is estimated that more than 200,000 people from
various nations died in Mauthausen during the course of the war.[37]
At least 10,500, or, more probably, 12,000 Spaniards were sent to
Mauthausen.[38] The Amicale Nationale des Deportés et Familles de
Disparus de Mauthausen et ses commandos, an organization of survivors of the concentration camp, has in its possession the actual list
of Spanish republicans who passed from Stalag XI B into Mauthausen.
Kept with Nazi thoroughness, the list contains the name, birthdate,

birthplace, occupation, prisoner's number, and admission date of each victim admitted to the camp. The overwhelming number of names were Spanish; occasionally an entry denotes a citizen of another country, or simply, "Jew." From August 6, 1940 to December 20, 1941, there were 10,350 Spaniards signed into Mauthausen or satellite kommandos. The list inexplicably does not carry entries for the period September 18–November 3, 1941, nor for the period before August 6, 1940, although we know that Spaniards arrived as early as August 1, 1940.[39] Of the Spaniards incarcerated in Mauthausen, 80 percent had died by May 7, 1945, when the Americans and Russians arrived. The prisoners had previously driven out the remaining SS men.[40]

Mauthausen, Dachau, and the other Nazi camps to which Spaniards were sent were immeasurably different from the French concentration camps of 1939. The French camps were hastily thrown-together pens, while the German camps were well-planned extermination centers. Although the French camps were deficient in many respects they were not designed as death factories. The German camps were organized for the purpose of working people to death, or starving them deliberately, or killing them in any of a variety of ways.

A number of workers' companies drew assignments to rear areas and thus escaped the mass death and captivity suffered by their comrades of the front. The great L'Aigle hydroelectric project in the Massif Central was a center for Spanish workers' companies and for individual contract workers. A large number of Confederacion Nacional del Trabajo members found their way into this area, and it was later to become the nucleus of a revised anarchist movement and of resistance to the Germans and the Vichy government.[41] Several units worked in gunpowder and aircraft factories in Toulouse, others were utilized in expansion of submarine facilities at Bordeaux, and a number were sent to work in areas near Italy.[42] In their desire to leave the camps many Spaniards created new skills for themselves. Mariano Puzo was among the latter group. He took an unofficial course of instruction from some of his miner friends and succeeded in passing a mining examination. Thus, he was selected to work in a coal mine without ever having been in one. He worked a nine-hour day, ate inadequate food, and suffered the unrelenting insults hurled at the Spaniards by their French overseers.[43]

At the conclusion of the armistice most of these men and women, together with the survivors of the battles in the north, returned to the same camps from which they had ventured a few months before. Again they languished, uneasily contemplating the new and disastrous turn of events. Presiding over the free, or unoccupied zone was the Vichy government of Marshal Philippe Pétain, which reminded them more and more of the Spanish Nationalist government they had fled. In Paris sat the hated Nazi conqueror, posing an ever-present threat to their security. Eventually, the Nazis were to occupy all of France, and the feared conjunction of oppressive forces was to become a reality. From July 1940 to the liberation, the already battered Spanish republicans continued their antifascist struggle against their two new masters, Nazi Germany and Vichy France.

CHAPTER EIGHT

IN THE SERVICE OF
LE MARÉCHAL

I am advised that the *travailleurs etrangers* . . . continue to be
mobilization centers on behalf of the revolution. The responsible
leaders of these communist activities have been recruiting among
the Spanish Republicans . . . who, during the civil war in their
own country, showed that they were capable of furnishing the
core of an insurrectionary army. They are thus more
dangerous to the public order.

Vichy Ministry of Interior to prefects and police officials,
September 1, 1942

I F THE HUMILIATING DEFEAT of France was a time of un-
mitigated disaster for many, it was for some a back door to power.
Those who had for so many years decried the ineptitude and leveling
tendencies of parliamentarism, or yearned for the reimposition of the
monarchy, or found truth in Adolf Hitler's principles, now became
the rulers of a chastised France that sought the protection of a supreme
leader. Marshal Philippe Pétain, hero of Verdun, embodiment of former
French glory, assumed this mantle, surrounded by a group of men
who were disparate in their philosophies but united in seeking and exercising power under the old warrior.

A new slogan was heard in the land, supplanting the treasured
"Liberté, egalité, fraternité." Under the stern image of Pétain the watch-
words were now to be "Work, Family, Fatherland," and a new melange
of nationalism, authoritarianism, and corporatism was to emerge as
an eclectic philosophy. This reversal of values was stated by Pétain:
"The new regime will be a social hierarchy, will no longer rest on the
false idea of the natural equality of men, but on the necessary ideas of
the equality of 'opportunities' given to all Frenchmen to prove their
aptitude to serve."[1] The Spanish republican exiles knew better than
the French people what lay behind such statements. The words of
General Auguste Noguès came a bit closer to the reality that would
govern the lives of all who were in unoccupied France at that time: "The
moment has come for union, for obedience, and for duty."[2]

What forms these injunctions would take were at first unclear. What

124

mattered to the Spaniards was the recurrence of the spector of forced repatriation to Spain or wholesale delivery to the Germans. These fears were given substance by Pétain's strong friendship with the Spanish Caudillo, his desire to placate the Germans, and his obsessive suspicion that the Spanish republicans were communists or anarchists.[3] Apprehension was heightened when a policy promulgated in August 1940 permitted many foreigners to leave, except those wanted for police interrogation; in practice, nearly all Spaniards were in this category.[4] Later, the government assumed the power to intern all foreign men between the ages of eighteen and forty-five.[5]

There is no doubt about the cordial relations enjoyed by Vichy France and Franco Spain. Pétain and Franco met at Montpellier on February 13, 1941,[6] to review matters outstanding between the two counties, but from the very beginning France had cooperated almost fully with its southern neighbor. A list of eight hundred Spanish republican "delinquents," doubtless a euphemism for political leaders, was prepared by Félix de Lequerica, Spanish ambassador in Paris. The German Gestapo and the Vichy government arrested many of them, who were delivered to the nationalists or tried in French courts. Luís Companys, president of the Catalan republic, was handed over to Franco by Pétain and executed. Other Spanish republican leaders were prohibited from leaving France.[7] However, the mass return of Spanish exiles to Franco's justice was not permitted by Vichy. It is certain that Pétain was more cooperative with the Germans in this respect than with his friend Franco. In fact, the Vichy government delivered thousands of Spanish republicans to Hitlerian concentration camps and forced labor in German factories.[8]

François Pietri, Vichy ambassador to Spain, in a postwar defense of Pétain's policies, declared that the marshal had repeatedly vetoed suggestions that he expel the Spanish masses, even though they were regarded as "Reds."[9] The record would seem to confirm this insofar as there was no large-scale repatriation, but there is no doubt of the truth of Salvador de Madariaga's assertion that Vichy voluntarily handed over to Franco "many of the leading men of the exiled left."[10] A three-cornered cooperation between Germany, France, and Spain was also evident during this period, following a meeting of Franco and Hitler at Hendaye in October 1940. The chief of police of the Pyrénées-Orientales reported to the prefect on December 24, 1941, that a large number of Spanish refugees had passed through Perpignan on German safe-conduct passes. They were on their way to Vigo, Spain, to construct a new submarine base, probably intended for Nazi use. Two of the refugees said that the group had just completed construction of a submarine base at Lorient, involving the labor of fifteen thousand Spaniards. Other groups had constructed a similar base near Bordeaux and an airfield at La Rochelle. These facilities had been completed in the face of frequent bombardments by the British Royal Air Force.[11]

For its own reasons the Vichy government had decided to harness the massive production potential of the Spanish exiles and not to return them to Spanish nationalist control. But its approach was dominated by profound distrust of the political coloration of the refugees. The Spanish republicans were considered to. be of a piece with the French communists and the decadent remnants of the Third Republic. These dangerous elements were therefore hunted, arrested, tried, and sentenced with great vigor. The French police had been given administrative sovereignty in both zones and the price was vigorous action against dissidents. It was a price gladly paid, and Pierre Laval was able to report to the Council of Ministers on October 23, 1942, that recent police actions had netted four hundred leading terrorists, 5,460 communists, and forty tons of illegal arms. Earlier, *L'Oeuvre,* noting the ongoing trial of eleven alleged Spanish communists, reported that forty-two had recently been executed for this crime by the Gestapo and the French police.[12] The obsessive fear of leftists was to become a hallmark of the Vichy regime. Resistance was to be equated with communism. The hysteria escalated as events unfolded. Hitler's invasion of the Soviet Union in June 1941 resulted in a prowar turnabout by the French communists. The Allied assault on North Africa in November 1942, and the subsequent erasure of the unoccupied zone brought the menace even closer. The response to these actions was an enormous intensification of the Vichy police campaign against subversives and the massive involvement of the Gestapo in suppressing resistance.

To the previous list of crimes was now added that of being "anti national." A police circular of September 1, 1942, warned that the Travailleurs Etrangers were serving as mobilization centers for Spanish communist activity designed to build a revolutionary movement. The Spanish workers had proved, during the civil war, that they were capable of forming such an insurrectionary army. Thus, they were more dangerous to the public order than other groups. To counteract this revolutionary force, every department was ordered to compile lists of suspected Spanish communists.[13]

Vichy authorities also worried about the possibility of an uprising that would affect both sides of the Pyrenees. The regional intendant in Montpellier was concerned about a May 1942 report from the commander of the 427th Travaillers Etrangers Group, based at Perpignan, which indicated that Spaniards were making frequent clandestine crossings into Spain. He wanted to find out whether this activity was directed toward stirring up a revolution in both countries or in Spain alone.[14] The resulting investigation indicated that the majority of the department's six Travailleurs Etrangers groups did not appear to be involved in revolutionary activity. However, certain trustworthy persons had reported, without hard proof, that extremist militants were indeed active. The difficulty was that the known communists and anarchists had apparently been replaced by a new group, totally unknown to the informers and the police. They worked underground and used a secret code known only to insiders. Because of the permeability of the frontier, it had not been possible to apprehend any of the conspirators. The police had already prohibited Spaniards from visiting towns within twenty kilometers of the border. Orders would also be issued to prevent them from receiving mail at the homes of friends in Perpignan. As to the major question, it was impossible to determine whether the undoubted revolutionary activity was directed toward simultaneous uprising in France and Spain, or in Spain alone.[15]

On November 13, 1942, probably in reaction to the Allied invasion of North Africa, another and more urgent alarm was sounded. The menace of communist and anarchist propaganda and organization had increased, and there was evidence that the Spanish extremist parties— Communists, CNT-FAI, and the POUM—had made external contact with the Third International and with French anarchist sympathizers. This activity constituted "a source of permanent agitation in the camps and in the Travailleurs Etrangers, and a danger to the security of the state." To repress these movements all intelligence services would be centralized. A special file was to be developed, containing all relevant information on suspects. This was especially important, Circular 1125 noted, because Spaniards frequently disguised their names by substituting the maternal name for the paternal. Photographs of the suspects— full face and profile—were to be affixed to each card. Regular reports were to be prepared identifying those Spaniards arrested, sent to punishment camps, or deported.[16]

Typical of police actions against the menace of subversion was the city-wide raid carried out in Perpignan on December 12, 1942. Two hundred and ninety-eight police officers were mobilized. Sixty-one roadblocks were set up within the city, and 204 men, divided into small patrols, raided all types of public establishments, searched suspected apartments, and detained Spaniards without proper papers or those who did not have legitimate business in the city. The archives do not record the number of arrests and subsequent actions.[17] Although we know from other sources that serious organizing was going on within the Travailleurs Etrangers and in other places where Spaniards worked, police investigations of individuals, as well as reports complying with Circular 1125, reveal that the frantic Vichy police activity failed to destroy it, despite continuing, large-scale arrests. A report from the chief of the 427th Travailleurs Etrangers Group, based in Perpignan, disclosed that fifteen men of the unit had been arrested for communist-anarchist propaganda. Among the charges leveled against them were distribution of communist tracts, attempts to organize political meetings, fomenting danger to public security, efforts to disrupt a working party, and service as liaison agent between the communists of Toulouse and Perpignan.[18] Another report summed up the investigation of an alleged ring of communists in Perpignan. The chief culprit yielded by the inquiry was a young exmedical student. When seized he was found to be carrying a copy of *Reconquista de España,* a communist resistance newspaper. In his apartment police found forty copies of the newspaper as well as other subversive literature. He was sent to the military prison at Montpellier. Twenty additional names were cited in this report, but incriminating evidence was found on only two suspects. One had a copy of *Reconquista* and the other possessed hand-written copies of articles from that newspaper. Both men were to sent to the Montpellier prison. The conclusions of the report were that the international communist apparatus continued to function despite massive arrests, and that efforts to halt the distribution of *Reconquista* had been unsuccessful. Further, although the police had been successful in smashing this particular cell, it was unable to penetrate the headquarters from which communist activity was directed.[19]

The extent of the anti-Allied paranoia that swept the Vichy government in 1942 is suggested by the hysteria that developed around an improbable plot involving the Mexican legation. On April 17, 1942, the Vichy Foreign Affairs Ministry informed the Ministry of Interior that the Soviets were pressing the British for large-scale diversions in France to alleviate the desperate situation on the eastern front. The object of the diversions would be to immobilize a large number of German divisions in France, thus preventing reinforcement of troops in Russia. The vehicle for these disruptions was to be a force of Spanish republican guerrillas who would destroy military stocks, blow up bridges and depots, attack German troops, and generally play havoc with the Nazi forces. The Mexican government was accused of supplying the guerrillas with monthly stipends and supplies. The Mexican government had, indeed, been dispensing Spanish republican funds to needy Spaniards, but denied any complicity in the alleged Russian scheme. Prefects were instructed to conduct inquiries regarding specific

Spaniards. Reports on twelve suspects residing in the Pyrénées-Orientales failed to turn up evidence substantiating the French government's fears.[20]

The conflict with the Mexican legation was an indication of the steadily deteriorating relations between the two countries. In August 1940 Mexico had offered to accept an unlimited number of Spaniards, and Marshal Pétain had expressed appreciation for the gesture.[21] But a mere 5,900 Spaniards actually reached Mexico between 1940 and 1942.[22] Friction arose because of Vichy's feeling that the Mexicans were totally unsympathetic to its policies, and because the Latin Americans insisted on representing the interests of Spanish Republicans and members of the International Brigades. The Vichy attitude toward anything English was even more hostile, and this was extended to American personnel and programs in France. Dr. Henry Harvey, who worked in the Spanish refugee camps with the American Friends Service Committee from September 1941 to June 1942 as a conscientious objector performing alternative service, said that the Vichy authorities made it extremely difficult for his organization to carry on its programs. To be friendly or cooperative with Americans was politically dangerous, he noted. Officials refused to speak English even though they knew the language. Foot-dragging in granting approvals or in processing papers was the rule. The Friends were engaged in four major programs designed to alleviate the living conditions of refugees. Attempts were made to find contract work for men, enabling them to be reunited with their families. Extra milk was provided for children. Heated foyers were established in several camps to enable Spaniards to warm themselves and to engage in social and cultural activities. Two villages were resettled with refugee families who were equipped with machine tools to enable them to earn their own livelihoods. All of these activities, Dr. Harvey declared, were hampered by bureaucratic roadblocks placed in the path of the American organization. In the milk program, for example, the Vichy government insisted that the Friends buy powdered milk in Switzerland, which was then given as an American gift to the government for distribution to French school children. In turn, the government would provide a grant to the Quakers with which to finance their projects with Spanish and German Jewish refugees. The grant was given at the ratio of eighty francs to the dollar, when the official rate was forty-five to the dollar. Thus, the money available to purchase milk for the Spanish children was doubled with respect to the official rate but was about half what could be obtained on the black market. Similarly, in order to set up the cooperatives—one manufactured prosthetic devices for Spanish amputees, and the other designed and produced toys—the Friends were required to set up and maintain another pair of cooperatives for French refugees from the north.[23]

The wisdom of the Vichy decision to retain the Spanish industrial and agricultural workers was evident to *La Dépêche de Toulouse,* which noted, on September 4, 1940, that they had exhibited "qualities of endurance, sobriety, and courage that are characteristic of their race." However, the paper added, the large-scale unemployment then current among demobilized French soldiers and refugees forced the government to place the Spaniards in organizations like the Travailleurs Etrangers or to contract them out to individual farmers.[24]

Pablo Casals called the Travailleurs Etrangers "a modern version of organized slavery," a judgment in which Arthur Koestler concurred. The charge that Europe was sliding back toward the age of slavery had been used so often, he said, that it was considered to be a propagandist overstatement. But his observations of conditions to the TE group at Gurs camp convinced him that it was in every respect the equivalent of a slave gang.[25] Eleuterio Quintanilla, the eminent teacher, author, and anarchist thinker, served in a TE unit at Roanne Loire, until April 1943. In a 1945 letter he confessed that the experience "represented a series of hammer-blows that created physical and moral suffering" that had not diminished at the time of writing. Federica Montseny charged that the Vichy authorities used the TE organization to destroy the spirit of the workers.[26]

Vilanova estimated that at the end of 1940, some 220,000 Spaniards were engaged in labor for French or German enterprises in France. Of this total, 75,000 worked with TE units on fortifications in both zones, 20,000 worked in mining and agriculture in the occupied zone, 25,000 were members of the special Organization Todt, whch built the Atlantic Wall, and 100,000 were engaged in a variety of enterprises in the unoccupied zone.[27] An unknown additional number had already been requisitioned for work in German factories or were in Nazi concentration camps.[28]

In structure, the Travailleurs Etrangers resembled the pre-armistice workers' companies, but there were several important differences. The TE's were much larger, each comprising 2,000 to 5,000 men. Discipline was harsher, many commanders were frankly collaborationist, and the political ambience was based on the authoritarian principles of the Vichy government. German requirements for labor also created a new dimension of instability for the Spaniards. Many TE units were assigned directly to the Nazis for work in the occupied zone. German commissions entered the camps freely to recruit labor. And when recruiting proved unproductive, the Vichy authorities forced Spaniards to go. The prevailing view was that for every Spaniard who went to work in the occupied zone or in Germany, one Frenchman would stay at home.[29] Later, as German demands for men increased enormously, it was impossible to protect French workers and they too were requisitioned in large numbers. The relève program promoted by Pierre Laval also added to the number of French workers in Germany.

To the exhausted, starving survivors of the military debacle of May-June 1940, the important thing was to escape the long reach of the German army. Antonio Arribas Colero was typical of thousands of Spaniards. He arrived in Perpignan on June 25, 1940, nearly dead of fatigue and hunger, wishing only to return to Argelès, where at least there would be a morsel of food. He remarked that all of unoccupied France was covered by hungry bands of people—of many nationalities —all seeking shelter in the south.[30] But after this second ingathering, the Spanish exiles were forced to face the harsh reality that they were virtual hostages to two powers that regarded them as enemies. The Travailleurs Etrangers and the contract system of providing workers for French entrepreneurs were the symbols of their continued bondage to fascism.

In the complex system of work arrangements created by the Vichy regime, the camps retained their importance as refugee centers. In addition to those men and women unable to work, the camps housed Travailleurs Etrangers units, women, and children. Even those workers on detached service or living in the towns looked to the camp headquarters for administration and medical services. A census taken in the town of Rivesaltes (Pyrénées-Orientales) in April 1942 revealed 111 Spanish exiles living there either on contract work or as unemployables. Fifty-five persons (thirty-eight women and seventeen men) were unemployed; twenty-one of this group were either too young or too old to work. There were also forty-three agricultural workers employed on nearby farms, two manual laborers, six teachers, two maids, one coiffeuse, one merchant, and one shepherd. Of the twenty-five members of TE units on detached work service, only four men were twenty-five years old or less. Fourteen were between the ages of thirty and forty, two between forty and fifty, and six were older than fifty.[31]

The major problem within the camps was the health service, which reflected other deficiencies in camp administration, particularly the poor diet afforded the refugees. Although many French doctors were conscientious and worked well with their Spanish counterparts, they were hampered by the negative attitudes of their government and by the lack of supplies. Beginning with a violent, three-day storm and flood in October 1940, which devastated many areas within the Pyrénées-Orientales, the Aude, and the Ariège, particularly the jerry-built barracks and hospitals of the concentration camps, there had been an abnormally high illness rate among the Spaniards. The grinding work routine of the TE groups and inadequate food added to the ever-increasing patient load. The primitive and overcrowded clinic facilities in each camp were completely overwhelmed. Moreover, there were now over five hundred seriously ill exiles in the old St. Louis Hospital in Perpignan, which had been abandoned before the war. However, the departmental médecin-inspecteur refused to sanction their transfer to the old military hospital in Perpignan, which contained seven hundred beds and specialized facilities but then housed only twenty-six patients. An important reason for denying the move was the fact that the cost of treating a Spanish patient at the military hospital was thirty francs per day, whereas in the St. Louis Hospital it was fifteen francs.[32] Another unmet need was for pediatric care. The Spanish children suffered particularly from otolaryngological diseases because of their exposure to the constantly blowing sand and wind. Because Dr. Gérard Lefebvre, the pediatrician and medical chief at Rivesaltes, was unable to treat them, he issued passes to allow mothers to take their children to the St. Louis Hospital. When complaints were made concerning the volume of passes the doctor urged the creation of an otolaryngology clinic at Rivesaltes. The camp commander approved the request.[33]

Apparently Dr. Lefebvre was unusual in his devotion to his patients. An article by a Spanish refugee, in *L'Indépendant* cited the doctor as "un grand ami des enfants" ("a great friend of the children"). But it drew the fire of Gustave Humbert, camp commander of Rivesaltes, who suggested to the prefect that he talk to the editors about the dangers inherent in publishing such material, especially when written by a foreigner.[34] Dr. Lefebvre also seemed willing to risk official displeasure in other ways. In a uniqe series of memoranda written between May 24, 1941, and November 14, 1942, Dr. Lefebvre and several colleagues repeatedly drew attention to the shortcomings of the French medical services, the rapidly growing incidence of debilitating malnutrition, the high death rate, and the inadvisability of keeping children in the Rivesaltes camp. The first memorandum, May 24, 1941, drew attention to the overcrowding of the men's infirmary with patients displaying symptoms of malnutrition. He noted that the cumlative effects of prolonged physical and mental suffering made the Spanish republicans peculiarly susceptible to diseases stemming from nutritional deficiencies. "The caloric intake of the workers is very strongly inferior to that which is required for a normal day's work," he said. He emphasized the importance of correcting the situation before the arrival of the intense summer heat characteristic of the sun-baked Rivesaltes plateau.[35]

Not having received an answer to his report, Dr. Lefebvre again wrote to Humbert on June 29, 1941. He included a report from Dr. Ginies, medical chief of the male service. Dr. Ginies noted the sharp rise in admission of patients whose generally poor physical condition was attributable to inadequate diet. Twenty-one of the forty male patients on his service were in this category. Their extreme debility rendered them incapable of the least effort, and although an infirmary stay alleviated the symptoms they reappeared when the men returned to duty. Lefebvre also pointed out that German requisitions for the Organization Todt had left mainly older and weaker workers in the camp.[36] This letter likewise failed to bring response, and on July 8, 1941, Dr. Lefebvre again wrote to Humbert. He noted that the period of extreme heat had arrived, and he emphasized the urgency of an improved diet for the Spaniards. Dysentery had already made its appearance and the mortality rate was growing: there had been seven deaths in the first week of July. He requested authorization to provide an extra liter of milk daily to his patients.[37]

Dr. Harvey, who visited Rivesaltes in September 1941, was also struck by the harsh physical setting of the camp—a bare, windswept plain—and by the deficiencies of diet. The official guide made much of the fact that the refugees were the guests of France and asserted that they were being fed 1,750 calories per day, the same amount as the French population. It was obvious to the American, however, that this statement was false. The vast majority of camp inhabitants were women, children, and older men. Dr. Harvey visited the nursery and observed approximately thirty children. There were a number of eight- and nine-month old infants but they looked like newborns. Very few of the children were gaining weight normally. The hospital, a converted barracks, could house only a small proportion of the sick. Most of the ill refugees remained in their own barracks.[38]

Finally, on July 10, 1941, Humbert drew the attention of the prefect to Lefebvre's report and noted the gravity of the situation.[39] The prefect then responded by ordering Dr. Dorvault, medical inspector of Pyrénées-Orientales, to investigate the situation. Dr. Dorvault was not overly alarmed by what he found in his investigation. The malaise affected a relatively small number of individuals in the camp population of eight thousand. These patients were unable to defend themselves against infection because of weak or damaged constitutions, or because their bodies were prematurely aged through their experiences in war and emigration. Inevitably, there would be frequent deaths among them. He concluded that the dysentery outbreak was seasonal, not epidemic, and affected only the weaker members of the group. He did note some lack of nourishment and approved the granting of larger rations.[40]

Dr. Lefebvre's sustained attacks on the state of sanitation and health services finally impressed Dr. Augaleu, who eventually replaced Dr. Dorvault as medical inspector, and they also drew the attention of regional authorities at Montpellier. Responding to a June 1942 inquiry from Montpellier, Dr. Lefebvre noted some improvement but added new complaints concerning the lack of firewood in winter and the continued pollution of the water supply. The camp required twenty tons of coal monthly, but had received only ten tons per month during the 1941–42 winter. The water-purification unit promised to the camp had never arrived, but thanks to a donation from Swiss sources this problem was being solved and the danger of typhus and other epidemics was being reduced. The diet had improved after February 1942, lessening the number of malnutrition cases. The mortality per thousand had dropped from February's high of 15 per thousand to 2.75 per thousand in April and 3.6 in May.[41]

The attitudes displayed by Dr. Lefebvre and his colleagues were shared by thousands of individual Frenchmen, especialy those who fought with the Spaniards in the Resistance. However, many French functionaries mirrored the official policy of suspicion of Spaniards, and many French employers abused them. The difference between prewar and wartime France lay in the fact that under the Vichy government hatred of Spanish republicanism was an article of faith. The Spanish exiles who worked in the Travailleurs Etrangers were given ample evidence of this policy.

J. Plazas wrote that in his Travailleurs Etrangers group at Gragnague (Haute-Garonne) and later at Catus (Lot), the men almost starved and were forced to steal out of the camp to find herbs. After the war he saw pictures of German concentration camp survivors; their skeletal appearance reminded him of the way his TE comrades had looked. The French commander at Catus, an overt collaborator, delivered hundreds of Spaniards to forced labor with the Germans. Next, Plazas was assigned to work on a farm at Loupiac (Aveyron) under wretched conditions. On December 13, 1942, Plazas refused to work unless the food ration was increased. When the enraged farmer called him a Spanish *salaud* ("swine"), Plazas kicked him and triggered an onslaught by the man's two sons. Seizing a pitchfork, Plazas chased them into the house, from where they called the police. He was imprisoned and sent to a work-gang. Released after several months, he was assigned to another farmer who treated him humanely. But then he was ordered back to camp headquarters, from where he expected to be deported to Germany. In an ironic dénouement, he was helped to escape by a gendarme who was a secret *resistant*.[42]

Ramón Viscosillos was working in the forests of the Landes when the Germans arrived. The Spaniards were summoned to a formation in the camp and found themselves facing a firing squad of machine guns at twenty-five meters. The order was given to fire, but it was a simulated execution, designed to terrorize the prisoners. Some fell to the ground, believing they were hit, but the majority remained standing. Then the German commander made a speech. The company was now under German jurisdiction. For every Spaniard who escaped, ten would be shot. For every firearm discovered, ten additional Spaniards would be shot. The mock execution scene was repeated each morning for the three months the company remained at that site. Then, inexplicably, the Spaniards were returned to French control and sent to work near Mazères (l'Ariège). Viscosillos became ill, but the authorities refused to transfer him to a hospital. Thereupon, he escaped and made his way to Belleserre, where he found four Spaniards who had also fled from their units. They went into the woods and built a hut, and his companions cut wood and sold it clandestinely while Viscosillos recuperated. Later, they sought to hire themselves out to a farmer, but he became suspicious at their lack of identity cards and called the police. Returned to the camp, Viscosillos was sentenced to three months at hard labor. At the prison camp of Noé (Haute-Garonne) the symptoms of his earlier illness returned; he lost fifteen kilograms of weight in one month and felt that he was doomed to an early death if he remained in his cell, which measured two meters by one and one-half meters and dripped water constantly. Feigning madness, he was released and sent to Septfonds (l'Hérault). Later, in sheer desperation, he volunteered to work for the Germans at St. Malo.[43]

Working at St. Malo meant affiliation with Organization Todt, the special group that was building Germany's Atlantic Wall defenses against Allied invasion. From Bordeaux to the Netherlands thousands of workers were engaged in the construction of artillery emplacements, beach traps, submarine pens, trenches, and casemates. After the Allied invasion of Africa, in November 1942, the concept was extended to the French Mediterranean coast. Fritz Todt, the engineer who had built the Siegfried Line in Germany, directed this vast undertaking, and he had broad powers to recruit the necessary work force for the project. Many of the laborers were foreigners and by the end of 1942 some twenty-five thousand Spaniards were working on the wall itself or other

Todt projects. The Vichy government gave the German recruiting commissions full access to the camps and set up its own manpower requisition organization, the Service Travail Obligatoire.[44] In the occupied zone, moreover, those workers' companies that had been captured during the war were controlled by the Germans and assigned to Todt.

The choice given to the Spanish exiles was narrow: either enlist in Todt or other German work voluntarily or be assigned arbitrarily. The German commissions visited the camps and explained that volunteers would receive far better treatment than those who were forced into service, but even this tactic failed to produce significant numbers of enlistees. From August 17 to 19, 1942, a German commission recruited actively in the main camp and substations of the 427th Travailleurs Etrangers in Pyrénées-Orientales. Of the 1,898 men called before the commission, only 92 volunteered for Todt. Similarly, telegrams alerting the French Ministry of Labor and Todt to the arrival of volunteers spoke in terms of convoys of 100 to 130 men.[45] Francisco Fenestres reported that of the two thousand men in his TE unit only one volunteered to Todt.[46] Avoidance of labor service with the Germans became the prime objective of the Spaniards. A variety of techniques were employed, but desertion and flight to the mountains soon proved to be the most direct and efficient means. *La Defense de France,* a clandestine newspaper, urged workers to refuse to go to Germany and employers to assist them in every way possible. "All should band together to aid the workers to flee, to go to Switzerland or to Spain, to thwart the police."[47] Later, the groups of fugitives—Spanish and French—were to become the nuclei of armed resistance to Vichy and to the Germans. The ambivalence of Frenchmen toward their new regime was shown clearly by the aid many of them extended to Spaniards seeking to escape forced labor. In one TE group the French Captain Nicholas Rougier and his adjutant, Lieutenant Jean Benoit, warned the Spanish republicans two or three days before requisitions for the occupied zone were scheduled. In another, the French officers would pare the number of Spaniards by a number of devices. The first requisition called for 175 workers from that group. By a planned coincidence, the majority of Spanish names submitted by the French officers were those of men who were already working for German war industry in the Vichy zone and who were "indispensable." As a result, only fifteen Spaniards actually went to Todt. The next requisition found ninety Spaniards placed on the sick list, making them temporarily ineligible for shipment. In keeping with the mounting demands for manpower, the third requisition, in mid-1943, called for 475 workers. To circumvent this requisition, several new techniques were developed. In addition to the "indispensables" and those on sick call, the resourceful officials issued death certificates for some, claimed that a certain number had escaped, and that others had declared their intention of returning to Spain.[48]

Those who were caught in the Todt net found themselves living in conditions of virtual slavery and being forced to strengthen the Nazis. In addition, they faced the danger of almost daily bombardments from the British Royal Air Force. At Bordeaux, 3,000 of the 5,000 foreigners who built the German submarine base were Spanish. On arrival at the German camp, they were relieved of all identification, and each was issued a card with his name and photograph. They were lodged in barracks at Fort Niel and St. Medard and lived under strict military discipline. For those on the day shift, the day began at 4:00 A.M. with a roll-call, and the working hours were from 6:00 A.M. to 6:00 P.M. Since construction proceeded around the clock, the workers alternated weekly on a 6:00 P.M. to 6:00 A.M. night shift. They were marched everywhere and frequent roll-calls were conducted, even at night. Heavily guarded by German soldiers at all times, they lacked the most elementary privacy. Nevertheless, acording to Dr. José Pujol, the Spaniards managed to maintain their morale and frequently outwitted the Germans.[49] For even under these conditions the Spanish exiles managed to organize resistance to the occupier, and many even managed to escape to the Maquis. In a special issue, July 19, 1942, marking the sixth anniversary of the start of the civil war in Spain, *Treball* ("Labor"), a Catalan underground newspaper, reported a number of instances of economic actions undertaken by Spanish workers to better their conditions. At Bordeaux, a strike of 1,500 workers protesting brutal treatment at the hands of their German guards and miserable living conditions resulted in ameliorative measures. A similar action was successful in Brittany. In the Loiret region, the workers refused to honor an order extending the work-day by two hours; it was rescinded. At Sarrebourg (Moselle), a German guard who was hated for sadistic behavior was stabbed to death. A strike to force payment of back pay was successful in the Morbihan area.[50]

Resistance was the natural state for the Spanish exiles in France. For them, the French dilemma over loyalty to Pétain was nonexistent. They were in France because they had resisted an authoritarian push against their republic; their struggle against fascism dated from July 17, 1936, not September 2, 1939. A simple Gothic unity pervaded their collective consciousness: the keystone was the ultimate reconquest of their homeland, but in order to uproot Francisco Franco it was first necessary to destroy German and Italian fascism, as well as Pétainism. Therefore, the common enemy was Germany, that same power that had been crucial to the success of nationalist Spain. To resist this enemy, wherever he could be found and by whatever means available, was as necessary as breathing. In fighting for the liberation of France, they were struggling to liberate their own country.[51]

Spanish politics, as complex and divisive as ever, nevertheless bowed to the highest imperative, the struggle against the common foe. Communists and anarchists might organize separately and dispute their respective aims and political purity but they recognized that for the moment the antifascist battle was the overriding priority.

That the tyrants had to be resisted was obvious, but how to resist them was another matter in the period immediately following the French-German armistice. The political groupings that had been established in the camps before the war had been shattered during the German blitz of France. The process of resistance would now begin again, but under the considerable handicap of the Vichy obsession with state security and the vigilance of the Germans. The decision of the French government and of the German authorities to form all-Spanish units of the Travailleurs Etrangers facilitated political organization and the beginnings of organized resistance. Those Spaniards who had fled rather than submit to enemy authority were to form nuclei for those who later sought the same escape. They were to join with the French Maquis in three great zones of resistance: the Alps between the Mediterranean and the Swiss frontier, the rugged heights of the Massif Central, and the area of the Pyrenees. Their introduction into the occupied zone, through the Organization Todt, was to extend their operations throughout France. Their interdependence with the French, which began the moment they crossed the border in February 1939, was now to grow into a close cooperation in resistance and liberation.

In the autumn of 1940, however, the situation was amorphous. "We wanted to make some kind of resistance. We did not know how, but we had to do something," Mariano Puzo said.[52] As time went on, two types of opposition to the Germans and the Vichy government developed. Many Frenchmen joined the embryo Resistance movement. Living mainly in cities and towns, they carried on their daily lives and engaged in small sabotage missions or the distribution of literature. The Maquis were originaly made up of those Frenchmen and Spaniards who were escaping work in Germany or on the Atlantic Wall. As their numbers grew they moved into active resistance. Within the protective umbrella of the Travailleurs Etrangers it was possible for the Spanish

Maquis to plan sabotage in their work areas and to extend their range to targets outside the camps. Puzo reported that much damage was done to the mine in which he worked, but when in June 1941 he was warned that his name was on a requisition list for Germany he sought refuge in the Pyrenees and linked up with a group of Spanish Maquis. His experience highlighted what was at that time one of the major functions of the mountain groups—to welcome fugitives and to build the means for later action.[53]

However, the sharp political and ideological differences within the Spanish refugee community made themselves evident in the organizing activities of the Spanish communists and the anarcho-syndicalists. Through their relations with the French Communist Party, which was also operating clandestinely and included a number of former International Brigaders in its top echelons, the Spanish communists possessed a great advantage, particularly after the Germans brought the Soviet Union into the war. The Spanish communists were zealous in extending their organizing activities throughout the TE network and among the contract workers. By mid-1941 they had established units throughout the middle and south of unoccupied France, and by mid-1942 they could boast of having communist cells in every department in that zone. From this base they launched a movement to embrace all dissident Spaniards in the Unión Nacional Española (UNE) which was organized in Grenoble in November 1942. Ultimately, it claimed to have organized the occupied zone as well.[54] Although the communists asserted that the UNE included representation from all anti-Franco groups, the anarchists never joined the national organization but continued to operate on a separate basis. Nevertheless, the UNE became the major organization in the Spanish Resistance and was so recognized by the French Resistance.[55]

The Grenoble meeting of the UNE, which took place on November 7, 1942, the day of the Allied landings in North Africa, demonstrated the extent to which the struggle was tied to an ultimate return to Spain. It called for the neutrality of Spain in the war, amnesty for the Republicans in Franco's prisons, absolute guarantees of basic freedoms in Spain, and autonomy for the Catalans, Basques, and Galicians.[56] The UNE underground newspaper, *Reconquista de España,* issued a call for action against the Nazi and Vichy enemies: "Produce less and worse, sabotage more and better."[57]

The resurrection of the Spanish anarcho-syndicalist movement began more slowly than the communist organizing effort but ultimately created an effective organization that fought the fascists and served as a haven for all Spaniards needing assistance. Approximately two hundred members of the Confederación Nacional del Trabajo (CNT) were in TE units engaged in building the huge hydroelectric dam at L'Aigle in the Massif Central. They had lost all contact with their National Council and at a meeting in October 1941 they decided to build a new organization. Circular One, November 1941, announced the election of a reorganization commission, which, by January 1942, succeeded in establishing eight new groups with a total of eighty members. Contact was also made with local French Resistance units. Trusted militants were dispatched to other areas to find and organize anarchists. Thus, in September 1942 it was possible to hold the first regional meeting, followed by a national gathering in May 1943. In October 1942 the leader of the new CNT announced, in Circular Four, their decision to attend the Grenoble meeting of the UNE as observers, but the CNT subsequently refused to join the communist-led organization.[58]

Through their own organizations and participation in the work of Mano de Obra Immigrante (MOI), the Spanish resisters and International Brigaders became important elements in the nascent Resistance movement. Colonel Serge Ravanel, chief of the Forces Francaises de l'Interieur for the Toulouse region, where Spanish Resistance units began to operate in 1942, wrote that the French, unprepared for guerrilla combat, welcomed the "invaluable experience" of the Spanish fighters. "During the War of Spain our comrades had acquired the knowledge that we did not possess; they knew how to make bombs, they knew how to set ambushes, they had a profound knowledge of the technique of guerrilla war. I must also say that they conquered us with their valor, their fraternity, their gentleness, their self-denial. They were, for us, 'brothers in combat.' "[59]

During 1941 and 1942 French and Spanish resisters were largely engaged in sporadic attacks upon the enemy. During those years they were also organizing and consolidating their forces. Thus, beginning in 1943, they were able to mount increasingly larger-scale sabotage and ambush efforts and to expand existing escape networks from France. The Spaniards were also involved in guerrilla activity in Spain itself. In absolute terms the damage inflicted by these attacks was relatively small during the period July 1940 to December 1942. But it is important to note that they set the framework for the progressive growth of resistance activity in the crucial years of 1943–1944.[60]

One of the earliest manifestations of resistance was the establishment of networks of escape routes from France. Indeed, the Spanish republicans had from the very first moment of exile carried considerable clandestine traffic across the Pyrenees, passing guerrillas into Spain and removing from that country persons who were in danger. After the armistice thousands of people sought to leave France, including Frenchmen seeking to join de Gaulle, foreign refugees, and downed or escaped Allied airmen and soldiers. Thus began the development of an intricate network of escape routes that extended from Belgium to Morocco or Portugal. Frenchmen and Spaniards worked closely in the operation of a large number of networks. A number of British operatives were involved in the task, at least two of whom had utilized a primitive network in escaping from France after the armistice and who left with a trusted Spaniard two short-wave radios, and a sum of money to finance an escape group. Later, with the establishment of communication links and the beginning of parachute drops of supplies, a number of American officers were involved in the work. It seems entirely likely that some of the Belgium-to-Portugal networks were in operation by the autumn of 1940. Certainly the French authorities were aware of the activity from the beginning and made strenuous efforts to destroy it. On March 20, 1941, the police of Le Perthus, a border town in Pyrénées-Orientales, reported that at Le Boulou the Café des Sports was suspected of being an assembly point for clandestine passage to Spain. Four young Frenchmen, recently selected for work in Germany, were known to have spent the night there and then to have vanished. Similarly, the police at Cerbère were requested to interrogate a certain M. Ducros and his brother-in-law, the Spanish Diego La Porta, who were suspected of harboring similar voyagers.[61]

Although the Spaniards were involved in all phases of the work in both zones, they had the major responsibility for the final phase of the journey: guiding the escapees over the Pyrenees and through Spain to Gibraltar or to Portugal. Since every one of the Spaniards involved was a former republican soldier or supporter, they ran tremendous risks. Many in fact were apprehended and imprisoned or executed in Spain. Mariano Puzo, after his flight from a forced-labor requisition, took the name of Ramón Rius de la Puerta, joined a network and became a *passeur d'hommes* ("ferryman of men").[62] Ferrymen faced multiple dangers—the Vichy police, informers, German police, French and Spanish border guards, Spanish and Portuguese police. But even before this stage of the journey was reached, potential escapees and their escorts ran a gamut of deadly risks in moving from northern France to the south. A string of safe houses needed to be established, ferrymen made availabe for each stage of the journey, false papers provided, intricate travel schedules perfected, emergency routes provided, plans made for the unexpected, civilian clothing obtained for the escapees.

What this meant in practice was revealed by Thérèse Mitrani.[63] A

housewife with one child, she was aware that her husband was involved in some sort of secret work but she was totally immersed in
the difficult task of finding food for her family in Vichy France. She
was not really interested in the course of the war or resistance to the
Germans or Vichy. But on a day in September 1941, her husband appeared with René, pseudonym for an unidentified Englishman who
had escaped from a German prisoner-of-war camp, and Martín, a
Catalan. They had organized *un service d'evasion* and they proposed
now to involve Thérèse. Reluctantly, she became an escort, shepherding
escapees from Toulouse and other cities to Perpignan, where they were
assigned to ferrymen for the crossing of the Pyrenees. Martín was ever-
present during these journeys: he might be sitting some distance away
from the group in a train, or occupying the table next to them in a
restaurant. Thérèse's greatest fear was that someone would attempt
to strike up a conversation with one of her flock. In a railroad train
from Narbonne to Perpignan a German officer approached an English
pilot traveling with Thérèse. She trembled, but the German merely
asked for a match, which was promptly supplied. The two men nodded
at each other courteously and the officer went his way. Her closest
brush with capture came when several Gestapo men burst into the
rented house that doubled as her abode and as a safe house. Her
group had left barely twenty minutes before. After this, she insisted
that she would not expose her child to danger, and a separate place
was acquired as her home.[64]

One of the best-known ferry groups was the Reseau Pat O'Leary,
one of whose leaders was a Spanish anarchist, Francisco Ponzán, known
by the pseudynym of Vidal. He had come to France in February 1939
and had promptly been interned in the punishment camp at Le Vernet.
He was assigned to work for M. Benazet, a farmer who turned out to
be an active resister, and later in 1939 Ponzán organized a network
to facilitate the transfer of Spanish Republicans into and out of Spain.
At the start of World War II he returned to Spain, where he organized
a guerrilla group. Wounded in a skirmish with nationalist police in
July 1940, Ponzán recovered in a cave near Argius and returned to
France, where he continued to operate the escape network. In March
1941 he met with Louis Nouveau, another ferryman, who proposed
that they link up with an English captain, Ian Garrow, a member of
the British Special Operations Executive (SOE), which had a network
of agents in contact with the French Resistance; it also participated in
the rescue of Allied personnel, and later parachuted military supplies
to the resisters. The addition of Garrow enabled Ponzán's group to
move escapees from France to Lisbon or Gibraltar. In June 1941

Garrow was captured in Marseille and his duties were assumed by a Belgian, Dr. Albert Guèrisse, another member of the SOE. Dr. Guèrisse adopted the pseudonym of Pat O'Leary, from whence arose the name of the group. The Reseau Pat O'Leary extended its routes until it was receiving men from Belgium and the north of France for transport to Portugal or Gibraltar. In all, it helped approximately fifteen hundred men to escape. But this was accomplished at great cost. After the Germans occupied the former free zone the searches intensified and many members of the group were caught, making it increasingly difficult for the network to function. Ponzán himself evaded one raid but was arrested in October 1942. He escaped, but was detained again in the spring of 1944 and sentenced to death. On August 17, 1944, the Gestapo executed fifty-four French and Spanish resisters in a forest near Buzet-sur-Tarn, some thirty kilometers from Toulouse, just as the city was being liberated. It is believed that Ponzán was among this group. After the war the British government conferred posthumously on Ponzán the emblem of the Silver Leaf, and the United States awarded him the Freedom Medal.[65]

The silent service of evasion was important but it did not have as great an impact on the French public consciousness as did the more spectacular deeds of assassination and sabotage. The first known assassination of a German—the naval cadet Moser—took place in Paris on August 21, 1941, and served dramatic notice of the presence of an active resistance. The assassin was Pierre Georges (Colonel Fabien), a French veteran of the International Brigades.[66] Although 1941 and 1942 were years of organization, consolidation, and coordination of Resistance forces, there was nevertheless increasing activity against the enemy. But even in the last half of 1942 there were conflicting reports as to the extent of such organized sabotage and small-scale military resistance. An Office of Strategic Services (OSS) report quoted from a source who had been in Vichy France during the months of September and October 1942 and who questioned the prevailing American and British view that ninety percent of Frenchmen opposed the Pétain regime. His own impression was that while nearly all disliked the government, a far smaller proportion—perhaps sixty percent—felt that there was any alternative.[67] However, other reports indicated that resistance in occupied France was quite active. In August 1942, the Military Intelligence Division of the United States War Department received a report from a Spanish republican source who had worked on the construction of a submarine base at Brest. He stated that "sabotage is country-wide" and that Frenchmen and Spaniards were daily involved in a wide range of activities, including dissemination of clandestine newspapers and British radio propaganda, sabotage and work-stoppages in factories, assassinations, and actions against German troops and materiel. To the German announcement that for every Nazi killed ten Frenchmen would be shot, the resisters had scrawled the reverse threat on the building walls in the town. He cited an instance where fifty French chauffeurs and mechanics, thought to have been sabotaging their vehicles, had been replaced by fifty Spaniards. The sabotage increased, although the Spaniards pleaded ignorance of the mechanics of their machines. They too were dismissed.[68]

What type of resistance was possible in the second half of 1940? Certainly, dislike of the occupier was almost universal, and there was a large body of Frenchmen who decried the collaborationist tendency of the old marshal's Vichy government. But the means to demonstrate this hatred, whether through organized groups or meaningful actions, were largely lacking, which indeed made the "genuine resister" a "rare bird." But in thousands of small ways Frenchmen and Spaniards were able to convey their mood and to set a framework for later resistance. For example, in the department of Eure, even before the signing of the armistice, an anticollaborationist tract written by the Vengeurs de la Patrie was distributed. On July 5, 1940, the walls of Gaillon (Eure) were painted with signs that read, "Down with Hitler, Down with Darlan." The distribution of English propaganda continued unabated in the face of the anti-British campaign mounted by the Vichy authorities. Angel estimates that there were a hundred and fifty organized resisters in Normandy in mid-1941, so there must have been considerably fewer at the end of 1940.[69] Spanish workers in the Travailleurs Etrangers, as previously noted, engaged in isolated acts of sabotage and distributed anti-German and anti-Vichy propaganda. One such act was the destruction of a railroad bridge at St. Junien (Haute-Vienne). Others consisted of the sabotage of trucks, ambulances, and artillery.[70]

By 1942, the numbers of organized French and Spanish *resistants* had grown considerably; disciplined units were at work and were in contact with each other. Hostile acts by both Resistance movements, while still not on a massive scale, were directed against larger targets and inflicted heavier damage on the enemy. The assistant chief of staff for intelligence of the de Gaulle forces in England informed the American Military Intelligence Division in London, on July 23, 1942, of a number of Resistance actions that had taken place in the occupied zone in the recent past, including hand grenades launched at parading German soldiers, the dynamiting of a crowded German military canteen in Brest, the disabling of an electrical transformer near Lorient, Morbihan, the destruction of twelve trucks at Armentières, the derailing of a train at Le Havre, the wrecking of thirty railroad cars at Tours, and the audacity of thousands of people in many cities appearing in the streets on Bastille Day wearing tricolor armbands. They circumvented the German ban on large assemblies of people by walking in groups of two or three.[71]

Spanish republicans were also active in Paris in 1942. On March 10, 1942, they burned a German military garage. Two Spaniards of the MOI destroyed a German factory in Issy-les-Moulineaux with an incendiary bomb, killing three Nazis. A German official was shot and killed by two Spaniards as he stood in the doorway of a hospital in Clamart. On May 15, 1942, two Spaniards set fire to a recruitment office for work in Germany. Also in May, a Spaniard who was carrying explosives was stopped by a German officer; he killed the officer and escaped. On the morning of September 30, 1942, three Spaniards tossed a bomb into a formation of police in a headquarters courtyard, killing eight and wounding others.[72]

Similar work was going on in the south. In the department of the Aude, for example, members of the reconstituted Fourteenth Corps of Guerrillas, which had been part of the rear guard on the march out of Spain, blew up a transformer at the mine in Monthoumet on October 26, 1942; destroyed a supply train destined for Germany, November 17, 1942; cut electricity lines near Carcassonne, December 4, 1942; and sabotaged the central electric station at Limoux, December 10, 1942. Also at year's end, a supply train was dynamited in a tunnel at Perles-et-Castilet in l'Ariège, destroying the convoy and interrupting service for several days.[73] A special Spanish sabotage group in the department of Charente managed to perforate tins of meat, fish, and preserves, and sacks of grain and cereals. Another unit sabotaged an airfield at Cognac, and a joint French-Spanish team damaged an arsenal at Angoulème. The Spaniards also proved that it was possible to cooperate with the Germans and still carry out acts of sabotage. At Brest, a Spanish Travailleur Etranger was asked to straighten used nails, in view of the shortage. He was punctilious in his performance of this task, tapping slowly, and inspecting the results frequently. But he was a perfectionist and each nail demanded an hour of his time. Meanwhile, for each nail he straightened he threw a number of new ones into the ocean.[75]

That Resistance attacks against the Germans were of some consequence is proven by a report received by the OSS in September 1942, in which a Vichy French source cited a secret German report for the month of July. The occupied zone, the report noted, had suffered fifty-five sabotage incidents, "all of which were major explosions." The

OSS document added that the British were parachuting increasing quantities of explosives to the Maquis.[76]

The corner that was turned in November 1942 with the Allied invasion of North Africa opened new avenues for those resisting the invader and the collaborationist French government. At the end of 1942 all was still vague, still clouded with the reality of omnipresent oppression, but those in the Resistance were able to afford the luxury of hope for the first time since the debacle of 1940. The buildup of American forces in the British Isles, the reconstitution of a French fighting group, the renaissance of the British army, the stunning reversals of the German advances on Stalingrad and El Alamein, the increasing volume and variety of parachuted supplies, and the continued flight of Frenchmen, Spaniards, and other nationalities to the Maquis, were strengths that would grow until they spilled over into massive intervention from England and an increasing tempo of Resistance attacks. *Treball* predicted that France would again become a theater of war. In fact, the newspaper said, a second front already existed, created by the multiple centers of resistance that dotted the country.[77] The Spanish republicans in France were to play their part in the inexorable process of liberating France and pushing on into the heartland of the invader. In fact, according to J. P. Barthonnat, since the Spanish Republicans had opposed the Germans and Vichy before the Nazi attack on the Soviet Union in June 1941, their resistance had preceded that of the French communists.[78]

CHAPTER NINE

AGAINST TWO MASTERS

SPANISH GUERRILLAS IN THE RESISTANCE AND LIBERATION

For four years we have fought together to liberate France from
the Hitlerian invaders. We have created bonds that not even
death can break.

If I am proud of being a son of Spain, I am not less proud of
having helped, with success, in the liberation of France.

> Cristino García Grandas, a Spanish guerrilla leader who was
> later executed by General Franco in the post-war guerrilla
> campaign in Spain.

Spanish guerrilla: In you I salute your brave compatriots, for
your courage, for the blood that you have shed for liberty and for
France. Because of your sufferings, you are a French and Spanish
hero.

> General Charles de Gaulle, in presenting two medals to García
> Calero at a victory parade in Toulouse, September 17, 1944

GENERAL CHARLES DE GAULLE was fond of asking Maquis
how long they had been in the Resistance. Since the question was
ritual in nature, he wanted and expected a ritual response: "Since June
18, 1940, General," the date of his famous appeal to the French nation
to continue the struggle against Hitler. In Limoges, in September 1944,
the General asked the question of a colonel of the Francs Tireurs et
Partisans (FTP). "With all respect, General," came the reply, "before
you." Seeing de Gaulle's surprised reaction the colonel continued, "Yes,
I fought against the Germans during the war in Spain."[1]

Perhaps the fact that the FTP was the communist arm of the Resistance motivated the Colonel's reply, but the Spanish saw the war
against the fascists as a continuing struggle dating from July 1936.
It was true, as General de Gaulle said on another occasion, that the
participation and sufferings of Spanish refugees in the Resistance had
made them heroes of France and Spain.[2] The sense of solidarity felt by

Spaniards with Frenchmen in the common combat was expressed by Cristino García Grandas, an outstanding Spanish guerrilla, when he noted that men and women of both nations had fought together for four years. "If I am proud of being a son of Spain I am not less proud of having helped . . . in the liberation of France." Cristino García's own career gave powerful affirmation to the basic Spanish idea that the war against fascism would not end until the victorious Allies helped the Spanish Republicans oust Francisco Franco. After the defeat of Germany, Cristino García returned to Spain to organize a guerrilla campaign to achieve this end. He was captured and executed by the nationalist government.[3]

To understand the Resistance movement from 1943 until the liberation in 1944, one must first of all recognize the close collaboration between the French and Spanish fighters. Although the Spaniards were organized in their own formations, they were part and parcel of the French Resistance movement during that time. Where such organization was not possible, Spaniards fought in the ranks of the French Maquis. The extent of Resistance operations can be better appreciated when one realizes that no Allied troops appeared south of a line drawn from Nantes to Orléans to Dijon, and west of a line from Dijon to Avignon. Yet many of the territories within these limits were liberated before Paris and almost entirely by Resistance forces. Although they were particularly active in the Massif Central, the Alps, and the south and southeast, Spanish forces fought in forty-one departments in almost every region of France. The liberation of forty-nine cities in France was accomplished totally or in part by Spanish Maquis. In some instances, they were instrumental in liberating entire departments. The order of battle of Spanish guerrilla units in August 1944 demonstrates the extent of their infusion into the battle for France. They were behind the barricades in Paris, blew up bridges and railroads, and attacked retreating German forces and inflicted thousands of casualties upon them. Spanish guerrillas were present in the sacrificial battles of the Plateau of Glières, Vercors, and Mont-Mouchet. They also distinguished themselves in the ill-fated breakout attempt from the prison of Eysses. Incorporated into the regular French forces at the end of 1944, many Spaniards also took a large part in the only mass battle fought by men of the Resistance, the reduction of the last German Atlantic strongholds of Lorient, Royan (Charente-Maritime), Le Verdon (Gironde), and Pointe de Grave (Gironde). Thousands of Spaniards also fought in the regular forces of the new French army, notably in the First and Second Armored Divisions and in the Foreign Legion. Spanish tank crews of General Leclerc's Second French Armored Divi-

8 *Domingo Baños, member of the crew of the Guadalajara, a tank of the Ninth Company, all Spanish republican, of the Regiment of Chad, is greeted by liberated Parisians outside the Hotel de ville, August 24-25, 1944.*

9 *Spanish Maquis marching behind the republican flag at the liberation day parade in Toulouse, August 1944.*

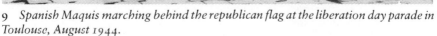

10   *General Leclerc, commander of the Second French Armored Division, talking with some Spanish troops of the Regiment of Chad, near Epinal, France.*

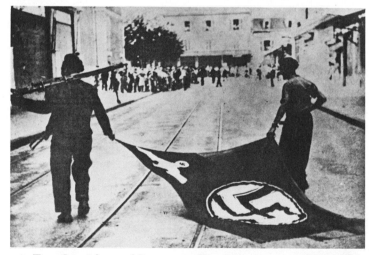

11   *Two Spanish republican guerrillas drag a captured Nazi flag through a street in Annecy, France, after the liberation of the town.*

12　Captain Raymond Dronne, Ninth Company, Regiment of Chad, plans an attack on the central telephone building, Paris, with two Spanish republican officers.

13　Spanish republicans man a barricade in the Paris street fighting, August 25-26, 1944.

14   *The half-track Teruel, with Spanish republican crew, enters Paris, August 24,*
1944.

sion were the first to penetrate Paris and reach the Hôtel de Ville.[4] In addition, the escape networks continued to rescue Allied soldiers and civilians. General de Gaulle noted that twelve thousand Frenchmen escaped the country through the French and Spanish networks.[5]

Spanish exploits were recognized by General de Gaulle and other high-ranking officers of the French liberation movement in the awarding of hundreds of citations to Spanish guerrillas. The Legion of Honor was conferred upon numerous Spaniards, including forty-two for their roles in the liberation of Toulouse and other southern cities, and six for being the first to penetrate the center of Lyon. Six Spanish guerrilla officers also won the War Cross for their actions in the liberation of Toulouse. Enrique Marco Nadal, ex-captain of the Spanish republican army, who, ironically enough, had escaped from a French concentration camp in 1939 and later joined the French army, was decorated on two occasions by General de Gaulle. In 1949, the General interceded with Spanish nationalist authorities to secure a commutation of the death sentence passed upon Nadal, who had returned to Spain to continue the battle and was captured.[6] The presence of the Spanish Maquis in the ranks of the French resistance "constituted an important contribution to the cause of the Allies," according to Colonel Serge Ravanel, chief of the Forces Françaises de l'Interieur for the Toulouse Region. "Valorous among the most valorous resistants, they sacrificed themselves with heroism and courage," he said.[7] Watching more than three thousand Spanish guerrillas pass in review before General de Gaulle in the victory parade at Toulouse, on September 17, 1944, Ravanel asked himself: "When will they be able to enter their own country? When will they be able to celebrate the liberty for which they fought so much at our side? What will the French nation do to help them, responding to the so-generous aid they gave us?" Twenty-four years later, when Ravanel wrote a preface for a book on the Spanish Maquis, the questions were still unanswered, he noted.[8]

At the beginning of 1943, however, victory parades in Paris or Toulouse—not to mention Madrid and Barcelona—were still far from realization. Throughout that year the influx of fugitives from forced labor in Germany presented the Maquis with growing challenges of supply and organization. By February 1944, the consolidation of Resistance forces was partly realized by the Comité National de la Résistance (CNR), which created the Forces Françaises de l'Interieur (FFI) as an umbrella over the numerous resistance groups that had evolved. The component elements of the FFI were the Armée Secrète (AS), which regrouped various Maquis elements in the southern zone under the title of Mouvements Unis de Résistance (MUR); the Francs Tireurs et Partisans Français (FTPF), and the Front National (FN), both dominated by the communists; the Organization de Résistance de l'Armée (ORA), composed of officers and men from the demobilized armistice army; and the Main d'Ouevre Immigrants (MOI), composed of foreigners fighting in France. Each department had a military leader, usually selected from the AS or FTP, and a chief of staff, generally assigned from the ranks of the ORA. The entire apparatus was linked to the CNR through the Commission d'Action Militaire (COMAC). Parallel to this organization was an administrative hierarchy, imposed by the Gaullist headquarters in London, to guard against the possibility of Communist hegemony and to coordinate the parachuting of supplies to the Resistance forces. The instrumentalities for this control were the Délégués Militaires National (DMN), Délégués Militaires Zonal (DMZ), and the Délégués Militaires Régional (DMR).[9]

Spanish units that had been working with the FFI as the Organización Militar Española of the Unión Nacional Española (UNE), the communist-led coalition, changed their designation in May 1944, becoming the Agrupación Guerrillera Española. In July 1943, command was decentralized into divisions and brigades based on regions and departments. Miguel Angel was appointed to represent the Spanish guerrillas at FFI headquarters, and Albert Luís Fernández was made joint commander with Ljubomir Ilitch of the MOI. It was understood by all concerned that the Spaniards would continue to operate in their own formations and under their own officers, although generally under the orders of the FTP and the FFI.[10] The UNE built a broad coalition grouped around the Spanish Communist Party. It included such disparate elements as monarchists, Navarrese traditionalists, and Gil Robles' Confederación Española de Derechas Autónomas (CEDA), a federation of small, independent rightist parties.

Successfully resisting the efforts of the UNE to bring them within its political and military orbit, the Spanish anarchists remained an independent fighting force within the French Resistance. Indeed, they organized their own coalition, the Alianza Democrática Española. Besides the Confederación Nacional del Trabajo (the labor federation of the Anarchists), the Alliance consisted of the Partido Socialista Obrero Español (Socialist Workers Party of Spain); the Unión General de Trabajadores (the trade union federation of the Socialist Party), Izquierda Republicana (the Left Republicans, a fusion of republican parties led by Manuel Azaña), the Independent Republicans of Felipe Sánchez Roman, the Federación Anarquista Ibérica (FAI), the Partido Nacionalista Vasco (Nationalist Basque Party), and Esquerra Catalan (the Catalan Left, which had been led by Luís Companys).[11]

The anarchists developed a separate understanding with the French Comité National de la Résistance and cooperated with the FFI and the confédération Générale du Travail, the French labor federation. Although committed to a strategy of sabotage rather than massive confrontation, they pledged to engage in the latter when an Allied landing occurred and the French people rose in national insurrection. Anarchist participants in the campaign would fight in their own units, commanded by their own leaders. They also reserved the right to regain their liberty of action when the war had been won, so that they could turn their full attention to liberating the Spanish homeland. In establishing official connection with the French, the anarchists felt that they had broken the communist "encirclement" of their movement and had preserved the separate identity and integrity of their organization. They had secured the cooperation of the FFI and gained the means to provide haven and support to those comrades who daily fled the threat of forced labor in Germany and wished to fight under their own banner.[12] Only in the regular French army and in predominantly French Resistance units would the anarchists submit to authority other than their own.

It has already been noted that requisition of French and Spanish labor for work in the Todt Organization or in German factories was perhaps the single greatest recruitment device for the burgeoning Resistance movement. In 1943 and the first half of 1944 the occupier's demands increased greatly, and the predictable result was that a great number of fugitives found their way into the Resistance. The labor requisitions had the effect of embittering the French population and turning it increasingly against Marshal Pétain's government. A secret report from the Direction de la Securité Militaire in Algiers, May 26, 1943, declared that "un vent de pillage souffle sur la France" ("a pillaging wind is blowing over France"). The country was being looted of its goods, its food, and, increasingly, of its men. There was a growing hostility to the labor requisitions—especially of the military classes of 1940, 1941, and 1942—and overt demonstrations against the departure of transports. In a single week in April, the document declared, only 6 out of 239 Mâcon men called for transportation had reported, 17 out of 120 men at Toulon (Var), and none of the 15 called at Lons-le-Saunier (Jura). That antideportation agitation had an effect on the growth of the number of fugitives was acknowledged by the Office of Renseignements Généraux of Lot. From March 12 to June 12, 1943, 168 members of the class of 1942 in Lot had been called for labor in Germany, and 148 had answered the requisition. But the following week, of 494 called, 139 failed to report. By August 25, only four out of eighty-five summoned at Cahors (Lot) responded, and on September 3, only two out of forty-six.[13] Another Algiers report in August 1943 said that there were strong indications that the gendarmerie did not appear anxious to escalate its struggle against *refractaires.* There were numerous instances where French gendarmes informed the Maquis of impending arrests or of requisitions for labor in Germany, thus permitting the intended victims to escape. "The intelligence service of the French Maquis functioned so well," Berruezo said, "that orders of detention emanating from Vichy were known to the Spaniards before they were received by the subprefecture." *La Defense de la France,* an underground newspaper, listed large-scale refusals to report for deportation in June 1943. In the department of l'Herault, 30 percent had failed to report, in Savoie 38 percent, in the Drôme 50 percent, in the Rhone 90 percent, in Isère 34 percent, in Haute-Savoie 42 percent, in the Haute-Garonne 63 percent, and in Corrèze 90 percent. These figures, the newspaper said, constituted a definitive answer to those who argued against resistance on the grounds that it was useless and impossible. A report issued by the American Office of Strategic Services in July 1943 noted that resistance to deportation had been vigorous from the very beginning. "Numerous strikes broke out, in spite of extremely severe punishment," the OSS observed, "In many cases, angry crowds freed the arrested workers." It asserted that the French peasantry, which had been told by Pierre Laval that the deportation of the workers would result in the return of their sons from German prisoner-of-war camps, was actively feeding and sheltering dissidents who fled to the countryside.[14] French officials in communes near the Spanish border were also perturbed by the discovery of large-scale distributions of *Combat,* a Resistance newspaper. The paper called for refusal to go to Germany, the formation of Resistance units, and death to Pétain and Laval, the subprefect of Prades suggested that the gendarmerie be instructed to inspect all mail boxes before dawn and remove copies of *Combat.* "In this fashion," he observed, the population will not be touched by such propaganda."[15]

The Travailleurs Etrangers were particularly vulnerable to requisitions for the Organization Todt and they responded with mass desertions. Reports in 1943 and 1944 from subprefects are replete with complaints from TE commanders and from private entrepreneurs who employed Spanish workers on a contract basis. Increasingly, such reports ended with the comment, "Je suppose que ces étrangers ont gagné le maquis" ("I suppose these foreigners have joined the Maquis").[18] The chief of the 427th Group of Travailleurs Etrangers, based at Perpignan, pointed out that of the 1,600 workers in his unit, 300 were on detached service for work in the forests and another 100 were employed in mines. He stated that he did not have enough police at his disposal to control these men. An idea of the profound resistance encountered in effectuating requisitions from the Travailleurs Etrangers may be gleaned from a report by Commandant Perramond of the 427th TE Group. A convoy of 165 TE's was slated to depart on December 30, 1943, for work in the northern ports of Calais, Lorient, Cherbourg, and Brest. Only sixteen were actually entrained. The rest avoided the requisition in a variety of ways. A total of eighty-six were exempted: twelve by the Prefecture, thirty-six by the German Placement Office, fifteen for "diverse reasons," and twenty-three because of illness. Sixty-three were listed as *refractaires*. The document provided a personnel report of the 427th Group for the last trimester of 1943. It listed the incorporation of sixty-four new members and the dispatch of forty-four workers to the Organization Todt. But it also noted 189 desertions, leaving the mean enrollment at 1,645.[17]

The predictable response to increased Maquis activity and to mass avoidance of labor service with the Germans was progressively more severe repression. With the elimination of the unoccupied zone in December 1942, the Vichy armistice army was dissolved and the German Gestapo and police extended their activities into the south. The Vichy government cooperated fully with the occupier. Moreover, having from the very beginning equated Resistance with communism and antinational sentiment, it entered into full collaboration with the Germans in attempts to suppress the Maquis. This effort was directed by Joseph Darnand, who became secretary-general for the maintenance of order in December 1943. Darnand, a declared fascist, waged an aggressive campaign against the Resistance, utilizing the Milice, a 45,000 man national police force. The Milice had been organized in January 1943 from the paramilitary arm of the Veterans' Legion, the Service d'Ordre Légionnaire. Under his leadership it engaged in virtual civil war against all who represented a threat to German victory, and it succeeded in decimating many Maquis organizations. It took part in the German reduction of a large Maquis force on the Plateau of Glières (Haute-Savoie). Miguel Angel related that a special force of Spanish Maquis in l'Ariège was betrayed to the Milice and thirty-four were captured in a surprise attack near Foix on April 22, 1944.[18]

But the Milice and other Vichy police forces also suffered heavy casualties, becoming the symbols of a constantly growing anti-Vichy feeling. An OSS report of March 15, 1944, received from a source in Switzerland, said that the vehemence of the Maquis attacks against the Milice was causing that body to lose some of its original enthusiasm, "because they are suffering heavily, and every member . . . knows that he is likely to have a bullet in his back at any moment." The report added that Vichy repressive efforts, which always began with great violence and then petered out, were destined for defeat by the very magnitude of the task. The informant noted that the French police and the gardes mobiles réserves were being used with less frequency because they were "either half-hearted or even in sympathy with the Resistance, and their action was generally quite ineffective."[19]

Controlling the activities of the Travailleurs Etrangers and the Maquis in the south proved particularly difficult because of the dispersed nature of their work, the inacessability of their strongholds in the Pyrenees, and the support of the local population. The prefect of Pyrénées-Orientales exhorted his commissaire central to greater efforts: "In this period it is more important than ever to impose a rigorous control and a particularly vigilant surveillance." In another letter to the regional prefect at Montpellier he urged a series of searches of private homes and sweeps throughout the region.[20] But despite these efforts and the increasing number of arrests, the authorities felt inadequate to the task and complained about the lack of sufficient police.[21] There was general agreement that in a situation of outright insurrection the vast majority of Spanish workers would constitute a dangerous force at the disposal of the Resistance. At least one official urged that they be evacuated from the Pyrenees border area. But this solution ran counter to the economic needs of the employers of the region, who found the Spaniards to be excellent workers: "They form an important part of the agricultural work force . . . If they were to depart in large numbers there would be quite a dislocation of the local economy."[22] As an alternative it was suggested that known or suspected resisters be imprisoned. A list of fifty-four such suspects, six of them women, furnishes an idea of what activities were considered dangerous by the Vichy authorities: the most common descriptions were "communist" (or variants) and "anarchist." But it was enough to be "considered as communist" or "engaged in procommunist activity." Other labels applied to suspects were "concubine of S——," "former member of International Brigade," "political commissar in Spain," "communist sympathizer," "exrevolutionary," "suspect from the national point of view," "noted as anarchist," "dangerous," "aided by Mexico," "accused by neighbors," and "listens to Gaullist radio."[23] In a report at the beginning of 1944 the commissaire principal of the Pyrénées-Orientales commented on thirteen Spaniards who were either arrested or interned. In addition to those labeled communist or anarchist, others had been detained for clandestine border passage, carrying a firearm, or voicing antinational sentiments.[24] Another letter noted the internment of twenty-five Spaniards in Le Vernet, and the arrest of fifty-four suspects.[25]

Despite the heavy damage inflected upon its groups in all parts of the country, the Resistance absorbed growing numbers of recruits, increased the pace and scope of its attacks upon the enemy, consolidated its organization, and played a considerable part in the liberation of France. Robert Aron said that the official number of maquisards armed by the Allies was 140,000, but he added that an unknown number of resisters acquired arms elsewhere. The official total of those killed in battle was 24,000, although Cookridge gives a figure of 30,000, and, in addition, lists 24,000 Resistance fighters executed by the Nazis and 115,000 deported to German concentration camps.[26] How many Spaniards fought in the Maquis, the French Foreign Legion, and the army is unknown. Anthony Eden declared that three out of five maquisards were Spanish republicans, but this proportion appears too high. Pierre Bertaux's estimate of 60,000 Spanish guerrillas is probably the closest approximation.[27] About 25,000 Spaniards died in the struggle, including those in concentration camps and regular army service as well as in the Maquis.[28]

The heaviest concentration of Spanish Maquis was in the southwest and the Pyrenees, but there were strong formations of them in many other areas. In the Alps, Spaniards fought in the departments of Haute-Savoie, Savoie, Isère, Ain, Jura, and Drôme. They participated in three of the largest Resistance engagements of the war—the Plateau of Glières, the Vercors (Isère and Drôme), and Mont-Mouchet (Auvergne) —as well as in hundreds of other actions.

Manuel Gutiérrez Vicente fought in the Spanish Civil War and was captured near its end. Escaping from a Franco prison he went to France and was interned in Argelès and Bram. Taken to Brest by the Organization Todt, he escaped and made his way to Dole (Jura), where he joined an FTP Maquis group commanded by the Frenchman Maurice Pagnon. One of the four companies in this group, "Pasteur," was manned entirely by Spaniards, and they were represented in each of the other companies. Always acompanied by Spaniards in his night forays, Pagnon began sabotage operations in October 1943. The Pasteur company was responsible for thirty-seven assassinations in the Dole area during this period. A railroad bombing engineered by the Spaniards resulted in eighty German troop deaths at Besançon. On February 24, 1944, Pagnon was wounded and captured, dying on March 10, 1944, at Dijon. Henri Guignard suceeded to the command and Gutiérrez became leader of the Pasteur Company, taking at this time the alias of

Pierre de Castro. His first action in this capacity was the destruction of gasoline supplies at a German airfield, an operation carried out by himself and one other man. On May 24, 1944, Gutiérrez was appointed to lead two new groups, with five hundred men, which eventually became the Batallon Maurice Pagnon. From this date to August 29, 1944, when Gutiérrez was caught by the Germans, the group engineered no less than one hundred and forty operations. These included cutting telephone lines, damaging railway roadbeds, punishing collaborators and spies, attacking German patrols and military convoys, and stealing ration tickets, tobacco, food, and money. Perhaps the most spectacular exploits of Gutiérrez' group were the destruction of the electrical generating station at Chambèry and of twenty thousand tons of aviation bombs and artillery shells in the munitions magazine at Crissey (Saone-et-Loire); Gutiérrez was apprehended by a German patrol on August 29, 1944, tortured, sent to Mauthausen, from which he was liberated in May 1945.[29]

The success of men like Gutiérrez demonstrated the effectiveness of the classic guerrilla pattern, wherein small, highly mobile groups attacked the enemy on their own terms, usually in surprise maneuvers. The negative dictum, that of avoiding at all costs the amalgamation of large groups of men in static positions and engaging the enemy in frontal combat, was to be disregarded by the Resistance in two instances—once in the Alps and once in the Massif Central—with catastrophic results.

The rapid growth of the Maquis, their contacts with London and Algiers, the parachuting of arms and materiel, the provision of funds that allowed units to pay their men ten francs per day and purchase their food and clothes, and the establishment of six training schools— all these may have contributed to a sense of aggrandizement and a tendency to minimize small group actions in favor of large-scale confrontations with the enemy. Misunderstanding of the strategic planning of the French headquarters in London and Algiers also contributed to the disasters. In Maquis circles it was believed that the Free French forces based in England and Africa had been divided into three groups: Force A would participate in the cross-Channel invasion, Force B was to be assigned to General Jean de Lattre de Tassigny for a landing on the southern coast, and Force C would be used for a parachute descent somewhere in the interior of occupied France. The latter force, once it had liberated and fortified a sizable zone, would establish Free French government and authority in the country even before it had been completely emptied of Germans. The general plan had originated in the Resistance and had been reviewed in London, which had refused to put it into operation. The maquisards, however, were never apprised of this decision and based their plans upon its activation.[30]

In January 1944 the Maquis, against the advice of the Spaniards and some French leaders, began to concentrate large numbers of men on the Plateau of Glières. Situated twenty kilometers from Annecy in Haute Savoie, the plateau, a rugged outcropping rising eighteen hundred feet above sea level, offered a strong defensive position and, in the eyes of De Gaulle's headquarters, could be converted into an offensive springboard at the proper moment, perhaps in support of an Allied Mediterranean landing later in the year. Under the command of a twenty-five old FTP captain, Théodore Morel, between 156 and 650 FTP and Armée Secrète men gathered on the plateau and built a fortified camp. Of this number, between fifty-six and eighty were Spaniards, organized as the Ebro Section.[31] In mid-February the Vichy government became aware of this unusual concentration of resisters, and Joseph Darnand sent 800 Milice and gardes mobiles to destroy them. In two battles the Vichy men were defeated, but Morel was killed and replaced by Captain Anjot. The failure of the Vichyites to control the situation led the Germans to send 8,000 men of an Alpine division to Glières. The reinforcement of the Milice and gardes mobiles to a strength of 1,500 men gave the enemy an overwhelming superiority, and on March 23, 1944, they launched an all-out attack. German planes saturated the plateau with bombs and machine-gun fire, and the infantry moved in behind the bombardment. The Maquis fought stubbornly until the evening of March 26, when the order to retreat was given. Reverting to guerrilla tactics, the survivors filtered down from the plateau in small groups. Casualties were extremely heavy, with 155 dead, including five Spaniards. One hundred and seventy-five maquisards were taken prisoner. The number of wounded is unknown. Of the six Spaniards among the prisoners, only one survived the torture, execution, and deportation that followed their capture. Shattered for the moment, the Resistance movement later revived and was instrumental in the liberation of Annecy and other towns in the area.[32]

Larger in scope than Glières, the Battle of Vercors involved 3,000 to 3,500 maquisards against a force of 15,000 to 20,000 Germans. Once again it underscored the controversy between those who saw the Maquis as a potential mass army and those who believed it should operate only in small, offensive, continuously mobile groups. Vercors is a thousand-meter high mountain, interlaced with almost inaccessable crags, ravines, cliffs, and grottos. Situated between Valence and Grenoble, it is sixty kilometers long by twenty kilometers wide and is dotted with a number of farming villages. Lying athwart the potential Allied invasion route to the German frontier, it proved an irresistible magnet to French Maquis, who envisioned planting a powerful force on its heights which, augmented by Allied paratroopers, could serve as a platform to pinion the enemy between Vercors and an Allied army advancing from the south. The plan was approved by Jean Moulin ("Max"), chief of the National Council of the Resistance, and General Delestraint ("Vidal"), chief of the Secret Army. It was forwarded to London for approval, but there is some confusion as to whether it was ever approved there and in Algiers. At least one important French Maquis leader decried the plan: Albert Chambonnier, regional chief of the MUR and the FFI opposed it on several grounds. The Maquis in the Vercors region, he said, were much too important to be used in a manner that did not correspond to the capabilities of the Resistance. It was dangerous to concentrate so many men on the plateau and to lock them into a defensive posture. He disputed the notion that Vercors was indestructible: "an impregnable fortress does not exist."[33]

However, the enthusiasts went ahead, believing that London had approved the plan and would furnish additional men and materiel at the proper time. Two guerrilla groups, comprising four hundred Maquis, fifty of whom were Spaniards, were already based on the mountain.[34]

Between early March and June 6, 1944, the guerrilla population increased steadily. On the latter day, when word came of the invasion of Normandy, it brought with it a widespread belief that a simultaneous landing would occur in the Marseille area. A call went out for all maquisards to concentrate on Vercors. General Pierre Joseph Koenig, supreme chief of the FFI, radioed from London on June 10 to apply the brake to this movement. He ordered the Maquis to break contact with the enemy, to avoid concentration of a large force, and to reorganize into small groups. It was impossible to provide sufficient arms and supplies for the Maquis, he said. But his message arrived too late. The mobilization was in full swing and 3,000 to 3,500 men were swarming over the mountain. Another 1,500 men, unarmed, also stood by, waiting for a parachute drop of supplies.[35]

The first German attack, on June 13, was repelled. Another Nazi assault on June 18 produced twenty-four Maquis deaths and a retreat from exposed positions in the lower reaches of the mountain. Arms and supplies were dropped to the Maquis on June 23, but they did not include artillery or the all-important mortar. At the beginning of July a small group of Allied officers and an American paratroop detachment parachuted into the area. Now the defenders of Vercors received reports of an ominous buildup of German bomber and fighter aircraft at a nearby airfield, but their plea for an immediate air strike was denied. Another large parachute drop of supplies was only partially recovered because of intense German bombardment of the area, and on July 20 the Maquis made a final plea for artillery. The next day the Germans launched simultaneous air and ground attacks, with a sizable force of glider troops establishing a position near the top of the mountain. For two days the area was bombarded almost ceaselessly while ground combat continued. By the evening of the twenty-third, Vercors was completely surrounded. As evening fell on July 24, the order to evacuate was given and the surviving maquis made their way to safety as best they could. The Germans were harsh in their treatment of maquisards and civilians. Five towns were burned and 250 civilians were executed. A number of wounded maquisards, a priest, four German wounded, and an American lieutenant recovering from an operation were discovered where they had been hidden in the grotto of Liure: the American lieutenant was treated as a prisoner of war, but the twenty-four maquis, the priest, and two doctors were shot. Seven nurses were arrested and deported to Ravensbruck. In all, the Maquis suffered 750 deaths, including those of 62 Spaniards.[36]

In light of Maquis expectations of major assistance, Glières and Vercors, as well as the Auvergne battle of Mont-Mouchet, may have been thought to represent the beginning of the national insurrection. Mont-Mouchet, pitting 10,000 maquis, of whom only 2,700 to 3,000 were armed, against 20,000 heavily armed Germans, was the third instance in 1944 where classic guerrilla warfare was abandoned for the tactic of mass combat.[37] Mont-Mouchet is situated at the juncture of the departments of the Haute-Loire, Cantal, and Lozère, and the Maquis felt that this rugged portion of the Massif Central could support three powerful redoubts. The *levée-en-masse* was ordered on May 20, 1944, and the Germans launched their first attack on June 2 with 800 men. It was repelled by a force of 3,000, including several hundred Spaniards. On June 10, eleven thousand Germans, supported by armored cars and a GMR unit, attacked again. Although the enemy was driven off it was clear that retreat was necessary, and on the next day the Maquis moved to a new position in the Truyère massif. The engagement had cost the Germans 1,400 dead and 1,700 wounded. At Truyère, there were 6,000 new maquis, but arms for only 800 of them. A parachute delivery made it possible to equip a total of 4,000 men, divided into thirty companies, but with ammunition for only one day of fighting. The heaviest German attack, consisting of 20,000 men with artillery, tanks, and aircraft was launched on June 20, and that night the Maquis were ordered to retreat as best they could toward the Lioran massif. The Spanish guerrillas distinguished themselves in the retreat by covering the withdrawal of several units.[38]

Throughout the central zone of France, Spaniards were numerous and active in many Maquis groups. Soleil, the French commander of a Resistance unit in the Dordogne, lauded their "unequaled valor" in combat and added that with them he was never afraid of treason or defection.[39] The career of Ramón, known as Raymond in the Resistance, created a legend that still finds people in the Rochechouart (Haute-Vienne) area referring to him as "the Spanish devil." After a short stay in a French concentration camp in February 1939, he returned to Spain and organized a guerrilla group. On one of his trips to Perpignan he was arrested and sent to work with the Todt Organization at Bedarieux (l'Herault). Notified by the French Resistance that the Gestapo was planning to arrest him, he escaped and, after working with several Maquis units, finally came to Rochechouart and organized an eighteen-man group. By the time of the liberation the unit had grown to over two hundred guerrillas. The list of his actions is long, but he is remembered for three major operations. Near Angoulême his group blew up a train, killing many German soldiers and coming into possession of the only antiaircraft gun known to have been captured. The unit also ambushed an entire armored train, taking hundreds of prisoners and a large quantity of machine-guns, rifles, and ammunition. Ramón's third major action resulted indirectly in the reprisal massacre at Oradour-sur- Glane (Haute-Vienne). Shortly after the June 6 invasion, a train filled with German soldiers was crossing a bridge over the Vienne River, near St. Junien (Haute-Vienne). Bridge and train were destroyed by Ramón and his men. The troops were on their way to' Normandy. In reprisal, an entire village, Oradour-sur Glane, was destroyed. Many of its inhabitants were either machine-gunned in the plaza or burned in the locked church. Six hundred and forty-two people were killed, including two hundred and fifty-two children. Among the dead were eighteen Spanish refugees. Ramón's revenge came swiftly. The village of Oradour-sur-Vayres (Haute-Vienne) was surrounded, and the German garrison was decimated: many were burned to death in a house, in the same fashion as the victims of Oradour-sur-Glane.[40]

Anarchist workers, as previously noted, were numerous in the Massif Central, and they organized resistance within the Travailleurs Etrangers groups working on the great L'Aigle hydroelectric dam project. Under the leadership of J. Montoliú and Manuel Barbosa, they formed four guerrilla groups, each consisting of fifteen men. Later, the groups were augmented by one hundred Spaniards and were active as the Battallon de la Barrage de l'Aigle, which was instrumental in the sabotage of roads and railroad tunnels and the liberation of a number of towns in the area. Apparently, anarchist refusal to join the UNE resulted in political strife for a time. The communists labeled the anarchists "bandits" in their regional newspaper, *Le Cantal Libre,* and attempted to incorporate a company of anarchist guerrillas stationed in Feixac (Lot) into the communist-dominated military organization. This move was successfully resisted.[41]

Other Spanish Maquis units were active throughout the central zone. A Spanish guerrilla group was among the first to enter Vichy and its initial act was to ocupy the Spanish embassy and replace the nationalist flag with the republican. Emilio Alvarez Canossa ("Pinocho") led a Dordogne guerrilla group that was responsible for numerous sabotages, including the destruction of twenty-seven locomotives in the repair shops at Perigueux and persistent dynamitings of railroads. On May 1, 1944, he led an attack that liberated eighty political prisoners from the jail at Nontron, including five members of the Central Committee of the Communist Party of France. In August his units, having distinguished themselves in blocking German troops from moving northward, participated in the liberation of Perigueux and Angoulême. In 1945 they joined other Maquis in the battles to reduce the last German strongholds on the Atlantic coast. Alvarez Canossa was named commandant of the 471st Brigade of Guerrilleros, and the French government made him a chevalier of the Legion of Honor and awarded him the War Cross with palm.[42] A Spanish unit, working with French Maquis, attacked the prison of Riom (Puy-de-Dôme) on August 22, 1944, and liberated 160 prisoners. Another Spanish force participated in the liberation of Limoges.[43]

Spanish Maquis organization and operations were perhaps most intense in the southwest of France. Bertaux observed that Spanish guerrillas had been in existence there even before the declaration of war, but their faces had been turned to the south until that event.[44] Nevertheless, these nuclei had formed the basis for a proliferation of Spanish republican combat against the Germans and the Vichy government. The Travailleurs Etrangers escaping from deportation found the Pyrenees and adjacent departments honeycombed with countrymen willing to take up arms in the Resistance movement. And it was in this region that the politics of the Resistance were most in evidence. Gaullists and French communists jockeyed for control against a background that had seen the Resistance movement, greatly influenced by communists, liberate the area largely through its own efforts and manpower. The Spanish communists, ubiquitous in nearly all of the Resistance groups, lent solid support to their French counterparts. Robert Aron, in one of his few references to the Spanish exiles, said that in the trial of strength between communists and noncommunists, the Spanish Reds had thrown their support to the former. He cited the presence of six thousand Spanish guerrillas in Toulouse who "were still imbued with the revolutionary spirit they had brought from beyond the Pyrenees." They were still estranged from the anarchists and were not prepared to accept the authority of General de Gaulle. "In August 1944," Aron wrote, "there was a great risk of revolution."[45] The general himself took cognizance of the Spanish guerrillas and remarked that they had stirred up a "considerable disturbance" in Toulouse.[46] Eventually, he succeeded in controlling the area, but he had acknowledged the pervasive character of the Spanish Resistance. Charles Foltz, Jr., noted the Spanish presence in a different way. In February 1939 he had seen the campfires of the Spanish refugees in the hills of southern France and again in the dark days of June 1940 he had seen the remnants of workers' companies camped before the Swiss border in attempts to reach safety. Now, in August 1944, he watched the German army departing from the Hendaye-Biarritz area. Again, he saw campfires in the hills and heard the sound of predawn maquisard rifle fire. When he investigated he found that the fires belonged to those same Spaniards. It was their only taste of victory in eight years of war and exile.[47]

Bertaux, who was appointed as de Gaulle's commissaire de la ré-publique in the Toulouse area, lauded the Spaniards for their role in liberating the city and for playing "the most important part" in Maquis action throughout the Pyrenees. But, he maintained, the liberation of Toulouse five days before that of Paris was not due exclusively to their efforts, nor those of the FFI. It was not even the result of a spontaneous rising of the people. If anyone deserved the credit, he said, it was the Germans themselves. When the Allies threw a column southeast of Paris and the Mediterranean coast was stormed on August 15, the Germans in Toulouse were imperiled by the possibility of a link-up between these two forces. Therefore, on August 19, they evacuated the city. Previously, however, the French and Spanish Maquis had maintained a consistent pressure on the enemy with bombings, assassinations, destruction of Germany convoys, disruption of communications, and industrial sabotage. On August 19, just before liberation of the city, the Spanish guerrillas had mounted a daring rescue of political prisoners in the Rempart Saint Etienne.[48]

Nowhere was the fighting more savage than in the department of l'Ariège, home of the punishment camp of Le Vernet and birthplace of the Spanish Corps of Guerrilleros in April 1942. In 1943 and 1944 the Third Brigade of the First Division, commanded by the Spaniard Royo, was very much in evidence in the department. Action escalated constantly during 1943, and key attacks destroyed an aluminum factory at Tarascon and a metal works at Pamiers. Resistance reached its peak after the Allied invasion of Normandy. Between June 6, 1944, and July 12, the Spanish Maquis executed seven major operations, which included blasting of railroad lines, attacks on two German convoys—resulting in seventy enemy killed or wounded—siege of a gendarmerie school and capture of a supply-laden truck, and breakouts from two German and Milice ambushes without loss.[49]

Between August 18 and 23 the Spanish guerrillas mounted their peak effort in l'Ariège, at the same time as their comrades and French Maquis were liberating other areas in the southwest. The official communique of the guerrillas listed their actions: August 18: under Spanish pressure, the enemy evacuated Pamiers, Varilhes, and Lavelanet. August 19: Spanish Maquis attacked Foix, headquarters of the German army in l'Ariège. The enemy retreated into a lycée after a brief street combat. With reinforcement from the Second Battalion, the school was assaulted and the Germans surrendered; 27 officers and 120 men were captured. In addition, ten vehicles and a large quantity of supplies were seized. August 20: A twenty-truck convoy was ambushed and, after a thirteen-hour battle, surrendered with fifty prisoners: twenty Germans were killed. August 21–22: the largest battle of the l'Ariège campaign was fought when the Germans attempted to retake Foix. In the late afternoon of the twenty-first, the Third Spanish Battalion and some French Maquis made contact with a strong German column near Rimont. The Second Battalion was called for reinforcements and the attack began. The enemy retreated, reorganized, and counterattacked. With its incontestable numerical and arms superiority it forced the Maquis to retreat. At midnight, the German column attempted to break out of the ambush and continue its movement, but it was stopped by constant machine-gun fire from a point directly ahead on the road. Thus, the guerrillas again suceeded in their main objective, that of forcing the enemy into immobility in an exposed position. Again, the Germans counterattacked a wing of the Maquis line, forcing a pullback. Sixty French reinforcements arrived and a new line was established. At 4:30 P.M. on August 22 the enemy made a last attempt to move, but suffered great losses. Frozen into immobility and thoroughly demoralized, the Germans surrendered. They had suffered 150 dead and wounded; 1,200 Germans were captured. Bertaux noted that the key action of the engagement, the harrassing machine-gun fire that had prevented the German breakout at midnight of August 21, was accomplished by a single Spaniard emplaced on the road. Alone, "firing like a crazy one," he had stopped the progress of thirteen hundred men. "But he was a Spaniard," Bertaux wrote, "a guerrillero." *Liberación,* a Maquis newspaper, published the official commendation of the Third Brigade for the action. An Allied mission, having observed the battle, termed the Spaniards "uniquely perfect guerrillas."[50]

The no-quarters savagery of the fighting in l'Ariège applied to both sides. During the two-day battle on the road to Foix, the Germans destroyed the village of Rimont, killing many of its inhabitants. On June 21, gendarmes discovered a large hole being hacked through the prison wall at Foix. Pincemin, chief of the gendarmes, decided to launch a reprisal raid on the Maquis at Roquefixade. A warning note, passed from inside the prison, failed to reach the Maquis in time, and thirty-two were massacred. When l'Ariège was liberated the victors exhibited a revolutionary violence which alarmed the Gaullist officials. A tribunal of the people was organized. At Pamiers, sixty to eighty people were condemned and executed within a few days. Mass arrests were made throughout the area. Bertaux finally appointed Ernest de Nattes as prefect. He immediately declared the tribunals illegal and liberated many prisoners taken by the Maquis. He received a letter on August 30 from the officers of the FTP of Saint Girons, who had arrested a number of Milice men and members of the Parti Populaire Français. "These traitors," the letter said, "having fought against France, arms in hand, ought to be killed by arms within twenty-four hours." If the provisional prefect was not willing to carry out this request the prisoners should be delivered to the FTP. The prefect later persuaded the FTP to withdraw the letter.[51]

Miguel Angel served as commander of the Fourth Division, which operated in the vast territory of the Pyrénées-Orientales, l'Aude, Tarn, Aveyron, and l'Herault. He described the key roles played by women. Nati and Carmen took many dangerous missions as couriers and later earned War Crosses. Mesdames Claudin and Consuela operated their homes as Maquis headquarters. The hotel of Madame Assezat in Perpignan was the workshop for creating false papers of all types. At one time Angel possessed three nationality cards and Wehrmacht stamps, which validated travel anywhere. In Carcassonne, Rafaela and Mercedes Núñez coordinated communications and supervised the establishment for providing false papers. A Maquis succeeded in securing a number of Spanish nationality cards from the nationalist consulate. Gestapo and Milice activity was all-embracing in this area, and they made frequent raids that disrupted Maquis operations. In mid-1943 the Gestapo arrested the members of two escape networks. In April 1944 many Maquis were captured in Carcassonne, and on May 10 the false papers workshop was seized, along with pictures of many leaders. Angel and others were forced to transfer their operations to new places. In l'Aude, Tarn, and l'Herault the repression was also severe. Despite the intensity of counter-Maquis activity, the guerrillas succeeded in pressing home a continuing flow of attacks. In late July and August 1944 they liberated much of this vast area. Enric Melich, known as Corporal Sanz, was typical of those fighting in the Resistance. An anarchist, he fought with the Jean Robert Maquis, which blew up the bridge at Saint Paul-de-Fenouilledes, the viaduct of Axat, and a German train at Quillan all in Pyrénées-Orientales. At the end of August 1944 the unit organized itself as the Bataillon Muriel and was incorporated into the Eighty-first Regiment of Alpine Infantry, First French Army. It then fought in Alsace and participated in the invasion of Germany.[52]

In other departments of the Southwest the Maquis carried out extensive operations that hindered the German war effort and severely damaged waning Vichy prestige. Their sabotage of railroads, in the south as elsewhere, was so effective that when General Revers, head of the Organization Résistance de l'Armée, took the train from Paris to Toulouse on June 6, 1944, to ascertain just how quickly the Germans might be expected to move troops to the north, it took him three days to complete the journey. Between June 1943 and May 1944, 1,822 locomotives and 200 passenger cars were destroyed or heavily damaged. In the single month of October 25 to November 25, 1943, the Vichy police reported 3,000 attempts against the railway system; of this number, 427 resulted in heavy damage and 132 caused derailment of trains.[53] Francisco Valentin, a Spanish anarchist, made the hundred mile journey from Mauriac to Limoges in eighteen hours on that same day. The train moved cautiously, and twice made wide detours because of bridges that had been dynamited.[54] In the Tarn-et-Garonne the Fourth Brigade, commanded by Ortiz de la Torre, specialized in railroad sabotage but also attacked German convoys and industrial targets. From April 6 to July 20, 1944, the group mounted nineteen major attacks, six of them in a single day.[55] In the Basses-Pyrénées, the Spaniards under Commandant Oria, known as Julio, harrassed German installations. At one point the Maquis were betrayed and the Germans raided a house where fourteen wounded resisters were recovering; all were shot. On August 21 the guerrillas surrounded a German force that was trying to escape into Spain. The Germans were willing to surrender, but not to Spanish guerrillas; they had been told that the

Spaniards would torture them. Angel claimed that their fears were unfounded: Prisoners were never harmed and were always turned over to the French authorities.[56] Tomás Guerrero Ortega, whose pseudonym was Camilo, escaped from the Le Vernet prison camp and organized a Maquis group of the department of Gers. Raymond Escholier, a French Maquis who fought with Camilo, described him as "a gloomy, dark Madrileño with eyes like hot coals, and only one leg—the other had been lost in the [Spanish] Civil War." He noted the delight of the four hundred Spaniards of Camilo when they were furnished with arms: "They were hard and audacious soldiers . . . They sustained the war against the Nazis without quarter . . . Nothing discouraged them. They were as tenacious in defense as in the attack." This group liberated Castelnau, (Landes), killing 250 Germans and wounding 350. The maquis suffered seventeen killed and twenty-nine wounded.[57]

In the south anarchists either fought with their own units or integrated into French groups because of their antipathy to communist control. José Cervera lauded the French command in the department of Lot, which greeted them cordially and respected their philosophy. A special Spanish unit of thirty-one men earned the respect of Soleil, the French commander, in a variety of missions. At one point, Cervera was suggested for a lieutenancy. The French communists objected, pointing out that Cervera was an anarchist, a member of the CNT, and that it was humilating for Frenchmen to serve under a Spaniard. Soleil replied that such considerations had no place in the Resistance. He cited Cervera's record of combat and the fact that he had volunteered for the most dangerous missions. Despite Soleil's stand, the promotion failed to materialize. Cervera and his group later joined the Libertad Battalion, an all-anarchist unit under the command of Santos, and took an active part in liberating Cahors and other towns.[58] Spanish guerrillas also fought in every department of southwestern France, participating in the liberation of Marseille and Toulon and harassing German troops retreating northward.[59] During 1943 and 1944 the Maquis managed to mount 535 missions in the Bouches-du-Rhone, including 98 military sabotages, 110 attacks against industrial and supply targets, and 74 assaults on German personnel. The Resistance movement had survived severe repression, including the gigantic round-up of citizens in Marseille on January 24, 1944, which had resulted in 2,000 deportations to Germany.

The departments of Lozère and the Gard, potential escape routes for the German army, saw heavy fighting. It was in Lozère that the Maquis group Bir Hakeim was betrayed, ambushed, and murdered. Cristino García Grandas operated in the Gard, participating in the rescue of political prisoners from the prison of Nîmes and in the classic guerrilla battle of La Madeleine.

Bir Hakeim was a mixed French-Spanish unit led by the French commandant Barreau. On May 28, 1944, it was assigned to receive a parachute drop of arms in the woods near Carnac. Betrayed by collaborators, the Spaniards who had taken up defensive positions around the drop area were attacked by German troops. In the battle that followed, Barreau was killed and the Spanish chief, Miguel López, took command. He was gravely wounded and the Germans captured almost the entire unit. Ninety-three French maquisards and twenty-three Spanish guerrillas were killed during the combat or executed afterward.[60]

After the capture of Marseille, interdiction of the German forces retreating through the Gard became the prime mission of the Area Resistance, and the Maquis pursued it with great vigor. Perhaps the most notable example of this guerrilla activity was the encounter between a predominantly Spanish group and a German column at the crossroads of La Madeleine, seventeen kilometers southwest of Alès. On August 22, 1944, Cristino García Grandas led thirty-two Spaniards and four Frenchmen in an ambush of a German convoy of 1,300 men, sixty trucks, six tanks, and two self-propelled cannons. At La Madeleine, the motor road and a railroad bridge passed over a stream. Both were dynamited. Some guerrillas then took positions on a hill near the Château de Tornac, which commanded the road, while others emplaced machine-guns for some distance along the ridge. At 3:00 P.M. the German column appeared and was halted by the roadblock. After a battle that lasted until noon of the next day, the Germans surrendered unconditionally. The struggle had resulted in three wounded maquis, against 110 Germans killed, 200 wounded, and more than 1,000 taken prisoner. The German commander, Konrad Nietzsche, committed suicide. Numerous actions of this type later caused the American General Jacob Devers to state that the support of the FFI during the northward advance of the American Seventh Army had been worth four or five divisions to him.[61]

Cristino García and Carlos Alonso were also responsible for planning and executing the rescue of fifty political prisoners from the jail at Nîmes on February 4, 1944. The resisters were awaiting shipment to Germany.[62] Prison rescues and breakouts, such as those at Nîmes, Toulouse, and Nontron, were frequent occurrences. The insurrection at the prison of Eysses (Lot-et-Garonne) was perhaps the most spectacular attempt of this nature, although it failed in its objective. Eysses was a regional facility for political recalcitrants and common criminals. In late 1943 it held twelve hundred prisoners, the majority French, but including eighty-two Spaniards and an unknown number of Russians, Poles, Englishmen, and Italians. One hundred and fifty-six political prisoners formed the Bataillon d'Eysses, with the intention of organizing a mass breakout. Assistance was given by local adherents of the National Front, who provided machine guns, small arms, grenades, and ammunition. A few guards were among the friendly forces.[63] François Bernard, an ex-International Brigader, was chosen as commander. It was agreed that the next prominent official to visit the prison would be isolated, captured, and held hostage. The prisoners would exchange garb with the guards and immobilize additional prison personnel. Several squads of rebels would assault the watchtowers. The balance of the resisters would appropriate some trucks and rush the main gate. Then they would storm past the gardes mobiles headquarters, situated about fifty yards from the gate, and escape into the nearby forest.

On February 19, 1944, the long-awaited opportunity arrived. An inspector from the prison bureau at Vichy visited Eysses and was taken on a tour of the facility by the commandant, Colonel Schivo. At 3:00 P.M. Schivo's group entered the kitchen and observed a number of prisoners preparing a Catalan pudding. Schivo inquired about a crude painting on the wall, a rooster imposed on a map of France, with rays of a rising sun illuminating the scene. He asked what it meant and a Spaniard responded: "It represents the sun that will rise tomorrow on a liberated France." Schivo took a backward step, drew his pistol, but did not fire. Quickly, the prisoners surrounded the officials, seized them, and disarmed them. The transfer of clothing was made. Other guards were captured and divested of their uniforms. Firearms were brought from their secret hiding place in the carpentry shop: twelve machine guns, some revolvers, and thirty-five hand grenades. The chapel was occuped and converted into what was named the "rat trap," to hold the newly-made prisoners. Those insurrectionists who were dressed in guards' uniforms began to infiltrate the courtyard, moving toward the five watchtowers. The plan was proceeding swiftly and efficiently. At this point the unforeseen happened. A group of common criminals who had been working outside the walls were marched back into the prison, two hours before their scheduled time. Upon seeing the rebels in guard uniforms, some of them began to shout. The alarm was given. The gardes mobiles went into action.[64] From every watchtower, machine-guns swept the main courtyard and the four prisoner blocks. Grenades were lofted: Spaniards picked them up and threw them back. Some pickaxes were found and a Spanish crew attempted to dig a hole through the wall; after a half-hour they abandoned the project. German reinforcements arrived. François Bernard was wounded. A council was held in the chapel. French survivors later recalled the parley:

The Spanish comrades propose to assault the northwest watchtower. They were all "volunteers of death" in the sister Republic, from 1936 to 1939. Their group comprises a dozen men. Whoever knows a Spanish brother in these difficult moments has a unique privilege. Is it our common struggle that has bound us more strongly still?

The following minutes are moving. Each wishes to shake the hands of these brave men. Do not some think that this attack is a folly and that it is insane to believe in its success? In this instant, before the calm confidence of these Asturians, these Castilians, these Catalans, one wishes above all to say thanks and to share their faith.[65]

Five times the Spaniards attempted to storm the watchtower, through the hail of machine-gun fire and grenade explosions. Some tried with pickaxes to enlarge the hole they had opened in the wall. But every effort failed. Serot, a key Spaniard, was wounded—six of his brothers had been killed, either by Franco or in the Resistance; soon he too would die. Finally, the Spaniards were prevailed upon to abandon their desperate attempts. Llanos, who had participated in the attacks, said simply, "We have done all we could. We have used a battering-ram against the walls, but dynamite is needed."[66]

It was now noon of February 20. The battle had raged since 3:00 P.M. of the previous day and the Bataillon d'Eysses was nearly out of ammunition. The insurrectionists tried to negotiate a surrender, but the Germans refused. Joseph Darnand arrived to take personal charge of the situation. Colonel Schivo telephoned his headquarters and said that he and the other hostages had been treated decently and he had given his word that there would be no reprisals. After the surrender, Darnand interrogated the insurrectionists personally, and a hastily-convened court-martial on February 23 condemned to death twelve resisters who had been wounded, including two Spaniards. Sentence was carried out immediately. On May 18, thirty-six members of the batallion were deported to Dachau, and during the next two months the remaining conspirators were deported to other concentration camps. *Paris-Soir,* on February 24, reported that "some prisoners, composed in the main of communists, foreign anarchists, and Spanish terrorists," had rebelled at Eysses. Having failed to achieve their objective they had been tried by a French court and sentenced to death.[67]

The spirit of the French and Spanish Resistance fighters, as exemplified by the Bataillon d'Eysses, had enabled them to survive ferocious repression from Germans and collaborationist French, to grow stronger in numbers and material, and finally to accomplish the liberation of the south virtually by themselves.[68] In the north and west of France, the character of the Resistance was to be somewhat different, tied as it was to the great military effort of the Allies. But in those areas too, Spaniards were to play a meaningful role in ridding France of the two masters who had ruled it so harshly from 1940 to 1944.

LIBERATION
AND VICTORY

FROM NORMANDY TO BERCHTESGADEN

[The Spanish soldiers] were both difficult and easy to command:
difficult because it was necessary that they accept for themselves
the authority of their officials; easy because when they granted
their confidence it was total and complete. They wished to
understand the reasons for that which was asked of them and
it was necessary to explain the why of things.

Captain Raymond Dronne, Commander, Ninth Company,
Regiment of Chad, Second French Armored Division

How many lands have my feet trod and my eyes seen! What
terrible scenes of desolation of death I witnessed in those years of
continual war. Adverse circumstances had made us, antimilitarists,
the most battle-hardened soldiers of the Allied armies.

Even today, all appears to me as a dream. And the most
extraordinary dream is that I survived so many battles while I saw
thousands die around me.

Murillo de la Cruz, in Federica Montseny, *Pasión y muerte
de los españoles en Francia*

THE SPANISH GUERRILLAS in the north were not as numerous
as their comrades in the south, but their presence was clearly felt
in the battles of liberation that began in June 1944. In this theater,
however, they were joined by their brothers who fought in French uniforms, those who had joined the Foreign Legion or escaped to England
after the defeat of France in 1940. These men had battled General Erwin
Rommel's Afrika Korps and had then prepared for the invasion of
France. They were to return to France in mid-1944, help to liberate it
from the Nazi army, and then to push into the heartland of Germany
itself.

In the summer of 1943, sixteen thousand soldiers, twenty percent
of them Spaniards, were activated in Africa as the Second French
Armored Division, under the command of General Philippe Leclerc.
They were drawn from diverse sources but all had seen considerable
action in the African campaigns. Equipped by the Americans, the di-

vision possessed the most modern armor. At about the same time General Brosset assumed command of the First French Armored Division and General Jean de Lattre de Tassigny was named commander of the French Army B.[1] These units were to become the visible symbols of the resurgence of French military vitality and the instruments through which France would rejoin the contest against Hitler.

Spaniards were spread throughout the ranks of the Second Armored, but were preponderant in the Infantry Regiment of Chad and the Ninth Tank Company of the Third Battalion. Commandant Putz, a French veteran of the International Brigades, was placed in charge of the Third Battalion, and Captain Raymond Dronne commanded the Ninth Company. Apparently, this latter assignment was not considered a prize by the French officers, several of whom had declined it before the selection of Dronne. "To tell the truth," he wrote, the company "inspired suspicion in everyone, and nobody wished to take the command." Dronne was finally chosen because he was fluent in Spanish, had spent much time in Spain before the war, and, perhaps most importantly, fulfilled the basic Spanish requirement of having been in the Resistance from the very beginning. The majority of the Spaniards were anarchists, and a number were socialists and moderates. When the Ninth Company landed in Normandy at the beginning of August 1944, there were 144 Spaniards in its ranks; only sixteen survived the drive through France and Germany.[2]

Dronne found the Spaniards "both difficult and easy to command." They withheld their confidence until the commanding officer had proved himself, but once they granted that confidence, it was "total and complete." They insisted on knowing the reasons for the tasks they were asked to perform, but once they were explained to the Spaniards' satisfaction and approval, they carried them out with single-minded determination. "They did not have a military spirit," Dronne said. "They were almost all antimilitarists, but they were magnificent soldiers, valiant and experienced. If they had embraced our cause spontaneously and voluntarily, it was [because] it was the cause of liberty. Truly, they were fighters for liberty."[3]

On April 4, 1944, the Second French Armored Division embarked from Casablanca for England. It was not earmarked for the actual invasion of Normandy, but landed in France July 31 to August 4. Almost immediately it went into combat, and on August 7 Andés García became its first casualty when he was wounded by an aerial bomb.[4] The Second Division, which was assigned to a corps commanded by the American general Gerow, began the push on Paris, General de Gaulle having received the assurance of General Omar Bradley that the honor of first entry into Paris would be given to the division. However, the Americans held up the order for the French to proceed. Instead, American strategy called for enveloping movements north and south of Paris that would threaten the Germans with encirclement and force them to evacuate the city without a battle. General Dwight D. Eisenhower expected Paris to fall in early September. General Leclerc bridled at the delay and made incessant inquiries about when he would be given the signal to plunge ahead. On August 21, before Argentan, he received word that the Resistance movement, which had risen in Paris on August 18, was engaged in severe fighting throughout the city. On his own initiative he sent a strong reconnaissance force towards Paris, but this movement was aborted by General Gerow. On August 23 the Second Armored reached Rambouillet, two hundred kilometers from the Normandy coast and only fifty kilometers from the gates of Paris. According to Dronne, at 7:30 P.M., August 24, General Leclerc came to him and asked why his unit had stopped. When told of General Gerow's order to hold its place in line, Leclerc replied, "It is necessary not to comply with idiotic orders." He took Dronne's arm, pointed with his walking stick to Paris and said, "Dronne, go directly to Paris, enter Paris." The captain replied, "If I understand correctly, I am to avoid any distractions, and to ignore anything I may encounter." Leclerc confirmed this, adding, "Pass by whatever means you can. It is necessary to enter Paris." Dronne surmised correctly that the objective of the move was not so much military as psychological. It was designed to raise the morale of the Resistance within the city. It was necessary for the people to see the only French force in the area and to know that they were the first Allies to enter the capital city.[5]

Dronne selected the Spanish-manned half-track sections of Second Lieutenant Elías and Sergeant Campos to spearhead the dash. His adjutant, Lieutenant Amado Granell, said the force was composed of twenty-two vehicles and 120 men. At 8:30 P.M., it entered Paris via the Porte d'Italie, where Captain Dronne placed himself at the head of the column. Then it moved rapidly through the streets and arrived at the Hôtel de Ville at 9:33 P.M. The first armored vehicles to reach the plaza were manned by Spaniards and bore the names Guadalajara, Teruel, Madrid, and Ebro, according to Granell. Dronne was greeted by Georges Bidault, president of the Comité National de la Résistance, and Daniel Mayer, Joseph Laniel, Georges Marrane, and Léo Hamon, members of the comité.[6] Robert Aron's and Adrien Dansette's accounts of the entry into Paris have credited French-manned tanks with being the first to reach the Hôtel de Ville. Aron cited a tank named Romilly for this honor, and Dansette declared that in addition to the Romilly, tanks named Montmirail and Champaubert drew up to the liberated city hall. Dansette, writing in 1947, gave no credence to the numerous reports of Spanish soldiers moving with the vanguard through the Paris streets. He claimed that these men were really Moroccans and added, in a somewhat arch footnote, "We have there an authentic and excellent example of the manner in which false news is born."[7] However, Captain Dronne states categorically that "half-tracks with Spanish names, manned by Spaniards of the Ninth Company, were the first to enter Paris" and to reach the Hôtel de Ville. At one point, after the lead vehicles took defensive positions in the plaza, Dronne went inside to converse with the Resistance leaders. An immense crowd flooded the plaza, climbing over the vehicles and congratulating the crews. Suddenly, a sniper sent a bullet into the Hôtel de Ville. Dronne remarked that when he went outside, the crewmen of the Ebro, freed from the restraining influence of the admiring crowd, which had fled at the first shot, were already in defensive positions against any possible German attack. The movements of the Forces Françaises de l'Interieur (FFI) resisters who flitted about in the shadows, he remarked at another point in his narrative, made the Spaniards restless and vigilant; their long experience with street fighting made them wary of a sudden assault.[8] Léo Haman, who rushed out to greet the arriving tanks, talked to their crews. "They did not speak French very well," he reported, "they were Spanish republicans enlisted in the Leclerc Division."[9] Lieutenant Granell's description of the advance group at the plaza noted that the tanks had Spanish names stencilled on their sides.[10] Chief Sergeant Jesús Abenza wrote that General Leclerc spoke to the Spaniards before the thrust into Paris and told them that he wanted them at the head of the column and that they would lead the liberating force. Abenza also recalled that during the passage from the Porte d'Italie to the Hôtel de Ville, the cheering populace had greeted them with shouts of "Vive la France!". When told that the tankists were Spaniards, they cried "Vivent les Espagnols!" ("Long live the Spaniards!"). Several of the tanks bore Spanish republican flags, and when they reached the plaza, Abenza emplaced the first cannon, named *El Abuelo* ("The Grandfather").[11]

The insurrection in Paris had been in progress since August 18, and the arrival of the advance party of the Second Armored, followed the next day by the bulk of the division and the American Fourth Division, fueled the battle for Paris. More than four thousand Spaniards participated in the insurrection and were prominent in battles at the Place de l'Opera, Place de la Concorde, Place de la République, the military school, and elsewhere throughout Paris. They linked up, in many cases, with the Second Armored Division and were active in attacking German strongpoints at the Luxembourg Gardens, Senate, and Invalides. In the Étoile district, a Spanish guerrilla named Pacheco took twelve German prisoners in the Hotel Majestic. Later, he captured a number of weapons at the Invalides and distributed them to the Resistance fighters. José Baron, leader of the Spanish guerrillas on the right bank of the Seine, died in the fighting at the Place de la Concorde. Another guerrilla, Trigomas, killed six defenders at the Senate building and appropriated their weapons. Charles Tillon noted the widespread activity of the Spanish guerrillas throughout the city. A group of Spaniards led by a former school teacher, Julio Hernández, occupied the Spanish embassy and replaced the nationalist flag with that of the Spanish republic.[12]

These actions were part of the continuing Resistance movement in the north of France, which had accelerated with the Allied landings. *La Defense de la France* detailed almost 500 separate Resistance efforts between April 1 and September 30, 1943, of which 278 were directed against the railroad system. Other missions included destruction of canal locks, telephone communications, munitions depots, and factories. The underground newspaper reported the killing of 950 Germans and the wounding of 1,890. More than 220 French collaborators were killed or wounded.[13] In Normandy and Brittany, the Spaniards who worked for the Organization Todt formed many Resistance groups. In Brittany and other areas, Spanish guerrillas blew up five transformers, a railroad station and switching area, and part of an aviation field at Saint Jacques de la Lande (Ille-et-Vilaine). Pedro Flores killed a German official, donned his uniform, and penetrated a movie house that was exclusively for the use of German personnel. He bombed it, with many casualties resulting from his action. On June 8, 1944, Flores was arrested, tortured, and shot by the Gestapo. At Saint-Malo in Normandy, the Spanish workers of Todt destroyed the electrical system in the work area. In November 1943, the Saint-Malo group was decimated by the Gestapo, but the unit was reactivated by a group of Spanish workers who had escaped from the Todt Organization on the Island of Jersey. A secret report from the Securité Militaire in Algiers, May 26, 1943, revealed the contents of a memorandum from the commandant of gendarmerie for the occupied territories to the Vichy French ambassador delegate in Paris. The commandant listed numerous acts of sabotage and assassination that had been performed by the French and Spanish Resistance. In Paris, the Spaniards had worked with many French Resistance units, including the Manouchian Group, which was betrayed in February 1944. All twenty-three of its members, including several Spaniards, were shot. Spaniards in the Manouchian

Group were responsible for the assassinations of General von Schaum-
berg, commandant of Greater Paris, and General Julius von Ritter,
who was responsible for the recruitment of workers for Germany.
The guerrilla Ortuño, after deserting the Todt Organization on Guern-
sey, formed a Resistance unit in the department of the Orne and harrassed German troops after the D-Day landing. From there his group
went to Paris and participated in the insurrection, in conjunction with
the Second French Armored Division.[14]

The Ninth Company was active in many parts of Paris on August
25th. The Germans had set up a number of strongpoints, and fighting
went on sporadically until General von Choltitz signed the surrender.
One battle may have ended, but another began as General de Gaulle's
forces and the communist-led portion of the Resistance movement
jockeyed for control of the city. Another engagement, perhaps not as
important, but indicative of the American attitude toward General de
Gaulle, took place when General Gerow issued a general order to
Leclerc forbidding the French Second Armored Division from marching in the victory parade down the Champs-Elysées, scheduled for
August 26th.

> Operating, as you are, under my direct command, you will accept no
> orders emanating from any other source. I believe you have received orders
> from General de Gaulle for your troops to take part in a parade this
> afternoon at 1400 hours. You will pay no heed to this order and you will
> continue to carry out the mission to which you are at present assigned to
> clean up all resistance in Paris and its neighborhood, within your zone of
> action.
>   The troops under your command will take no part in the parade, either
> this afternoon, or at any other time, except on orders personally signed
> by me.

De Gaulle replied, for LeClerc, that he had loaned one of his divisions to the American command but had a perfect right to employ it
in entering the French capital.[15] Gerow's prohibition was disregarded
by at least one unit of the Second French Armored Division, but he
never pressed the point. Aron noted that the guard of honor at the
Tomb of the Unknown Soldier came from the Chad Regiment of the
Second Armored. But he did not say that the unit was the ubiquitous
Ninth Company, whose tanks were drawn up before the Arc de
Triomphe.[16] Thus, the Spanish republicans, who had fought their way
from Madrid and Barcelona, across Africa, and into the center of Paris,
now stood at the military shrine of France in the hour of that country's
greatest triumph. The Spanish presence was felt in other ways on
August 26th. Lining the Champs Elysées were many trucks with huge

messages of greetings from the Spanish Resistance fighters, and across the entire avenue was strung an enormous streamer in the red, yellow, and maroon colors of the Spanish republic.[17]

The Leclerc Division—the Second French Armored—remained in Paris from August 24 to September 8, when it resumed its march to the east. When it left the capital it contained six clandestine Spanish members, whose mission looked beyond the defeat of Germany to the eventual return to Spain: in the first hours of liberation, six former members of the anarchist Durruti Division who were in the Paris Resistance had met some of their former comrades who were now with the Ninth Company. Sergeant Campos, a section leader, proposed to Joaquín Blesa and five comrades that they join the unit clandestinely, with the objective of recovering arms and ammunition from the battlefields and hiding them for future use in Spain.

They received uniforms, a truck, and weapons. Blesa was certain that Campos had received the unofficial blessing of a French officer for the venture. Campos instructed them in the operation of the tanks and their armament, and this knowledge was put to use when they were called into action during the crossing of the Moselle River. In November, for some unexplained reason, Campos told them to return to Paris. They had already made two trips to cache arms and now, provided with safe-conduct passes, they moved back along the division's trail, gathering a harvest of hidden arms intended for later use in the guerrilla campaign in Spain.[18]

Moving toward the East, the Leclerc Division engaged in strenuous fighting along the whole route against a stubbornly resisting enemy. At Chatel-sur-Moselle (Vosges), on September 16, 1944, the Germans launched a strong counterattack directly against the Ninth Company. Federico Moreno assumed command of his section when the commander was killed, and he rallied his men to halt the drive. The citation awarding him the War Cross with silver star declared that he had not yielded a single inch of territory despite the ferocity of the enemy. The action of the Ninth Company on the Moselle brought exclamations of praise from the French officers who, according to V. Echegaray, a member of the unit, lauded the Spaniards for their "bravura, combat spirit, and initiative." Moreno and Fermín Pujol subsequently received the Military Medal and War Cross with palms for their action in the liberation of Nancy.[19] On November 22, after destorying a strong concentration of German tanks and artillery, the Ninth Company and a battalion of the American Seventy-ninth Infantry Division were the first to enter Strasbourg. From that date until February 1, 1945, the LeClerc Division was engaged in extending the

Allied line along the approaches to the Rhine River. On January 31 they linked up with elements of the First French Armored Division and the Foreign Legion, which had reentered France in the landings in Provence and Var on August 15, 1944, and moved northward through the Alps. The Spaniards in both units occupied adjoining portions of the line until March 3, 1945, when the Leclerc Division was sent to a rest camp. The division had been in almost uninterrupted combat for eight months. The Third Regiment of Chad had suffered 116 killed, 494 wounded, and 20 missing. Among those killed in action were Lieutenant Colonel Putz and Commandant Puig. The losses inflicted upon the enemy—as estimated by the regiment—were 2,200 dead and 5,870 taken prisoner (in addition to the 20,000 taken in Paris and 9,000 in Strasbourg). Seventy-two tanks, 127 cannons, and 872 other vehicles were also captured.[20]

After resting in central France the Second French Armored Division was assigned to attack the remaining pockets of German resistance on the Atlantic coast. Leclerc objected to being sidetracked from his primary objective—Berlin—and committed only two tank regiments. The remainder, including the Spaniards, crossed the Rhine on April 27 and continued the march through Germany. One column captured Augsburg and Munich. Another, slicing south, reached Sigmaringen, the Vichy government headquarters in Germany, but were able to seize only a few officials. On May 4, 1945, the Ninth Company approached Berchtesgaden. It encountered heavy German resistance and fields sown thickly with mines. "Take great care," Lieutenant Martín Bernal told Moreno, "or not a single Spaniard will live to tell what happened." No casualties were sustained, but when the Spanish soldiers reached Adolf Hitler's Eagle's Nest two French units had already arrived. Nevertheless, according to Pons Prades, the Spaniards relished the delight of entering Hitler's sanctuary as conquerors.[21]

The Spaniards of the First French Armored Division, with whom those of the Second Armored had linked up in Alsace on January 31, 1945, had also covered much territory during the war. Originally, they had signed with the French Foreign Legion and fought in Syria and Africa. When the First Armored Division was formed, in 1943, they were incorporated into its ranks and took part in the Italian campaign. More than a thousand Spaniards were in the newly created fighting · force. On August 15, 1944, they landed at Saint-Tropez, participated in the clearing of the Mediterranean coast, and then struck due north. Their first meeting with the Resistance fighters was at Valence, and José Millán Vicente was surprised to see so many Spaniards among them. After the capture of Lyon the First Armored Division liberated Besancon and Colmar (Haut-Rhin) before it connected with the French

Second Armored Division. From Alsace it turned eastward and captured a number of German towns. For Millán Vicente the end of the war came none too soon. Together with Enrique Marco Nadal and a number of other Spaniards, he had been captured and placed on a northbound train. The train, which was carrying a full load of tanks, cannons, and munitions, displayed the Red Cross prominently as it sought to avoid aerial bombardment. Nevertheless, near Nuremberg it was bombed, and Millán, Marco, and four other Spaniards escaped. They hid in a forest, determined to wait for Allied troops. A group of German soldiers, apparently deserters, sought to surrender to them, but the Spaniards, as Millán put it, engaged in "a weird ballet" with their enemies. When the Germans approached, hands in air, the Spaniards melted away and found another hiding place. A few days before the end of the war in Europe they encountered a group of American tanks and finally reunited with their unit. Millán estimated that of the thousand men who began the campaign in Africa, no more than a hundred survived to V-E Day.[22]

While the Spaniards of the First and Second Armored Divisions swept through Germany in April 1945, their erstwhile guerrilla countrymen in France had been incorporated into the regular French forces. They were slated to take part in the only all-French battle of the invasion, the reduction of German garrisons bottled up in the Atlantic ports of Lorient, Saint Nazaire, La Rochelle, Royan, and at Le Verdon-Pointe-de-Grave. From 69,000 to 90,000 well-armed, strongly entrenched enemy soldiers had been by-passed in the initial Allied surge toward Paris, but in mid-August 1944 they represented to General de Larminat a splendid opportunity to achieve several objectives with one throw of the military dice. Colonel Paul de Langlade felt that the operation was unnecessary because of the inevitability of Allied victory, but he sensed the reasoning behind de Larminat's plan. The maquisards, in de Larminat's view, now represented a potential danger to the new French state and certainly to the rapid acquisition of power by General de Gaulle, who had given every indication of being aware that "an army of guerrillas is always a revolutionary army." The nationalization of the Maquis would eliminate this danger, but it would also serve another useful purpose. An all-French victory would present to the Allies a national army, disciplined and powerful, thus undercutting any idea of leaving an Allied occupation force in France.[23]

General de Gaulle accepted de Larminat's plan, and on August 23, 1944, a decree offered the Resistance fighters enlistment in the regular army or a return to civilian life. From thiry-five to fifty percent of the FFI abandoned their arms; the others donned military uniforms. The Spanish guerrillas were divided on the question. Some felt that the main priority now was the reconquest of Spain, and they hoped to transfer their units intact to the Spanish border and await Allied arms and materiel for this task. Others, who loathed military combat and hoped to return to Spain through peaceful means, left their units. Still others thought that their presence was no longer necessary in view of the existence of the powerful Allied army. In the end, a sizable number of Spaniards enlisted in the regular forces because they felt that their strength would be needed until the very end of the conflict. Among these were the anarchists of the Confederación Nacional del Trabajo. The national committee of the CNT entered enthusiastically into the task of recruiting for an enlarged role in the war effort. The Libertad Battalion was expanded to regimental strength under the command of Santos. The Basques also enlarged their Guernika Battalion, with Ordoki as commander. Altogether, about 6,000 Spaniards were part of the 73,000-man force assembled for the campaign to reduce the German Atlantic bastions. General de Larminat was given command of the entire force.[24]

The assault, originally scheduled for late 1944, actually took place between April 14 and 19, 1945. Most of the Spanish soldiers were assigned to the Pointe-de-Grave sector and opened the attack on April 14. Progress was slow because the German position was protected by marshy terrain, minefields, and three concrete forts that sheltered artillery and machine-guns. The French 75-mm gun had very little effect on the thick concrete walls of the bastions, which, ironically, had been constructed by the Organization Todt. Finally, the Basque infantry took the position after three hours of combat. On April 16, the Second Company of the Libertad regiment captured Montalivet (Gironde) and followed this on April 18 by liberating Soulac-sur-mer and, incidentally, taking a German admiral as a prisoner. By April 19, 1945, the campaign was ended. General de Gaulle reviewed the troops at a parade in Cognac and saluted both the Basque and Spanish republican flags carried by the soldiers. Spanish soldiers earned eleven War Crosses and many other medals during this campaign.[25]

On May 8, 1945, V-E Day, the war in Europe ended. The Spanish republicans had fought the Germans since 1936 in Spain and Africa and on the western and eastern fronts of Europe. They had fought too for the right to gain Allied support in the liberation of their homeland. Thousands were already anticipating a campaign in Spain, and the guerrilla war there had never really ceased. It was hoped that the new United Nations Organization would throw its weight behind the effort to reestablish the Spanish republic.

THE BRIEF TIME OF EUPHORIA, 1945·1946

Today, when the Sun of Liberty shines.
Today, when the World comes out of the abyss,
It raises songs of Victory to the sky.
Can it be that this World without commiseration
Will not do justice to your epic heroism?
It would be the most unique case in History!

Juan Ceron

THE ILIAD of the Spanish republicans spanned three continents. In their nine-year struggle against dictatorship they had been brutally assaulted in their homeland and deprived of their hard-won freedom. As refugees in France they had been derided, hunted, imprisoned, and forced to labor for two French regimes and the Nazi occupier. They had experienced suffering, maltreatment, humiliation, martyrdom, and death. Finally, they had reasserted their enmity to dictatorship through their participation in the Resistance and liberation. The defeat of Hitler and Mussolini meant survival for those Spaniards who had not died on the battlefields of Europe or Africa, been executed by the Gestapo or the Vichy Milice, or perished in German concentration camps. The Spanish republicans had paid a heavy price for their antifascism. Their long struggle had, as Murillo de la Cruz said, made them the most battle-hardened soldiers in the Allied armed forces. Gabriel Jackson wrote of their conduct in the civil war: "The majority fought to preserve Spain, and Europe, from tyranny. They were conquered, but they were not humiliated in their souls."[1] The same could be said for those Spaniards who had escaped to France and continued the struggle during World War II.

For them the struggle against Germany had been indivisible from the necessity to unseat the nationalist government in Spain and reinstate the republic. As partners in the common conflict they hoped and expected that the Allies would finally recognize the justice of their claims and their considerable role in the liberation, and that Allied power would be unleashed on behalf of the Spanish republic. Francisco Franco, announced enemy of democracy and the last remaining fascist dictator in Europe, would be swept into oblivion to join his discredited friends.

After the liberation of France and the end of the war in Europe, the golden moment for the restoration of the republic seemed to be both inevitable and imminent. The exiles basked in what has variously been called "The Age of Euphoria" and "The Age of Hope."[2] Certainly, in 1945 and 1946 this attitude received powerful encouragement. The German and Italian war machines were destroyed. The new Charter of the United Nations provided no place for the likes of the Spanish nationalist government. At the Potsdam meeting in July 1945, leaders of the Big Three had castigated Franco's regime. Out of the common struggle for liberation had come a new comradeship with France and therefore the expectation of solid support. The victory of the British Labor Party in the July 1945 election offered the certainty of influential advocacy of the republican cause. In the United States and the Soviet Union, sentiment appeared firm for the restoration of democracy in Spain. In Spain itself, the Allied military victory seemed to deepen already serious political and economic difficulties. The world knew that the Western powers could, with the flick of a finger, topple the Spanish dictator. The Spanish republicans waited impatiently for the signal to be given.

Spanish consciousness was reasserted in an upsurge of political and cultural life. Emerging from secrecy, the exiled political parties and the anarchist movement began to reconstitute their organizations with a vitality fueled by the promise of the moment. The newspaper of the Agrupación Militar saluted its French comrades on Bastille Day, 1945, by demonstrating solidarity with France, "our second country." Drawing a parallel with July 19, 1936, the date of Franco's insurrection in 1936, the paper declared, "We Spanish republican soldiers are confident that this will be the last 19th of July that we pass in exile." *Adelante,* a socialist newspaper, asserted that Franco was "condemned by the world," and that his days were numbered. A cartoon in the same newspaper showed the dictator quaking before a hooded messenger holding an hourglass. Only a few grains of sand remained. The caption said, "Abandoned! The last grain of the clock of my life is running out."[3]

Dr. José Giral y Pereira, who had been appointed premier of the Spanish republican government-in-exile on August 17, 1945, noted that the Spanish republic, which had been the first country to fight fascism, was now "called to represent the last act of the tragedy." In a series of statements after his arrival in Paris on February 8, 1946, he called upon the Spanish refugees to have faith in the United Nations, which had already repudiated the nationalist government. Although he understood their impatience and shared their pain, he urged them to maintain the hope that had sustained them in their unhappiness. In a joint statement with José Aguirre, president of the Basque republic, he declared that the international situation was increasingly favorable and strong historical currents would facilitate the liberation of Spain.[4] Indalecio Prieto, one-time minister of war and leader of a powerful socialist faction, declared his certainty of Franco's fall before the end of 1945 and urged that all necessary plans be prepared for a take-over of the government.[5]

Perhaps the intensity of emotion felt by the republican exiles was best expressed by one who called himself Patria and addressed a letter to "Mother Homeland" in the *Boletín* of the Agrupación Militar, in July 1945:

> The day of your liberation is near!
> During the time of your tribulations it tears my heart to see your suffering and illness, that your existence is seriously menaced. But your sons, your true sons, hear your entreaty and have sworn to revenge you. It is a Law, a sacred, indestructible Law, to continue loving you as always, freely, passionately. And to fight until victory or death to save you, because our conscience demands it, our honor, our destiny, our rights, our duties, our dignity and responsibility and, in the end, all our strength.
> Yes, Mother Homeland . . . soon we shall be able to offer you . . . PEACE, JUSTICE, AND LIBERTY.[6]

The apogee of euphoria was reached with the victory of the British Labor Party in the July 1945 election. The Spanish socialists in particular saw the triumph not only as a crushing defeat for nationalist Spain, but on a par with the French Revolution as the greatest event in history. Rodolfo Llopis, secretary general of the Spanish Socialist Workers Party (Partido Socialista Obrero de España), declared his full confidence in the government of Clement R. Attlee to fulfill its campaign promise to resolve the Spanish question as soon as possible. The splendid innocence of the Spanish republicans was never more in evidence than in this instance. Great Britain had, in their eyes, betrayed the republic during the civil war of 1936–1939 with its policy of nonintervention. A government led by the Conservative Winston Churchill would be pro-Franco, but a brother socialist party would serve as a strong right arm to smite the enemy and restore democracy to Spain. The visage of Ernest Bevin, the new British foreign minister, smiled out at his Spanish comrades from the front page of *Adelante,* giving little hint in August 1945 that his policy would parallel Churchill's in almost

every respect and that he would lead the republicans into fruitless negotiations with the Spanish monarchists and conservative republicans.[7]

Despite the optimism voiced by nearly all sections of the refugees,
there were those who were less confident of the intentions of the Great
Powers. The anarchist groups in particular were wary of the ultimate
outcome, and as time wore on without decisive commitment and action there was more and more talk of taking the initative and carrying
the fight to Franco by means of guerrilla action.

As early as April 1945, while the war was still in progress, the Confederación Nacional del Trabajo asserted that the Allies did not seem
to wish to precipitate the fall of Franco. The policy seemed to be one
of moral condemnation of the Franco regime, but without any action
to bring about a restoration of the republic.[8] *Ruta,* organ of the anarchist youth federation (Federación Ibérica de Juventudes Libertarias),
denounced the "passivity" of the democracies. It asserted that their wartime promises to eliminate all vestiges of fascism and assure popular
liberties had not been honored. The conscience of the world could not
continue sleeping while terror reigned in Spain.[9] The Agrupación Militar, in June 1945, complained that the Spanish problem appeared to
have passed to "a secondary plane" of importance in the world, except
among the French. The Allies had forgotten "that there still exists a
ramification of the cancerous tumor of fascism and its immediate ex-
tirpation is indispensable."[10] By November 1945 even the usually optimistic *Adelante* was dismayed because "against all reason and all
logic," fascism remained alive in Spain. It asked the democracies to
choose between the republic and Franco.[11] The pessimistic strain in
Spanish republican attitudes found expression in a poem by Juan
Ceron:

> How many times has it been said that in life
> All is a lie and the truth does not exist?

He recalled the ordeal of the Spanish people, who had suffered the
first wound in the struggle against fascism, and railed at the lack of
action to unseat Franco. He cried out in just anger:

> No, do not speak to me of democracy.
> To live in this world is shameful:
> Justice? Liberty? All is a lie![12]

This latent fear of Allied intentions opened another avenue for reclaiming the Spanish homeland. Premier Giral, in February 1946, declared that if diplomacy failed to dislodge Franco another civil war
might arise. An *Adelante* editorial, ushering in the new year of 1946,

said that although hope still existed, the republicans must also be prepared to "exercise our muscles" if it became necessary to enter Spain by
"the road of action." The theme was reinforced by the Agrupación
Militar, which inveighed against the "cerebral myopia" of the Allies
and warned of the possibility of returning to armed struggle against
fascism, with even more tragic repercussions than the war of 1936–
1939.[13]

That detestation of the nationalist government was unanimous
among the Great Powers was incontestable. But even in 1945 it was
apparent that serious differences existed among them concerning the
manner in which it should be removed and what kind of government
would be substituted. The question of when the change should be made
was vital to the Spanish republicans, but appeared of little moment to
the Allied governments.

French attitudes toward the Spanish republicans had undergone a
profound change during the war. Thousands of Spanish exiles had
fought in the Resistance and liberation, and their heoic actions had
earned a new respect and admiration for their fighting prowess and
human qualities. It could justly be said that relations between the
French and the Spanish republicans had changed for the better. For
the Spaniards the ordeal of the humiliating reception and treatment they
had received in the French concentration camps in the winter and spring
of 1939 had been largely forgiven if not forgotten. They had made
common cause with the French people against the Vichy government
and the German occupation, and they had come to regard France with
great sympathy and affection. For its part, the Free French government
had recognized the participation of the Spaniards in the war effort and
had awarded many benefits to soldiers, Maquis, and deportees. "Because of your sufferings, you are a French and Spanish hero," General
Charles de Gaulle told a Spanish Maquis as he decorated him. Pierre
Bertaux, commissaire for the republic at Toulouse, noted that many
Spaniards were among the survivors who were returning from German
camps in the spring of 1945. He noted that the Spaniards had been
particularly affected by their experiences and ordered that special measures be taken to facilitate their return and adjustment.[14]

The French government displayed the most aggressive attitude toward
Franco's Spain among the Western powers. General de Gaulle told the
Consultative Assembly of his desire to see Spain embark on the road to
democracy. *Combat,* a Resistance newspaper, declared that as long as
Franco remained in power it could not be said that "liberty and human
dignity have been reestablished." Vincent Auriol, the then president of
the French National Assembly, addressing a congress of the Spanish

Socialist Workers Party in Toulouse, declared that "my presence here
. . . is equivalent to recognition of the Spanish republic." Félix Gouin,
who in May 1945 was president of the French Consultative Assembly,
acknowledged the error of the policy of nonintervention and called for
the proclamation of "the undoubted right of the republic to reinstall
itself in Spain." *L'Aube,* a Catholic newspaper sympathetic to the
Mouvement Républicain Populaire (MRP), compared the situation of
Premier Giral with that of General de Gaulle during the war years—
both represented the popular will. The Spanish republican government,
it added, was the legal government of Spain. Several socialist leaders declared that if an insurrection erupted in Spain the Allies should provide
assistance. Lieutenant Colonel Aubert, commandant of the French
Forces of the Interior in the department of L'Ariège, wrote that it would
never be forgotten that the capital of the department was liberated by
Spaniards. He assured the Spanish people that their French comrades
would fight at their side for the liberation of Spain.[15]

The British attitude toward the Spanish question was more ambiguous than the French. It did not forgo official condemnation of the
Franco regime, but the search for a solution involved something less
than direct confrontation with the Spanish nationalists. The shift to Labor power in England, which had aroused such great expectations
among the Spanish republicans, resulted finally in a policy that was an
almost exact copy of the Churchill approach. The supple uses of diplomacy by the British led them to a flirtation with the Spanish monarchists looking for restoration of the Bourbon monarchy in Spain, and
then to a delaying action in the United Nations against a forthright
declaration and action to oust the dictator.

Churchill, on May 24, 1944, less than two weeks before the cross-
channel invasion, astounded and confused public opinion when he
praised Spanish neutrality as an aid to the Allied cause. He felt no sympathy for those who, as he put it, wished "to injure the Spanish government." And he sounded the keynote of British policy when he declared
that "the internal political problems of Spain concern only the Spaniards. We must not interfere in those matters." In January 1945 he re-
versed himself partially in a letter to Franco, taxing the Caudillo with
following "a policy not of neutrality, but of non-belligerence." But he
never renounced his insistence that the ultimate fate of Spain was an
internal matter.[16] Although it was widely expected that the new Labor
government would adopt a stiffer attitude toward Franco, the first policy statement made by Foreign Secretary Bevin in August 1945 demonstrated a startling similarity to that of the previous government. Mr.
Bevin declared that England would not intervene in Spain or "permit or

encourage civil war in that country." He also refused a suggestion by the House of Commons that Great Britain break relations with Franco. Sir Anthony Eden, the previous foreign secretary found nothing to criticize in Bevin's program and added that he and Mr. Bevin had never disagreed about foreign policy during their four years together in the wartime coalition cabinet.[17] Responding to a French note proposing that the Spanish case be brought before the United Nations Security Council, the British demurred. They replied that the Spanish regime did not pose a real threat to international security and that Spanish affairs belonged exclusively to the Spanish people. Britain repudiated the idea of immersing itself in the domestic politics of a foreign country and doubted the efficacy of economic sanctions leading to a change in Spain.[19] The *New York Times* had earlier interpreted a British refusal to permit Juan Negrín, premier of the Spanish Republic, to use its overseas broadcast facilities to address a rally in the United States as indicative of British indecision and disinclination to be implicated in the overthrow of Franco.[19]

There were those in England who disputed the official policy and fought to change it. Harold J. Laski, chairman of the Labor Party's National Executive Committee, declared on August 12, 1945, at the French Socialist Party Congress, that the Spanish republicans would return home "in a few months, if not weeks." He asserted that "the British Government will keep its promises made during the election campaign regarding aid for the Spanish Republicans." His remarks prompted a stormy debate in Parliament, where he was repudiated by Prime Minister Attlee and Viscount Addison, Labor leader of the House of Lords, who said Laski was speaking only for himself. Foreign Secretary Bevin reiterated his stand for nonintervention in domestic Spanish affairs.[20] Attlee's statement was in direct contradiction to the message he had conveyed in June 1945 to the Junta Espanola de la Liberación at the organizing conference of the United Nations in San Francisco. Referring to fears that a Mexican resolution barring Francoist Spain from membership in the organization might be defeated, he urged the republicans not to worry if this should happen. "Labor will win the [July] election," he declared, "and will break relations with Franco. We shall give you great support with the other nations."[21]

Support for the republican cause was forthcoming from many sources in the British Isles, ranging from Britons who had fought with the Spanish exiles to left-wing elements within the labor movement. Cristobal García García, a former Spanish republican infantry lieutenant who had later fought with the French army, wrote of his conversation with a British colonel. "I know very well the truth of your tragedy," the

Colonel said. "It is a debt, an obligation, for my country to help you throw out the tyranny which has been imposed on your country." In Parliament, 105 members of all parties expressed their confidence in the Spanish republican government-in-exile and asked their own government to do all in its power to secure United Nations aid in helping the Spanish people to recover their liberty. The executive committee of the British Communist Party demanded the rupture of diplomatic relations and cessation of all trade with the Franco government. The support given by the British government in continuing these activities constituted "an intervention in favor of Franco against the Spanish people," it declared. The *Daily Worker,* the British communist newspaper, reported that English trade with Spain had increased markedly in February 1946, particularly in chemicals, motor vehicles, iron and steel, and electrical equipment. The *Tribune* decried "the declarations and fulminations" that obscured the need for an honest decision on the Spanish question. Francis Noel-Baker, Labor member of Parliament, addressing a congress of the Spanish Socialist Workers Party, said that the Spanish situation was complicated but that his government was working toward an early solution. He hoped that the next Socialist congress would take place in Madrid. The arrival of a new Spanish ambassador in London provoked angry claims that Great Britain was supporting the Franco dictatorship, but Bevin countered that it was well known that "we not only detest the man but we also detest the regime." However, he added, it was necessary to maintain some sort of contact with Spain.[22] His dislike for the nationalist regime likewise did not prevent him from speaking out against a proposed blockade of Spain when it was discussed by the British cabinet. He felt that without the active participation of the United States it could not succeed, and he feared Spanish reprisals on the economic front that would damage Britain's recovery efforts. His refusal to intervene in the internal affairs of another country was apparently not a rigid article of faith with the foreign secretary, because he told the cabinet that Britain could not overlook the internal suppression of rights in the communist countries. He proposed to continue his intervention through constant criticism.[23]

Initiation of an economic blockade and the rupture of diplomatic relations would almost certainly have toppled the Franco regime. The underlying reason why Britain and the United States were hesitant to undertake these measures may have been, as R. Badiou, mayor of Toulouse, believed, that they feared the restoration of the Spanish republic because it would almost certainly have led to a social revolution in Spain.[24]

Ernest Bevin, moderate trade unionist and long-time detractor of the

Soviet Union, assuredly shared Churchill's view that communism would rush in to fill the vacuum created in many countries, including Spain if the Franco regime were displaced. The American attitude in the period immediately following the cessation of hostilities showed very little trace of this attitude. President Franklin D. Roosevelt, in March 1945, a month before his death, declared that Franco's government "justly inspires mistrust." President Harry S. Truman expressed a willingness at the Potsdam meeting of the Big Three to consider Stalin's request for action against the Spanish dictator.[25] The State Department released a series of documents demonstrating Franco's close collaboration with Hitler and appeared ready to advocate a strong move to unseat him. However, the department appeared uncertain as to the proper course to follow, short of actual intervention by force. The Spanish regime, along with that of Argentina, was labeled a "bush-league Axis" by senators Joseph R. Ball of Minnesota and Warren D. Magnuson of Washington. Both legislators demanded action to eliminate these regimes, but a House resolution calling for a break in relations failed to pass. The United States was urged by Harry Hopkins, confidential advisor to presidents Roosevelt and Truman, to use its diplomatic power to derail the nationalist government of Spain.[26]

The aspirations of the Spanish republican exiles and their postwar plight in France and other countries excited the generous sympathies of a large number of Americans. A number of organizations were formed to foster the Spanish Republican cause and to influence American governmental action in their favor. The *New York Times* took the unusual step of publishing an editorial urging support for the fund-raising efforts of the Joint Anti-Fascist Refugee Committee, a group that was later cited as subversive by the House of Representatives and tried for contempt because it refused to produce its records. The editorial called the exiles "people without a country" and cited their wartime service in the Allied armies and their role in liberating many French towns. The executive council of the American Federation of Labor urged recognition of the Spanish republicans as the legitimate government of Spain.[27]

The call for forceful diplomatic action through the rupture of relations with the Spanish nationalists was not, however, heeded by the United States government. The French desire to introduce such a proposal into the United Nations Security Council was rejected by the Americans and the British. In turn, they pressured the French to participate in a note that fell far short of the French proposal for rupture of diplomatic relations and placed the responsibility for change directly upon the shoulders of the Spanish people themselves. This action and other manifestations of hesitation produced the first signs among the

Spanish exiles that the Age of Euphoria was coming to an end. *Adelante* said that the British-American actions signified a return to the disastrous nonintervention policy and pointed out that while the American people was solidly against Franco the government continued to sell war materials to Spain, including airplanes.[28]

The Soviet Union, along with France, demonstrated not only hatred for Franco but the will to take aggressive action to precipitate his downfall. But this forthright Russian attitude was overshadowed by the swiftly developing Cold War and encouraged the United States and Great Britain to proceed with caution. From the beginning, they attempted to isolate the Soviets from discussions concerning policy toward Franco's Spain and to reach consensus among the three great democracies. There is no doubt that fear of a communist victory in post-Franco Spain motivated these moves.

At Potsdam, Stalin introduced the Spanish question with the recollection that the Franco government had been imposed on the Spanish people by the Axis powers and was still giving shelter to German and Italian fascists. "This regime should be changed," he declared. "It harbors great danger to the United Nations." President Truman responded with a statement that "I hold no brief for France. We shall give the matter further study," but Churchill quickly put the brakes on Truman's inclination to agree with the Russian Generalissimo.[29] Later, when the French position conformed more nearly with that of the other democracies, the Soviet Union continued to be the chief supporter of moves within the United Nations to put an end to Franco's regime.

Pravda, the Russian newspaper, editorially approved the resolution passed by the French Consultative Assembly in January 1946 that called for rupture of relations with nationalist Spain. It said that the question of international sanctions against France was ripe for discussion, but warned that serious study of the problem could only be made with the participation of all the Great Powers. Another article hinted that the Soviets would like to join the three democracies in their ongoing talks on relations with the Franco regime.[30] In March 1946 the tripartite note calling for Spanish self-determination was promulgated; this was seen as a U.S.-Britain move to forestall increasing pressure from Moscow and Paris for more drastic steps.[31] Russian Foreign Minister Vyacheslav Molotov, in an interview with Spanish Republican Premier Giral, gave assurances that the Soviet Union continued to consider Franco a war criminal, would not establish relations with his government, and would stand staunchly with the republicans in their efforts to return triumphantly to their homeland. An article published in the bulletin of the Soviet embassy of Mexico gave urgency to the Spanish problem with a declaration that the Spanish people knew very well that return to Spain was a matter of "now or never."[32]

Recognition of the danger involved in the increasing tensions between the Soviet Union and the Western powers prompted many partisans of the Spanish republican cause, particularly the French and Spanish communists, to cry alarm and to call for the continued maintenance of unity. Speaking at a meeting of the Spanish Communist Party in Toulouse, December 1946, Dolores Ibarruri, La Pasionaria of civil war fame, warned that the reconquest of Spain could only be guaranteed through a common approach by the victors of World War II. "If the unity among the great powers should be broken," she asserted, "it would be a true catastrophe for republican Spain." Jacques Duclos, a French communist leader, called for pressure by working-class groups on the American and British governments to bring about a common rupture of relations. There is no doubt that by the spring of 1946 the republicans began to see the developing diplomatic situation as a replay of the tragic nonintervention policy of 1936, and that meant betrayal of their aspirations. In 1961, Fernando Valera, then a minister in the republican government-in-exile and later to be its premier, asked the central question of why the democracies had, from the exiles' point of view, betrayed the Spanish republicans after World War II. Overwhelming fear of Russia, he declared, was the primary reason. The Allies committed the blunder of believing that to confront the hypothetical aggression of communism, all the possible allies, including Franco's Spain, were necessary and valuable. The consequence of this policy, he added, was the death of the hopes of the Spanish people.[23]

If fear of communism increasingly dominated the thinking of the Western democracies, not the least of their bogies was the possibility—strong in their minds—of a communist triumph in a reborn republican Spain. The leaders of the democratic nations lacked confidence in the ability of the Spanish republican government-in-exile to blunt the communist drive for power. The image that persisted of Spanish democratic politics was one of factionialism and weakness, qualities that were not conducive to building a stable government that could contain the inevitable communist thrust. It is important to note that the democracies were desirous of seeing parties of the republican right, as well as the monarchist and Catholic groups, included in a broad-based coalition. Thus, although the democratic powers gave respectful attention to the representations made by government-in-exile leaders, they did not respect their authority and never permitted them to play a significant role in determining international policy toward the nationalists. Hugh Thomas dismissed them with the comment that "the republican leaders passed their years of exile quarreling over their phantom power, and over the financial assets remaining to them." Republican sentiment was still very strong both inside and outside of Spain, but, as C. L. Sulzberger of the *New York Times* wrote, seeking to put his finger on the source of the Spanish political malady: "The trouble is that, as is unfortunately usual in Spanish history, violent individualist, separatist, tribal and generally centrifugal forces which are apparently traditional to the proud Spanish character, have tended to dissipate the energies which otherwise might have broadly combined in an over-all republican movement." He acknowledged that the republican elements had been trying desperately to resolve their differences, but estimated that despite their numerical inferiority the right wing and monarchist elements within the opposition were stronger organizationally than the leftist groups. Under these circumstances, it was virtually impossible for the Spanish republicans to heed the injunction of the Western powers to build a broad national coalition that could act as an interim government in the event of Franco's political demise. The joint American-British-French note issued on March 4, 1946, in addition to representing a defeat for France and the virtual abandonment of a policy of direct confrontation with Franco, was seen as a bid to the Spanish republicans to end their frictions and cooperate in the construction of the broadest possible political base.[34]

The stamp of disunity and ineffectuality thus placed upon the successive Spanish republican governments-in-exile was bitterly refuted by the refugees. Fernando Valera said that these Western prejudices too often served as a pretext for not taking decisive action against Franco. By the "fatal law of exile" the Spaniards were dispersed, but not divided, he asserted. Each time that circumstances had demanded unity it had been achieved, he said, and pointed to the broadly representative nature of the republican governments-in-exile. In the immediate postwar years, he added, they had included a wide range of Spanish political ideologies, from the Right to the Left. Valera argued that the real reason for the failure to oust Franco was Spain's peculiar geographical position, which made it a pawn in the Cold War.[35]

Although the government-in-exile may have been weak and riddled by faction, it is quite unfair to lay the failure to unseat Franco entirely at its door. A measure of national coalition was achieved, although it never met the Allied desires for solid inclusion of the center-right opposition groups. Composed in 1945 of a coalition of socialists, moderate republicans and anarchists, the cabinet of Premier Giral was later broadened to include communists, a move that met with opposition from the socialists and certainly alienated the Western democracies.

Over the years, however, it gradually became a government of the republican parties. The communists never held more than one or two portfolios. Although men of great individual ability and stature were prominent in the various governments, their intensely personal leadership served to further the process of factionalization. Their parties were either tiny (as were the republican parties), or struggling to overcome the effects of intraparty politics (as were the socialists and anarchists). Without the financial support of the Great Powers the exiles were unable to conduct their affairs on the scale that the situation demanded.

It is clear that Great Britain mistrusted the government-in-exile and sought to further the claims of Don Juan Borbón, son of the deposed Alfonso XIII, for restoration to the throne of Spain. The presence of communists in a government of national coalition was not welcomed by either the United States or Britain. But the conclusion of Valera and others that republican Spain was entirely a victim of global politics in postwar Europe as well as in the civil war period has been challenged. It cannot be denied that European political pressures and needs influenced the course of events, José Borras said, but the Spanish republican governments were not simple marionettes manipulated by foreign hands. They cannot escape responsibility for their failure to eliminate "a castrating exclusivism" that prevented the development of a stable and respected government-in-exile. Because they were unable to renounce partisanism in the conduct of their internal politics, the Spanish republicans in exile were unable to achieve that concert of will and effort that was vital if they were to work in tandem with the Allied powers toward the derailment of Franco's dictatorship.[36]

Many Spanish guerrillas fighting in Spain also regarded the republican government-in-exile with contempt. In 1948, a writer for *Ruta* interviewed several members of a guerrilla band in Asturias. They were disdainful of the achievements of the politicians, calling them "boys on a man's errand," and "panderers." In response to a statement about the difficulties of creating union among the numerous Spanish republican parties, a guerrilla replied: "Union? Here we have had it from the first day we reached this mountain. Look, we have here many socialists and anarchists. We have been together for six years and there is nobody who speaks ill of anyone else. Here we all fight against the regime. Union? I believe in it, but with arms in hand, face to face with our enemies." One year later an editorial in the same newspaper condemned the lack of activity by the government-in-exile and said that the frantic efforts of the immediate postwar years had given way to the silence of desolation. It declared that the "gentlemen" members of the government were passing their time frivolously. If they really wished to favor the just aspirations of the Spanish people they would simply disappear.[37] Both sides of the question were illuminated by Albert Camus, writing in *Combat* in December 1944. On the day that all the allies recognized the sole legitimacy of the Spanish republican government, he said, all doubt and uneasiness would disappear and the liberation of Spain would be accomplished. But the Spaniards must help in the process, he added, by giving substance to their legal government-in-exile.[38]

In 1945–46, the period of greatest hope for a return to Spain, there was in fact a government of the Spanish republic, first in the form of a permanent committee of the Cortes, the Spanish parliament, followed by the constitution of a formal governmental structure. The leaders of this government were active in presenting their case to the powers comprising the newly formed United Nations, but tangible results were far from noteworthy. Enthusiastic receptions, testimonials to the rectitude of the republican cause, and opportunities for meeting with top officials of the Allied governments existed in plenitude, but commitments to aggressive action or recognition of the legality of the government-in-exile were not forthcoming, except in a few cases. The Spanish republican claim to belligerent status in the war was ignored. An invitation to the San Francisco organizing meeting of the United Nations was not extended. In short, the respect and attention that were tendered to the exile governments of Norway and Czechoslovakia, for example, were denied the Spanish republicans. How much of all this was due to the weakness of the Spanish republican leadership is open to question. Certainly, the Spanish exiles lacked a figure of commanding force, a General de Gaulle. Just as certainly, the divisions within the Spanish republican government permitted the big powers to claim that it did not represent the broadest spectrum of Spanish political life. Ernest Bevin, for example, was able to exploit the bitterness between the Spanish socialist rivals, Premier Juan Negrín (who resigned in August 1945) and Indalecio Prieto, former minister of war, to involve the latter in ill-fated and procrastinating negotiations with Don Juan. The Spanish exiles, therefore, remained outsiders—supplicants—and therefore vulnerable to the destructive conflicts of big-power interests. The overriding fact remains, however, that in 1945 and even into 1946, Great Power unanimity on the question of Spain would have encouraged, not ignored, any Republican government-in-exile. If the Great Powers had been determined to destroy Franco, they could have displaced him with Allied power and helped a new republican Spain to restore its democratic institutions. That the Great Powers did not achieve this unity was a reflection of their own fears of the consequences of republican restoration, as well as the early development of East-West tensions.

As previously noted, the communists, socialists, and anarchists had managed to reconstitute their organizations clandestinely during the period of occupation and Resistance in France. However, it was in Mexico, where many political leaders had taken shelter, that the roots of the Spanish government-in-exile were to be found. In mid-1942 a group of republican and regional autonomist parties formed an inter-party committee that affirmed the latent desire of the exiles to establish political unity. The group lacked substance, however, because the socialists felt that the moment was inopportune for such activity and the communists became involved with their own organization, the Junta Suprema de la Unión Nacional. In October 1943, a meeting sponsored by the Union of Spanish Emigrant Professors produced the Declaration of Havana, which provided a basis for broader political activity.

The Declaration of Havana announced the belligerent status of the Spanish republicans in the struggle against fascism and asserted that under the terms of the Atlantic Charter the Spanish republic had the indisputable right to recover its sovereign power in Spain. It called for the formation of a political organization in exile that would co-operate with the Allies, liberate Spain, and prepare for a return to power there. The document invoked the moral and physical support of the United Nations in these tasks. A month later the socialists and their trade union arm, the Unión General de Trabajadores, joined in the signing of a unity pact with the bourgeois parties. The communists did not participate, but the anarchist Confederación Nacional del Trabajo subscribed to the provisions of the pact. Each participating party retained the liberty to advance its viewpoints in discussions, but agreed to respect the principles of the pact. It was considered significant that the agreement relied on the strength of parties rather than on political, military, or intellectual personalities. Affirmation of the principle of autonomy for the Catalan and Basque regions also broadened the base of the pact.

After ratification by the participating parties on November 25, 1943, the Junta Española de la Liberación came into existence. Diego Martínez-Barrio, the last president of the Cortes in 1939 and leader of the small Unión Republicana party, was named president, and Indalecio Prieto became secretary. For the first time, then, the Spanish republic possessed an instrument of fairly broad representation, one that could speak in the name of the exiles. The program of the Junta was an activist application of the principles enunciated by the Declaration of Havana, and it drew support from committees in Latin America and the United States. Perhaps its greatest service to the cause was its invocation of the Atlantic Charter, which had promised that all governments deprived of liberty by force should be restored. It coupled the destruction of Nazism and fascism with that of Falangism in Spain and exerted moral pressure upon the great democracies to demonstrate fidelity to the principles they themselves had formulated.[39]

In 1942 there was also activity on the part of the permanent committee of the Cortes, which represented a thin lifeline to the last meeting of the full parliament, February 1, 1939, at Figueras, Spain. Poised for flight into exile before the arrival of the nationalist troops, the Cortes had provided for a committee of twenty-one members to maintain legislative continuity and to call new elections when such a step became feasible. Meeting at Mexico City, July 27, 1942, the committee, known as the Diputación, passed a resolution addressed to the United Nations and "the conscience of the world." It condemned the formation of a Cortes by the Franco government as illegal and asserted its own sovereignty. The enthusiasm that greeted this affirmation of republican legality created a demand for a meeting of the full Cortes, which would name a government to represent the Spanish republic at the organizing meeting of the United Nations in San Francisco.[40]

Such a meeting, however, proved to be difficult to arrange. It was not until January 1945 that the body finally met, not until August that a government was finally organized, and not until November that a cabinet was finally formed. The continuing rivalry between Dr. Juan Negrín and Indalecio Prieto had grown acrimonious and entirely personal in nature. Although both were socialists, Negrín had drawn the support of the left wing of his party, some republican party elements, and the communists. Prieto was influential in the moderate wing of the Socialist Party and also had the adherence of a number of republican party leaders. Negrín was subjected to constant criticism, both for his conduct of affairs during the last months of the civil war and for the quality of his leadership after the defeat.

Prieto, the secretary of the Junta, was strongly opposed to the convening of the Cortes, feeling that it would reinforce Negrín's position and that the duality of organizations would be prejudicial to the cause of the republic. Nevertheless, Martínez-Barrio persisted and the meeting was finally scheduled for January 10, 1945, in Mexico City. Of the 470 constitutional members of the Cortes, only 76 attended. One hundred and twenty-seven deputies had died in the interim, and forty-nine were living in other countries. The boycott of the meeting by the communist and Catalan Deputies makes it difficult to know how many of them were still alive. Parliamentary wrangles, initiated by Prieto, effectively killed the possibility of action that, it was hoped, would resurrect the Spanish republican government. He claimed that a legal quorum of the Cortes did not exist, that absentee votes were invalid, and that the socialists, therefore, would not take part in the discussions. Despite Martínez-Barrio's response that Article 63 of the 1931 republican constitution gave the Cortes power of deliberation even in the absence of a quorum, the members voted for suspension of the session. A date for reconvening of the Cortes was left open.[41]

The embattled Negrín, who had thought to profit from the meeting of the Cortes, came to Mexico in July 1945 to report on his activities and to press for a meeting of the legislature. Before a large public gathering, he declared that it would be a mistake to change the composition of the government-in-exile because such a move would increase the danger of crises and water down the power of the executive. Moreover, a new administration would not have the authority of the government chosen freely during the civil war. Instead, he called for the formation of a true national coalition government, and he admitted the necessity of a vote of confidence in his administration. He offered to resign in the interests of unity if such a vote were not forthcoming. He criticized the tendency toward government by junta or committee and declared that such extralegal bodies could not provide the conviction that a stable republican regime was in existence. The socialists claimed that Negrín was usurping the functions of the Cortes and called instead for a session of that body, given the prior assurance that Martínez-Barrio would consent to serve as president of the group. The Cortes finally met on August 17, 1945, with ninety-six deputies present. Negrín delivered his government's resignation to President Martínez-Barrio. The deputies considered the candidacies of Negrín and Dr. José Giral y Pereira and chose the latter by a large majority.[42]

Giral immediately encountered political difficulties and entanglements. He offered a vice-presidency to Negrín, who refused, claiming irreconcilable policy differences. The communists also refused to enter the government, because they would work only with a Negrín government. Prieto also declined a cabinet post and alarmed the Cortes with a statement that if the masses in Spain "spoke differently" his wing of the Socialist Party would follow them, although later he cast an affirmative ballot in a vote of confidence for the Giral government. José Tarradellas, a Catalan leader, was also offered a portfolio and refused it. The government, as it finally emerged, had a distinctly bourgeois stamp, despite the small number of members claimed by the republican parties. The Izquierda Repúblicana (Left Republican Party) had three seats. Unión Repúblicana, the moderate center party of Martínez-Barrio, had one seat. Two other Catalan autonomist, moderate parties had a single seat each—Esquerra Repúblicana de Cataluña and Accion Repúblicana Catalana. The Partido Nacionalista Vasco (Basque Nationalist Party) also had one seat. The Unión General de Trabajadores (the socialist trade union federation) occupied one post, and the Confederación Nacional del Trabajo accepted two positions.

By November 1945, therefore, the Spanish republican government-in-exile was in place and ready to attack its major problem: convincing the Allies to oust Franco and restore it to power in Spain. The Junta dissolved itself on August 31 despite Prieto's objections, and the Mexican government transferred an unknown amount of Spanish funds to the new government. On November 7, 1945, the Cortes met to ratify the new administration and to hear their premier present a policy of "justice without vengeance." He asked: "How and when shall we return to Spain? We shall try with all our strength to persuade those who direct international life that a pacific and legal solution depends principally on them. [We shall] convince them to abandon this second phase of nonintervention and to implement the Potsdam Declaration," which barred Francoist Spain from membership in the United Nations. He promised free elections after the reconquest of the homeland, freedom of religion, respect for the principle of antonomous regions, and a nonpolitical army. He declared that he would seek recognition of his government as the legitimate representative of Spain. But he warned that violent action might become necessary if a peaceful solution were not found.[43]

By the end of 1945, recognition had been extended to the Spanish exile government by Mexico, Guatemala, Panama, and Venezuela. The list of recognitions was not to grow much longer. The Foreign Affairs Committee of the French Assembly asked its government, in December 1945, to break relations with Madrid. At the first meeting of the United Nations General Assembly in February 1946 a resolution was adopted affirming the San Francisco and Potsdam declarations and recommending that member nations be guided by their provisions in relations with the Franco government. The members of the Spanish republican government-in-exile initiated a furious round of appearances in the capitals of the Allies, where they conferred with officials, addressed parliaments, and sought to arouse public opinion for their cause. It was true, as del Valle remarked, that at the end of 1945 international opinion was very hostile to the Franco regime and increasingly favorable to the exiles, but the Giral government failed in its major objective of fomenting decisive action against the Spanish nationalists. After the rather ambiguous action of the United Nations General Assembly in December 1946, which was to become the high-water mark of the anti-Franco campaign, the Giral government came under increasing attack and was forced to resign in February 1947. Rodolfo Llopis, general secretary of the Socialist Party, replaced Giral.[44]

The Age of Euphoria, 1945–46, was of brief duration. It was a time of deliverance from the Nazis and the Vichyites, a time to exult in the mere fact that one was still alive, a time to savor a rare victory, a time of renewed Spanish consciousness, a time to ride the flood tide of victorious democracy straight through to Barcelona and Madrid. The voices of caution and disbelief found very few listeners. Gradually, however, they were to become stronger as the "Spanish question" was debated, negotiated, and made the object of a tug of war in the struggle of East against West.

Two roads were open to the Spanish republicans in 1945: diplomacy and guerrilla warfare. They were to move down both roads, with disastrous results. They were to be frustrated in their efforts to re-establish the republic through United Nations action. In Spain, they were to fight a guerrilla campaign in an attempt to generate a popular insurrection that never came. The Spanish people, crushed by war and repression, were too tired and too fearful of new bloodshed to rise en masse against Franco.

STALEMATE, REVERSAL, AND FINAL BETRAYAL

In the great democracies the most dazzling speeches are made,
singing the imperishable glories of Liberty. Nevertheless, the
reality contrasts singularly with the rejoicing tone of the songs.
And Franco, Salazar, and Peron . . . are sustained in their criminal
empires by the same ones who proclaim the delights of democracy.

Ruta, June 12, 1946

THE QUEST of the Spanish republicans for reconquest of their homeland passed through three distinct phases in the postwar era. The short-lived time of high expectations and euphoria extended from 1945 into 1946. The chief achievement of this period was passage of a United Nations General Assembly resolution on December 12, 1946, banning Franco's Spain from membership in the United Nations or its specialized organizations and recommending withdrawal of ambassadors from Madrid. The promise of this action, which was seen as limited by some friends of republican Spain, never materialized, and from 1947 to 1949 the international pendulum swung gradually in favor of the retention of Franco in power. The drive of the United States to recruit allies in a potential war against the Soviet Union marked Spain as a prime strategic area in the period 1949–1955. A powerful effort to reverse the resolution of 1946 was finally launched by the Americans and bore fruit in 1952 with the admission of nationalist Spain to the specialized organs of the United Nations. In 1953 a military-economic aid pact was signed between the United States and the Spanish regime. In 1955 Spain was admitted to full membership in the international organization. This final betrayal of Spanish republican aspirations may be fairly attributed to the Cold War requirements of the United States, the increasing ennui and helplessness of those nations that were friendly to the republicans, and the progressive decline in power and effectiveness of the successive Spanish governments-in-exile.

With the flush of victory still in the air in mid-1945, a series of actions and declarations seemed to augur an early success for the Spanish republicans. The organizing meeting of the United Nations in San Francisco in the spring of 1945 was the first public opportunity to present the claims of the republic. Although they were not invited as official participants, the Junta Española de la Liberación and many individual Spanish republican leaders sought to present a convincing case to the assemblage. They lacked sufficient financial resources and were not officially apprised of the names and locations of other national delegates, though they managed to find most of them. In a seventy-page document the Junta noted that although Hitler and Mussolini had been defeated, Franco still remained in power. Spain, it said, should "not remain as a monstrous exception in a world free of the totalitarian tyranny." The Junta appealed to the conscience of the member nations, urged that diplomatic recognition of Franco be withdrawn, and declared that "the moral repudiation of the United Nations would be sufficient for the Spanish tyranny to fall" without the ravages of a new civil war. "We seek the exclusion of Franco, not Spain," declared the Socialist leader Indalecio Prieto, "and we appear in San Francisco representing the authentic [republican] Spain." Premier Negrín and Basque president José Aguirre objected to the organizing committee's exclusion of the Spanish republic, which was based on the grounds that it had been neutral in the war. They asserted that republican Spain had fought Nazism for two and one-half years before 1939 and throughout the Second World War. Recognition of Spanish republican belligerency was also advanced by the republican press, which insisted that it was absurd to compare the Spanish situation with that of any other country. However, despite these activities it was apparent that the Spaniards were not speaking with a single voice. When Aguirre suggested that the Junta delegates have dinner with himself and Negrín as a demonstration of unity, Prieto refused categorically to have any relationship with Negrín.

Speaking to a Mexican proposal to bar nationalist Spain from membership in the new United Nations, the Junta document outlined four steps in the reestablishment of the Spanish republic. Following repudiation of Franco by the delegates at San Francisco, the nations of the victorious alliance would break relations with the dictator. A provisional republican government would then be formed by the Cortes, and the members of the United Nations would recognize the new administration. Not a single delegation spoke against the Mexican resolution, and it passed handily.[1]

Following swiftly upon the conclusion of the San Francisco meeting, the Potsdam Conference of the United States, the Soviet Union, and

Great Britain emerged with what appeared to be still another positive statement regarding the hopes of the Spanish republicans. Equally, however, it was clear that in this opening round of the Great Power struggle for control of Europe and the world, Spain was more of an ideological testing ground than a case of rank injustice that must at all costs be rectified. Joseph Stalin regarded the American attitude toward Franco as "an acid test" of its intentions and he pressed for inclusion of Spain on the agenda. Truman's offhand remark that he held no brief for Franco gave no clear answer to the Soviet leader's inquiry, but the Russian's call for a complete rupture of relations with the Franco regime brought forth the Churchillian concern for self-determination in the Spanish case. "I do not think we should interfere in the internal affairs of a state with whom we differ in views," the British prime minister said. Further, he was afraid that such a step could have the effect of uniting the proud and sensitive Spaniards around Franco. It has been previously noted that Churchill's concern for Spanish democracy was motivated by his belief that in the event Franco fell the communists would be most likely to seize power. Stalin, fearing that he had alarmed the British and the Americans, retreated from his proposal for complete rupture and asked that other, more flexible means be considered, but Churchill countered with the observation that every government was free to make its views known on an individual basis. Truman then modified his stance to bring it more into line with Churchill's policy. He had no desire to participate in a new Spanish civil war, he said. He would be happy to recognize another government instead of the Franco regime, but he thought that was a matter for Spain herself to decide. The question of possible action was referred to the foreign ministers. They agreed on a statement that halted at the brink of direct confrontation with the Franco regime, but declined to invite Spain to join the United Nations. The policy on membership requirements for the United Nations made it clear that an application by Franco would not have been favored because his regime had been founded with the support of the Axis Powers and had in turn been closely associatively with them during the war. Charles Mee called this public position of the Big Three "presentable and meaningless."[2] In fact, although it aroused enthusiasm among the Spanish republicans and their supporters, it left a good deal of room for later maneuver in the matter of how Franco's downfall would be accomplished and exactly what kind of alternative government would be acceptable to the Great Powers.

France, the only nation among the allies with a common border with Spain (excepting Britain and its Gibraltar holding) and still licking the wounds of Nazi occupation and Vichy authoritarianism, was more sensitive to the presence of the Spanish dictator in Madrid. The influence of communists and socialists in the French coalition government almost insured a hostile policy toward Franco, but the Christian Social Mouvement Républicain Populaire was equally unfriendly, insisting that it felt no sympathy for the Franco regime. Moreover, the close ties of the French with Spanish republicans who had fought at their side in the Maquis or in the army created public sympathy for the exiles in their battle to oust the Caudillo. Generally, during 1945 and much of 1946 the policy of the French provisional government toward Spain was closer to that of the Soviet Union than that of Great Britain and the United States.

As early as May 25, 1945, the Foreign Affairs Committee of the French Consultative Assembly urged the Allies to insist upon the immediate abdication of Franco in favor of a democratic coalition. Declaring that appeasement of the nationalist leader was definitely ended, the committee added that, if he did not abdicate, the democratic nations should break relations with Spain. A security zone was set up along the French-Spanish frontier. The French National Assembly passed a near-unanimous resolution on January 15, 1946, praising the French government for suggesting to the British and Americans that diplomatic relations with Franco be broken. Two days later, the Assembly approved a motion calling for rupture of relations. Even at this stage, however, France was apprehensive about unilateral action. Foreign Minister Georges Bidault declared that a final decision depended on an understanding with the Great Powers. In accordance with this limitation on French action, Bidault sent a note to the United States and Great Britain, on December 23, 1945, urging that the Security Council of the United Nations consider a break in relations with Franco and the possibility of recognizing the Spanish republican government-in-exile. The aggressive attitude of France toward the Spanish regime was strengthened when Félix Gouin replaced General de Gaulle as president of the provisional French government in January 1946. A socialist and staunch advocate of the Spanish republican cause, Gouin declared that France would not forget the Spanish exiles. He desired to see Spain become democratic and pledged that the French government would work to destroy the last vestiges of Nazism and fascism. On February 27, 1946, France ordered its Spanish frontier closed as of March 1. It called on the United States and Great Britain to adopt a common approach against Francoist Spain, on the grounds that it was a danger to international security. The French government reiterated that the Spanish issue should be brought before the United Nations.

This stand was taken despite the fears of some French foreign affairs advisors that the Soviet Union and the French Left had pushed France into an intemperate action. The move aroused sympathy in the Western democracies. C. L. Sulzberger, correspondent for the *New York Times,* estimated that as much as seventy percent of the Spanish population opposed Franco, but an editorial in that newspaper characterized as "delicate" the question of what to do about Franco's repressive regime. Armed intervention was unlikely, but the *Times* speculated that internal Spanish opposition, particularly within the army, might succeed in breaking the power of the Spanish dictator.[3]

The French suggestion was rejected by the United States and Britain, but accepted by the Soviet Union. The American government now was firm in its belief that the replacement of the Spanish Caudillo was exclusively the concern of the Spanish people. It hoped sincerely that the change would be made as rapidly as possible, and by pacific means. The British doubted that the Security Council held jurisdiction over the Spanish question. Beyond that, its attitude was based in part on a fear that overt action against the dictator might once again make Spain the cockpit of a battle for and against communism. The political antipathy of the Labor government toward Franco was thus modified by the developing struggle with the Soviet Union.[4]

French willingness to use aggressive tactics to oust Franco was thereby eroded, and the countersuggestion of the United States was accepted reluctantly and resentfully. Foreign Minister Bidault even threatened to take the issue to the Security Council in spite of the American-British stand, but the move came to nought. The tripartite note on Spain was issued on March 4, 1946, and hardened the policy of nonintervention in Spanish affairs. It reiterated the Big Three's belief that a Spain led by Franco could not participate in the United Nations, but it declared that "there is no intention of interfering in the internal affairs of Spain." The three governments voiced their horror at the thought of another civil war in Spain and hoped that the peaceful withdrawal of Franco could be accomplished. In the event of such a development, a representative caretaker government would be established to guarantee free elections. The caretaker government would receive diplomatic recognition and economic aid from the three powers and other freedom-loving peoples.[5]

The resurrection of the nonintervention policy, considered by many to be one of the chief causes of the defeat of the Spanish republic in 1936–1939, aroused bitter protest. Premier José Giral pointed out the impossibility of action within Spain by an oppressed and disarmed people. The most effective means of destroying Franco was still the

rupture of diplomatic relations and the recognition of the Spanish
republican government-in-exile, he said. Rodolfo Llopis, general secretary of the Spanish Socialist Party, called the Big Three policy a "cruel
hypocrisy and a tremendous injustice against the Spanish people," while
Adelante said that Franco was the only one pleased by the note. Sumner
Welles, former under secretary of state for the United States, agreed
with Giral that it was obvious that the Spanish people were in no position to expel Franco. The exclusion of the Soviet Union from the
deliberations leading to the three-power note was contrary to the spirit
of the United Nations, he added. For its part, the Soviet Union called
the tripartite note inadequate because it left Franco in power. The
Russians favored a statement by the Big Four that would recommend
a complete break with the Spanish Nationalist regime.[6]

Not all Spanish and international opinion reflected these beliefs. An
address by U.S. Secretary of State James F. Byrnes gave the impression
that the United States intended to create a new regime by separating
General Franco from his own military leadership. The dissident officers would take power temporarily pending free elections. Such a
move would provide the Spanish republicans with time to resolve their
political differences. Others, who shied from the thought of any military regime, be it Falangist or republican, saw in Byrnes' reference to
the creation of an international force an indication that the United
States and Great Britain would supervise the resulting elections.
Adelante summed up the general evaluation: "something is worth more
than nothing."[7]

Whatever difficulties the tripartite note may have portended, the
Spanish republicans were still largely optimistic about their prospects.
The arrivals in Paris of Premier Giral on February 8 and of President
Martínez-Barrio on March 12 gave tangible evidence that a Spanish
republican government-in-exile existed, and the Spanish refugees in
Paris gave the leaders a rousing welcome. One refugee, shaking Giral's
hand, said, "You are our de Gaulle." On balance, it appeared that
progress was being made. Six countries had recognized the exile government by April 1946, and thirteen had either broken relations with
the nationalist regime or were considering such action.[8] The ominous
fact still remained, however, that neither the United States nor Great
Britain showed any inclination to move in this direction.

Basking in the aura of these first successes and near-triumphs, the
government-in-exile set up shop in a two-room office furnished by the
French government. The nine ministers each had one office worker and
shared several typewriters and other equipment. Giral took up residence in a student room at the Cité Universitaire. A reporter who visited

the office in mid-March 1946 noted animated action in the crowded space. Couriers arrived from Spain, their garments worn and ragged, their faces tired and unshaven. They carried newspapers that had been printed with ancient, hidden equipment, as well as other information that had been requested by the exile government. In a few days they would begin the journey back to Spain, carrying documents and instructions. The newspapers reminded the reporter of French wartime resistance folios, with their messages of hope, faith, and struggle.[9]

If the French were dissuaded from introducing the Spanish issue into the United Nations, the Soviet bloc was under no such inhibition. Poland introduced a resolution in the Security Council on April 17, 1946, under Article 34 of the United Nations Charter, charging that the existence and activities of the Spanish regime had led to international friction and thus endangered peace and security. Invoking Articles 39 and 41, the resolution called upon member nations of the UN to sever diplomatic relations with the Franco government.[10] The resulting Security Council discussion of the question was to furnish an excellent example of how the machinery of the United Nations could be and was used to blunt the major issue. Jurisdictional questions, amendments, subcommittees, subsidiary reports, compromises, all worked finally to ease the problem from the Security Council to the General Assembly, where definitive action would be much more difficult to obtain and less effective than in the Security Council. From the direct thrust of the Polish solution, which would have simply united the community of nations in withdrawing all formal contact from the Spanish dictator and thus making his position untenable, the problem was convoluted and transmuted into a matter for further study, for delicate fence-top walking that sought to determine whether Franco's Spain represented an imminent danger or a latent danger. The reservations that had characterized the British and American attitudes and that found expression in the tripartite note's thesis of Spanish self-determination were thus elevated to United Nations policy and became the touchstone of subsequent actions. Although the universal condemnations of Franco and his regime gave the appearance of a collective desire to eliminate him from the scene, the actions of the British and Americans, followed by their dependent nations, militated against such an eventuality, served to diffuse effort and energy, and eventually brought the movement for republican restoration to a pathetic halt and reversal.

The case presented by the Polish delegate, Dr. Oscar Lange, was on its face a powerful indictment of the fascist origins, structure, and actions of the nationalist regime in Spain. Dr. Lange refreshed the memories of the delegates: "The Franco regime was brought into power against the will of the Spanish people by the armed forces of the Axis powers which have waged war against the United Nations." He recalled the aid given to Germany and Italy during the war, as detailed in a White Book issued by the U.S. State Department, and produced documents showing that Spain was at that moment harboring thousands of Nazi officials, soldiers, and German-owned businesses, as well as fugitive Vichyites. There was tension along the French-Spanish border, he continued, resulting in the closing of the frontier. For all of these reasons, Dr. Lange declared, the Franco regime was not merely an internal Spanish affair but was the concern of all the United Nations. Dr. Lange's contentions were supported by Georges Bonnet of France, who said that the situation endangered international peace and security. As for the fear that collective action might strengthen Franco's hand, the French spokesman was of the opinion that "the Spanish people will bear the Allies no grudge for offering a helping hand."[11] The Soviet delegate, Andrei A. Gromyko, also attacked the notion of nonintervention in the internal affairs of Spain. Intervention was clearly authorized in Article 2 of the charter, he said, when the internal situation of a country constituted a danger to international peace and security. Spain, as a breeding ground of fascism, past and present, represented such a threat. He added that the policy of nonintervention practiced by the League of Nations and applied in the 1936–1939 war in Spain had encouraged German fascism and led to World War II.[12]

The opposition to the Polish resolution presented itself as a force for moderation. The core of the argument seemed to be that everybody hated Francisco Franco, but . . . The "but" in the presentation of Dr. Eelco Nicolaas van Kleffens, delegate of the Netherlands, was that passion must not be allowed to rule the deliberations of the nations. Sentiment was not always a safe guide, he said, and the question must be judged "coolly and dispassionately." He raised the oft-stated fear that action against the Caudillo might actually rally his people behind him and result in a new civil war. The Poles had failed to make a convincing case that the Spanish regime was an international threat. In the absence of such danger, the question of Franco's continuation in power rested solely with the Spanish people. The American delegate, Edward R. Stettinius, reiterated his government's dislike of the Spanish regime and reaffirmed its major policy objectives: that the nationalists be removed from power by the Spanish people themselves and that this be accomplished without bloodshed. Whether or not the Security Council was entitled to act in the absence of a prior finding of a threat to the peace was a question raised by Sir Alexander Cadogan for the United Kingdom. The Polish delegate had not proved, he said, that recent Spanish actions could be described as aggressive. The Franco government had begun to hand over German assets to the Allies and was in process of repatriating German fugitives from Allied justice. Thus, under Article 36, the only recourse of the Security Council was to recommend appropriate procedures or methods of adjustment. There was, he added, no compelling need for collective severance of diplomatic relations.[13]

A third point of view was represented by the Australian delegate, Lieutenant Colonel William Roy Hodgson, who did not accept the interpretation of either side. He proposed the formation of a five-nation subcommittee that would investigate the Polish allegations and report factually to the council. The Poles countered with an amendment to Hodgson's proposal which called for rupture of relations with the Franco regime. The subcommittee report, rendered on April 29, 1946, affirmed that the problem was international in character rather than internal, but that, since no menace to the peace had been established, it was impossible to order coercive measures under Articles 41 and 42 at that time. Nevertheless, the facts unearthed about the Franco regime were so grave that other actions within the purview of the Security Council were indicated. Even if the situation did not constitute a "present menace," it could properly be called a "latent menace." The subcommittee recommended sending the matter to the General Assembly, which could recommend rupture of relations in September 1946 if the Franco regime were still in power then. The British declared their preference for sending the Spanish problem to the assembly with no recommendation at all.

Tortuous and labyrinthine as the discussions had been up to this point, they were to undergo further twists and turns in what seemed to be an orgy of wrangling and petty disagreements. In a surprise move Gromyko vetoed the subcommittee proposal in order to determine, as he said, just how far the member nations were prepared to go in opposing Franco. He received his answer when the motion was defeated on June 24, 1946, at which point Dr. Lange submitted a new resolution calling upon the Security Council to maintain the question on its agenda and to reexamine the situation before September 1. The British and Australian delegates immediately produced a substitute resolution. It differed from the Polish proposal in the extent to which the Franco government was labeled a menace to peace. The Polish resolution called the regime "a serious danger to the maintenance of peace and international security," while the British-Australian one said that the "persistence of the situation in Spain could place peace and international security in danger." Both resolutions would have kept the item on the agenda. Gromyko charged that the Anglo-Australian formulation was "loose, without just appreciation of the gravity of the Spanish situation and the possibilities inherent in the existence of the Franco regime." The British-Austrailan resolution was approved, nine votes to two, but Gromyko declared that his negative vote constituted a veto. Castillo Najera of Mexico, council president, ruled that the issue was procedural rather than substantive and therefore not subject to a veto. Gromyko finally agreed to a compromise formula eliminating those phrases he found objectionable.[14]

The confused and apparently aimless bickering that had characterized the discussion resulted in equally jumbled interpretations of what had really transpired. Spanish republican Premier Giral declared himself dissatisfied with the final resolution, in view of the case that had been made that Franco was a serious danger to the peace, but he added that the importance of the action lay in the fact that the Spanish dictator had been formally condemned by the Security Council. Del Valle later said that the Gromyko vetoes had vitiated the general agreement on ultimate rupture of relations with the Spanish nationalists, while Security Council President Najera felt that in abusing his veto power, the Soviet delegate had given satisfaction to Franco by leaving the problem unresolved. On the other hand, the *New York Times* believed that the Russian's stand for Security Council action was motivated by his fear that the necessary votes for positive action might be lacking in the General Assembly.[15] It may also be fairly inferred that Gromyko was well aware that the powers of the General Assembly were limited to recommendations to member states, whereas the Security Council could order specific actions.

As what was becoming ironically known in Spanish republican circles as the "Spanish case" moved from the Security Council to the meeting of the General Assembly in October 1946, the lines of agreement and disagreement had become somewhat more defined. In general, the Soviet bloc and several Latin American nations emerged as the proponents of swift, decisive action against Franco, while the English-speaking powers and their adherents appeared hesitant to follow their moral condemnation of the Spanish regime to its logical outcome. While the United States and Britain encouraged the Republicans to oust Franco and take control of the country, nevertheless they wanted this accomplished without a renewal of bloody civil war. How Franco was to be induced to surrender power voluntarily was not prescribed beyond vague generalities. The suspicion persisted that what the Americans and British really wanted was the creation of pressure against the Spanish dictator by a combination of monarchist, military, and center-right republicans in Spain, with the tacit support of the Western powers. If such a bloc could be brought into existence, a double objective could be achieved: Franco's departure as well as the consequent control of the country by a politically safe alignment that would merit the support of the United Nations and eliminate the dire possibility of a communist or anarchist surge to power in a post-Franco Spain.

The experience with the Security Council had already disillusioned several important sectors of Spanish republican political life. The prospect of continuing the debate in the General Assembly was dreary and hopeless to the anarchists. "It is useless to believe in the efficacy of diplomacy," *Ruta* said. "The end result will be another exchange of international banalities." It also pointed out that the United States and Britain were interested in securing the Spanish output of tungsten, and this dictated their go-slow policy toward Franco. *Adelante* declared that as time went on the confidence placed in the United Nations was more and more revealed to be unwarranted. A *New York Times* editorial worried about whether the drive of the communist bloc and leftist groups in other countries on behalf of republican Spain would have the end result of dividing the United Nations. And Léon Blum exhorted the working class in England to pressure the Labor government to adopt a stronger anti-Franco position, more in keeping with its ideology and its campaign commitments.[16]

The judicial gyrations that had so aroused the ire of Soviet Ambassador Gromyko in the Security Council were transferred to the arena of the General Assembly in October 1946. The Polish resolution that had been defeated in the council was reintroduced, but this time it faced the opposition of another resolution promulgated by the American delegation. Whereas the Polish motion retained its simple emphasis on the rupture of relations with the Franco regime and the exclusion of it from membership in the United Nations and its specialized organizations, the American proposal stressed action by the Spanish people as the major impetus for change in Spain. Senator Tom Connally agreed with the Poles that the incumbent Spanish regime should be excluded from the United Nations, but he carefully refrained from urging diplomatic isolation of the nationalist government. The crux of his argument was that the Spanish people ought to prove to the world that they could form a government that stemmed from the consent of the governed. Obviously, he did not believe that the Giral government met this definition. He called, either from naivete or calculated cynicism, on Franco to deliver his powers to a provisional government that would install democratic institutions and call free elections. The resulting government, purged of all fascist connections, would reestablish Spanish legitimacy and thus be eligible for membership in the international organization.[37] The message of the United States to General Franco was clear: You are so badly tainted that you have very little chance to survive. If you wish to preserve the traditional cast of Spanish life you will turn over power to conservative elements within and outside of Spain. If not, the deluge of social revolution will not only sweep you away but destroy all that you have tried to accomplish.

A sense of hardening positions and growing antagonism pervaded the assembly discussions. Spanish republican Premier Giral circulated a document which declared that the Spanish people would regard as a deception any failure of the United Nations to put an end to the Franco tyranny. Such a refusal to honor its moral obligations would be equivalent to denying the Spanish republic a peaceful way to change the regime and would force it to use the more violent methods that all nations deplored. Soviet Foreign Minister Vyacheslav Molotov charged that the efforts of "certain great powers" to avoid diplomatic rupture with Franco made them responsible for the continued existence of fascism in Europe. The Soviet ambassador to the United Nations, Andrei Gromyko, charged that the U.S. resolution represented diplomatic obfuscation and was utterly inadequate to remove Franco from power. This was echoed by Zuloaga, the Venezuelan delegate, who decried "platonic declarations" that did not have the practical effect of excluding Franco Spain from the international community. The United Nations had already engaged in too many discussions on the Spanish issue, Léon Jouhaux, the French delegate, said, and the moment had arrived to take a concrete decision. He taunted the United States for believing that General Franco would renounce power voluntarily, and said that it was unimaginable that UN intervention on behalf of the Spanish republic would be interpreted by the Spanish people as an affront to their honor.[18]

Supporting the American resolution, Sir Hartley Shawcross, the British delegate, asserted that rupture of diplomatic relations would not be in the best interests of the Spanish people because it would suppress all possibility of communication and judicious intervention in Spain. He was also opposed to economic sanctions, which would "constitute a brutal interference in world commerce." Moreover, he noted, the form of the Spanish government was exclusively the concern of the Spanish people. And since the Security Council had not clearly indicated that the Spanish question constituted a present menace to peace, there was absolutely no doubt that the problem was one of internal politics. If the Spanish people were truly enthusiastic for democracy and liberty they would forge their own salvation.[19]

The final resolution that emerged from the process of negotiation and accommodation combined important features of the Polish and American proposals, but insofar as it recommended the withdrawal of ambassadors from Madrid it represented a partial victory for those who favored strong action against the Franco regime. It was equally important that, for the first time, the Big Four voted unanimously on a major proposal in the General Assembly. The vote, taken December 12, 1946, was thirty-four in favor and six opposed, with thirteen abstentions. The resolution declared that the origins and nature of the Franco regime made it clear that it did not represent the Spanish people, thus making impossible the participation of Spain in United Nations affairs. If, in a "reasonable" period of time, which, according to the understanding of the Security Council, meant by September 1, 1947, Spain did not possess a government that emanated clearly from the will of the people, the Security Council should study adequate means for remedying the situation. Member states were urged to report what actions they had taken to effect the resolution at the next session of the General Assembly.[20]

That the passage of the resolution was at best a limited success was generally acknowledged. Premier Giral of the Spanish government-in-exile declared that although it was not entirely satisfactory it at least furnished a basis for further progress. The true triumph, he added, lay in the fact that the United States and Britain had been induced to abandon their narrow position of moral condemnation and to accept the possibility of recalling their diplomatic representatives from Madrid. Whatever the merits of the premier's evaluation, it was apparently not shared by the constituent parties of his government coalition. On December 17, 1946, two days after the assembly resolution, he was attacked by Indalecio Prieto. Prieto was unimpressed with the notion of diplomatic rupture, and he thought that the lack of economic sanctions in the resolution eliminated the only real possibility of throttling General Franco. He was convinced that the Giral government would never achieve the common goal of restoring the republic, and he advised the Socialist Party to withdraw immediately from the Giral government. His statement touched off a chain reaction of criticism of Giral's performance. The socialists and anarchists seemed particularly displeased, while the republican parties were split in their reactions. It was noteworthy that, beyond criticism of Giral's leadership in the United Nations discussions, there emerged a significant move to follow the British initiative and bring monarchist and center-right elements into a post-Franco provisional government in order to gain American and British support. Prieto stated this explicitly in his blast against Giral. It drew support from the Prieto wing of the Socialist Party and a faction of the anarchist movement. Sánchez-Guerra, a conservative republican serving in the Giral government as the representative of an anti-Franco group in the interior of Spain, declared that it was "necessary and urgent" to arrive at an agreement with center-right, monarchist, and Catholic organizations in the interior. Only in this manner could Franco be derailed by legal and pacific means.[21]

Giral called a cabinet meeting on January 22, 1947, and presented his program for future action. He called for the unification of antifascist forces in the interior through formation of a Council of the Resistance. The strengthened Resistance movement would then intensify its struggle. The combined force of these actions would make Franco's position untenable. Giral also proposed to widen the base of the government, increasing the number of conservative ministers, mainly from inside Spain. Sánchez-Guerra doubted that Giral was the man to carry out such a program successfully. He felt that the government had exhausted all of its national and international possibilities. Trifón Gómez, head of the General Union of Workers, and Enrique de Francisco of the Socialist Party drafted a joint policy statement. It decried the UN resolution as "insufficient and not energetic enough to be an efficient instrument of action." A new and decisive stage was opening in the political life of the emigration, the statement said. The Giral government would be unable to exploit the possibilities offered by the United Nations because it had failed to win the confidence of the Resistance forces within Spain or of the great democratic powers. For these reasons the Giral government should be replaced. The anarchist labor federation (CNT) also expressed lack of confidence in the Giral government. Giral then resigned his post and the cabinet followed his action.[22] Rodolfo Llopis, secretary-general of the Socialist Party, became the new premier and organized a cabinet that included representatives from the republican parties, Basque nationalists, socialists, communists, and anarchists. Llopis, in contrast to Giral, accepted the formation of an eventual provisional government in Spain that would incorporate center-right, Catholic, and monarchist groups. From the diplomatic point of view the new government appeared to be in a stronger position to accomplish its mission. Its willingness to entertain an alliance with conservative groups created a favorable impression in Great Britain, where Foreign Minister Ernest Bevin admitted on February 19, 1947, that he was engaging in extensive conversations with the Llopis government on his cherished idea of reinstituting a constitutional monarchy in Spain.[23]

The advent of the Llopis government at the beginning of 1947 accelerated the development of factionalism among the Spanish republicans and resulted in an inability to plan a successful follow-up in the United Nations. The government was able to survive only until August 1947, when it gave way to a new administration headed by Alvaro de Albornoz. *Adelante* characterized the Albornoz government as one "without Socialists, without the CNT, without the UGT, without Communists, without Basques, and without Catalans." In fact, the Albornoz cabinet was composed almost exclusively of representatives of the small republican parties.[24]

Two major issues were responsible for the fall of the Llopis government and the deterioration of Spanish republican politics. The first was the question of whether to include communists in the exile government. At its congress in 1946, the Socialist Party approved a resolution that it would not countenance the presence of communists in the government. At the Socialist Party Congress of July 25, 1947, in Toulouse, Llopis was castigated for offering a cabinet post to the Communist Party, despite the fact that the republican parties had sanctioned the move and declared that exclusion of the communists "would be a grave error." Prieto insisted that Llopis should have resisted all pressures for communist inclusion. He said that the Western powers would "never give their approval to a regime in which they see a danger of communist dominance." The Giral government, he said, had fallen into the orbit of the Eastern nations and this had hardened the attitude of the West. He stressed his belief that the democratic powers wielded the decisive power in the United Nations. Defending his policy, Llopis asserted that he had consulted the socialists in Spain on the question of communist inclusion. They had been "surprised and disconcerted" by the anticommunist resolution of the Socialist Party. They added that it would be "inopportune and politically unjust" for the anti-Franco elements struggling in Spain to adopt a similar attitude. However, Prieto was successful in securing from the 1947 congress a reaffirmation of the anticommunist stand of the Socialist Party.[25]

Whether the Spanish republicans should have heeded Ernest Bevin's desire for the restoration of the Bourbon dynasty as part of the plan for the expulsion of Franco furnished the fuel for the second great conflagration that seared Spanish politics in 1947 and 1948. Juan de Borbón, son of the deposed Alfonso XIII, was living in Portugal and giving every sign that he was available for the throne, whether the restoration was initiated by the Franco government or its opponents. The Spanish dictator issued a law of succession on March 31, 1947, in which he stipulated that his successor must be of royal blood and must be Catholic. Juan rejected this law with the assertion that he was already king and needed no other tests of his fitness, although he met both conditions. He carried on fitful negotiations with Franco's emissaries and even with conservative dissidents within the Franco government, but without result. A committee of monarchist partisans also negotiated with a special political committee of the Socialist Party, headed by Prieto, in an effort to create an acceptable formula for Juan's accession to the throne. The arrangement was to be that, first, Juan would be named king, and, second, a plebiscite would be held in which the voters would choose between a monarchy and a republic. But Juan refused to agree to step down in case of an adverse decision at the polls, and this stalled the negotiations, which eventually just petered out. In early 1947, however, Prieto was working assiduously to consummate the project, and in the process he was creating deep divisions among the various republican groups. If the idea of the plebiscite were rejected, he argued, then Juan might be installed as king by Franco himself, in which case all hope of republican government would be lost. But there was a great probability of republican victory in the plebiscite, he held, and the monarchy would be repudiated in decisive fashion. Even if the monarchy should be restored, he said, a large number of republican delegates would almost certainly be chosen in elections for a constitutional assembly. This would assure a liberal monarchy, with sufficient restraints on the king's powers. Thus, the alliance with monarchist and conservative elements would avoid the possibility of protracted internal struggle, in which the republican elements could only butt their heads ineffectually against the wall formed by the police and the army.[26]

Opposition to the monarchist-republican negotiations split the Spanish republican political organizations, especially the bourgeois left and the moderate parties. Premier Albornoz, speaking at a Congress of the Izquierda Repúblicana (Left Republicans) in December 1947, dubbed Prieto's call for Spanish solidarity the "solidarity of the wolf and the lamb under the mask of philanthropy." He called for a Spain that would be an arbiter between East and West, and not a partisan of one side or the other. But the strongest opposition came from the Left Republican Party in Spain itself. Meeting clandestinely, it passed a resolution that accused Great Britain of being the driving force for the monarchist alternative. As such, the resolution said, it was the greatest enemy of the republic: "We accuse the Anglo-Saxon governments of being responsible for Franco's continuance in power, for the hunger, for the misery and the ruin of the nation." Esquerra Catalan (the leftist Catalan nationalists) took umbrage at these statements and called upon the complainers either to withdraw from politics or to range themselves openly on the side of the Soviet bloc. It simply would not do to ask aid of the English-speaking countries and then insult them. Prieto, in discussing the Marshall Plan and European developments, asserted that "if Europe divides itself into two blocs . . . Spain will be in the Western camp."[27]

Prieto's role in Spanish and international politics was curious and disconcerting to many of his compatriots. Refusing all offers of ministerial portfolios and thus direct responsibility for the conduct of affairs, he maintained his power base in an important section of the Socialist Party and pursued his own objectives, which were often outside of and in direct contradiction to the official government program. He was a constant critic of whatever government happened to be in power, and he wrote voluminously for the Spanish refugee press, advancing his own notions and exercising a considerable influence among Spaniards of diverse political persuasions. His violent antipathy toward the Spanish communists and the Soviet Union made it easy for him to identify with the West, and with Britain in particular. His advocacy of a partnership with monarchists and conservative republicans in the construction of an interim government stemmed from his own fears of communist hegemony in any new Spanish government and the fact of Ernest Bevin's strong interest in such a solution. He corresponded with the British foreign secretary and there is evidence that he had a continuing secret relationship with the British Foreign Office. It is entirely possible that Prieto remained aloof from the day-to-day frustrations of the government-in-exile because he was convinced that factionalism and ineptitude would inevitably taint the reputations of its politicians. He may have believed that by pressing the British plan he would emerge in a dominant position in a reconstituted Spanish republic, for there is no doubt that he was an ambitious man.

Certainly, during 1947 and 1948, Prieto's attitude reflected an accurate assessment of the state of affairs. The Security Council, which had promised to examine the situation if Franco were not removed in a "reasonable time," meaning by September 1, 1947, took no action whatever in that year. A vicious circle had been closed: the key Western powers hesitated to make a decisive move because they felt that the republican exiles had failed to achieve the necessary degree of unanimity among themselves. On the other hand, unanimity escaped the Spanish republicans because Western demands for the inclusion of monarchist and conservative elements in the coalition had fostered increased political fragmentation and bickering. Moreover, a growing number of Spaniards were losing confidence in the desire of the United Nations to act with decision.

Evidence that the balance of forces was beginning to turn against the Spanish republicans came also at the 1947 session of the General Assembly, when a Polish resolution reaffrming the 1946 vote to withdraw ambassadors from Madrid failed by one vote to register the required two-thirds majority. However, this failure did not remove the December 1946 resolution from the United Nations books. The resolution that was passed on November 17, 1947, merely urged the Security Council to exercise its responsibilities whenever it should consider that the Spanish situation required action. The *New York Times* noted that the debate "was short and surprisingly lacking in fire."[28] There were many other significant straws in the wind. France, which had closed its border with Spain in March 1946, reopened it on February 10, 1948. The 1948 General Assembly did not even discuss the Spanish question, but a new spirit was nevertheless evident. Whereas in 1946 the representatives of Franco's Spain had tiptoed gingerly around the fringes of the meeting, in 1948 they were strongly in evidence. They circulated openly among the delegates, strengthening their ties with the Arab and Latin American nations, hosting expensive lunches. Although the majority of countries still professed hostility toward General Franco, it was evident that he sensed a change in the air. Premier Albornoz took notice of these trends in a press conference on October 30, 1948. He complained that even countries that had condemned the Spanish nationalist regime were negotiating treaties of commerce and other agreements. With the attenuation of the 1946 assembly resolution, he said, the slackening of the international conscience had strengthened the Caudillo's position.[29]

The final turn of the screw, which virtually ended all possibility of the restoration of the Spanish republic for another twenty years, came during the period 1949–1955. With the Cold War at its height the United States and Britain became increasingly desirous of annulling the 1946 resolution banning diplomatic relations with Spain, although they continued to withhold ambassadors from Franco. France, which was having difficulties with communists in its own internal politics, also now wished to remove the 1946 resolution. In early 1949, a many-sided campaign began for repeal of the resolution and for the gradual recognition of the nationalist government by the United Nations. Officials of the U.S. State Department and the British Foreign Office let it be known that their governments would not be averse to recognition, but that they would not act while the resolution remained in force. U.S. Senators Pat McCarran of Nevada, Owen D. Brewster of Maine, and Tom Connally of Texas visited Spain and returned calling for the immediate appointment of an ambassador to Madrid. James A.

Farley, a prominent Democratic politician who was also an important Catholic layman, joined the movement for recognition of the Spanish nationalist government and its admission to membership in the United Nations. Assistant Secretary of State Dean Rusk hinted that the United States would back a move to repeal the ban. Senator Robert A. Taft demanded that the State Department cease following what he called the communist line on Spain and send an ambassador to Franco. Senator McCarran told Secretary of State Dean Acheson that he would attempt to cut the State Department budget unless it eased its policy on Spain. These pressures coincided with an attempt by four Latin American nations to introduce a resolution in the General Assembly of the United Nations rescinding the ban on diplomatic relations with Spain, but it was defeated by four votes. These diplomatic moves were accompanied by tentative consideration of a U.S. Export-Import Bank loan to Spain, a $25 million dollar loan by the Chase National Bank, and a first-time visit to Franco Spain by four U.S. navy ships. The government denied that these two initiatives were official policy or indications that a military pact was contemplated. They pointed to the exclusion of Francoist Spain from the newly formed North Atlantic Treaty Organization as evidence against the existence of a Spanish-United States military agreement. In this welter of activity the Spanish republican government-in-exile was relegated increasingly to the background. It made very few ripples in international waters when, after the General Assembly failed to discuss the Spanish problem at its 1948 meeting, the government of Premier Albornoz resigned. And it made even less impact when he was appointed to succeed himself.[30]

The clamor for recognition of the Franco government and for its admission to the United Nations gathered force in the United States during 1950. Perhaps the urgency was due not only to the American desire to make an ally of the anticommunist Franco but to the fact that Spain was virtually bankrupt. On January 9, 1950, Representative John Kee of West Virginia, chairman of the House Foreign Affairs Committee, told the committee that the United States should renew full diplomatic relations with Franco's Spain. He indicated that his address had been coordinated with the State Department. Kee denied that the sought-for change was a simple desire to enroll Spain in the anticommunist alliance; he viewed it, rather, as an effort to influence Franco to democratize Spanish institutions. Kee's address was followed ten days later by a pivotal letter from Secretary of State Dean Acheson to a number of congressional leaders. The secretary informed them that the United States was now "ready to support a United Nations resolution freeing each power to restore normal diplomatic relations" with Spain, without implying approval of the Franco regime. The 1946 resolution had failed to achieve its objective of replacing the Caudillo; on the contrary, it had helped to solidify his power. Acheson also indicated that Spain could now apply to the Export-Import Bank for a loan on the same basis as any other nation. The *New York Times,* in commenting on the Acheson letter, predicted that a move for repeal of the 1946 resolution would succeed at the next session of the General Assembly.[31]

However, Franco's staunch supporters in the Congress preferred to utilize the mechanism of the European Recovery Program (Marshall Plan) to advance economic aid to Spain. On August 1, 1950, the Senate approved a $100 million dollar loan to Franco as part of this program. President Harry S. Truman and Secretary of State Acheson criticized the loan on the grounds that Spain should instead apply to the Export-Import Bank for assistance. The *New York Times* supported the president's objection and claimed that the action of the Congress could harm the U.S. position in the United Nations. The loan was subsequently cut to $62 million dollars in the House-Senate conference committee. A rather curious compromise was reached when the Marshall Plan administrators announced that the loan would be floated through the Export-Import Bank. Despite the furious complaints voiced by such groups as the Congress of Industrial Organizations and the Americans for Democratic Action, the Franco government greeted the action as "the first gesture of friendship toward Spain" since the hostile General Assembly resolution of 1946.

Other and more friendly actions were soon to be taken. On November 4, 1950, the General Assembly rescinded the 1946 ban on diplomatic relations with Spain, as well as the restriction on its membership in the specialized organizations of the United Nations, despite a steady stream of protest from the dwindling number of organizations that still pressed for the restoration of the Spanish republic. A statement by seven prominent French writers directed a "fervent call" to their government to refuse to work cooperatively with the fascist government of Franco. But the halcyon days of leftist influence in French politics had long since gone, and France itself was engaged in a bitter campaign against the communists. One hundred and sixty Spanish communists were among those seized by the French authorities on September 7, 1950, and their organizations and newspapers were suppressed.

The profound anger and sense of betrayal provoked by the rescission of the 1946 UN resolution found its deepest expression in the resignation of Indalecio Prieto from his Socialist Party post as chief negotiator with the monarchists and from political life. He called the vote "an outrage to the democratic conscience." He declared: "My failure is complete. I am responsible for having induced our party to trust itself to the powerful democratic governments who did not merit such confidence . . . By my guilt my party has been the victim of an illusion that had dazzled me . . . Our Party and the U.G.T. have made the greatest efforts . . . but today, that which predominates is the insensate desire to unite Franco to the anti-Stalinist alliance, ignoring all scruples." Rodolfo Llopis, secretary-general of the Socialist Party, declared that "Europe has spoken in the United Nations. And Europe has abstained . . . Not a single country of Europe led by the socialists has voted against Franco. Not one." The second Albornoz government resigned on November 30, 1950, in view of the assembly vote.[32]

The wall isolating Franco was further breached on November 19, 1952, when Spain was admitted to the United Nations Educational, Scientific, and Cultural Organization (UNESCO). The vote was forty-four in favor, four opposed, and seven abstentions. The United States and Great Britain voted yea. Pablo Casals resigned from the music committee of UNESCO in protest against the action.

These political events were soon to be matched in the military and economic spheres. Despite the denials of official Washington, contacts had been established and informal talks held between Spain and the United States for several years. Hanson W. Baldwin, military commentator of the *New York Times,* reported on June 22, 1951, that U.S. congressmen were exerting a growing pressure for arms aid to Spain. On July 14 of that year several U.S. senators had conferred with Franco on Spain's possible role in the Western military alliance. Secretary Acheson declared on July 19, 1951, that the United States was aiming for active Spanish participation in the defense of Western Europe. Despite the opposition of Great Britain and France, who wished to slow down the drive for military aid to Spain, Acheson asserted that the military-strategic factors superseded the political. The upshot of all this was the signing, on September 26, 1953, of a ten-year military and economic aid pact between the United States and Spain. In return for dropping its traditional policy of neutrality, Spain was to receive $226 million dollars in military and economic aid to modernize its armed forces and its economy. The United States was granted the use of air and naval bases and both countries would gear their efforts toward strengthening Western defenses against any possible Soviet threat. *Arriba,* the Falange newspaper, greeted the pact with high enthusiasm. In a choice of words that could only evoke memories of the recent past, it declared: "We have become today the decisive axis of the political world."[33]

There remained only one final step to be taken in the rehabilitation of Franco Spain. On December 14, 1955, nationalist Spain became a full member of the United Nations. The vote was part of a package deal arranged by the Western and Eastern blocs. On Spain, the vote was fifty-five in favor, none against, two abstentions.[34]

Although the world had turned upside down in the little more than nineteen years since the beginning of the Spanish Civil War, the concept of nonintervention in the affairs of Spain had remained constant. The refusal of the great democracies to aid republican Spain in the 1936–1939 struggle had, in the most concrete fashion, proved to be decisive assistance to General Francisco Franco. Despite the repression, death, and destruction rained on the countries of Europe by Nazi Germany and fascist Italy, activities Franco had supported wholeheartedly, the Spanish dictator had avoided the fate of Adolf Hitler and Benito Mussolini. Once again, the idea of nonintervention had been of service to Franco, this time to preserve him in power. The demands of the Cold War had made his anticommunism respectable. He had become a pillar of strength and virtue in the campaign against the Soviet bloc.

The Spanish republicans had surely been betrayed by their friends, victims of the fear of social revolution and the clash of ideologies. For those who had waited so long and endured so much it was easy to believe, with Federica Montseny, that Europe was a moral desert and that the Spanish republicans had deserved a better fate. After all their sacrifices, they were still pariahs to the democratic world. If they were guilty of any major blunder or weakness, it was that after the Second World War they had repeated the error of placing their trust in those governments that did not believe in them.[35]

THE PRISONS CONSUMED A GENERATION OF FIGHTERS

"And what will you do now?"

"Since it must be done. I return to Spain.
There the battle has not ended."

"Take good care, Ramón. Take good care."

He shrugs his shoulders.

"Today or tomorrow, I know already that I must fall. Struggles
like ours need victims. And one can never think of saving his life.
If one survives it is good luck. If one falls, then it is a debt already
paid. Until now death has respected me. If it comes, here or there,
what more can be given?"

"I see him stand before me. [He is] the spirit and the symbol of
invincible and indestructible Spain, of the new Spain, the eternal,
the perennial, that of yesterday and of tomorrow, which all of
Franco's guns all of Franco's schools, all of Franco's work of
material and moral destruction, will never be able to annihilate."

A conversation between Federica Montseny and Ramón Capdevila,
from Federica Montseny, *Pasión y muerte de los españoles
en Francia*

THAT OTHER ROAD, the way of the guerrilla, was taken by those
Spanish republicans who had no confidence in the futile exercise
of diplomacy practiced by the United Nations. Both efforts were doomed
to fail, one dying in a savage war of extermination in the mountains and
streets of Spain, the other strangled by diplomatic red tape. The militant branch of the anarchists, who from the beginning mistrusted any
solution imposed by liberal capitalist governments, declared that Spain
"must not beg for its liberty in the chancelleries . . . It must conquer it,
arms in hand, grabbing it from the claws of Fascism." In response to
the Western fear of another bloodbath in Spain, Confederación Na-

cional del Trabajo, the anarchist trade union federation, countered that "there is no solution of the Spanish problem other than with blood." The communists were willing to play the diplomatic game, but their participation had been held to a minimum by the strong objections of the moderate Spanish socialists and the great democracies. They organized the Unión Nacional, which was designed to be an umbrella organization, but was of arguable effectiveness. They too, saw the necessity for a guerrilla campaign in Spain, both in terms of its potential effectiveness and in order to organize solidly for the post-Franco political scramble. The socialists, despite the efforts of their many valiant guerrilla fighters, were largely dedicated to the diplomatic route, and the republican parties, as one guerrilla put it, "slept in their houses."[1]

Thus, between the end of 1944 and 1950, there was a shadow war in Spain. Although it was to continue sporadically right up to the point of Franco's death—witness the killings of Ramón Capdevila and the urban guerrilla Sabaté in the Sixties and the execution of Puig Antich in 1974—those years represented the height of activity and of confidence that a classic guerrilla campaign could succeed. It was a legend even before it began, because everyone anticipated that, once finished with the war against Germany, the Spanish republican Resistance fighters in France would turn their attention to their homeland. Juan Molina, who fought in the French Resistance and returned to Spain to fight as a guerrilla leader until caught and imprisoned, wrote that it was impossible to capture the true dimensions of the clandestine struggle and noted that although more than twelve thousand books had been written about the Spanish Civil War, there was not a single one dealing with the post–World War II guerrilla campaign.[2] Molina himself labored ten years to produce a volume on the clandestine war, but he admits that it is sadly incomplete. The reasons are fairly easy to catalogue. The severe, and for the most part efficient, actions of the Spanish police and army wiped out thousands of guerrillas and imprisoned many additional thousands. Even when former guerrillas survived punishment and emerged from prison, they could not relate their stories to Molina for fear of incriminating others who had not been captured. Most of the records of the guerrilla fighters, as well as those of local and regional committees, were seized by the authorities and impounded or destroyed. The government has never released this material nor the records of the police forces, and there is no indication as to when it will. Thus, there are very few documents available concerning the methods of the police and Guardia Civil, the trials of guerrilla prisoners, their tortures, or their executions. All these, Molina said, were "carried out without publicity in the shadows of the prisons." Molina's extensive collection of clandestine periodicals, manifestoes, reports of guerrillas on their experiences after entering Spain from France, official directives of the national executive committee of the anarchist movement in Spain, was inexplicably stolen while he was writing, and thus this invaluable body of material was lost to posterity. His narrative was largely reconstructed from his personal experience in clandestine activities, his extensive contact with the interior Spanish Resistance since 1939, and the personal memoirs of some combatants.

The mystery of the guerrilla, the image of the lonely, isolated groups of Spanish Maquis prowling the Guadarrama or Pyrenees mountains, descending swiftly and silently to attack a Guardia Civil post and then retreating just as silently, quickly, into their mountain fastness, has excited the imaginations of people. There is a romantic aura about the Spanish guerrilla that is linked to the tradition of the irregular, irreverent fighters of the past. They are the stuff of Goya paintings.

How many guerrillas there were, how many were killed and captured, and what effect they had is almost impossible to determine because of the scarcity of records. Estimates of the number of guerrillas who fought in Spain vary from 5,000 to 30,000; the most generally accepted figure is 15,000. The number killed, wounded, and captured is even more difficult to estimate. A 1969 article in *A.B.C.*, a Francoist newspaper, lauding the Guardia Civil for its long battle against "bandits," claimed that 5,548 guerrillas were killed between 1943 and 1952, and that 624 wounded guerrillas were captured, of whom 256 later died of their wounds. Detained as accomplices were 19,407, a rather startling figure, for if true it indicates an extensive network in support of guerrilla activities. The article gives no details as to where and when these accomplices were apprehended, nor what happened to them.[3]

Most Spanish republican guerrillas were communists or anarchists who had fought the war of 1936–1939 and then fled to France, where they had been put into French concentration camps. They had fought with the French forces in May–June 1940, either as soldiers or as members of worker's companies. Some, such as Amadeo Cinca Vendrell, were captured in the German blitz and sent to concentration camps. If they survived to be liberated in 1945, they returned to France, vowing, as Cinca Vendrell did, "to fight with equal or greater fervor than ever."

José Mata, a socialist and a battalion commander in Asturias when that region was conquered by Franco in 1937, went into the hard Asturian mountains with two thousand comrades and fought there until October 1948 when, sitting in the forest, he suddenly said to himself, "Franco, you have won the first round." Then he took his surviving comrades, thirty-two men and one woman, into France.

Cristino García Grandas followed the typical pattern—retreat into France, the beach camps, the Resistance. Operating in the department of the Gard, he became famous for his leadership in the classic guerrilla battle of La Madeleine and other bold coups. He returned to Spain after the war, where he was finally captured and condemned to death, along with ten comrades. Despite a tremendous outcry—the French government appealed to Franco for clemency and great meetings were held in many countries to protest the sentence—he and his comrades were executed on February 22, 1946.[4]

Francisco Sabaté Llopart ("El Quico") became the most feared guerrilla in Barcelona, number one on Franco's most wanted list. When, in the early 1950s, the CNT abandoned the guerrilla campaign, he fought on alone with almost maniacal intensity. In January 1960, he was trapped, wounded three times, escaped, commandeered a train, abandoned it, and was finally hunted down and killed in the streets of the small town of San Celoni.

Almost every issue of every publication of the Spanish refugee press contains the names of comrades who were reported killed in Spain. *Ruta,* in November 1949, acknowledged heavy losses and declared that the guerrilla movement was facing a "difficult hour." It called for more volunteers to fill the gaps. Franco's repressive forces, who were at first reluctant to engage in combat with the guerrillas, were reinforced and reorganized and became extremely efficient and ruthless in their work. Harsh discipline, poor food, and indiscriminate conscription at first led to widespread desertions from the Spanish army in 1946 and 1947, but this gradually ceased. As the silent war continued, Molina said, the guerrillas slowly succumbed to ferocious counterattacks, which were facilitated in no small measure by French informers. Thus, a U.S. naval intelligence report on April 20, 1945, recounted the crossing of twenty Spanish guerrillas from France into Spain, each a chief who was destined to take command of a unit somewhere in the country. They were ambushed by the armed police, who killed two, wounded two, and captured four. The military reporter said that "the Spanish military intelligence . . . has very complete information regarding Spaniards in France and that these make the mistake of trusting the French who provide the Spanish authorities with information." The Franco government offered its Moorish border patrols a bounty of one hundred pesetas for every deserter captured alive, and fifty pesetas for every dead one. A report of the U.S. Office of Strategic Services described the interrogation of a Spanish army deserter by French authorities in Perpignan. He claimed that he was the first of his unit to desert, but said that many others would soon follow. He wished to join the fight against Franco.[4]

There is no doubt that guerrilla operations were extensive and that some of them, such as the strikes organized in Barcelona and the Basque provinces, involving as many as 250,000 people, had an impact on the regime. The *A.B.C.* article reported a total of 8,275 "unlawful deeds" between 1943 and 1952, and presumably many more went unreported. Most of the guerrilla attacks were directed at the stations and personnel of the Guardia Civil. Many electrical installations, street-cars, and government buildings were also destroyed, and nationalist officials were assassinated. These actions were executed by the gueril-leros, while the politicos were responsible for agitation and propaganda, which included the printing and dissemination of clandestine news-papers, political organization, and the fomenting of strikes and civil dis-orders. From January 1945 through March 1946, the *New York Times* reported a series of guerrilla actions in many parts of Spain, as did French and American intelligence sources. C. L. Sulzberger of the *Times* declared that this activity proved the error of official Spanish statements that communism was dead in Spain. In March 1946 Sulzberger inter-viewed a Communist Party representative called Felipe, who claimed a Communist Party membership of 25,000, a figure Sulzberger found be-lievable. Felipe spoke of a central resistance committee directed from communist headquarters in France. The Spanish communist claimed that there were between 9,000 and 12,000 active guerrillas of all parties and organizations, but the majority, he added, were communists. The greatest need was for arms, which was the greatest weakness of the guerrilla movement, but he hoped that more would soon be smuggled into the country.[5]

This widespread guerrilla campaign was part of what the Francoist Tomás Cossias called "a slow invasion, silent and clandestine, of in-dividuals and isolated groups that did not begin their labors until they reached their destinations." They were the fighters whom Emmet John Hughes had in mind when he wrote: "Each night hundreds of men check their rifles, fasten the cords of their sandals, stock their miserable cartridge boxes. Silently they march in the night air, crossing forests and hills, torrential rivers and streams . . . Today it is a police post that they attack, tomorrow a farmhouse or a large warehouse to procure food." And there was also the demolition expert who came to Asturias from France to blow up a special target, a metallurgical factory. He met his guide and they walked in the early morning to the mountain headquarters of the guerrilla unit. Midway up the mountain he turned and looked at his objective in the morning sunlight:

"What are you looking at?" his guide asked.
"The target. It will fall beautifully," the dynamiter replied.
"That is not important," the guide said. "The important thing is that it fall."[6]

The so-called silent invasion—small groups that infiltrated Spain from France and melted into the mountains—came after a few large invasions had taken place during and just after the conclusion of World War II. The best-known of these was the battle of the Aran Valley, in the Basque country. A force of Spanish guerrillas, estimated at 2,000 men, invaded the valley in December 1944, armed with supplies parachuted by the Allies for use in the French Resistance. They seized sixteen villages and held on for ten days while Franco rushed 45,000 troops to the area. Eventually they were forced to withdraw, both by the pressure of the Francoist forces and because of the orders of the Allies. The hoped-for result, that of raising the cry of insurrection and rallying the populace to the Spanish republican banner for a triumphal sweep to Barcelona and Madrid, did not eventuate. Pierre Bertaux, the commissaire of the provisional French republic at Toulouse, who knew and admired the Spaniards and had fought with them during the Resistance, tried to dissuade them from the adventure, but they promised "to be gentle with the priests" and continued their preparations. Bertaux forewarned the French gendarmes at the frontier and instructed them to allow the guerrillas to pass. There was widespread criticism of the Aran action, which the Spanish republicans also hoped would force the Allies to support and supply a massive invasion of Spain. Borras thought that it was "an absurd battle" with heavy casualties (although he supplies no figures), but Santiago Carrillo, the present Spanish communist leader, who was also active in Communist Party activities during World War II, called it a success after the conclusion of the withdrawal into France. "When . . . after achieving their objectives, the guerrillas withdrew . . . the inhabitants said farewell in the streets with embraces, tears, and gifts, while the priests gave them their benediction," Carrillo wrote, perhaps with slight exaggeration.[7]

The anarchists, refusing to join the communist-dominated Unión Nacional, formed the Alianza Nacional de Fuerzas Democráticas (ANFD). In contrast to the communists, their order of battle was highly decentralized, although they related closely to Alianza in Spain and the anarchist organizations in France. When Serge Groussard interviewed a number of guerrillas and asked about the existence of a national command, the anarchist Marcelino Fernández replied that he commanded the guerrillas of three provinces, divided into small groups of ten to fifteen men each. "We live in the mountains or the forests where it is difficult to penetrate. We move around continuously. They chase us more than they do the wild boars and the wolves, who are very numerous here . . . Under these conditions you will understand that it is very difficult to have a general headquarters for all of Spain." Juan Molina described the difficulties associated with the guerrilla effort. Without the help of anyone, with inefficient arms, some of which were rusted and dated from before the Civil War, the guerrillas faced regular army regiments and the Guardia Civil. Despite all the handicaps, he added, the guerrillas succeeded in bringing half of Spain into a state of permanent war.[8] But they were doomed almost from the beginning because, unlike the Maquis of the French Resistance during the later stages of World War II, they received very little outside support and were met with apathy and even hostility by large sections of the Spanish populace. Unlike guerrillas in sucessful campaigns, they were unable to swim like fish in the ocean of the people, receiving shelter, nourishment, and support from them. The people, for the moment, were tired and battered; they wanted nothing more than to be left alone and earn their morsel of bread.

How can one evaluate the achievements of these isolated fighters? They did not succeed in stirring up a popular insurrection, to say nothing of bringing down Franco's regime. They were not effective in stimulating diplomatic action; in fact, their impact on the Western powers was negative and revived fears of social revolution. What, then, did they acomplish by their presence in the mountains, by their assaults on the Franco establishment, by their suffering, imprisonment, and death? Were they the Don Quixotes of the twentieth century, immersed in a fantastic dream and wearing tattered rags for armor? Were they simply zealots and revolutionaries who didn't know when to acknowledge defeat? Or were they heroes, anonymous idealists whose exploits, told and retold in the villages, would keep hope alive? The answers to these questions will not be known until the full story of the guerrillas is unearthed and written. We do have the opinions of some of the men who participated in the effort, as well as those of some professional observers. That the Franco government did not take these men lightly is shown by the report, dated July 23, 1957, of a civil governor who attributed the guerrilla effort almost entirely to the Communist Party. The guerrillas had been trained in France and sent in small groups to Spain, he said. He gave the communists credit for organizing a comprehensive network of operations, but he hinted at the anti-Franco feeling in the countryside when he declared that the guerrillas had profited by "circumstances" that still existed in many provinces. He asserted that the guerrillas were well armed with machine-guns, hand grenades, and other explosives, in contrast to Felipe's complaint that they lacked modern arms. No judgment was made as to the guerrilla's effectiveness, but the propaganda purpose of the report is underlined by the governors' consistent use of the word "bandits" and "communists" to describe the guerrillas.[9]

A more realistic evaluation, and certainly one based on more direct experience, was made by the anarchist Juan Molina, who had served a fifteen-year prison term for his guerrilla activities. When the Alianza Nacional de Fuerzas Democráticas (ANFD) had disappeared in 1948–49 the guerrilla movement had languished, he said "until it was practically eclipsed at the end of 1949." The guerrilla assaults planned by the anarchists and other groups diminished, there were no further planning meetings of resistance groups, and the number and frequency of clandestine periodicals declined. Molina's final judgments were somber, but he was aware that the men of the guerrilla movement had lived an immortal saga that would some day be told:

> The prisons consumed a generation of fighters, defeated this time irremediably. Years later they will emerge in a very restricted, provisional liberty, after having completed fifteen or twenty years of prison. Wounded in morale, like sleep walkers or shipwrecks of social torment, they will dedicate themselves exclusively to reorganizing their lives in the sunset of their years and by reconstructing their family lives. Some of them will not even be recognized by their own children, who were not able to communicate with them for all those years.
>
> They had complied with a grave and heavy historical mission, but one would not be able to count on them ever again for an active role.
>
> The fall of the Franco regime was not realized because of many negative factors, and the interior Resistance, which had taken a decisive step, without a return ticket, found itself abandoned, alone, facing the most terrible police and military apparatus in Europe. . .
>
> All strength in life has its limits and this limit was amply exceeded by the Resistance, in almost inhuman endurance. But it had to succumb.[10]

Molina did not forget how and why the Spanish republicans had been deceived: "The world, the democracies above all, had consummated the betrayal . . . Under the pretext of containing Communism . . . the democracies signed [Spain's] death sentence, pushing the people into the blackest era in Spanish history."

Another guerrilla declared that: "In the field we found help, but it was a curious kind of aid. Curious, no, defensive . . . in the city, nothing. The fear weighed heavily, the terror, the war . . . It is clear that this was an era of hope. Perhaps here was our greatest error. In not taking into account that we were fighting the battle alone. But who was able, at that time, to see it?" He recalled how relations with the French had changed favorably through Spanish republican participation in the French Resistance, but he blamed de Gaulle for stifling the readiness of Frenchmen to engage personally in the Spanish Resistance. He too castigated the democracies for their role in postwar diplomacy, but he was sad at the continued belief of the Socialists in United Nations action. In Spain, when the guerrillas arrived, they were faced with a hard reality:

> "Hardly had we entered Spain and begun to speak with the people, when we understood that all was not the color of a rose. One sector of opinion believed that the people were ready to rise when the guerrillas arrived. We believed that . . . But in the interior the sympathy was more for the republic than for the guerrillas. They too believed that the chancelleries would resolve the problem. The return to the struggle was very difficult, almost impossible. And, in spite of all, we continued forward. In truth, I do not know how we were able to resist for so long.
>
> When we decided to return to Spain it appeared that our decision was correct. And we were convinced. Nobody among us then doubted the necessity of the guerrilla. Perhaps one could call us crazy, but those who did so were perhaps cowards, people who always hope that [the task] would be done for them, that others would resolve the problems. We were already in the country, months later, when we understood that the conditions for victory did not exist.[11]

Two contrasting evaluations of the guerrilla campaign were offered by Americans who were closely involved with the Spanish situation. Abel Plenn, who served as press-attaché for the American embassy in Madrid, felt in 1946 that the guerrilla movement might be the harbinger of a general uprising against Franco. He recounted stories of massive arms shipments flowing across the border, of guerrilla activity almost everywhere, and of a general feeling of unrest among the people that could easily be translated into insurrection. But he qualified his judgment by asserting that the Spanish were led to believe—perhaps falsely —that deliverance from the Falange was imminent. On the whole, however, his evidence suggested the beginnings of a groundswell that could bring Franco down. Charles Foltz, Jr., who was sympathetic to the republican cause, was nevertheless dismayed at the volume of optimistic propaganda broadcast by the Spanish republican radio in Toulouse, which exaggerated the extent and success of the effort and again led to false hopes. He cited a broadcast from the Toulouse radio which proclaimed that "masses of demonstrators against the Fascist regime had to be dispersed by the machine-gun fire of Franco's police" in Madrid's Puerta del Sol. At the very moment when the demonstration was supposed to have taken place, Foltz had been sitting in an outdoor cafe in Puerto del Sol, peacefully sipping his coffee: there was no evidence of disorder. If one multiplied what Foltz called "such nonsense" by months of daily broadcasts concerning every region of Spain, it is easy to understand why he thought that Spaniards at that time had little confidence in the Spanish republican exiles.[12]

The men who volunteered to reenter Spain to fight the guerrilla campaign were those for whom the wars of 1936–1945 were the central facts of their existence. Nothing else mattered. They were imbued with a single idea: Franco must go. They were tough, nurtured on the hard fare of war and privation, had lived with death every day for ten years. They were convinced that victory could be achieved only with gun in hand; all else was fruitless. They distrusted the normal channels of diplomacy and especially the manipulations of Great Britain and the United States. Even when they realized the impossibility of victory, some of them continued the struggle into the 1950s and 60s. Like Ramón Capdevila, they expected death as their portion.

Certainly they saw the situation from an extreme point of view. Perhaps they were men deranged by too much frustration, too much bitterness, too much anger and hate. Perhaps some of them wanted to die rather than accept reality. But most of them were Spanish idealists, to whom politics and social action were the core of life; if Franco had thwarted the expressed will of the people, the injustice had to be corrected.

Many of the guerrillas survived the battle and returned to France, to take up a long exile and to continue to do what they could to bring about their enemy's downfall. The examples of two men who came back are symbolic of those who risked everything in what was bound to be a fruitless endeavor.

Mariano Puzo was twenty-three years old when he entered France in May 1939 after escaping from a Franco prison camp for republican soldiers. He spent some time in the concentration camp at St. Cyprien, wangled his way into a miner's job during the *drôle de guerre* of September 1939 to May 1940, and later worked as a baker's assistant under the Vichy regime. He managed to increase the bread order by two hundred loaves, which he carried dutifully every day into the hills to an encampment of men who had escaped the summons for forced labor in Germany. One day he was informed that the Gestapo was looking for him, and five minutes later he was on his way to join the others in the camp and to become a member of an escape network. Like most Spaniards, he enjoyed the brief time of euphoria when it seemed like he might be returning to his native province of Lérida. But he soon became disillusioned with what he once called "the waltz of the liars" in the United Nations. In 1946 he volunteered for guerrilla duty in Spain and went there, not in triumph but as a fugitive fighter. After a series of successful missions he was wounded by a hand grenade that exploded just as it left his hand. He lost fingers on both hands, as well as sustaining internal wounds. He returned to France, finished as a guerrilla but not as an anarchist. Despite his handicaps he succeeded in making a new life in Perpignan. The Spanish Refugee Aid, an American organization, gave him a hook for his right hand and with that he managed very well. He acquired a pushcart and sold peanuts and candy on the sidewalk before the Castillet Theater. His stand was a center for anti-Franco activity. Men would stop and talk, exchanging information and the latest news. Mariano would open a drawer in his cart and, with his pincers, delicately extract the latest copy of *Frente Libertario,* an anarchist newspaper, or a report of some meeting or other. He continued, in this way, to fight the war against Franco every day.

In 1977 Puzo visited his old village in Spain, which had been an anarchist stronghold in the old days. He returned disillusioned and heartsick, his spirit dented by what he had found. "The old things are gone," he complained. "Everyone is becoming Americanized. Everyone is either a little capitalist or trying to become one. I know a man who was captured by Franco in 1937 and tortured. The fascists mangled both of his arms so that he could never have full use of them again. Today he is running around, trying to buy choice property lots because a tourist-building boom is beginning in the area. Everything has changed in Spain." On New Year's Day, 1978, he suffered a heart attack. He died three weeks later. His wife said his heart had been broken by what he saw in Spain.[13]

Pascual Ortiz also served his time in a French camp and was enrolled in a worker's company. He was digging fortifications near the Belgian border when the Germans overran his unit and he was made prisoner. They refused to accept the Spanish prisoners as members of the French army and sent them to Mauthausen concentration camp, along with 12,000 to 14,000 other Spanish republican prisoners. Ortiz was one of 2,000 Spaniards who survived this ordeal. What he remembers most is that one day a guard said he would be willing to smuggle out a letter for Ortiz. The prisoner wrote a message to his wife, using a nail as a pen and his own blood as ink. The guard disappeared, but Pascual hid the letter and carried it triumphantly to freedom when the camp was liberated by the Americans on the last day of the war. But Ortiz was burning with a sense of vengeance and with shame for having allowed himself to become a prisoner and thereby having lost the opportunity to fight the Germans in the Resistance. So he joined the Spanish Resistance and crossed into his native land as a guerrilla. He survived three years of mountain fighting and came back to France, painfully aware that the Franco regime still lived, but somewhat content at having struck a few blows against it. With his wife and young children he bought a small vineyard, which prospered. Then he bought fifty hectares that adjoined the property. One evening, three years later, he said to his wife, "We now own one hundred hectares. In two years we shall probably own two hundred hectares, and maybe even more after that. Do you realize what is happening to us? We are becoming big landowners." So they promptly sold the property, and he became a worker again. Today he is retired and enjoys his large family. Friendly and gregarious he will talk about the Spanish Civil War, Mauthausen, the Spanish Resistance, for hours, at the slightest invitation. The events of those years are still the core of his existence. In April 1978, Perpignan enjoyed a special week-long showing of films about the Spanish Civil War. Pascual Ortiz was there. One of the old newsreels showed a street-fighting scene in the Barcelona of July 1936, when the people of the city rose and aborted the take-over attempt of the insurgents. Suddenly Ortiz jumped in his seat. "That is me!" he shouted, pointing out a young worker creased against a building wall and firing a rifle. The scene seemed to offer a motif for the film-maker, for it flashed on the screen again and again.[14]

Mariano Puzo, Pascual Ortiz, and all those who went back to Spain as guerrilla fighters knew why they did it. They knew that the attempt had to be made and that they had to make it. Perhaps the best epitaph for the guerrilla campaign and those who died in the struggle was expressed by a bricklayer at a memorial service for Francisco Sabaté Llopart in Perpignan: "When we were young, and the republic was founded, we were knightly though also spiritual. We have grown older, but not Sabaté. He was a guerrillero by instinct. Yes, he was one of those Quixotes who come out of Spain." And so were they all.[15]

EPILOGUE

"We are an accusation and a living protest against the world."

Luís Bazal, *Ay de los vencidos*

FRANCO REMAINED IN POWER primarily because the United States and Great Britain feared the possibility of a Red Spain more than they feared the actuality of a fascist one. The United States and its allies were preoccupied with political and military planning for a possible war against the Soviet Union, and they saw the Mediterranean as a base of operations against the communists. Because of its strategic importance, Franco's Spain became an ideological and military bastion against the Soviet Union.

With the admission of Spain to the United Nations in December 1955, the Spanish republican refugees entered the fifth phase of their exile. Now they had nothing more to contemplate than a lifetime of separation from their homeland and futile exercises of opposition. Activity continued on a large scale, with political parties, publications of all types, and even the mounting of clandestine operations within Spain. But while this might appease their hunger for action, the scope of what they could accomplish was severely constricted. Any meaningful opposition to the Caudillo must now arise in Spain itself, born of repressive conditions and the coming of age of a new generation of dissidents. Although there was contact between the Spaniards in France and those within Spain, the pivot of action had shifted decisively to the interior. Many of the younger opponents of Franco had a measure of disdain for the older generation and considered them guilty, first, of having lost the civil war and, second, of carrying on an inept opposition.[1]

Successive amnesties declared by the Franco regime lured an indeterminate number of exiles back to Spain. In 1969 there was a general and unconditional amnesty, save for a few "undesirables," and larger numbers of refugees returned. Many Spaniards returned to the homeland only for visits with families. Among the hard-core exiles there was contempt for the amnesty and for those who took advantage of it. "They go back to Spain to die," Mariano Puzo said.[2] Large numbers of Spanish refugees took advantage of the liberal French offers of automatic naturalization. Their children were born French, married French mates, and entered fully into the culture and life of that country. Although the exiles themselves generally remained close to the bottom of the economic ladder, many managed to become small businessmen and skilled craftsmen, and their children have entered professional and administrative jobs that were closed to their parents. "My children know their Spanish background and are sympathetic to the cause," one refugee said, "but they will not do anything to aid it."[3] There are those of the older generation, however, who cling fiercely to their Spanish nationality. They proudly display their identity cards, point to the designation "Spanish refugee," and say "Siempre" ("Always"). The generation of Spanish exiles is dying off at a rapid rate now. Privation, war wounds, and physical and mental disabilities are combining to decimate their ranks. In 1979 the French government changed the Spaniard's status from "refugee" to "Spanish national."

The death of Franco in November 1975 brought a quiet satisfaction but no dancing in the streets. He had been in power too long, consolidated his regime too well, thwarted reconquest hopes. The refugees in France have watched the unfolding of events in Spain with a measure of cynicism. Their attitude is colored by a disbelief in the sincerity of the reforming government. They feel that they have suffered too much, seen too much, been betrayed too often, to accept as genuine the developments now unrolling in their native land.

Time has given the Spanish people the type of government that Ernest Bevin envisaged for them in 1946, a limited monarchy leavened by conservative republicanism. The relative freedom entailed by this change has lightened the atmosphere in Spain. Ideas circulate more freely, and political parties, even the feared Communist Party, are part of the parliamentary apparatus. The communists represent a comparatively small segment of the electorate, but the socialists are the second largest party in the nation. A coalition of center-right parties governs in Madrid. The anarchists still remain outside the formal structure, although they have experienced a considerable rejuvenation. In a sense the situation has returned to the period 1933–1935, although without the excesses perpetrated by the ruling coalition of that period. A new constitution has been written. There is some moderation of police power, and the people are free—within limits—to demonstrate, to publish and read a wide variety of books, periodicals, and newspapers. The Church has modified its stand on a number of issues and taken a more liberal approach on social and economic questions. Where all this will lead, nobody can predict at the moment. It is entirely possible that after a period of several years things will come full circle and Spain will return to the situation of February 1936 and the politics of the popular front. In that case, the major question would become: will the army permit the flowering of legislation it thinks inimical to the Spanish tradition, of which it considers itself the guardian? And what if a new Franco arises to move against a left-liberal government? There lies the great uncertainty of Spanish politics. Nobody can say that events will repeat themselves exactly, and everyone hopes they will not. We shall have to wait and see.

For the aging Spanish refugee population in France, as well as for those exiles who have returned to Spain, these are lively speculative questions. But the central fact of their generation's existence is still the span of time from 1931 to 1955: 1931–1936 was the time of their knighthood, as the eulogist for Francisco Sabaté Llopart said; 1936–1939 was the time of their struggle to retain the Second Spanish Republic; 1939–1945 was the time when they gave their strength to Resistance and liberation; 1945–1955 was the time when hope for reconquest of the republic gradually dimmed and was extinguished by world forces beyond the exiles' control. This was more than enough for any generation of men and women to endure.

Appendixes

Notes

Bibliography

Index

A P P E N D I X   A

MEMORANDUM FROM JOAQUÍN CAMPS ARBOIX, SPANISH REPUBLICAN CONSUL AT PERPIGNAN, TO RAOUL DIDKOWSKI, PREFECT OF THE DEPARTMENT OF PYRENEES-ORIENTALES, APRIL 23, 1938.

Translated by Silvie Larrimore

The war in Spain can still present us with many surprises. Moreover, surprise is a factor in war, most especially in the paradox that reigns over the destinies of Spain.

It is not outlandish at the present time to foresee the possible victory of Franco. This victory would create political problems in France which are not mine to analyse.

Other problems of a humanitarian nature would also result, and I take the liberty to point out and formulate some suggestions regarding these.

I am talking about the problems that will surely ensue at the end of the Spanish tragedy in the form of internal convulsions, both deep and contradictory, and in the form of the mass exodus to the French border which will result. I know that a solution to the latter problem has been anticipated thanks to the insight of the French officials.

But I believe it has been considered only in regards to the damming in of emigrant masses in French territory.

I believe that it would be desirable for all that this problem should not arise; or in any case that it not arise for France in an acute way.

It is this hope that prompts this report.

The Spanish passion, inherent in the character of the race, is what easily leads to extremes that range from an unlimited cruelty to the most chivalrous generosity.

The present war abounds with both types. Thus every Spaniard, especially if he is not Catalan, bears within him a surprising complex of Torquemada and Don Quixote.

All the civil wars in Spain, as numerous as they have been in the country's history, have always been without quarter.

Consequently, the possibilities of Franco's approaching victory have created in the mind of every man the fear of appalling disasters.

One need only listen to perceive that two stages, of horror and ignominy, are taking shape in everyone's imagination.

First stage: foresees the loser's despair, which could translate inself into criminal madness and violence: plunders and conflagrations against real or imaginary fascists, against personal enemies out of desire for revenge or else with the intention of leaving nothing useful or nothing that could benefit the conqueror.

Second stage: the conquerors arrive, almighty, haughty, uncompromising, fiercely proud, not to bring a reign of justice and equality, but to impose their despotism, yielding to an inquisitorial and implacable hatred, that is to say, to establish precisely the opposite of what should be a policy of logic and basic understanding.

This double prospect is similar to a dagger that is turned in a raw wound.

In Catalonia, which is more sensitive, more understanding, in a nutshell, more European, this mental state causes an indescribable torment. To fathom this psychological state is both poignant and painful.

France with her spiritual sensitivity, which is hers alone, cannot remain indifferent to this reality, both because of her humanitarian disposition and because of the imperious force of the right of the people.

France could avoid this violence by finding a pretense in the facts themselves.

Indeed, in Spain, and particularly in Catalonia, everyone more or less has it in mind to seek refuge in French territory when the time comes to escape death no matter whence it come.

This desire is all the greater given that as a matter of honor, eternal France keeps the gates to her border open, and especially that one can reach this border within two days walk.

It is probable that the exodus will be massive, yet it is difficult to estimate the number of refugees. Neither can the conflict which this might produce in France be determined. What matters is avoiding it. How?

Simply by decreeing a truce, if not a respite, when Franco's victory would be imminent. This would be accomplished by a pact contracted among France, England, and Franco's accredited officials, and imposed on the latter with no option.

This agreement would consist in recognizing his exploits and his victory. But it would be limited on one point, namely the formation of one or several Spanish zones in which the right of asylum or of provisional extraterritoriality would be temporarily recognized.

France and England would insure and guarantee the lives of the refugees, as well as order, within this or these zones, they would take care that the refugees would not be returned to Spanish territory, and they would prevent the emigration of the others.

The most interesting zone or hinterland for France would be that of northern Catalonia, along the Andorra border to Cerbère (including the passes of Cerdagne, Perthus, and Cerbère). Its width would be such that it would reach the Rio Tordera and the mountain range of Montseny, that is to say, that it would correspond to the limits of the old province of Gerona.

In this project we would not dispute the victor's victory; his triumph, an established fact, would be unquestionable.

The defeated would be spared the anticipated initial cruelty and violation of common rights, which would be followed up and punished.

We would also avoid the extermination of Franco's supporters remaining in the loyal zone. Their goods and wealth would be sheltered from destruction.

And finally this would allow France and England to act as counterpart to the politics of the established fact, so dear to the totalitarian states.

This would place a trump card in the hands of the former, should the latter, unfaithful to their word, wish to maintain positions already established in Spain.

We do not ignore the difficulties of adopting and starting such a plan, these difficulties born of the military facts and the sinuosity of international politics.

But all will benefit from the advantages of a general order that could be obtained by the adoption and application of such a plan.

A P P E N D I X   B

The "List of Spaniards who passed through Stalag XIB before being sent to Mauthausen Concentration Camp" was the official record of the German Headquarters at Mauthausen, and is now in possession of the Amicale Nationale des déportés et familles de disparus de Mauthausen, Paris. The list contains the dates of reception, name, birthdate, birthplace, occupation, nationality, and concentration camp number of each Spaniard who entered Mauthausen between August 6, 1940, and December 20, 1941. It is not complete because Spaniards entered both before and after these dates. Also, there are gaps between September 17, 1941, and November 3, 1941, and between November 3, 1941, and December 20, 1941. Below is a tabulation of the number entering on the different dates of reception.

	Date	Number Entering
1940	August 6–8	561
	August 13	91
	August 25	430
	August 30	22
	September 8	201
	September 27	28
	October 14	1
	November 30	3
	December 23	846

	Date	Number Entering	Date	Number Entering
1941	January 24	841	June 7	21
	January 25	775	June 8	20
	February 2	1,506	June 15	15
	February 17	1,184	June 29	8
	March 3	254	June 30	500
	March 29	600	July 22	61
	April 3	358	July 23	19
	April 7	200	August 5	25
	April 8	500	August 8	62
	April 26	469	August 31	108
	April 29	28	September 5	7
	May 15	25	September 11	40
	May 22	22	September 12	25
	May 23	3	September 17	12
	May 24	34	November 3	51
	May 25	34	December 20	342
	May 29	12	Total	10,350
	May 31	6		

NOTES

INTRODUCTION

1. Gabriel Jackson, *The Spanish Republic and the Civil War, 1931–1939* (Princeton: Princeton University Press, 1971), p. 498.

2. Gerald Brenan, *The Spanish Labyrinth* (Cambridge: Cambrige University Press, 1967), p. 231. First published in 1943.

3. Lawrence Fernsworth, *Spain's Struggle for Freedom* (Boston: Beacon Press, 1957), p. 130. See also Hugh Thomas, *The Spanish Civil War* (New York: Harper & Row, 1961), pp. 21–30.

4. Thomas, p. 86.

5. *Paris Soir,* quoted by Brenan, p. 300.

6. Based on an interview with Jordi Planes, director of the Fondation Internationale d'Etudes Historiques et Sociales Sur la Guerre Civil d'Espagne, April 18, 1974, Perpignan. The foundation moved to Barcelona in 1978.

7. Thomas, p. 616.

1. RISING TIDE: THE FIRST REFUGEES, 1936–1938

1. Carmen Ennesch, *Emigrations politiques, d'hier et d'aujourd'hui* (Paris, Editions I.P.C., 1946), p. 161.

2. *Ibid.*

3. Guy Hermet, *Les Espagnols en France* (Paris: Les Editions ouvrières, 1967); and Javier Rubio, *La emigración española a Francia* (Barcelona: Editorial Ariel, 1974). Both writers speak of this difficulty throughout their works.

4. The flight of Napoleon's sympathizers in 1814, Spanish liberals in 1814 and 1823, and Carlists in 1840 and 1849. Gregorio Marañon, *Españoles fuera de España,* 6th ed. (Madrid, 1968), pp. 43, 45, cited by Rubio, p. 69.

5. Rubio, pp. 69, 89, 119, 125. The 1911 French census listed 105,760 Spaniards. During World War I, 125,000 Spanish emigrants came to France. The 1931 Census counted 351, 864 Spaniards.

6. Rubio, p. 201, claims 200,000 Spaniards were involved. This is disputed by George Bidault's statement that 340,000 refugees had been registered at the beginning of 1938. See also *L'Aube,* February 16, 1938. Michel Legris, "Les Espagnols en deça des Pyrénées," *Le Monde,* January 8, 1964, asserts that 156,00 Basques crossed into France during 1936–37. Of this group, 63,000 eventually returned to Nationalist territory, 32,000 chose to go to Catalonia, and 60,000 remained in France. Rubio, p. 206, also claims that the net number of refugees remaining in France at the end of Spring 1938 was 40–45,000. It should be noted that Rubio consistently shows a smaller number of refugees in France, either emigrating or remaining. In the present instance, however,

he has used figures supplied in a dispatch from the ambassador of Spain to France, official, no. 783, June 14, 1938 (MAE R-1.780,25).

7. *Mouvements migratoires entre la France et l'étranger* (Paris: Imprimerie nationale, 1943), pp. 104–5, cited by Hermet, p. 27.

8. Rubio, p. 193.

9. Ennesch, pp. 162–63. According to Rubio, p. 195, some 300 Franco sympathizers were repatriated when Irun fell, on September 4, 1936; *La Dépêche de Toulouse,* September 4, 1936.

10. *Le Populaire,* March 30, 1937.

11. Rubio, pp. 195–96. For information on repatriations see Conference Internationale d'Aide aux Refugiés Espagnols, *Recensement des refugiés espagnols* (Paris, July 15–16, 1939), cited by Rubio, p. 197.

12. Thomas, p. 251.

13. *Le Temps,* August 31, 1936.

14. Ibid., September 6, 1936. Hugh Thomas, p. 251, puts the figure at 560 soldiers.

15. *L'Humanité,* May 1, 4, 1937; July 4, 1937. Shipments of refugees that were reported for 1937 in *L'Humanité* and *La Dépêche* were: May 6, the *Havana,* 4,000 children; May 8, *Izarra,* 500, and 600 by train to Bayonne; May 9, ship unknown, 180; May 10, French ships *Chateau-Margeau, Chateau-Palmer,* and *Carimare,* 2,000; May 24, *La Galea,* 879, and *La Zuriola,* 759; May 25, *Cabo-Corona,* 1,100, *Somme* (French), 83, and 500 by train to Brive; June 2, *Havana,* 3,000 (escorted by British destroyer *Foxhound*); June 28, *Marion Maller* (British) 1,670; *Perros-Guirec,* 1,239; July 8, *Stancroft* (British), 1,950; August 22, *Seven Seas Spray* (British), 2,000; August 25, unknown ship, 500; August 28, *Cantabria,* 45. See *La Patriote des Pyrénées,* August 20, 21, 30, for estimate on evacuees from Santander. Rubio, p. 199, says, "We do not know with precision the number of refugees arriving in France at this time, nor the proportion which preferred to remain in France."

16. Servicio de Información de la Secretaria General del Jefe del Estado, no. B-21.556, August 31, 1937.

17. Servicio de Información de Fronteras del Norte de España, no. 16.995, October 5, 1937. Archivo del Ministerio de Asuntos Exteriores de Madrid (hereafter referred to as MAE), R-1.060,217, cited by Rubio.

18. Spanish consul, Bordeaux, official no. 194 to Spanish ambassador in Paris, MAE, R–631, 164, cited by Rubio, p. 200. David Wingeate Pike, *Vae Victis: Los republicanos españoles refugiados en Francia, 1939–1944* (Paris: Ruedo Ibérico, 1969), notes that 600 men of the Irun militia were permitted to traverse France and rejoin the Loyalist forces in Catalonia. See also *L'Humanité,* October 24, 25, 1939.

19. *La Dépêche,* April 3, 4, 1938, June 17, 1938. Thomas, p. 628, and Pike, p. 5, agree with this figure. Sir John Hope Simpson, *Refugees: A Review of the Situation Since September 1938* (London, 1939), p. 164, places the number at 8,000. *L'Humanité,* April 8, 1939, reported that 10,000–12,000 refugees entered Fos. See also April 9, 11, 19, 1939.

20. *La Dépêche,* April 4, 1938, June 19, 1938; ambassador of Spain to France, official no. 286, June 22, 1938; MAE, R–1.784,11, cited by Rubio, 205; *L'Humanité,* April 5, 1939.

21. See note 6. Jacques Vernant, *The Refugee in the Post-War World* (London: George Allen & Unwin, 1953), p. 274, says, "only women, children and elderly remained in France."

22. Cited by Pike, p. 2, minister of interior to police commissioners, March 22, 1937; telegram, General Menard to minister of war, April 10, 1938, cited by Pike, p. 5.

23. *La Liberté,* October 5, 1937; General Menard, chief of Seventeenth Army Corps (Toulouse) to the prefect of Haute Garonne: no. 21869, October 9, 1937, classified VERY SECRET, quoted by Pike, p. 4.

24. Albert Petit, *Journal des debats* (n.d.), cited by Pike, p. 6.

25. *L'Epoque,* July 10, 1937; *Le Petit Parisien,* April 2, 1938.

26. *L'Action française,* April 9, 1938; *Le Journal de Toulouse,* December 25, 1938, cited by Pike, p. 7.

27. *Le Matin,* May 7, 1938.

28. *Le Journal de Toulouse,* August 15, 1937; Pike, p. 8.

29. Pike, p. 8.

30. Thomas, p. 575.

31. Firmin Bacconnier, *La Production française,* cited by Pike, p. 8.

32. *Le Nouvelliste de Lyon,* April 2, 1938. Other newspapers, such as the extreme right-wing *La Garonne* (Toulouse), published a string of articles that castigated the conduct of Spanish refugees in France; Pike, p. 9.

33. *L'Humanité,* April 21, 1938.

34. Pike, pp. 9–10; *L'Humanité,* May 3, 1938. Arturo Barea, *The Forging of a Rebel* (New York: Reynal and Hitchcock, 1946), pp. 736–737, reported that it became increasingly difficult to secure renewals of papers. The French government ordered a number of Spaniards out of Paris. But one young Basque, who had secured a safe-conduct from Franco's government through the efforts of his father, a San Sebastian businessman, was told by the French authorities that "we've nothing against you, but it is high time we cleared France of all those Reds."

35. Hem Day, *L'Espagne nouvelle,* October 1938. Mr. Day was president of the International Committee for Anarchist Defense. *L'Humanité,* May 4, 1938; *Le Jour,* September 3, 1938.

36. Perpignan, near the Mediterranean coast, some forty kilometers from the Spanish border, had 23,000 refugees in September 1937, according to *L'Action française,* September 18, 1937. In the 1931 Census, Perpignan had a population of 73,962, according to F. Villaceque, *Le Département des Pyrénées-Orientales* (St. Germain-en-Laye: Editions M.D.I., 1970), 36.

37. Many refugees had relatives or friends who had come to France before the civil war and were thus in position to help. Private organizations also sheltered individuals or groups of refugees.

38. Louis Guilloux, "Refuge in Limbo," *Living Age,* 354 (July 1938):440–

445. The diary was translated by D. S. Bussy and appeared first in the section on "Life and Letters Today," *London Literary Monthly*. The quotations in the next few paragraphs are all from "Refuge in Limbo."

39. Guilloux, pp. 444–45. In France in those days it was customary for a new mother to remain in the hospital for twelve days after delivery of her baby.

40. *L'Humanité*, October 1, 1937.

41. Ibid., June 19, 23, 1938.

42. Letter and memorandum from Joaquín Camps Arboix to Raoul Did-kowski, April 23, 1938, no number, departmental archives, Perpignan. The memorandum is printed in full in Appendix A. As far as I am aware, this document is being presented in print for the first time. It does not appear in any of the standard accounts of that period.

43. *Le Midi socialiste*, January 24, 1939; *L'Oeuvre*, January 24, 1939; *L'Indépendant* (Pau), January 25, 1939; *La Dépêche*, January 25, 1939; Pike, p. 12; Thomas, p. 575.

44. *Le Midi socialiste*, January 26, 1939; *L'Action française*, January 28, 1939; *La Dépêche*, January 26, 1939.

45. *L'Action française*, January 28, 1939; *L'Oeuvre*, January 24, 1939; *Le Midi socialiste*, January 26, 31, 1939; *L'Indépendant* (Pau), January 26, 1939.

46. *Le Midi socialiste*, January 29, 1939.

47. Pike, p. 12.

48. *La Dépêche*, January 29, 1939.

49. *Le Petit Parisien*, January 24, 1939, cited by Pike, p. 13.

2. THE LONGEST MONTH

1. Pierre Izard, *La Petite Histoire, Argelès-sur-mer 1900–1940* (Perpignan: Editions Massana, 1974), p. 119.

2. Recensement de la population de 1936 à 1954, Archives, Département des Pyrénées-Orientales, Perpignan.

3. Villaceque, pp. 1–36. In 1967 there were 21,270 farms in the department. Of these, 60.3 percent consisted of one to ten hectares and 9.2 percent of less than one hectare.

4. Izard, pp. 119–120.

5. Ibid.

6. Thomas, pp. 570, 572; Izard, p. 120.

7. *Le Populaire*, January 14–19, 1939; *Le Midi socialiste*, January 14, 1939. The latter newspaper, the leading organ of the Socialist Party in Southwestern France, published many of the articles which appeared in *Le Populaire*, particularly the columns of Leon Blum and the reportage of J. M. Herrmann.

8. Thomas, pp. 572–73.

9. *Le Midi socialiste*, January 20, 21, February 1, 1939.

10. *L'Action française*, January 23, 1939.

11. Pedro Vallina, *Mis memorias*, vol. 2 (Mexico City: Ediciones Tierra y Liberatad, 1971), p. 159.

12. Ibid., pp. 159–60.

13. Ibid., p. 160.

14. *Le Midi socialiste,* January 24, 1939.

15. Federica Montseny, *Pasión y muerte de los españoles en Francia* (Toulouse: Ediciones "Espoir," 1969), p. 9. First printed in 1951.

16. Pierre Broué and Emile Témime, *The Revolution and the Civil War in Spain* (London: Faber and Faber, 1972), p. 517. First printed in French in Paris, 1961. The Spanish edition was published in Mexico City, 1971.

17. *Le Populaire,* February 9, 1939; *Daily Express,* February 13, 1939.

18. *La Dépêche,* February 22, 1939; Pike, p. 41; *Le Midi socialiste,* February 6, 1939. Companys went to Paris, then to St. Nazaire; he was detained by the French government on the outbreak of war and later turned over to Franco by the Vichy government. He was executed in 1942.

19. Pike, p. 41; Constancia de la Mora, *In Place of Splendor: the Autobiography of a Spanish Woman* (New York: Harcourt, Brace, 1959), p. 398.

20. Pike, p. 41; *Le Populaire,* March 10, 1939.

21. *Gringoire,* February 16, 1939.

22. Stanley Payne, *Franco's Spain* (New York: Crowell, 1967), pp. 110–112. Montseny, pp. 14–15, related that after her ordeal on the road she was recognized by a Spanish government official who took her to a French general at the frontier. Because she had a passport the general admitted her immediately. On the way to see the general she endured the curses of the waiting thousands. Realizing how useless any answer could be, she knew she was being treated differently because of her prestige. She asked the general when the others would be admitted and "he opened his arms in a sign of impotence and ignorance." He said the decision was not his to make. "The government continues deliberating. Undoubtedly the frontier will open. But the preparations . . . have not yet been made."

23. *Le Midi socialiste,* February 1, 1939. The same headline and story appeared in *Le Populaire,* January 31, 1939.

24. *New York Herald-Tribune,* February 7, 1939.

25. *Le Midi socialiste,* February 1, 1939; Jean Olibo, *Parcours* (Perpignan: Editions du Castillet, 1972), p. 52; Gustave Regler, *The Owl of Minerva* (London, 1959), p. 321; Montseny, p. 56; Thomas, p. 574. Also, Pierre Rouzard in *La Garonne,* January 30, 1939; *L'Humanité,* January 29, 1939.

26. These themes recur in every account of the flight.

27. De la Mora, p. 387.

28. Vallina, p. 162; Isabel de Palencia, *Smouldering Freedom: The Story of the Spanish Republicans in Exile* (London: Victor Gollancz, 1945), p. 40; de la Mora, p. 389.

29. Montseny, pp. 10–11.

30. De Palencia, 38–40. See also de la Mora, pp. 389–392; *Le Midi socialiste,* January 29, 1939; *Le Populaire,* January 29, 1939. In the latter, one refugee recounted how two airplanes had killed seventeen children with low-level strafing. See also *L'Action française,* January 29, 1939.

31. Vallina, pp. 162, 165–168.

32. Montseny, p. 22; *Le Populaire,* February 9, 1939, charged that the government had not prepared a plan and "does not want to understand, even today, the urgency and the breadth of necessary measures."

33. Pierre Rouzard, *La Garonne,* January 31, 1939; *L'Action française,* February 1, 1939; *Le Journal des debats,* February 1, 1939.

34. *Gringoire,* February 2, 1939. *L'Indépendant* (Pau), February 8, 1939, reported that a young woman of Gerona, who had had a child five days before the retreat from the city, had been told that when the Moorish soldiers arrived they would eat all infants. Thereupon she was persuaded to be evacuated, and her husband pushed her to France in a wheelbarrow. See also Vladimir d'Ormesson in *Le Figaro,* February 5, 1939.

35. De la Mora, p. 392.

36. *Gringoire,* February 2, 1939.

37. P. J. Sautes, *L'Action française,* February 1, 1939. Jean Taillemagre, in *La Garonne,* February 8, 1939, said that "the strange and growing terror" of the fleeing peasants was due to "a misunderstanding." He predicted that they would "pass to a more prudent attitude" when they realized that "they had nothing to fear from Franco."

38. *La Dépêche de Toulouse,* January 29, 30, February 1, 1939; Ennesch, p. 165.

39. *Le Populaire,* January 25, 1939.

40. Ibid., February 2, 1939; *Le Petit Parisien,* January 25, 1939; *Le Midi socialiste,* January 29, 1939; *L'Indépendant* (Perpignan), January 31, 1939. This prescription for felicitous reception of refugees was clearly not followed. Almost every account of the exodus notes that refugees were not fed for at least two and three days after entry. As will be seen, the first food for many was apt to be one loaf of bread for five or more persons.

41. Izard, p. 8; Pike, p. 5.

42. *Le Midi socialiste,* January 25, 26, 27, 1939; Izard, pp. 121, 124, 127.

43. *Le Midi socialiste,* February 22, 1939. Rous used the arguments advanced by Richard Klen, *The Laws and Usages of Neutrality,* vol. 2, par. 156.

44. Interview with author, March 20, 1974, Perpignan. *Le Midi socialiste,* February 1, 1939, interviewed a young woman who had just been permitted to enter France at Le Perthus. A worker from Barcelona, she had been on the road for five days carrying her fifteen-month old infant. Her husband had been killed in the defense of Catalonia. "I have waited twenty-seven hours in the rain for my turn to enter France," she said.

45. Broué and Témime, p. 518.

46. *L'Action française,* February 1, 1939; Izard, p. 124.

47. *New York Times,* February 5, 1939.

48. *Le Midi socialiste,* January 30, 1939, February 1, 1939. The newspaper's correspondent told of four young children being taken care of by their thirteen-year-old sister. "Mama has remained on the other side," the youngster said. "She did not want to abandon Papa but he cannot walk

very fast; he has a foot and a hand amputated. Now we are waiting for them here [Le Perthus]."

49. Izard, pp. 123, 132; *Le Midi socialiste,* January 31, 1939.

50. *New York Times,* February 7, 1939.

51. Izard, pp. 120–24. "Create a camp, with utmost urgency!" Izard relates how, after his mobilization in September 1939 and subsequent capture by the Germans in 1940, he met Boutillon in a German prisoner-of-war camp. They were behind barbed wire, and they realized that they were now in the same kind of trap they had built for the Spaniards.

52. Ibid., p. 124.

53. Ibid., p. 124–25.

54. *Le Midi socialiste,* February 1, 2, 1939; Izard, p. 125; *La Garonne* February 2, 1939; *L'Action française,* February 1, 2, 1939; *Le Populaire,* February 9, 1939.

55. *Le Midi socialiste,* February 1, 2, 1939.

56. *La Dépêche de Toulouse,* February 2, 1939.

57. *Gringoire,* February 2, 16, 1939.

58. *Le Midi socialiste,* February 6, 1939; *Le Populaire,* February 6, 1939.

59. Herbert L. Matthews, *New York Times,* February 7, 1939.

60. *Le Midi socialiste,* February 7, 1939. The figure of 10,000 is generally accepted as accurate. *L'Action française,* February 11, 1939, drew attention to the fact that there were only 500 hospital beds available in the Midi for the 8,000 Spanish wounded who had already arrived.

61. *Le Midi socialiste,* February 7, 1939; *L'Humanité,* February 9, 1939; *Le Figaro,* February 7, 1939, spoke of "the great misery of the wounded, with their ragged dressings and bloody plaster casts."

62. *Le Midi socialiste,* February 11, 1939. Before the decision was taken to admit the wounded, *Le Midi socialiste,* February 1, 1939, reported that some wounded, including amputees, had been lying on pallets for several days. "If only there were some gauze I would change their dressings," a Spanish doctor told the reporter.

63. Interview with author, Perpignan, June 19, 1974. *L'Humanité,* February 9, 1939, reported that some citizens of Perpignan, noting that a convoy of wounded had been left lying on the ground in the courtyard of the old military hospital for several hours, carried the men indoors themselves.

64. Montseny, pp. 55–57.

65. Interview with author, Perpignan, March 19, 1974.

66. Montseny, p. 16. *L'Action française,* January 31, 1939, noted the deaths of many young children "who succumbed following long marches in the snow and under the rain." The exodus never should have taken place, the newspaper said.

67. Hermet, p. 29. Pike, p. 64, says that it is probable that the largest part of this number were escapees. In a visit to the refugee cemetery at St. Cyprien, I saw that many of the Spanish graves were unmarked, and the crosses on others had sunk into the marshy ground to such an extent that markings were

invisible or obliterated. Also, many families had later claimed the remains of victims and reinterred them elsewhere. *Le Midi socialiste,* February 10, 1939, reported that at La Tour-de-Carol thirty-five deaths had occurred among the wounded during the previous night.

68. *Petit Bleu,* quoted in *L'Action française,* February 11, 1939.

69. Theo Ripoll in *L'Action française,* February 10, 1939. This particular accusation does not appear elsewhere.

70. *Gazette de la Haute-Loire,* quoted in *L'Action française,* February 4, 1939.

71. Leon Blum, *Le Populaire,* February 8, 1939; *Le Midi socialiste,* February 9, 1939.

72. *La Dépêche,* February 3, 1939.

73. Ibid., February 2, 1939. Ibid., February 5, 1939, published a *France-Presse* photo showing French mountain troops digging trenches near Osseje in order to prevent what was called a possible invasion of the Spanish republican troops.

74. Thomas, p. 575; H. L. Matthews, *New York Times,* February 6, 1939; Pike, p. 23; *L'Indépendant* (Perpignan), February 6, 1939; *Le Midi socialiste,* February 6, 1939; Broué and Témime, p. 538.

75. Regler, p. 321.

76. Ibid, p. 323.

77. De la Mora, pp. 393–395.

78. H. L. Matthews, *New York Times,* February 7, 1939.

79. J. M. Herrmann, *Le Populaire,* February 7, 1939; *Le Midi socialiste* February 7, 1939. There were some 1,500 to 1,800 members of the International Brigades still remaining in Spain when Catalonia fell. Many—particularly Germans and Italians—had taken Spanish citizenship. Others had been too severely wounded to depart in November and December, 1938. Jean Olibo, p. 196, wondered whether the forcible removal of arms was linked to the acceptance of "dishonorable conditions" by the democracies. He asks: "Don't they understand that our drama will, in a short time, be their drama?" See also Arturo Barea, p. 738.

80. Interview with author, Perpignan, May 17, 1974: Mr. Gomez is now a cobbler in Perpignan. *L'Humanité,* February 8, 1939, called for the trans-shipment of republican men and arms to the portion of Spain still under their control. *L'Action française,* February 9, 1939, thought otherwise. Trans-shipment would constitute a hostile act against Franco. Rather, men and arms should be sent to Franco.

81. Mariano Constante, *Les Années rouges, de Guernica à Mauthausen* (Paris: Mercure de France, 1971) pp. 129–132. *L'Indépendant* (Pau), February 9, 1939, reported the presence of 200 railroad wagons in the yards at Cerbère. They were filled with war materiel destined to go to Spain when the frontier was opened for a brief time. The material was still in crates. Pike, p. 24, pointed out that the French government made it clear that Spanish troops would not be transshipped to their native country. Such a

maneuver would probably have been in violation of the Hague Convention, V, art. 2. At the inaugural session of the French Conference for Aid to Spanish Refugees, Paris, June 10, 11, 1939, it was argued that "since the republican army was not a belligerent one, the soldiers ought to be returned to Valencia and not interned as prisoners of war."

82. Luís Bazal. *Ay de los vencidos! Testimonio de la guerra de España, 1936–1939* (Toulouse, 1966), p. 280.

83. José Gros, *Abriendo camino: Relatos de un guerrillero comunista español* (Bucharest: Coleccion Ebro, 1972), pp. 13–14.

84. *Le Midi socialiste,* February 11, 1939; H. L. Matthews, *New York Times,* February 12, 1939.

85. *Le Midi socialiste,* February 11, 1939; H. L. Matthews, *New York Times,* February 12, 1939; Antonio Herrero, quoted in Montseny, pp. 59–60.

86. Olibo, pp. 194–196, 199. *Le Midi socialiste,* February 8, 1939, found a grim irony in the fact that the jettisoned Spanish arms "are those which until yesterday served to protect us. They are mute witnesses, terrible accusers."

87. *Le Midi socialiste,* February 15, 1939.

88. *La Dépêche,* February 10, 1939.

89. *Le Midi socialiste,* February 9, 1939; Broué and Témime, 518.

90. *L'Action française,* February 10, 1939. *Gringoire,* February 16, 1939, also likened the republican army to a mob, "without leaders or discipline."

91. Valière, in an untitled report to the Chamber of Deputies, March 9, 1939, gives a figure of 440,000 Spanish refugees; Valière was president of the Commission on Finances; cited by Rubio, p. 210. Previously, a committee of the Ministry of Foreign Affairs under the presidency of Jean Mistler, had declared, on February 15, 1939, that a total of 340,000 Spanish refugees had entered France. Pike, p. 28, comments that the Mistler figure quite possibly did not take into account those who crossed the frontier without passing control points or passed these posts without being processed. *Le Midi socialiste,* February 19, 1939, presented a figure of 450,000, which had been calculated by a socialist parliamentary delegation that visited the camps. This figure was corroborated by *La Dépêche,* which estimated that 349,000 refugees had entered France before February 10, 1939. The estimates of *Le Midi socialiste* and *La Dépêche* were later confirmed in the pamphlet *La verité sur les camps de concentration en France,* issued by the Centrale sanitaire Catholique, Section Belge (Brussels, n.d., but probably in April 1939). This pamphlet said that by April 1939 refugees were scattered in camps or other shelters in seventy departments of France. It said these places contained 200,000 soldiers, 250,000 civilians (125,000 children, 100,000 women, 25,000 men). Guy Hermet, p. 27, puts the total of refugees at "more than 500,000" in mid–1939, quoting *Mouvements migratoires entre la France de l'étranger* (Paris, 1943), pp. 104–5. Michel Legris, *Le Monde,* January 9, 1964, says that 550,000 Spaniards entered France during 1939.

3. The Great Fear of 1939

1. Izard, p. 129. Janet Flanner, *Paris Was Yesterday, 1925–1939* (New York: Viking, 1972), p. 201. Under the pen name of Gênet, Flanner wrote a monthly column from Paris for the *New Yorker* for many years.

2. Ibid., p. 126.

3. Ibid., pp. 129–130.

4. Ibid., p. 126.

5. Ibid. *L'Humanité,* January 30, 1939.

6. Flanner, p. 127.

7. *Gringoire,* February 23, 1939.

8. *L'Action française,* February 3, 1939. The FAI is the international federation of anarchists. *Gringoire,* February 9, 1939, carried the headline, "The Anarchist Scum Is in France."

9. *La Garonne,* February 7, 1939.

10. *L'Action française,* February 12, 1939.

11. *La Dépêche,* February 3, 1939; Vladimir d'Ormesson in *Le Figaro* February 6, 1939.

12. *Gringoire,* January 26, 1939.

13. *Gringoire,* February 16, 1939.

14. Georges Ravon, *Le Figaro,* February 3, 1939.

15. Ibid., February 1, 2, 1939. George Orwell, in *Homage to Catalonia* (New York, Harcourt, Brace & World, 1952), p. 229, wrote that after leaving Spain in 1937, he and his wife stayed three days in Banyuls (Pyrénées-Orientales). The "little town seemed solidly pro-Franco," he said, and marked coolness was displayed toward the English couple when it was learned that Orwell had fought for the republic.

16. *L'Action française,* January 30, 1939. The same newspaper charged on February 6, 1939, that members of the French Communist Party were hiding Spanish Reds in their homes throughout the Pyrénées-Orientales. While this charge has been confirmed in some instances by Spanish communist sources, there is no evidence that the practice was as widespread as the newspaper indicated. On the other hand a cartoon published in *Gringoire* on February 16, 1939, shows a disarmed Spanish soldier seeking instructions from a man who is obviously an officer and Red commissar, complete with red star in his cap." What can we do now, without arms?" the soldier asks And the answer is: "Propaganda!" *L'Indépendant* (Perpignan), February 3, 1939, reported that an inspection of refugees had revealed that two hundred were carrying concealed arms.

17. *La Garonne,* February 6, 1939. Dolores Ibarruri, known as La Pasionaria, was a communist leader who was noted for her fiery speeches. She fled first to Paris and then to the Soviet Union. She returned to Spain in 1977 and now sits as a communist deputy in the Cortes.

18. Ibid., January 29, 1939.

19. Salvador de Madariaga, *Spain: A Modern History* (New York: Frederick A. Praeger, 1958), p. 581.

20. John Hope Simpson, *Refugees: A Review of the Situation since September 1938* (London: Royal Institute of International Affairs, 1939), p. 56.

21. *La Dépêche*, February 5, 1939. Pike, p. 19, says Persis Miller, director of the Unitarian Universalist Service Committee, told him she saw refugees refuse margarine. Also, they did not drink the proffered milk and threw it to the poultry. However, the "potato purée" was more often apt to be a weak and watery lentil soup.

22. Ibid.; *La Garonne*, February 7, 1939; *L'Action française*, February 4, 1939; *L'Indépendant* (Pau), February 7, 1939. The latter newspaper reported that the Spaniards had gone so far as to express their wish that France would become embroiled in war with Germany and Italy.

23. *L'Indépendant* (Pau), February 9, 1939; *L'Action française*, February 12, 1939.

24. *La Garonne*, February 7, 1939. Taillemagre asserted that "the one hundred and thirty-five journalists who are following the operations share my sentiment."

25. *L'Action française*, February 7, 1939.

26. *L'Indépendant* (Perpignan), February 5–6, 1939. *L'Action française*, February 4, 1939, also reported that French priests and nuns had been insulted by Spaniards.

27. *La Dépêche*, February 5, 1939.

28. Izard, pp. 131–32.

29. Ibid., p. 131.

30. Ibid., p. 132. He recalled that a year and a half later, thousands of Frenchmen had to endure the same trials on the roads of France as they fled from the Nazi army. French prisoners of war who also were shepherded into the German version of "el campo" were able to "understand and excuse in 1940 the acts which they had condemned in 1939."

31. Ibid., p. 133.

32. Francisco Fenestres, interview with author, Perpignan, March 19, 1974.

33. *La Garonne*, February 5, 1939.

34. Ibid., March 14, 22, 1939.

35. Izard, p. 134.

36. *L'Action française*, February 10, 1939.

37. *Le Figaro*, February 5, 1939.

38. *Gringoire*, February 16, 1939.

39. *L'Indépendant* (Pau), February 5–6, 1939.

40. *La Garonne*, February 3, 1939.

41. *La Dépêche*, February 7, 9, 1939.

42. *Le Midi socialiste*, February 3, 1939. The funds were appropriated through a decree based on Article 41 of the Law of 30 April 1921; Thomas, p. 576. There is no way in which the total of French and foreign governmental and private assistance can be determined, but it amounted to a considerable sum.

43. *New York Times*, February 16, 1939; Associated Press dispatch in

New York Times, February 19, 1939; *Le Midi socialiste,* February 9, 1939, reported the detention of eleven trucks bearing the reserves of the Bank of Spain and guarded by troops under the command of Colonel Lister. A French resident of Perpignan, who refused to allow the use of his name, told the author that as a boy of eleven he had accompanied his father to market near Le Perthus. They encountered a Spanish convoy in which one truck had broken down. A Spanish soldier offered the boy's father several hundred francs if he would allow the Spaniards to load the disabled truck's contents into his vehicle and take it to Perpignan. The father refused. "We looked into the truck and saw that it was filled with gold. My father was a naturally suspicious man and refused to become involved in what looked like a dirty transaction, and he didn't trust the Spaniards anyway," the informant said. See also de la Mora, p. 410.

44. Thomas, p. 576.

45. *La Garonne,* February 2, 3, 1939.

46. Herbert L. Matthews, *A World in Revolution: A Newspaperman's Memoir,* (New York: Scribner's, 1971), p. 37.

47. Constante, pp. 137–38; *The Times,* February 23, 1939.

48. Montseny, pp. 26–27.

49. Antonio Vilanova, *Los olvidados: Los exilados españoles en la Segunda Guerra Mundial,* (Paris: Ediciones Ruedo Iberico, 1969), p. 9.

50. Izard, p. 132.

51. *L'Action française,* February 4, 1939.

52. De la Mora, p. 407.

53. De Palencia, pp. 45–46.

54. Interview with author, Perpignan, April 17, 1974.

55. *Le Midi socialiste,* February 9, 1939.

56. *Le Midi socialiste,* February 1, 1939. De Palencia, p. 44, reported that in some instances the gardes mobiles and the police "scoffed at papers and safe-conducts signed by the French premier himself."

57. Ibid., February 14, 1939.

58. Vilanova, p. 5.

59. Izard, pp. 132–33. He remarks that in 1940 when he became a prisoner of war in Austria, "I was not cold because it was summer. But I too was hungry."

60. Ibid., p. 132; *Le Midi socialiste,* February 3, 1939.

61. *Le Midi socialiste,* February 10, 1939.

62. Ibid., February 9, 1939; *Le Populaire,* February 9, 1939.

63. *La Garonne,* February 5, 1939.

64. *La Dépêche,* February 13, 1939. The group also created a Comission for Aid to Spanish Children, led by Mme. de Montbrisson. See also *L'Indépendant* (Perpignan), April 2, 1939. *L'Aube,* February 9, 1939.

65. *La Dépêche,* February 6, 13, 1939; *Le Midi socialiste,* February 7, 1939.

66. *L'Indépendant,* Perpignan, February 17, 1939.

67. De Palencia, p. 41.

68. Vilanova, p. 13.
69. Interview with author, Toulouse, April 2, 1974.
70. Ibid.
71. Letter to author, July 5, 1974.
72. De Palencia, p. 52.
73. Vilanova, pp. 3–4. Vilanova, p. 75, also says that many French authorities were able to display "their hatred of liberty" in their treatment of the Spaniards. De Palencia, p. 41, claimed that fascist tactics had already "begun to interpenetrate every official aspect of France."
74. Miguel Angel, *Los guerrilleros españoles en Francia 1940–1945* (Havana: Editorial de Ciencias Sociales, 1971), p. 27.
75. Montseny, p. 58.
76. Ibid, p. 18.
77. De Palencia, p. 44.
78. Montseny.
79. Del Vayo, p. xi.
80. Francisco Fenestres, interview with author, Perpignan, March 19, 1974.
81. Angel, p. 28. Montseny, of course, also notes the aid given to the Spanish anarchists and others by French sympathizers, but she does not claim that "the people" adhered to the principles of "the democratic organs," that is, "the Communist Party."
82. Del Vayo, p. xi.
83. *La Dépêche*, March 15, 1939.
84. Interview with author, Perpignan, April 17, 1974.

4. IN THE EYE OF THE HURRICANE: THE BEACH PARTY

1. *Le Midi socialiste*, February 10, 1939; report of the socialist parliamentary delegation, February 15, 1939; *La Dépêche*, February 10, 1939; Pike, p. 32; Vilanova, p. 15; *Status of Construction*, memorandum, February 21, 1939, department archives, Perpignan.
2. *Le Midi socialiste*, March 1, 1939.
3. Hermet, p. 27; J. B. Climent, "España en el exilio," *Cuadernos Americanos*, 126, no. 1 (Mexico City, January-February 1963): 98–102, cited the last census conducted by the Mexican legation in Vichy France, June 1942, which listed 3,892 officers and subofficers; 1,743 doctors; 1224 lawyers; 431 engineers, architects, and technicians; 216 secondary school teachers, 156 university professors; 243 writers and journalists; and 4,649 public officials. Mention of large numbers of bourgeois and professional entrants into France was also made by Juliette Minces, *Les Travailleurs étrangers en France* (Paris, Editions du Seuil, 1973), pp. 61–62.
4. Conference Internationale d'Aide aux Refugiés Espagnoles, *Recensement des refugiés espagnoles* (July 15–16, 1939), vol. 1, pp. 2–6, quoted by Rubio, pp. 230–33. Many of the practitioners of liberal professions emigrated to Latin American countries. Thus, of eighty male adult refugees embarking from Marseilles to Argentina or Brazil, January 15, 1941, there were sixteen lawyers and ten doctors, plus a number of businessmen, MAE, R–1, 268, 29.

Jay Allen, in "Hostages of Appeasement," *Survey Graphic,* 28, no. 11 (November 1939), listed the following occupations: 2,063 school teachers, 2,440 printers, 2,909 electricians, 5,922 woodworkers, 17,000 builders and masons, and 10,272 mechanics.

5. Rubio, pp. 234–36. The departments surveyed were Aveyron, L'Herault, and the Gard.

6. Olibo, p. 207.

7. *Le Populaire, Le Midi socialiste,* February 13, 1939.

8. *La Dépêche,* February 2, 1939; de Madariaga, p. 734; Pablo Casals, *Joys and Sorrows* (New York, 1970), p. 233.

9. Olibo, pp. 202, 204.

10. Herrero, quoted in Montseny, p. 61.

11. Constante, p. 138.

12. An official memorandum of February 21, 1939, regarding the status of construction stated that barracks had been completed for six *ilots* ("sections"), each containing 27 barracks, for a total of 162; departmental archives, Perpignan. Vilanova, pp. 9, 14. Flanner, p. 202.

13. *Le Midi socialiste,* February 24, 1939, *L'Humanité,* February 7, 1939; interview with the police commissioner of Perpignan, Emile Severac, *Le Figaro,* March 3, 1939.

14. *Le Midi socialiste,* February 11, 1939; *Le Populaire,* February 9, 1939.

15. *La Dépêche,* March 18, 1939, recounted the escape of fifteen refugees from Argelès. A former refugee, who refused to permit use of his name, told me that he and many others had escaped by swimming around the perimeter of Argelès when the weather warmed up. A Spanish captain who had escaped from St. Cyprien and was recaptured, killed himself rather than return there. There are many other documented stories of prisoner escapes. Pike, pp. 52–53.

16. Vilanova, p. 11.

17. *L'Humanité,* February 13, 17, 1939. Other signers were François Billoux (Bouches-du-Rhone), Raymond Guyot (Seine), Virgile Barel (Alpes-Maritimes), Benenson (Seine-et-Marne), Marcel Brout (Seine), Cossonneau (Seine-et-Oise), Sulpice Dewez (Nord), Emile Fouchard (Seine-et-Marne), Demusois (Seine-et-Oise), Charles Benoit (Seine-et-Oise), Fernand Grenier (Seine), Darius Le Corre (Seine-et-Oise), Jacques Gresa (Seine), Georges Levy (Rhone), André Mercier (Seine), Adrien Mouton (Bouches-du-Rhone), René Nicod (Ain), Albert Petit (Seine), Auguste Touchard (Seine). Stories on camp conditions were printed in, among others, *The Times,* February 18, 24, 1939; David Scott, *Yorkshire Post,* February 27, 1939; *Time,* March 20, 1939; *Picture Post,* April 15, 1939; Jose F. Rojas, *Excelsior* (Mexico City), July 11, 1939; *Nation,* vol. 148, no. 19, May 6, 1939. Pike, p. 64n, reported that when the English journalist Lord Forbes arrived in Toulouse, April 13, 1939, his visit was monitored by the Sureté Nationale, which believed that he had been sent by the British government; principal inspector Policía Especial, to director general, Sureté Nationale, no. 180, May 29, 1939. The attack against Prefect Didkowski was pursued avidly by the Communist Party, in contrast

to the hands-off attitude of the socialists who, while they disapproved of his administration, did not call for his transfer. The communist deputy François Billoux accused Didkowski of "at least tolerating and encouraging" acts of severity against Spaniards. He intimated that the prefect was overzealous in carrying out governmental policy because of his rightist bias. Didkowski, for example, refused to meet with the communist delegation because it included André Marty, whom he accused of fomenting disorder in the camps. It should be noted that Didkowski was ultimately transfered to another prefecture. On January 24, 1944, he and eleven other prefects were removed from their posts and sent to a German concentration camp.

18. *Le Midi socialiste,* February 19, 1939, "Report of the socialist parliamentary delegation regarding conditions in the concentration camps for Spanish republican refugees." The report was actually completed by February 14 and portions of it were released at a press conference in Paris, February 15. The full text was published on February 19. Leading members of the socialist delegation were Vincent Auriol, Jules Moch, André Le Trocquer, Marx Dormoy, Lucien Hussel, Roucayrol, Auderguil, Castagniez, Parayre, and Louis Noguères.

19. Ibid. Pierre Izard, in a letter to me, January 22, 1976, declared: "I knew the camp of Argelès especially in its first months, from January to March 1939. There were contacts at the Mairie between the mayor and the camp commander, but the army would refer matters to its chiefs and the Mairie to the prefecture. Let us say that in this matter it was necessary to 'improvise'. There was no unity of command and decision."

20. *Le Midi socialiste,* February 19, 1939. The socialist delegation reported the case of a soldier who staggered because of a deep neck wound. There was nobody present to assist him.

21. Ibid. The committee saw French soldiers appropriate a wrist watch from a refugee. A French sympathizer who objected when four pencil cases were taken from Spanish soldiers was threatened with arrest by gardes mobiles.

22. Ibid. When Spanish soldiers greeted the socialist delegation with "Viva Francia," they were beaten by Senegalese soldiers. When a loudspeaker truck outside the gates blared nationalist propaganda the refugees threw stones at it and were in turn attacked by Spahis.

23. Ibid.

24. Ibid. The report took note of a certain amount of promiscuity as a result of the indiscriminate mixing of men and women during the first days of camp life. In addition to Spanish men, members of the French security forces and civilian officials were involved. Montseny, pp. 35–36, mentions "the continuous intercourse in the shelters and on the sand" and charges coercion by "those who had the right of power" over the women. The guilty women were disciplined by other Spanish women who stripped them in public and gave them "such a cudgeling [which] would make them think again before backsliding." However, she says, most of the women maintained their dignity. "They never lost their modesty, their desperate efforts to main-

tain themselves morally clean in the midst of that horrible wreckage." Izard, p. 136, also remarks on promiscuity in Argelès.

25. The earliest such list was compiled by the Spanish Socialist Workers Party and was printed in *Le Midi socialiste* on February 8, 1939. Other papers followed suit.

26. Report of the socialist parliamentary delegation. The socialist newspapers *Le Populaire* and *Le Midi socialiste* were finally admitted into the camps on February 23, according to *Le Midi socialiste*, February 24, 1939.

27. Ibid. *Le Midi socialiste*, February 15, 1939, declared that "France has covered itself with shame," and an editor who signed himself "D," in the same paper, February 19, 1939, said, "I do not feel proud of being French." The report recalled that when a French army under General Bourbaki had retreated into Switzerland during the Franco-Prussian war of 1870 the Swiss had received them with kindness and cordiality.

28. Léon Blum, "Nos Hôtes espagnoles," *Le Populaire*, February 17, 1939; *Le Midi socialiste*, February 17, 1939. The Council of Ministers had scheduled a discussion of the issue for February 14, but it was delayed until February 18. *Le Populaire*, February 15, 1939, ascribed the postponement to a campaign against Interior Minister Sarraut because he was "guilty of not having approved the *franquiste* zeal of [Foreign Minister] Bonnet."

29. *Le Midi socialiste*, February 13, 1939. The newspaper listed four army camps that were available for use by the refugees: La Valbonne (Gard), Caylus (Tarn-et-Garonne), Larzac (Dordogne), and La Courtine (Creuse).

30. *L'Humanité*, February 17, 1939; *La Dépêche*, February 15, 1939. The friendship group was composed mainly of leftist members of the chamber.

31. *Le Midi socialiste*, February 15, 1939; *L'Indépendant* (Pau) February 16, 1939.

32. *Le Populaire*, February 19, 1939; *L'Indépendant* (Pau) published the official communique without comment.

33. *Le Midi socialiste*, February 15, 1939.

34. *Le Populaire*, February 20, 1939; Izard, pp. 136–37; *Le Midi socialiste*, February 23, 1939. Deputy Noguères also wrote a strong article in the same paper, February 24, 1939, entitled "Videz Argelès" ("Empty Argelès").

35. Memorandum from Cazes, engineer-in-chief of Service Speciale d' Amenagement des Camps d' Hebergement des Refugiés Espagnoles, to engineers in camps, February 26, 1939, departmental archives, Perpignan. *Le Figaro*, March 2, 1939, declared that General Menard and Didkowski had agreed that, in the future, only Argelès, St. Cyprien and Barcarès would function as camps in Pyrénées-Orientales. See also *Le Midi socialiste*, March 3, 1939. Among new camps set up as a result of this policy were Gurs (Basses-Pyrénées) mainly for Basques and International Brigaders; Bram (l'Aude) for the elderly; Agde (L'Herault), mainly for Catalans; Mazères (L'Ariège), and Vernet-les-Bains (Pyrénées-Orientales).

36. *Le Populaire*, March 11, 1939; *L'Indépendant* (Pau), March 12–13, 1939. It is worth noting that *Le Populaire* devoted much space to the verbatim comments of the debaters, but *L'Indépendant* ignored Deputy Rous's

remarks entirely. It supported the contentions of Ybarnegaray, who represented the Basses-Pyrénées in the Chamber. *La Dépêche,* March 11, 1939, printed Rous's comments as well as Ybarnegaray's. Editorially, it flayed both the extreme left and right for their attitudes and declared that the government's policy of humane actions, tempered with its need for French security, was correct. It should also be noted that when Spanish Navarrese troops arrived at the French border, *Le Petit Journal* quoted Ybarnegaray as saluting their arrival with "Long live free Spain . . . we know that this [kind of] Spain is traditionally the friend of France," February 15, 1939. See also *La Dépêche,* March 15, which lauded a Chamber of Deputies speech by Sarraut in which he predicted the reconciliation of the two Spains: "All of Spain will then remember the hospitality of France, which has always understood the moving call of humanity."

37. Fenestres, interview with the author, March 19, 1974, Perpignan. He said that two wells were dug about 20 meters from the shore, but they were dirty and contributed to the spread of dysentery. This, in turn, created a sanitation problem because there were too few latrines. Women, especially, suffered embarrassment because the open beach served as the only place where one could relieve oneself. J. Plazas, quoted by Montseny, p. 48; Vilanova, pp. 7–9; *La Garonne,* February 8, 1939. However, Tixier-Vignancourt in the same newspaper, February 24, 1939, indicated that the situation was due almost entirely to the idleness, indifference, and lack of discipline among the refugees.

38. Izard, p. 121.

39. *La Dépêche de Toulouse,* February 10, 1939.

40. Ibid., February 16, 1939. Castan reported that Argelès contained sixty sheds, each inhabited by twenty-four men, whereas they were constructed to house ten or twelve at a maximum; sixty similar sheds were under construction, affording shelter to a total of 2,880 men. J. M. Herrmann, of *Le Populaire* and *Le Midi socialiste,* February 16, 1939, disputed this figure, asserting that only 750 men were under shelter.

41. Izard, p. 137.

42. An order for wood to construct 250 barracks at Barcarès was confirmed on February 20, 1939, Francis Dorlet Co. to Louis Malet, engineer in charge of procurement; no. R–8400, February 20, 1939, departmental archives, Perpignan. A memo from Malet to a Mr. Robert, engineer, states that construction at Argelès had begun on February 24, 1939; April 28, 1939, departmental archives, Perpignan. On March 5, 1939, Aldo Lombardi of Arudy (Basses-Pyrénées) was given a contract to install 350 barracks at Barcarès, beginning March 10, 1939, according to a memorandum signed by engineer Robert, departmental archives, Perpignan (Jacques Petry, director, Société de Construction des Hautes-Alpes, to chief of engineers, Prefecture, Pyrénées Orientales, February 22, 1939, department archives, Perpignan). There is no confirmation in the archives as to whether the offer was accepted, but Izard, p. 137, notes that some time in March "some prefabricated barracks arrive . . . solid" (Mayor of Bayonne to Prefect Didkowski,

February 22, 1939, departmental archives, Perpignan). Lieutenant Colonel Moufflet informed Malet that he had ordered 800 latrine containers; no. 537, March 3, 1939, departmental archives, Perpignan. In April 1939 the prefect signed an agreement with Jean Birot, of Montpellier for the installation of three distribution stations for sterilized water at Argelès and St. Cyprien; departmental archives, Perpignan. Jean Humareau of Bordeaux undertook to construct a service road at St. Cyprien; May 16, 1939, departmental archives, Perpignan. Charles Gambres, of Industrie Electrique Ecoiffier, Perpignan, contracted to install electricity at St. Cyprien, at a price not to exceed 120,000 francs; May 15, 1939, departmental archives, Perpignan. Similarly, Henri Groud, director, Societé Hydroelectrique, Perpignan, agreed to construct an electrical network at Argelès, at a price not to exceed 150,000 francs; February 25, 1939, departmental archives, Perpignan.

43. Memorandum, Cazes to Colonel Gauthier, commandant of forces in Pyrénées-Orientales, February 19, 1939. An unaddressed memorandum mentions the fact that forty-nine Spanish army trucks were being used at Barcarès; departmental archives, Perpignan.

44. "Besoins en main d'oeuvre espagnole," Barcarès, February 25, 1939, departmental archives, Perpignan.

45. General Menard to camp commanders, May 8, 1939, no. 2576/31; note du service from Colonel Gauthier, May 11, 1939, no. 958/31; note du service from Colonel Gauthier, May 11, 1939, no. 958/GRM; note du service from Lieutenant Colonel Bois, May 9, 1939, no. 2682-d; all from departmental archives, Perpignan.

46. *New York Times*, March 1, 1939.

47. *Le Midi socialiste*, March 1, 1939. Dr. André David, a deputy from Haute-Garonne, inspected the camps. He told *Le Figaro*, March 3, 1939, that even when construction supplies were sufficient, "absolutely nothing has been done." On the other hand, a contractor at Barcarès complained of the lack of wood for construction; another, at Argelès, blamed incessant rain and cold for the lack of progress. See A. Lombardi to engineer Berthelout, March 7, 1939, and Henri Perdrix to lieutenant colonel commandant of engineers of camps, March 23, 1939; Lieutenant Colonel Moufflet, commandant of troops, camps, and service, sixteenth Military Region, no. 181/GC. All of these citations are from the departmental archives, Perpignan.

48. Lieutenant Colonel Moufflet to Prefect Didkowski, March 18, 1939, no. 29/G.C.; no. 781/G.C., departmental archives, Perpignan.

49. *Time*, March 20, 1939.

50. *The Times*, February 24, 1939; report of Dr. Peloquin to Parliamentary Group of French-Spanish Friendship, February 23, 1939.

51. Constante, p. 141.

52. Jaime Mas Torne, in Montseny, p. 54, testified: "Mental troubles made inroads among us . . . The lack of food, the cold, the hopelessness, wrecked our reason."

53. John Stevens, "The Driven People," *New Republic*, 98 (March 15, 1939):158–59.

54. Pike, p. 38.

55. Chavarría, in Montseny, p. 52. He says, "In those days at St. Cyprien, if one went to the infirmary it was to die." Later, contagious disease patients were evacuated to one of the two hospitals in Perpignan that received Spanish refugees.

56. *New York Times,* February 25, 1939.

57. *Le Midi socialiste,* February 27, 1939.

58. Ibid., February 26, 1939. Dr. José Pujol, Montseny, p. 29, corroborates the impossibility of arriving at the total number of deaths. "No statistics were kept. Many times [the refugees] were buried without even their names being known. In the mairies of Argelès, Barcarès, St. Cyprien and Agde, no detailed registry exists."

59. Bills from Pompes Funèbres Générales, Perpignan, January 31, 1940, February 29, 1940; departmental archives, Perpignan. However, it is impossible to give credence to Palencia's claim, p. 160, that at least 140,000 Spaniards died in France between 1939 and 1946. Vilanova, p. 10, asserts that in the first six months of 1939, 14,672 Spaniards died in the camps. He attributes this figure to "the French authorities," but does not cite any document or report.

60. Report of Dr. Peloquin to Parliamentary Group of French-Spanish Friendship, February 23, 1939. Dr. Peloquin had granted a lengthy interview to *L'Humanité* on February 11, 1939, in which he stated his recommendation for the use of French army supplies. In another *L'Humanité* article on the same date, Emile Decroix recounted the recommendations of a group led by Dr. Dervaux, of the Centrale Sanitaire, which had met with Health Minister Rucart in Perpignan and urged the development of a supply depot at Elne which would serve the health and sanitation needs of the camps and hospitals in the Pyrénées-Orientales.

61. Report of engineer, Barcarès, May 10, 1939, departmental archives, Perpignan. At Argelès in mid-April there was still a need for 300 additional latrine-containers; Lieutenant Colonel Moufflet to M. Malet, April 14, 1939, departmental archives, Perpignan.

62. García-Bastide, unpublished manuscript, made available to the author. There is no date for the cited entry, nor is any place named.

63. *Commonweal,* 31 (March 15, 1940):443.

64. "Spaniards in Exile," *The Nation,* 148, no. 2 (May 13, 1939):556–58; *The Times,* February 24, 1939.

65. *Le Populaire,* March 9, 1939; *Le Midi socialiste,* March 10, 1939; *Le Figaro,* February 22, 1939.

66. Thomas, p. 713; Vernant, pp. 58, 279; Simpson, p. 59, cited by Pike. France undertook to pay high Spanish officials 1,500 francs per month, with 500 additional francs for a wife and each child, up to a maximum of 2,500 francs, according to Madariaga, p. 738. Militiamen were supposed to receive a subsidy of 450 francs monthly, but many did not receive it; *Au Secours des républicains espagnols,* p. 26, quoted by Pike, p. 60.

67. Vilanova, pp. 7, 11; Dr. Pujol in Montseny, p. 33; Gros, p. 16.

68. Controller General Sallet to the prefect, Pyrénées-Orientales, March 7, 1939, departmental archives, Perpignan. *Le Figaro,* February 3, 1939.

69. Ibid. A letter from director-general of Territorial Police to prefect, Pyrénées-Orientales, no. 1.994, February 1, 1939, informed him that "a number of particularly suspect individuals, members of the FAI," have been reported as being in France. In particular, T.C., a member of the National Committee of the FAI, is wanted for participating in a number of assassinations; departmental archives, Perpignan. I have used only the initials of suspects, rather than the full names contained in the police reports.

70. Head of Prefecture Office (Pyrénées-Orientales) to divisional Commissioner of Special Police in Perpignan, April 29, 1939, departmental archives, Perpignan.

71. Central Commissioner of police, Sureté Nationale, to prefect, Pyrénées-Orientales, no. 5399, March 19, 1939, departmental archives, Perpignan; head of Prefecture Office, Pyrénées-Orientales, to central superintendent, April 12, 1939, departmental archives, Perpignan. J.J.B. was a naturalized French citizen.

72. *Le Figaro,* February 19, 20, 26, 1939.

73. Special inspector of radio, Port Vendres, to chief of police, no. 38, February 5, 1939, departmental archives, Perpignan.

74. Among the more notorious of these camps were: Collioure, Le Vernet, Noë, Bram, Ste. Sulpice, Eysses, Toulouse, Montpellier, Lodève, Moissac, Bergerac, Noutron de Castres, Gaillac, Foix, Tarbes, Riom, Montlucon, Perpignan, Nîmes, and Mont-Louis. Women were sent mainly to Rieucros. Mayor Baudru of Perpignan worried about the length of time the anarchists could be kept in jail in the absence of specific charges and a trial, *Le Figaro,* February 12, 1939.

75. Montseny, pp. 63–64.

76. Vilanova, pp. 19–21.

77. Angel, pp. 197–98.

78. Pierre Brandon, *Asile et travail aux refugiés espagnols,* p. 45; *Temoinages sur Collioure,* pp. 1–6; *Le Midi socialiste,* May 22, 1939; Madeleine Braun, letter of June 12, 1939, *Nation,* 149, no. 2 (August 12, 1939):160; *Au secours des républicains espagnols* (Paris, 1939), p. 10; Pike, pp. 58–59, 65.

79. Montseny, p. 65.

80. Arthur Koestler, *Scum of the Earth,* (New York: Macmillan, 1968), pp. 101–131; first published in 1941. Pike, p. 66. Montseny, p. 63.

81. Koestler, pp. 106–7, 116, 131.

5. Requiem for a Republic: Recognition, Repatriation, Resettlement

1. Broué and Témime, p. 520.

2. *Le Midi socialiste,* February 8, 1939; and *L'Indépendant* (Pau), February 8, 1939.

3. *Le Populaire,* February 9, 1939; Ennesch, p. 166.

4. This section is based on the accounts of Broué and Témime, pp. 519–522; Jackson, pp. 464–477; and Thomas, pp. 579–604.

5. General Rojo, when he resigned his commission rather than continue a useless struggle, quoted by Julian Zugazagoitia, *Guerra y vicisitudes de los españoles* (Paris: Librería Española, 1968), vol. 2, p. 232, first published in Buenos Aires under the title of *Historia de la guerra de España*, 1940.

6. Broué and Témime, p. 521; Jackson, p. 465; Thomas, p. 577.

7. Jackson, p. 467.

8. Herbert L. Matthews, *New York Times*, February 6, 1939.

9. De la Mora, pp. 412–14.

10. Julio Alvarez del Vayo, *Freedom's Battle,* translated by Eileen Brooke, (Boston: Houghton-Mifflin), p. 278.

11. Jackson, p. 467.

12. Ibid., pp. 467–472. For Mera, the anarchist general, the suppression of the communist uprising must have been a sweet victory. In effect he was exacting revenge for the communist putdown of the anarchists in May 1937. At the end of the war Mera escaped to French North Africa and was interned. But on February 20, 1942, he was delivered to Franco by the Vichy government in response to a specific demand for extradition. Mera was then imprisoned by the nationalists and sentenced to death. Later, this punishment was revoked.

13. Jackson, p. 477.

14. Rubio, p. 215, gives a total of 15,000. Vilanova, p. 26, puts the number at 20,000. In his later indictment of Colonel Casado, Alvarez del Vayo said that only 2,000 had left, whereas at least 30,000 should have been able to do so, as quoted in Broué and Témime, p. 538. It would appear from figures pertaining to Spanish refugees in French North African concentration camps that del Vayo grossly understated the number and that the actual total lies somewhere between the estimates of Rubio and Vilanova.

15. Broué and Témime, p. 538; Rubio, p. 214; Thomas, p. 602.

16. Joaquín Raluy, in interview with the author, Toulouse, April 3, 1974.

17. Rubio, pp. 214–15.

18. *L'Action française,* February 3, 1939; *L'Indépendant* (Pau), February 8, 1939; *Le Figaro,* February 3, 1939. It should be noted that Senator Bérard, who had been a close friend and supporter of Poincaré during the 1914–18 war and the nineteen-twenties, later became a loyal adherent of the Vichy government and was appointed by Marshal Pétain to the post of ambassador to the Vatican.

19. Thomas, p. 580.

20. *Le Midi socialiste,* February 19, 1939; "Non, non, et non," *Le Populaire,* February 14, 1939.

21. Léon Hudelle, *Le Midi socialiste,* February 17, 1939.

22. *La Dépêche,* February 16, 1939; *Le Midi socialiste,* February 18, 1939; *Le Populaire,* February 8, 1939.

23. *Le Figaro,* February 3, 1939; Gabriel Péri, "Do We Dare Recognize Franco?", *L'Humanité,* February 13, 1939; *Le Midi socialiste,* February 17, 1939. *Le Populaire,* March 10, 1939, accused the newspapers that favored the

Daladier-Bonnet policy of seeking to prepare French public opinion to accept mass repatriation "without rebellion."

24. Robert O. Paxton, *Vichy France: Old Guard and New Order, 1940–1944* (New York: Alfred A. Knopf, 1972), p. 169.

25. *Le Midi socialiste,* February 13, 1939; *Le Populaire,* February 13, 1939; *L'Humanité,* February 11, 12, 14, 1939; Hermet, pp. 27–28, wrote: "Desirous of disembarrassing themselves quickly of these exiles, the French authorities did not always reserve for them a welcome above reproach. [They] offered them a choice only between a return to Spain, dangerous for their liberty, and even for their lives, and internment in the camps." The French also recruited soldiers for the Foreign Legion.

26. *New York Times,* February 13, 1939; John Stevens, "The Driven People," *New Republic,* 98 (March 15, 1939):158–59.

27. Jean-Maurice Herrmann, *Le Midi socialiste,* May 19, 1939.

28. *Excelsoir,* February 23, 1939; *Petit Parisien,* February 25, 1939. *Excelsior,* February 22, 1939, called for a complete break with the Spanish republican government.

29. *Le Figaro,* February 9, 14, 23, 1939.

30. *Le Matin,* February 3, 1939.

31. *L'Action française,* February 3, 1939.

32. *République,* February 4, 1939.

33. *L'Indépendant* (Perpignan), February 5–6, 1939; *L'Indépendant* (Pau), February 8, 1939; *La Dépêche,* March 15, 1939; Robert Brasillach, *Histoire de la guerre d'Espagne* (Paris, 1939), pp. 444–45.

34. *Le Figaro,* February 24, 25, 1939; *New York Times,* February 24, 25, 1939; Thomas, 583; *Le Midi socialiste,* February 28, 1939.

35. *Le Figaro,* March 15, 1939; Lois Elwyn Smith, *Mexico and the Spanish Republicans* (Berkeley: University of California Press, 1955), p. 209.

36. *Le Midi socialiste,* February 15, 1939; *New York Times,* February 25, 1939; Jackson, p. 466; Pike, p. 27.

37. Principal inspector of the Special Police to the director general of Sureté Nationale, no. 105, April 29, 1939, quoted by Pike, p. 57.

38. *Le Midi socialiste,* February 20, 1939. The article was signed with the initials M. D.

39. Stevens, *New Republic,* March 15, 1939; Francis G. Smith Jr., "Spaniards in Exile," Ibid., 148, no. 2 (May 13, 1939):556–58.

40. *Le Figaro,* March 15, 1939. Jean Claire Guyot, *L'Illustration,* March 15, 1939, said that general French opinion demanded that "the rabble . . . anarchists of POUM . . . communists of the UGT," be made to leave the country.

41. *Le Midi socialiste,* April 8, 1939; circular no. 6.656, Ministry of Interior to prefects, no date, quoted by Rubio, pp. 219, 221; *Lettre datée du 30 mai denonçant les Traitements infligés aux Espagnols refugiés en France,* quoted by Pike, p. 58; *La Dépêche,* March 15, 1939.

42. *Lettre datée du 30 mai,* quoted by Pike, p. 58.

43. Jesús Abenza in Montseny, p. 235.

44. *Le Peuple,* March 8, 1939.

45. *Le Midi Socialiste,* April 5, 8, 1939.

46. *New York Times,* March 29, 1939. The Paris newspapers cited by the *New York Times* were not identified.

47. Rubio's own calculations, pp. 219–220, are double-edged. On the one hand he adopts the figure of 440,000 refugees entering France that was advanced by the Valière Commission (see Chapter 2 of this book). If this figure is accurate, then the subtraction of 340,000 repatriates would leave only 90,000 exiles remaining in France in mid-December 1939. On the other hand, although he labels as "fantastic" Guy Hermet's projection in *Les Espagnols en France* that 528,000 refugees entered France, a similar subtraction would leave 188,000 exiles still in France. Actually, Rubio uses the total of 140,000 that was stated as the number of Spaniards still in France by the minister of interior in a report to the Chamber of Deputies, December 14, 1939, and printed in the *Journal Officiel,* December 15, 1939, 2, 133. On page 229, Rubio puts the net emigration of Spanish republicans at 190,000, including 140,000 to France, 25,000 to North Africa, 15,000 to Mexico and other Latin American countries, and 10,000 to the Soviet Union. Hugh Thomas, in the second edition of his book, uses the figure of 140,000 Spaniards remaining in France. The figure of 250,000 repatriates was first used by Victor Alba, *Histoire des républiques espagnols* (Vincennes: Les Editions Nord-Sud, 1949), p. 402. The cumulative totals of 50,000 and 70,000 repatriations for February and March were reported by the *Manchester Guardian,* March 3, 1939; Jackson, p. 466; Simpson, p. 57; Thomas (first edition), p. 712; *Le Monde,* January 8, 1964; Hermet, pp. 26–28. Hermet used as his sources *Mouvements migratoires entre la France et l'étranger* (Paris: Imprimerie nationale, 1943), pp. 104–5, and the figures of the Mexican Embassy, obtained through J. B. Climent, "España en el exilio," pp. 98–102. Vilanova, p. 3, also bases his estimates on the Climent statistics.

48. Sheean, "Spain: The Aftermath of Defeat," *New Republic,* 100, no. 1292 (September 6, 1939):125–127. Patricia W. Fagen, *Exiles and Citizens: Spanish Republicans in Mexico* (Austin: University of Texas Press, 1973) pp. 110–113.

49. Material for this section was gathered from Fagen, pp. 22–39; Lois Elwyn Smith, *Mexico and the Spanish Republicans* (Berkeley: University of California, 1955), p. 223; and Pike, p. 84–88.

50. Fagen, pp. 34–35. Salvador de Madariaga, p. 589, describes how a group of Spanish refugees, who had been "living the life of wealthy South Americans" in Deauville after leaving Spain in February 1939, loaded the treasure on the *Vita.* Madariaga estimated the worth of the treasure at $50,000,000. See also Lois Smith, pp. 229–30. Prieto happened to be in on the scheme because he was returning from his assignment as Spanish republican representative at the inauguration of the president of Chile.

51. *Acuerdo adoptado por la Diputación Permanente de las Cortes, reunida*

en Paris el 31 de junio de 1939, published by JARE, 99, quoted by Fagen, p. 36.

52. Pike, pp. 84–85.

53. Pike, p. 80; Kershner, pp. 121–22.

54. Patricio G. Quintanilla, *Comité Técnico de Ayuda a los Españoles en Mexico: Memoria,* the official records of SERE, quoted by Fagen, p. 36.

55. Silvia Mistral, *Exodo: Diario de una refugiada española* (Mexico: Ediciones Minerva, 1940), p. 149.

56. De Madariaga, p. 738.

57. Fagen, pp. 37–38, Lois Smith, pp. 237–38. Smith lists 1,800 passengers for the *Sinaia,* and 2,085 for the *Mexique.* Sir John Hope Simpson, p. 62, noted the strong professional representation in the first official sailing: thirty-seven professors, twenty-eight doctors, seventeen lawyers.

58. Fernando Solano Palacio, *El éxodo: por un refugiado español* (Valparaiso: Editorial Más Allá, 1939), p. 79. Solano said that in a later voyage of the *Mexique,* and in the first trip of the *Winnipeg* to Chile, up to 86 percent of the anarchist applications were rejected while those of other groups were accepted almost in entirety. See also *Boletín de los antifascistas descontentos de los campos internacionales,* no. 2, n.d., quoted by Pike, p. 83.

59. Ibid., p. 103.

60. Vilanova, p. 13.

61. Interview with author, Perpignan, March 19, 1974.

62. Mauricio Fresco, *La emigración repúblicana: Una victoria de Mexico* (Mexico City: Editores Associadas, 1950), pp. 9–10, defends the Mexican officials. Mistral, pp. 148–158, details the prejudiced nature of the interviews. Fagen, p. 37, n. 43, interviewed a number of Spanish refugees in Mexico who supported the contention that selection procedures were biased in favor of Negrín supporters and Communists. Solano, quoted by Pike, pp. 83–84, was especially bitter toward Negrín.

63. Lois Smith, pp. 236–37.

64. Solano Palacio, p. 89.

65. Fagen, p. 37. See also Pike, p. 81.

66. Ibid., p. 38; Pike, pp. 87–89.

67. Ibid., pp. 36–38. Fagen says that the Dirección's figures probably err on the conservative side. Félix Fulgencio Palavicini, *Mexico: Historia de su evolcuión constructiva,* 4 vols. (Mexico City: Distribuidora Editorial Libro S. de R.L., 1945), p. 272, said that the emigration counted at least 15,000 exiles. Fresco, p. 53, estimates about 16,000. Other estimates are higher, ranging between 20,000 and 40,000. The Spanish embassy in Mexico was closed between 1939 and 1945, thus precluding the existence of official records; Vernant, p. 662.

68. Fagen, p. 39, n. 51. See also note 55 of this chapter.

69. José R. Marra-López, *Narrativa española fuera de España* (Madrid: Ediciones Guadarrama, 1963), p. 52.

70. Mistral, p. 158.

71. Barea, pp. 738–39.

6. "Father Don Quixote, Deliver Us . . ."

1. *Le Midi Socialiste*, April 13, 1939. The minister of labor was given sole responsibility for the mobilization, assignment, and regulation of working conditions of foreign workers. Minister of agriculture Queuille told a Senate Committee that he strongly favored the use of "certain foreigners" to aid production on French farms; *Le Figaro*, February 1, 1940; Vilanova, p. 52. In *Le Figaro*, August 4, 1939, January 18, 1940, it was emphasized that the decrees of July 20, 1939, and September 4, 1939, made foreigners liable for military and labor service. The latter decree specified that foreigners who had resided in France for less than two years could serve in the armed forces only at the discretion of the French authorities. Two additional decrees, *Journal Officiel*, February 27, 28, 1940, mobilized all foreigners for any service required by the State, and authorized the requisition of all agricultural workers, including foreigners.

2. Kershner, pp. 30, 33–34.

3. Pike, pp. 55–56. These figures are by no means definitive. For example, they do not include 1,600 wounded and sick who were in French hospitals, nor 3,440 Basques maintained by the Basque government-in exile, nor 6,250 children housed in special foyers, nor unknown thousands—mainly women— who lived in unoccupied buildings or in private homes. Simpson, p. 114, says that 350,000 refugees were housed in official institutions and private homes. He put the number of Basques at 60,000 and estimated the population in Barcarès at 80,000 instead of the 70,000 cited above. Additional corrections, gleaned from other sources, appear in the following pages.

4. See Chapter 4. General Menard announced that overcrowding would be reduced by the establishment of new camps in the departments of Tarn, Garonne, and l'Ariège. Barcarès and Argelès were to be reduced to populations of 40,000 to 50,000 each, and the new camps would hold no more than 15,000 to 20,000 each. The target was apparently met in Argelès, but not in Barcarès. However, the new camps fulfilled the French government's expectations in terms of their refugee populations.

5. The camp at Argelès had eleven sections, as follows: transients and amputees; former police; infantry (four sections); artillery; supply services; frontier guards and tax collectors; sailors; aviation; civilians; Basques; International Brigades; and cavalry.

6. Instruction Générale no. 3, Cazes, chief engineer of the camps, February 19, 1939, departmental archives, Perpigan; Dr. José Pujol, in Montseny, pp. 3–32; Pike, p. 68.

7. Interview with author, Perpignan, March 12, 1974.

8. *Manchester Guardian*, as condensed in an article in *Current History*, July 1939, p. 49.

9. *Le Midi socialiste*, April 4, 1939.

10. *L'Indépendant* (Pau), May 4, 1939. The paper gave 20,000 as the camp population, in contrast to the 16,000 cited by Pike and shown in the table in this chapter.

11. *La Dépêche*, May 6, 1939. The refugee population of Montoliou is placed at 17,000 in the article, but Pike lists it as "indeterminate."

12. Francis G. Smith, Jr., "Spaniards in Exile," *The Nation*, 148, no. 20 (May 13, 1939), pp. 556–558.

13. *La Dépêche*, May 6, 1939.

14. Olibo, p. 239.

15. Dr. José Pujol, in Montseny, p. 36.

16. Madeleine Braun, general secretary of the Comité International de Coordination et d'Information pour l'Aide à l'Espagne Républicaine, *The Nation*, 149, no. 2 (August 5, 1939), p. 158. Miss Braun's letter had been written on June 12, 1939 in response to the positive picture painted by Francis G. Smith. She also forwarded a letter from Emile Kahn, secretary of the League for the Rights of Man, written on June 8, 1939. He reported excessive brutality toward prisoners and made the assertion concerning Collioure.

17. Pujol, in Montseny, pp. 30–31, 36.

18. Report of the engineer of bridges and roads, *Protection contre les Crues du Vieux Tech de l'Hôpital construit sur la rive droite de ce cours d'eau,* August 22, 1939, departmental archives, Perpignan.

19. Pujol, in Montseny, p. 37. *Le Figaro*, May 19, 1940, reported a decree permitting foreign doctors to practice in France.

20. Ibid., pp. 39–40.

21. Ibid., p. 38. As a corollary, Dr. Pujol reported that after having separated Spanish families, the French authorities required passes to be issued for Sunday visits to the camps. When the number of requests for passes increased, the practice was abruptly terminated.

22. *Le Midi Socaliste*, May 10, 1939.

23. Minister of interior, n. 9647, September 13, 1939, classified as secret, quoted by Pike, p. 100.

24. Principal inspector of special police to subprefect Saint-Gaudens (Haute Garonne), February 6, 1940; Divisional General Michel (Toulouse), n. 70–1870D, March 5, 1940, classified VERY SECRET, quoted by Pike, p. 100–101.

25. Ministry of Interior, telegram, October 2, 1939, confirmed in circular on October 9, 1939, quoted by Pike, pp. 101–2; David T. Cattell, *Soviet Diplomacy and the Spanish Civil War* (Berkeley: University of California Press, 1957), pp. 126–132. Kershner, pp. 145–46, points out that the sudden Russian concurrence with Germany heightened the already active distrust of Spaniards which had previously marked French attitudes; Pike, pp. 92–93.

26. *Le Figaro*, July 26, September 2, 8, 1939; Miguel Angel, *Los guerrilleros españoles en Francia, 1940–1945* (Havana, 1971), p. 29; Pike, pp. 92–94; decree of the interior ministry, June 24, 1939; Madariaga, pp. 738–39.

27. *Le Figaro*, July 11, 25, 26, 1939.

28. Ibid., September 11, 1939; April 15–May 10, 1940.

29. *L'Indépendant* (Pau), May 11, 30–31, 1939; *Le Midi socialiste*, July 21, 1939.

30. Olibo, p. 236.

31. Broué and Témime, p. 539.

32. Prefect of Haute-Garonne to minister of interior, February 29, 1940, CONFIDENTIAL; decree of minister of interior, May 20, 1940, quoted by Pike, pp. 102–3.

33. Pike, p. 103. Although Negrín was officially the chief executive of the government, he did not carry much weight with his own people. Other center parties were also represented in this group.

34. José Berruezo, *Contribución a la historia de la C.N.T. de España en el exilio* (Mexico City: Editores Mexicanos Unidos, 1967), pp. 26–28.

35. Pike, pp. 68–74.

36. Juan Comorera in *La Voz de los Españoles*, August 12, 1939.

37. *Boletín de los Antifascistas Descontentos de los Campos Internacionales*, no. 1, n.d.

38. Pike reports that on July 4, 1939, one hundred and fifty internees, mainly members of the International Brigades, requested such a separation.

39. Constante, pp. 139–140, 142.

40. Ibid., pp. 143–44.

41. Gros, p. 16.

42. Miguel Angel, pp. 35–37. Angel's claims to the leading role of Spanish Communist Party are disputed by the anarchists and other groups, although all agree that the party and individual Spanish communists were prominent in the Resistance. It is interesting to note Angel's use of communist lexicon in this connection: "During all this time [exodus and in the later phases of Resistance] the Spanish communists, inside and outside the concentration camps, held high the banner of the party and against the calumnies and odious propaganda orchestrated by the French and international reaction. Conserving their organization and the unity of the ranks, they worked indefatigably for the united action of the democratic forces in the emigration, fighting against bad treatment and suffering by the refugees in the camps and preparing themselves to prosecute the combat on French territory and in the interior of Spain," p. 29.

43. Vilanova, p. 239.

44. Juan de Pena, "Arena" [Sand], *Arena y viento* (Barcelona: Gráficas el Tinell, 1973), pp. 86–90. The first edition was published in Perpignan, 1949. The poems were written in 1939 and 1940 while de Pena was interned in a French concentration camp. Fifteen woodcuts that accompany the poetry were also created in the camps.

45. Ibid., "Misfortune," p. 62.

46. Olibo, p. 199.

47. De Pena, "Nostalgia," p. 46.

48. Léon Felipe, "Allí No Hay Nadie Ya," in Dario Puccini, *Romancero de la resistencia española* (Mexico City: Ediciones Era, 1967), p. 186. First published in Italian as *Romancero della Resistenza Spagnola*, 1960, translated into Spanish by Juan Goytisolo.

49. J. Atienza, "Nosotros Queremos Ser," in *Rossellon*, vol 1, no. 3, August 31, 1939. *Rossellon* was published by a group of artists and writers who had

been given shelter at the Chateau Valmy, near Argelès-sur-mer. The poems and articles were written in longhand and hand-copied to the number of twenty-five copies. The author is indebted to M. Pierre Izard for making available one of the few copies in existence. The copy is in the archives of the Mairie at Argelès-sur-mer.

50. Fagen, p. 83.

51. J. M. Corredor, *Conversations with Pablo Casals* (Paris, 1955), p. 215, This book was later translated into English by André Mangeot, London, 1956. Corredor was secretary to Casals for many years and now lives in Perpignan, where he teaches at the university.

52. *Nostra Terra,* May 1939. This newspaper was printed with some French assistance. A copy was made available to the author by Jordi Estevill, director of the Centre Pluridisciplinaire des Sciences Humaines et Sociales, of Perpignan University.

53. Berruezo, pp. 195–96. The exhibit contained ten sections as follows: "Factors of Social Disorder," "The Road of the Revolution," "History of the Spanish Revolution," "Scenes from the War," "Men of the War and of the Revolution," "The Constructive Work of the Revolution," "In Exile," "Art Against Fascism," and "Conquered and Conquerors."

54. Montseny, pp. 34–35.

55. Based on a study of *Le Figaro, L' Indépendant* (Pau) and *Le Midi socialiste,* June-September, 1939.

7. Deja Vu: War and Defeat Again

1. Michel Legris, "Les Espagnols en deça des Pyrénées," *Le Monde,* January 9, 1964. When two hundred Spaniards working for the Societé Nationale des Constructions Aeronautiques asked to return to Spain, the minister of labor informed the minister of interior that it was very important to keep them in France; minister of labor to minister of interior, November 2, 1939, in Pike, p. 99. See also *Nation,* 152, no. 16 (April 19, 1942):461–62, which quoted Adolf Hitler to the effect that he considered the Spanish republicans as "presumptive enemies no matter where they go."

2. Mariano Puzo, interview with author, Perpignan, March 12, 1974.

3. Vilanova, p. 16; *Le Figaro,* August 21, 1939.

4. Vilanova, pp. 52, 320; Flanner, p. 202; Rubio, p. 244, quoted by Georges Mauco, "The Cultural Assimilation of Immigrants," supplement of *Population Studies* (London and New York: Cambridge University Press, March 1950); Spanish ambassador to France, dispatch no. 66, April 4, 1939, MAE R–10578; Ibid., no. 452, April 9, 1940, MAE, R–1.342, p. 2.

5. *L'Indépendant* (Pau), September 16, 1939. The *New York Times,* April 15, 1939, saw the French interest in the Spanish refugees as a warning to Italy that she "would arm masses of veteran republican fighters if Rome does not take her troops out of Spain." It is worth recording the words of Enrique Ballester Romero, who spoke for many Spaniards when he gave his reasons for joining the Foreign Legion: "For me this war represents the continuation of that of Spain . . . I prefer the risks of the soldier in the field to the humiliat-

ing condition of the refugee among the barbed wire that surrounds us, the wide horizon of the battlefield to the limited space of the concentration camp, the fraternity of the combatant to the entangling hostility of an unhappy comrade. And, when the war is over, if I live, to be able to shout to the whole world that I gained my liberty with my rifle in hand." Vilanova, pp. 321–22, 67; Pike, p. 92; Antonio Soler, in Montseny, p. 100.

6. *Le Midi socialiste*, July 17, 19, 1939; Pike, pp. 89–91; *Pasión y muerte de los españoles in Francia*, p. 83. Montseny implies that the Spanish government-in-exile and SERE, the aid organization that would have furnished the funds for the cooperative project, were not aggressive enough in pursuing it with the French government.

7. Constante, pp. 141–42; Vilanova, p. 51; J. Plazas, in Montseny, p. 48, said that he was forced to join a worker's company.

8. Julio Alvarez del Vayo, *Freedom's Battle* (Boston: Houghton Mifflin), p. x; Olibo, pp. 242–5, 251; Montseny, p. 99; Pedro Alba, in Montseny, p. 216.

9. Eduardo Pons Prades, *Republicanos españoles en la Segunda Guerra Mundial* (Barcelona: Editorial Planeta, 1975), pp. 37, 40.

10. Vilanova, pp. 16–17, 51.

11. Del Vayo, p. 221n.

12. Angel, p. 30; Mario Montagnana, *Ricordi di un operaio torinese* (Roma: Rinascita, 1949), vol. 2, p. 174, quoted by Pike, p. 98. Montagnana was an Italian member of the International Brigades who was imprisoned at Le Vernet. Rinascita is the publishing arm of the Italian Communist Party.

13. Vilanova, pp. 325–29. The figure of nine hundred dead is given by Michel Legris, *Le Monde*, January 8, 1964.

14. *Le Figaro*, April 22–28, May 1–30, June 11, 1940; *La Dépêche*, April 25, 1940; *Le Midi socialiste*, April 14–28, May 1–30, June 1–11, 1940.

15. Georges Blond, *La Légion étrangère* (Paris: Stock, 1964), p. 279.

16. M. J. Torris, *Narvik* (Paris: Arthème Fayard, 1946), p. 157; Vilanova, p. 329.

17. Vilanova, p. 321.

18. Ibid.

19. Antonia Soler, in Montseny, pp. 100–102.

20. Pedro Alba, in Montseny, pp. 216–224.

21. Constante, p. 149; Pons Prades, p. 43.

22. Manuel Razola Romo, in Pons Prades, p. 42.

23. Joan Pagés, in Pons Prades, p. 48. See also Amadeo Sinca Vendrell, in Pons Prades, p. 50.

24. Pons Prades, pp. 56–7; Vilanova, p. 71.

25. José Cercos Redon, interview with author, Perpignan, March 14, 1974.

26. Carmelo Ibañez, in Vilanova, p. 72; Ibid. See also Pons Prades, pp. 57–58.

27. The 117th Workers' Company was captured at Dunkirk, along with remnants of other units, according to Secundino Pinto Cortino, a member of the 117th, in Pons Prades, pp. 51–52.

28. Joan Pagés, in Pons Prades, p. 48.
29. Constante, pp. 140–49, 153; Pons Prades, pp. 43–44. Constante gives the date of capture as June 20, 1940, whereas in Pons Prades he gives it as June 21, 1940.
30. José Ortuño Lopez, in Pons Prades, p. 47.
31. Amedeo Sinca Vendrell, in Pons Prades, pp. 49–50.
32. Manuel Razola Romo, in Pons Prades, pp. 42–43.
33. *España Nueva* (Mexico City), vol. 1, no. 2, December 8, 1945.
34. Casimiro Climent Sarrió, in Pons Prades, pp. 41–42.
35. José Luís Fernández Albert, in Pons Prades, pp. 40–41.
36. Vernant, p. 188.
37. Angel, p. 218.
38. Vernant, p. 217.
39. Amicale Nationale des deportés et familles de disparus de Mauthausen et ses commandos, *Liste des espagnols qui sont passés au Stalag XI B avant d'aller à Mauthausen* (Paris: Angle), p. 218. I have seen and counted the Amicale list; see Appendix B.
40. Angel, p. 218; Manuel Razola and Mariano Constante, *Triangle Bleu: les républicains espagnols à Mauthausen 1940–45* (Paris: Gallimard, 1969), p. 194; Constante, pp. 153–245. Montserrat Roig, *Els Catalans als camps Nazis* (Barcelona: Edicions 62, 1977), pp. 367–528.
41. Berruezo, pp. 18–23.
42. J. Plazas, in Montseny, pp. 48–49; Pons Prades, p. 58.
43. Mariano Puzo, interview with author, Perpignan, March 12, 1974.

8. IN THE SERVICE OF LE MARECHAL

1. Philippe Pétain, "Message (sur la politique de Redressement National)," *La France nouvelle* (Paris: Fasquelle, 1941), p. 78. Eugen Weber observes that "in its moments of crisis, modern France traditionally turns toward old men, *patres patriae*, whom habit has endowed with the authority the nation yearns to abdicate"; Hans Rogger and Eugen Weber, *The European Right* (Berkeley: University of California Press, 1966), p. 112.
2. *La Dépêche*, August 12, 1940.
3. Paxton, p. 170, declared that the "presence of so many 'Reds' made French conservatives nervous." Pétain had been the first French ambassador to Franco's Spain and strengthened his old friendship with the Caudillo. See also Abel Plenn, *Wind in the Olive Trees: Spain From the Inside* (New York: Boni & Gaer, 1946), pp. 221–224.
4. Seventeenth Military Region (Vichy): 69717/S August 24, 1940, quoted by Pike, p. 104.
5. Ministry of the Interior, *Bulletin officiel*, no. 10 (October 1940), quoted by Paxton, p. 170. "Thus," he remarked, "Vichy had already set up its own concentration camp system."
6. Pike, p. 106; Angel, p. 39.
7. Vilanova, pp. 17–18. Angel, p. 39. Other prominent leaders turned over to the Spanish government were Ministers Julián Zugazagoitia and Juan

Peiró Belia; and deputies Teodomiro Menéndez and Francisco Cruz Salida. In 1941, fifteen members of the POUM were tried at Montauban and sentenced to a collective total of one hundred years in prison.

8. Broué and Emile Témime, p. 449. José Salvador, who worked in the Office of Obligatory Work (Service du Travail Obligatoire) during that period, told David Wingeate Pike that "Vichy delivered Spanish Republicans to the Germans, but not to Franco"; Pike, p. 108.

9. François Pietri, "vis-à-vis des Espagnols," *La vie de la France sous l'occupation, 1940–1944* (Paris: Plon, 1957), pp. 701–2, translated by Philip W. Whitcomb for the Hoover Institution of War and Peace, Stanford University.

10. Madariaga, p. 703. See also Alberto E. Fernández, *La España de los Maquis* (Mexico City: Ediciones Era, 1971), p. 104.

11. Richard Herr, *An Historical Essay on Modern Spain* (Berkeley: University of California Press, 1974), p. 229. He says that although Franco resisted entry into the war, he allowed German submarines to use Spanish ports. Report from principal commissioner, chief of District Police, Pyrénées-Orientales, to prefect of Pyrénées-Orientales, no. 11596, December 24, 1941; Zimmermann, principal inspector of the National Police, to M. Bondurand, commissioner of information services, Perpignan, no. 111/42, February 23, 1942. Both citations from departmental archives, Perpignan.

12. Général Bridoux, "Journal," October 23, 1942, quoted by Paxton, p. 296; *L'Oeuvre*, September 12, 1942.

13. Henri Cado, for the secretary of state, Ministry of the Interior, circular No. 900 POL. JUD. 6.T, September 1, 1942, to prefects, governor general of Algeria, from departmental archives, Perpignan.

14. Letter for the regional intendant of police (Montpellier), no. 5459 R.G., to prefect, Pyrénées-Orientales, July 2, 1942. He referred to a report from the prefect of Pyrénées-Orientales to the secretary general of police, Vichy, May 16, 1942, departmental archives, Perpignan.

15. Letter from principal commissioner, Perpignan, to prefect, Pyrénées-Orientales, No. 7837, August 19, 1942, in response to letter from the prefect requesting the inquiry, July 26, 1942, no number, departmental archives, Perpignan.

16. Henri Cado, for the state councillor, secretary general of police, circular no. 1125 POL JUDI, to prefects, police prefects, and police intendants, November 13, 1942, from departmental archives, Perpignan.

17. Report of divisional commissioner, chief of information, No. 12322, to prefect, Pyrénées-Orientales, December 12, 1942. The action was initiated by the regional intendant of police, no. 390/199–112–1148, telegram no. 08416 Very Urgent, departmental archives, Perpignan. *La Dépêche*, October 16, 1940, reported a somewhat more limited operation where three hundred suspects were searched and fifty detained for further questioning.

18. Letter from chief, 427th Travailleurs Etrangers group, to prefect, Pyrénées-Orientales, marked secret, January 7, 1943, no. 8268/C/EC, departmental archives, Perpignan.

19. Letter from Aime Blachas, superintendent of Judicial Police, to divisional commissioner, chief of the Fourteenth Regional Brigade of the Judicial Police, Montpellier, no. 48/10.156, January 26, 1942, from departmental archives, Perpignan.

20. Note from Ministry of Interior, no date, no number, to prefects, April 17, 1942; letter from secretary general of police, Vichy, no. 1385/POL.JUD. 2/T, to prefect of Pyrénées-Orientales, May 15, 1942; letter from prefect of Pyrénées-Orientales to subprefects, no. 2896, May 19, 1942; letter from prefect of Pyrénées-Orientales, to the principal commissioner of general information, Perpignan, no. 5560, transmitting the reports on suspects compiled by subprefects. All citations from departmental archives, Perpignan.

21. *La Dépêche*, August 22, 23, 1940.

22. Patricia W. Fagen, *Exiles and Citizens: Spanish Republicans in Mexico* (Austin: University of Texas Press, 1973), p. 38. The figure is an approximation because it includes all of 1940, not merely those who came after August and because the government was unsystematic in its method of counting. Fagen believes they erred somewhat on the conservative side.

23. Dr. Henry Harvey, in interview with author, May 11, 1975, Littleton, Massachusetts.

24. *La Dépêche*, September 3, 1940, October 10, 1940.

25. Corredor, p. 215; Koestler, p. 257.

26. Ramón Alvarez, *Eleuterio Quintanilla, vida y obra del maestro* (Mexico City: Editores Mexicanos Unidos, 1973), p. 403; Montseny, pp. 83–84.

27. Vilanova, p. 59. These figures cannot be considered totally accurate. They present an averaging of varying estimates, but they serve as a valuable indicator of the level of utilization of Spaniards by Vichy and the Nazis.

28. Ibid., pp. 200–201, quoting Casimiro Climent Sarrió, who served as a secretary in the office at Mauthausen.

29. Vilanova, p. 55. He quotes a memorandum from the Vichy government to the ministers of interior, war, and labor, regarding the desirability of having Spaniards substitute for Frenchmen in German projects, but he fails to give proper documentation for this assertion.

30. Montseny, p. 93.

31. Letter from the commissioner of police of Rivesaltes to prefect, Pyrénées-Orientales, No. 1.101, giving census figures as requested in note from prefect, March 21, 1942, departmental archives, Perpignan.

32. *La Dépêche de Toulouse,* October 19, 1940. It was the worst storm since 1892. Letter from inspector of health to prefect, Pyrénées-Orientales, April 10, 1941; report of secretary of state for family and health, to prefect, Pyrénées-Orientales, May 28, 1941, departmental archives, Perpignan. The secretary pointed out that rooms and other facilities in St. Louis Hospital would be "absolutely impossible to repair." Dr. José Pujol described how the wind tore off the roofs of the barracks, allowing the rain and sand to inundate the residents, in Montseny, p. 41.

33. Letter from Dr. Gérard Lefebvre, chief doctor of Infant Sections and chief physician of the camp of Rivesaltes, to camp commander, May 16,

1941; note of confirmation to camp commander's approval, from Dr. Lefebvre, May 17, 1941, from departmental archives, Perpignan. At a meeting of camp commanders in Vichy, September 22, 23, 1941, the proceedings recorded the need expressed for the establishment of a sanatorium for tuberculous Spaniards.

34. Letter from Gustave Humbert, commander of Camp Rivesaltes, to prefect, Pyrénées-Orientals, May 9, 1942, no number, departmental archives, Perpignan.

35. Memorandum from Dr. Gérard Lefebvre, chief physician of the camp of Rivesaltes, to Gustave Humbert, camp commander of Rivesaltes, May 24, 1941, no number, departmental archives, Perpignan.

36. Letter and memorandum from Dr. Lefebvre and Dr. Ginies to Gustave Humbert, camp commander, June 28, 1941; letter from Dr. Lefebvre to inspector general of camps, Vichy, no. 5125/SA, November 13, 1941. Both citations from departmental archives, Perpignan.

37. Letter from Dr. Lefebvre to Commandant Humbert, July 8, 1941, departmental archives, Perpignan.

38. Dr. Henry Harvey in interview with author, May 11, 1975, Littleton, Massachusetts. The figure of 1,750 calories per day made French intake the lowest in Western Europe, according to Paxton, pp. 359–60. It is reasonable to suggest, therefore, that with food so scarce the caloric intake of the Spaniards was even lower.

39. Letter from Gustave Humbert to prefect, Pyrénées-Orientales, no. 2495/DI, July 10, 1941, departmental archives, Perpignan.

40. Report by Dr. Dorvault, inspector of health, Pyrénées-Orientales, to prefect, Pyrénées-Orientales, no. 741 Hy, July 17, 1941, departmental archives, Perpignan.

41. Report from Dr. Gérard Lefebvre to the director of regional health services, Montpellier, June 8, 1942, no number, in response to the latter's note, no. 2658, June 4, 1942. Both citations from departmental archives, Perpignan.

42. J. Plazas, in Montseny, pp. 49–52.

43. Ramón Viscosillos, in Montseny, pp. 85–88. Miguel Angel, p. 49, reported that at another Todt camp each morning roll call would feature a harangue by a German officer. He told the Spaniards that they were magnificent soldiers who had been betrayed by their leaders. Also, he said, the French merited disapproval because of the shoddy reception they had given the refugees.

44. Vilanova, p. 59.

45. Telegram from Delage and Recruitment Commission for TODT, to minister of labor, no. 11938, August 24, 1942; telegram from prefect, Pyrénées-Orientales, to prefect, Gironde, no. 879, August 17, 1942; prefect, Pyrénées-Orientales, requisitioning ten gendarmes to accompany one hundred workers from Perpignan to Montpoint, August 27, 1942; telegram from Delage to Commissariat de lutte contre le chomage, no. 00955, informing it of the

transport of 125 workers, August 27, 1942. All citations from departmental archives, Perpignan.

46. Francisco Fenestres, interview with author, March 19, 1974, Perpignan.

47. *La Defense de France,* no. 21, November 1, 1942.

48. Vilanova, p. 55. Paxton, p. 292, remarks that "it was Hitler who did most to mobilize young people for the Resistance by trying to mobilize them for work in German factories." A report to the American Office of Strategic Services (OSS) from a Frenchman who had recently escaped to London told of the posting of a list of names of railroad workers in Lyons who were being requisitioned for labor in Germany. The entire shop walked out and threatened to stay out if the list were not removed. The next morning it was gone. Similar incidents were reported from Toulouse and Limoges, A–9821216, marked SECRET, November 21, 1942, National Archives, Washington, D.C.

49. Vilanova, pp. 64–65; Dr. José Pujol, in Montseny, p. 41.

50. *Treball,* July 1942. The newspaper was published by the Partido Socialista Unificado de Cataluña (PSUC), which was the ruling party in the autonomous Catalan republic. It cooperated very closely with the Communist Party of Spain.

51. *Treball,* July 19, 1942; Arthur London in Henri Noguères, *Histoire de la résistance en France, juin 1940–juillet 1941* (Paris: *Robert Laffont,* 1967), quoted by Angel, p. 45. Colonel Serge Ravanel, chief of the Toulouse Region, Forces Françaises de l'Interieur, in Angel, p. 12, recalled his conversations with Spanish guerrillas in the spring of 1944. He said that all considered that the liberation of France and Spain were the same struggle. They hoped that after the war the Allies would do everything necessary to reestablish the Spanish republic.

52. Mariano Puzo, interview with author, March 12, 1974, Perpignan.

53. Ibid., see also Angel, pp. 54–56; and Vilanova, pp. 240, 257–59.

54. Angel, pp. 55–56; Vilanova, p. 239. Fernández, p. 23, claims that the UNE was actually organized in Montauban earlier in November but was proclaimed officially at the meeting in Grenoble.

55. Angel, pp. 45–49, 56, says that the Communist-led UNE was "an anti-Francoist, patriotic, and democratic movement," which contained "militant republicans, socialists, and anarchists." The most important task facing the party, inside and outside of Spain, he added, was "to forge the unity of the anti-fascist forces."

56. *Reconquista de España,* November-December 1942.

57. Ibid.

58. Berruezo, pp. 25–42. Berruezo, who participated in the organizing meetings, saved the texts of circulars, against instructions to the contrary. In May 1941, the French authorities intercepted a letter and questionnaire which showed that small anarchist groups were trying to establish connections with other militants and seeking advice as to how to proceed in reorganizing the CNT; letter from divisional commissioner of Special Police,

Toulouse, to prefect of Haute-Garonne, no. 4511, marked SECRET, May 29, 1941, from departmental archives, Perpignan.

59. Statement by Colonel Serge Ravanel, chief of Toulouse Region, Forces Francaises de l'Interieur, in Angel, pp. 11–12. See also statement by Arthur London, a leader of the MOI, in Angel, p. 45.

60. Paxton, p. 292, states that direct action by the Resistance subsided after the fall of 1941. There is at least a good case to be made for the reverse, as far as the Spaniards were concerned, if one includes the growing operations of escape networks and sabotages in factories, mines, and depots.

61. Pons Prades, p. 295; Montseny, pp. 107–8; report from special commissioner of Le Perthus to prefect, Pyrénées-Orientales, no. 698, March 20, 1941, and divisional commissioner, Cerbère, to prefect, Pyrénées-Orientales, no. 693, February 26, 1941, both citations from departmental archives, Perpignan.

62. Mariano Puzo, interview with author, March 14, 1974, Perpignan; Pons Prades, p. 300.

63. Thérèse Mitrani, *Service d'Evasion* (Paris: Editions Continents, 1946), pp. 16–17. The reference to the Avenue de la Gare carries interesting connotations. At the time Thérèse used it, the street was actually known as Avenue du Maréchal Pétain. After the war it was renamed Avenue Général de Gaulle.

64. Ibid., pp. 30–34, 61–63.

65. Material for this section was gathered from Pons Prades, pp. 296–309, including a letter from Pilar Ponzán, sister of Paco Ponzán, who had been with him throughout the period of his escape work, dated March 22, 1973; Montseny, pp. 108–124; Antonio Tellez, *La guerrilla urbana: Facerías* (Paris: Ruedo Ibérico, 1974), pp. 25–29. All of these sources agree substantially on the details of Ponzán's (Vidal's) career. See also E. H. Cookridge, *Set Europe Ablaze* (New York: Crowell: 1967), pp. 52, 286. Cookridge relates the betrayal of the Reseau Pat O'Leary through the work of a German agent who infiltrated the network.

66. Paxton, pp. 45, 223, 292; Angel, p. 52. Paxton attributes the great increase in direct Resistance action from June to October, 1941, to the sudden switch in the French Communist Party line after the invasion of the Soviet Union by Germany in June 1941. The French communists immediately engineered a series of assassinations and sabotages. This activity subsided after the autumn of 1941 and accelerated again after the Allied invasion of North Africa in November 1942.

67. Report to Office of Strategic Services from unnamed source, no. A698, C.I.D. 25071, marked SECRET, December 4, 1942, National Archives, Washington, D.C.

68. Report from Lieutenant Colonel Joseph Rodrigo, G.S., military attaché, Lisbon, to Military Intelligence Division, Washington, D.C., no. 5790.2990, marked SECRET 20773, August 27, 1942, National Archives, Washington, D.C.

69. Marcel Baudot, *L'Opinion Publique sous l'occupation, l'example d'un département française, 1939–1945* (Paris: Presses Universitaires de France, 1960), pp. 95–97. Baudot pointed out that the pro-Vichy attitude of the Eure press resulted in a 1941 loss of readers by *Le Journal de Rouen,* the circulation dropping from 1,098,000 to 678,000. The Paris press, he claimed, lost two-thirds of its readers.

70. Angel, p. 60.

71. D'Alary Fechet, lieutenant colonel, infantry, assistant Military attaché, for the assistant chief of staff, G–2, Fighting French Forces in British Isles, to Military Intelligence Division, W.D.G.S., London, no. 5970, marked CONFIDENTIAL, 19401, July 18, 1942, National Archives, Washington, D.C.

72. Vilanova, p. 279; Angel, p. 54.

73. Angel, pp. 57–59.

74. Ibid., p. 48.

75. Ibid., p. 50; Montseny, p. 97.

76. Report of Office of Strategic Services, from unnamed source, No. 4652, marked SECRET, 21367, September 24, 1942, National Archives, Washington, D.C.

77. *Treball,* July 19, 1942.

78. J. P. Bartonnat, *Le Mouvement social,* no. 103 (April 1978), pp. 122–140.

9. AGAINST TWO MASTERS: SPANISH GUERRILLAS IN THE RESISTANCE AND LIBERATION

1. Pierre Bertaux, *Libération de Toulouse et de sa Région* (Paris: Hachette, 1973), p. 90.

2. General Charles de Gaulle, in presenting two medals to García Calero at a victory parade in Toulouse, September 17, 1944; Alberto Fernández, *Emigración republicana española 1939–1945* (Alcorta: Ediciones Zero, 1972), quoted by Pons Prades, p. 83.

3. Colonel Rol-Tanguy, Regional Chief of the Forces Françaises de l'Interieur, Ile-de-France, in preface to Angel, p. 9.

4. Vilanova, pp. 310–315; Angel, pp. 7, 9, 85–87, Bertaux, p. 57. Vilanova lists Spaniards as fighting in more than fifty departments. Pons Prades quotes Noguères, p. 66, as saying that Spaniards fought in three-quarters of the departments.

5. Charles de Gaulle, *The Complete War Memoirs of Charles de Gaulle* (New York: Simon and Schuster, 1972), vol. 2, p. 581.

6. Vilanova, pp. 311–12; Pike, p. 113n.

7. Colonel Serge Ravanel, in prefatory note, Angel, p. 11.

8. Ibid., p. 13; Pons Prades, p. 19, quoting a letter from Captain Dronne. See also Vernant, p. 221.

9. Robert Aron, *France Reborn: The History of the Liberation,* trans. Humphrey Hare (New York: Scribner's, 1964), pp. 163–65.

10. Pons Prades, p. 65; Angel, pp. 74, 82, 85, 91.

11. Berruezo, p. 248; Jackson, pp. ix–x; *Manifiesto* of the Spanish refugees

of Draguignan (n.d.); *A Todos Los Antifascistas,* manifesto announcing formation of Alianza Democrática Española in Marseilles (October 1944). Luís Companys, as noted previously, had been handed over to Franco and executed.

12. Berruezo, pp. 108–112.

13. Report of Direction de la Securité Militaire, Algiers, May 26, 1943, marked SECRET 38267, from National Archives, Washington, D.C.; Bertaux, p. 37.

14. Report of Direction de la Securité Militaire, Algiers, August 31, 1943, marked SECRET 44115, National Archives, Washington, D.C.; Berruezo, pp. 110, 154; Report of Office of Strategic Services, "Labor Deportations and Resistance," CONFIDENTIAL 39014, written June 19, 1943 and distributed July 19, 1943, National Archives, Washington, D.C.

15. Report from Captain Leveque, commandant of Gendarmerie, Ceret, to prefect, Pyrénées-Orientales, SECRET, no. 68/4, May 15, 1943; Letter from subprefect of Prades, to prefect, Pyrénées-Orientales, no number, May 25, 1943. Both citations from departmental archives, Perpignan.

16. Letter from M. Lazare Perramond, chief of 427th Group, Travailleurs Etrangers, to the prefect, Pyrénées-Orientales, no. 6553 MO/AM, August 2, 1944, on "Desertion Massive de Travailleurs Etrangers," reported the desertion of twelve Spaniards from a forest work crew; thirty-five desertions were reported from another forest gang near Ballestavy, in a letter from the prefect of the Pyrénées-Orientales to the secretary general of the Maintenance of Order, no. 288, August 2, 1944. The same letter reports on the desertion of twenty-eight Spaniards from an unnamed location on June 7, 1944, and relates the disappearance of seventeen Spanish miners who apparently received word that they were scheduled for arrest and transfer to a punishment camp. See also the memo from the secretary-general of the Vichy police to the prefect, Pyrénées-Orientales, no. 15176 Police Sureté 6/RB, December 18, 1943, which expresses annoyance at reports of mass desertions from the Organization Todt and demands a comprehensive inquiry and decisive action. Another letter from Perramond to the prefect of Pyrénées-Orientales, no. 6429 MO/AM, July 27, 1944, reports the desertion of twenty-one workers, all Spaniards. All from departmental archives, Perpignan.

17. Note de Renseignements, from Commandant Lazare Perramond, 427th Travailleurs Etrangers Group, to prefect, Pyrénées-Orientales, no. 153, January 12, 1944, departmental archives, Perpignan.

18. Paxton, p. 298, says that under Darnand French-German collaboration against the Resistance reached it's climax. See also Angel, p. 196. Angel, pp. 72–73, cites the report of the Eighth Brigade of Security Police to the principal commissioner at Toulouse, no. 2.38/436, May 8, 1943.

19. Report no. TB–104, Office of Strategic Services, "Darnand Campaign Against the French Resistance," SECRET 62365, March 16, 1944, National Archives, Washington, D.C.

20. Letter from prefect, Pyrénées-Orientales, to central commissioner, Perpignan, no number, January 25, 1944; letter from prefect, Pyrénées-Orientales, to prefect, Regional Office for the Maintenance of Order,

Montpellier, no. 213 Cabinet, May 22, 1944; both from departmental archives, Perpignan.

21. Letter from Second Group of Travailleurs Etrangers, Toulouse, to regional prefect, Toulouse, no. 1002/AP, March 4, 1943. The commandant complained that Spanish miners working near the Col de Puymorens were virtually unreachable because the snow blocked access to their locale. He was aware that they were stealing dynamite and arms and conveying them to Andorra, which was only four kilometers away; departmental archives, Perpignan.

22. Letter from principal commissioner of General Information, Pyrénées-Orientales, to divisional commissioner, Montpellier, no. 3493, January 6, 1944; Letter from principal commissioner of General Information, Le Perthus, to subprefect, Ceret, no. 641, March 10, 1943; Letter from Joseph Landi, police inspector, Criminal Investigation Department, no number, May 21, 1943.

23. Letter from principal commissioner, Perpignan, to prefect Pyrénées-Orientales, no. 4440, August 20, 1943, departmental archives, Perpignan.

24. Letter from principal commissioner, Pyrénées-Orientales, to prefect, Pyrénées-Orientales, "Repression of Subversive Menaces on Our Territory," no. 84, January 22, 1944, departmental archives, Perpignan.

25. Letter from principal commissioner to prefect, Pyrénées-Orientales, no. 3582, June 18, 1943, departmental archives, Perpignan.

26. Aron, 208; Cookridge, pp. 197, 246.

27. *España Libre*, January 2, 1963, quoted by Nancy Macdonald, "Spanish Refugees: Waiting," *New York Times*, January 30, 1976; Bertaux, p. 57.

28. Vernant, p. 279; *Le Socialiste* (Paris), December 29, 1966. The newspaper's figure of 25,000 includes 10,000 to 12,000 Spaniards who died in German concentration camps.

29. Pons Prades, pp. 240–246. On November 8, 1945, Gutiérrez (Castro) was commended by Colonel Claude Monod, chief of FFI, Burgundy, Franche Comté, for refusing to divulge information about his Resistance group despite German torture. See also Vilanova, pp. 260–264.

30. Aron, pp. 171–174.

31. The narrative on the Battle of Glières was drawn from the accounts of participants who related their experiences to Montseny, pp. 172–178; Vilanova, pp. 303–305; Pons Prades, pp. 254–261; and Angel, pp. 90, 156–158. The figure of 56 Spanish participants out of a total of 465 is given by Vilanova, p. 303, and is in near agreement with the projection of Angel, p. 156, who put the number of Spaniards at 60 out of the total of 457. J. Barba, who participated in the battle, said there were 80 Spanish Maquis on the plateau and a total of 650 maquisards.

32. Ibid. Barba, in Montseny, p. 177, said that there were 115 graves in the cemetery near the plateau, but he added that others who were killed in action were buried elsewhere.

33. This account is based mainly on the full-scale treatment by Paul Dreyfus, *Histoire de la Résistance en Vercors* (Paris: Arthaud, 1975), and those of

Pons Prades, pp. 262–269; Vilanova, pp. 301–2; and R. Aron, pp. 171–208. Dreyfus and Aron mention Spanish participation minimally. Chambonnet's objection to the Vercors plan appears in Dreyfus, p. 89. Hugh Dalton, head of the British Board of Economic Warfare, which supervised the SOE, had enunciated the policy to guide Resistance fighters. While acting with sufficient vigor to cause constant embarrassment to the enemy, they should avoid any attempt at large-scale risings or ambitious paramilitary operations; Cookridge, p. 17.

34. Pons Prades, p. 262.

35. Dreyfus, p. 130–31.

36. Dreyfus, pp. 153–239; Pons Prades, pp. 262–269; Vilanova, pp. 301–2; R. Aron, pp. 171–208.

37. Amicale Nationale des Anciens Combattants de la Résistance, *La France des Maquis* (Paris: Editions Denoal, 1964), cited by Pons Prades, p. 200.

38. R. Aron, pp. 177–182; Pons Prades, pp. 200–202; Amicale National, p. 167, cited by Germaine Willard, et al., eds., *Le Parti Communiste Française dans la Résistance* (Paris: l'Institut Maurice Thorez, 1967), p. 300; Vilanova, p. 305, claimed that 68 Spaniards were killed in the battle.

39. Vilanova, p. 292. Pedro Alba, a sergeant of the first battalion of the Dordogne Brigade, won the War Cross with bronze star for heroism at Saint Astier, August 20, 1944. A direct shell hit on his position killed two Spaniards and wounded six, but Alba maintained fire in spite of constant bombardment.

40. Vilanova, pp. 287–289; Pons Prades, pp. 224–226; Montseny, pp. 147–151. Cookridge, p. 219, says that the massacre was in retaliation for the killing of a German officer in Oradour-sur-Vayres. He also notes that the Das Reich Division arrived in Normandy ten days behind schedule.

41. J. Montoliú in Montseny, pp. 138–140; Berruezo, p. 121; Vilanova, p. 281.

42. Vilanova, pp. 289, 265–268; Pons Prades, pp. 184–185.

43. Angel, p. 171; Casto Ballesta, in Montseny, pp. 141–144.

44. Bertaux, p. 55.

45. Aron, pp. 375, 387–88.

46. De Gaulle, pp. 682–83.

47. Charles Foltz, Jr., *The Masquerade in Spain* (Boston: Houghton Mifflin, 1948), pp. 57–58.

48. Bertaux, pp. 99, 34–35; Angel, pp. 95–96.

49. Angel, p. 96; Bertaux, pp. 57–58.

50. Bertaux, pp. 58–59; Fernández, pp. 46–49; Angel, pp. 101–108.

51. Bertaux, pp. 58–59, 64–67. Pon Prades, p. 69, related that Captain Miguel Sanz Clemente was captured by the Gestapo while transporting arms. He was ordered to be shot. While awaiting execution by firing squad he suddenly seized a machine-gun from a truck and killed his firing squad. Then he escaped into the forest. For this exploit he was awarded the Medal of Resistance and the War Cross. Pons Prades (p. 102) told the story of Manolo Morato, who was captured in Carcassonne and ordered deported to

Germany. Before crossing the French border he managed to dislodge some floor boards in the train and drop to the roadbed. Badly injured, he dragged himself into forest where he was found by guerrillas. He recovered and fought with them until the liberation.

52. Angel, pp. 136–152; Pons Prades, p. 95.

53. R. Aron, p. 143; "Les Resultats de l'action de la Résistance dans la SNCF, l'Histoire de le FFI," unpublished mss. by Major R. A. Bourne-Paterson, Captain Lucien Galimard, and Captain Marcel Vigeras, quoted by Cookridge, p. 198; Report of Vichy minister of interior, quoted by Cookridge, p. 198.

54. Berruezo, pp. 113–117.

55. Angel, pp. 110–112.

56. Ibid., pp. 115–119.

57. Angel, pp. 120–122; Raymond Escholier, *Maquis de Gascogne* (Geneva: Editions Milieu du Monde, 1945), cited by Angel, p. 121, and Pons Prades, pp. 121–123. Guerrero Ortega ("Camilo") received the War Cross and the Liberation Medal.

58. José Cervera, in Montseny, pp. 199–203.

59. Pierre Guiral, *Libération de Marseille* (Paris: Hachette, 1974), pp. 79–99. The German troops wished to surrender but were afraid of civilian and Maquis reprisals. They were assured that they would be treated as prisoners of war and protected from mob action.

60. Pons Prades, pp. 116–117; Angel, pp. 129–130.

61. Charles Tillon, *Les FTP: la guerrilla en France* (Paris: Editions Julliard, 1962), p. 249; Pons Prades, pp. 110–111; Angel, pp. 134–135; Vilanova, pp. 272–276. On October 25, 1946, the commander of the Ninth Military Region, General Olleris, issued a posthumous citation for Lieutenant Colonel Cristino García Grandas. In lauding his achivements, the general said that García's men had taken thirteen hundred prisoners and killed six hundred Germans; Vilanova, p. 276. There is some disagreement as to the rank held by the German commander. Tillon, p. 249, and Angel, p. 35, said he was a lieutenant general, but Pons Prades, p. 111, and Vilanova, p. 275, called him a lieutenant colonel. R. Aron, p. 317.

62. Angel, p. 132.

63. L'Amicale d'Eysses, *L'Insurrection d'Eysses* (Paris, Editions Sociales, 1974), pp. 47, 64–66; Pons Prades, p. 167.

64. Amicale, pp. 94–97; Pons Prades, pp. 171–72.

65. Amicale, pp. 114–117.

66. Ibid., p. 117.

67. Amicale, pp. 118, 129–135, 137–140; Pons Prades, p. 172; Angel, pp. 212–215.

68. Alberto Fernández, *La España de los Maquis* (Mexico City: Ediciones Era, 971), p. 141, gives what he calls an incomplete table of Spanish republican guerrilla activities during the Resistance in France. Spanish units engaged in combat with enemy forces 512 times, took 9,800 prisoners, killed 3,000, liberated 200 political prisoners, destroyed 80 locomotives, downed

150 railroad bridges, cut 600 electrical lines, demolished six central electrical stations, dynamited 20 factories, and sabotaged or inundated 22 mines.

10. LIBERATION AND VICTORY: FROM NORMANDY TO BERCHTESGADEN

1. Pons Prades, p. 362; Vilanova, pp. 371–372; Aron, p. 309.

2. Raymond Dronne, *Le Serment de Kouffra* (Paris: Editions du Temps, 1965), quoted by Vilanova, pp. 372–373; Pons Prades, p. 415, quotes Federico Moreno, a member of the Ninth Company, on the figures concerning the original complement and survivors of the campaign, from a letter written by Moreno on July 7, 1974.

3. Dronne, quoted by Vilanova, pp. 373, 380. Angel, p. 190, quoted Dronne as saying in a 1968 television interview, "My company was composed almost totally of Spanish Republicans, and I assure you that these were men who knew how to make war."

4. Pons Prades, p. 370.

5. Captain Raymond Dronne, quoted by Vilanova, p. 424. Robert Aron skirts the issue of disobedience of American orders at this juncture. He does not mention the role of General Gerow and says merely that General Leclerc, on August 23, "received the orders to march on Paris for which he had been waiting for four years"; Aron, *France Reborn*, p. 257. See also Pons Prades, pp. 388–389; Angel, pp. 190–192.

6. Captain Raymond Dronne, quoted by Vilanova, pp. 426–428; Pons Prades, p. 389; Angel, pp. 191–192.

7. Dronne, quoted by Vilanova, pp. 426–427; Pons Prades, p. 389; R. Aron, pp. 257, 284; Adrien Dansette, *Histoire de la Libération de Paris* (Paris: F. Brouty, J. Fayard, 1947), pp. 350, 354.

8. Dronne, quoted by Vilanova, pp. 428–430.

9. Léo Hamon, quoted by Pons Prades, p. 390.

10. Lieutenant Amado Granell, quoted by Vilanova, p. 447.

11. Jesús Abenza, in Montseny, p. 236. V. Echegaray, another tankist, wrote in Montseny, p. 242, that two French tanks rolled up to the City Hall after the first Spaniards had arrived. He also noted that the first FFI men who greeted Dronne's force mistook them for Americans or Englishmen and had to be informed of their nationality.

12. Angel, pp. 88, 192–193; Gaston Laroche, *On les nomment les étrangers* (Paris: Editions Français Reunits, 1965), p. 190, quoted by Angel, p. 192; Tillon, p. 541; Vilanova, pp. 279–280. Vilanova, p. 278, wrote that the German commander, General von Choltitz, complained to French Vichy officials about the "great quantity of foreign terrorists who have arrived in Paris."

13. Marie Granet, *Le Journal "Defense de la France"* (Paris: Presses Universitaires de France, 1961), p. 244.

14. Angel, pp. 66–68, 70–71, 178–182; Pons Prades, pp. 276–279; report from Securité Militaire d'Alger to Office of Strategic Services, marked SECRET 38267, May 26, 1943, National Archives, Washington, D.C.

15. R. Aron, *France Reborn*, p. 298.

16. Ibid.

17. Vilanova, p. 281; Dansette, p. 329.
18. Joaquín Blesa, in Pons Prades, pp. 408–410.
19. General order no. 66, October 31, 1944, headquarters of Second French Armored Division, quoted in Pons Prades, p. 401; decision note no. 374, official diary, November 11, 1945. The citation noted that on November 17, 1944, Moreno had again assumed command at a critical moment and led his unit to victory over a numerically superior force, in Pons Prades, p. 403. V. Echegaray, in Montseny, p. 243. Echgaray was wounded on November 12, 1944, terminating his participation in the war.
20. Pons Prades, pp. 405–407.
21. Ibid., pp. 412–414. After the reduction of the Atlantic ports the two tank regiments rejoined the Second Armored Division and completed the dash across Germany.
22. Ibid., pp. 498–499; Murillo de la Cruz, in Montseny, pp. 230–233; Vilanova, pp. 355–356.
23. Colonel Paul de Langlade, *En Suivant Leclerc* (Paris, 1964), p. 383, quoted by Vilanova, pp. 305–306. R. Aron, *France Reborn,* pp. 430–436. Aron puts the number of Germans in the Atlantic pockets at 69,000.
24. Vilanova, pp. 305–306. R. Aron, in his discussion of this campaign, in *France Reborn,* pp. 430–436, does not mention the Spaniards.
25. Vilanova, pp. 309–310.

11. THE BRIEF TIME OF EUPHORIA, 1945–1946

1. Jackson, p. 498.
2. José María del Valle, *Las Instituciones de la República Española en exilio* (Paris: Ruedo Ibérico, 1976), p. 191.
3. *Boletín de Información de la Agrupación Militar de ex-Combatientes de la República Española* (Toulouse), vol. 1, no. 5, July 1945; *Adelante,* vol. 1, no. 42, August 9, 1945; ibid.
4. Del Valle, pp. 191, 148, 211; *Adelante,* vol. 3, no. 68, February 10, 1946.
5. *Adelante,* November 1945.
6. *Boletín de la Agrupación Militar,* vol. 1, no. 5, July 1945.
7. *Adelante,* vol. 1, no. 41, August 2, 1945; ibid., vol. 1, no. 47, September 13, 1945.
8. *Boletín Interior de la C.N.T.* (Toulouse), second series, no. 6 April 21, 1945.
9. *Ruta* (Toulouse), vol. 2, no. 25, December 5, 1945.
10. *Boletín de la Agrupación Militar,* vol. 1, no. 4, June 1945.
11. *Adelante,* vol. 2, no. 57, November 1945; ibid., vol. 3, no. 7, March 8, 1946.
12. *Boletín de la Agrupación Militar,* vol. 1, no. 5, July 1945.
13. *Adelante,* vol. 2, no. 68, February 10, 1946; ibid., vol. 2, no. 63, January 6, 1946; *Boletín de la Agrupación Militar,* vol. 1, no. 5, July 1945.
14. *Boletín de la Agrupación Militar,* vol. 1, no. 4, June 1945; General Charles de Gaulle at the victory parade for the liberation of Toulouse, September 17, 1944.

15. *Boletín de la Unión de Intelectuales Españoles*, vol. 3, no. 15, February 15, 1946; *Combat*, quoted by *Adelante*, vol. 1, no. 30, May 20, 1945; del Valle, 189; *L'Aube*, quoted by *Adelante*, vol. 2, no. 69, February 17, 1946; *Adelante*, vol. 1, no. 2, October 14, 1944; ibid., no. 26, April 20, 1945; ibid., no. 39, July 22, 1945; Angel, reproduction of news article on unnumbered page.

16. Del Valle, 81; see ibid., pp. 81–84, for Spanish reaction to Churchill's speech; Fernándo Valera, *La République Espagnole dans le cadre de la politique internationale* (Mexico City, 1961), p. 31. See also *New York Times*, January 19, 1945.

17. *New York Times*, August 22, 1945; Ibid., January 24, 1946.

18. *Le Républicain* (Perpignan), March 19, 1946. This newspaper was edited by the Resistance forces after the liberation and did not assume its old name of *L'Indépendant* until 1955.

19. *New York Times*, January 31, 1945.

20. Ibid., July 29, 1945; August 13, 16, 21, 1945. See also *Adelante*, vol. 1, no. 43, August 16, 1945. The Labor Party policy toward Spain was expressed in its platform statement, "Let Us Face the Future."

21. Del Valle, p. 110.

22. *Boletín de la Agrupación Militar*, vol. 1, no. 4, June 1945; *L'Espagne Républicaine*, August 17, 1946, quoted by del Valle, p. 192; *Le Républicain* (Perpignan), February 20, March 23, 1946; *The Tribune*, quoted by *Adelante*, vol. 2, no. 82, May 17, 1946; ibid., vol. 2, no. 84, June 3, 1946; ibid., vol. 2, no. 60, December 16, 1945.

23. Minutes of cabinet discussion, 1947, quoted by *Le Monde*, January 5, 1978; *The Times* (London), January 7, 1978.

24. *Adelante*, vol. 1, no. 37, July 8, 1945.

25. Franklin D. Roosevelt to Norman Armour, American ambassador to Spain, quoted by Charles L. Mee, *Meeting at Potsdam* (New York: M. Evans, 1975), p. 243; Valera, p. 31; Mee, p. 31.

26. *New York Times*, March 5, 1946, July 29, 1945, and January 30, 1946; *Adelante*, vol. 1, no. 48, September 20, 1945.

27. *New York Times*, June 22, 1945, January 30, 1946.

28. *New York Times*, March 5, 1946; *Adelante*, vol. 2, no. 63, January 6, 1946, and vol. 2, no. 68, February 10, 1946. Secretary of State James F. Byrnes denied that machine guns had been sold to Spain but acknowledged the sale of five transport planes, *New York Times*, January 30, 1946.

29. Mee, pp. 91, 101.

30. Del Valle, p. 148; *New York Times*, January 14, 1946.

31. *New York Times*, March 5, 1946.

32. Del Valle, p. 206; *Boletín de Información* (Soviet embassy, Mexico), vol. 3, no. 13, March 30, 1946.

33. Andrés Sorel, *Guerrilla española del siglo XX* (Paris: Collección Ebro, 1970), p. 36. Ibid., p. 32, Valera, p. 35.

34. Thomas, p. 949; *New York Times*, March 3, 5, 1946.

35. Valera, pp. 15–17.

36. José Borras, *Políticas de los exilados españoles, 1944–1950* (Paris: Ruedo Ibérico, 1976), pp. 9, 269.

37. *Ruta,* vol. 5, no. 154, August 27, 1948; ibid., vol. 6, no. 210, October 1.

38. Borras, p. 284.

39. Del Valle, pp. 72–76, 78–80. The anarchists attacked Martínez-Barrio and Dr. Juan Negrín on December 1, 1946, for not having reconstituted the government-in-exile during the war years and for not having declared war on the Axis; Borras, p. 270. In January 1945, Negrín declared that Republican Spain had been a belligerent in the war because of the participation of Spaniards on many fronts, *El Patriota del Suroeste,* January, 1945.

40. Ibid., pp. 61–65.

41. Del Valle, pp. 84–88; *New York Times,* January 4, 5, 11, 21, 31, 1945. The figure of ninety-six attending deputies was given by the *New York Times.* Del Valle put the number at seventy-two.

42. Del Valle, pp. 113–119; *New York Times,* July 21, August 3, 9, 1945; *Le Républicain,* July 10, 1945; *Adelante,* vol. 1, no. 18, February 11, 1945 (for criticism of Negrín's stewardship).

43. Congreso de los Diputados, Mexico City, November 7, 1945, quoted by del Valle, pp. 119–135; *Adelante,* vol. 2, no. 57, November 25, 1945; *New York Times,* August 3, 1945.

44. *L'Espagne Républicaine,* quoted by del Valle, p. 149; del Valle, pp. 195, 144–145.

12. Stalemate, Reversal, and Final Betrayal

1. Del Valle, pp. 91–112; *Adelante,* vol. 1, no. 10, December 17, 1944; *Documentos políticos para la historia de la República española,* vol. 1 (Mexico City, 1945); *España* (Mexico City), June 9, 1945; *Le Républicain* (Perpignan), May 12, 1945.

2. Mee, pp. 66, 91, 101, 142–146; *New York Times,* July 29, August 3, 1945.

3. *New York Times,* May 26, August 4, 1945, January 18, 1946; *Adelante,* vol. 1, nos. 31, 27, 1945; ibid., vol. 2, no. 61, December 23, 1945; del Valle, p. 147; *Le Républicain,* January 30, 1946; *New York Times,* February 27, 1946.

4. *Le Républicain,* March 13, 1946; *New York Times,* March 3, 12, 1946.

5. *New York Times,* March 5, 22, 1946; ibid., April 7, 1946; *Le Républicain,* March 2, 1946.

6. *New York Times,* March 7, 1946; *La Nouvelle Espagne,* March 15, 1946; *Adelante,* vol. 2, no. 72, March 8, 1946; ibid., vol. 2, no. 73, March 15, 1946; *New York Herald,* quoted in *Adelante,* vol. 2, no. 73, March 15, 1946; *Pravda,* quoted in *New York Times,* March 10, 1946.

7. *New York Times,* March 3, 1946.

8. The six countries that had recognized the Spanish Republican government-in-exile were Guatemala, Mexico, Panama, Venezuela, Poland, and Yugoslavia. Those who either had no relations with Franco or had broken them were the Soviet Union, China, Czechoslovakia, Austria, Hungary,

Bolivia, Bulgaria, and Romania. Considering rupture were Cuba, Equador, Peru, Uruguay, and France; del Valle, pp. 148, 151, 160, 163.

9. *Le Républicain,* March 13, 1946.

10. *New York Times,* April 18, 1946; del Valle, p. 163.

11. Transcript of proceedings, United Nations Security Council, April 17, 1946, in the *New York Times,* April 18, 1946.

12. Ibid., April 19, 1946.

13. Ibid.

14. Del Valle, pp. 175–187.

15. *La Nouvelle Espagne,* June 11, 1946; *L'Espagne Républicaine,* June 6, 1946; del Valle, p. 187; *New York Times,* June 27, 1946.

16. *Ruta,* vol. 3, no. 66, November 12, 1946, and vol. 3, no. 45, June 12, 1946; *Adelante,* vol. 2, no. 101, October 10, 1946; *Le Populaire,* October 26, 1946; *New York Times,* quoted in *Adelante,* vol. 3, no. 111, December 12, 1946.

17. Del Valle, pp. 211–22, 216.

18. *La Nouvelle Espagne,* November 23, 1946; del Valle, pp. 213–215, 219.

19. Del Valle, p. 218.

20. *Nations unies, Résolutions adoptées par l'Assemblée générale pendant la seconde partie de sa première session du 27 octobre au 15 décembre 1946* (Lake Success), quoted in del Valle, 221–223.

21. Del Valle, pp. 224–225; *Adelante,* vol. 3, no. 111, December 12, 1946.

22. *L'Espagne Républicaine,* January 25, 1947; *Espagne Libre,* February 1, 1947; del Valle, pp. 225–227.

23. Del Valle, pp. 229–232.

24. *Adelante,* vol. 3, p. 145, September 4, 1947.

25. Del Valle, pp. 253–257.

26. *L'Espagne Républicaine,* March 8, 1947; ibid., June 21, 1947; del Valle, pp. 232–233.

27. *Adelante,* December 25, 1947; *L'Espagne Républicaine,* January 16, 1948; del Valle, pp. 273–276; *L'Espagne Républicaine,* July 19, 1947.

28. *New York Times,* November 18, 1947; del Valle, pp. 264–271.

29. *L'Espagne Républicaine,* February 13, 1948; *Libertad,* November 6, 1948; del Valle, pp. 275–276, 288–290, 292.

30. *New York Times,* February 3, 4, 10, 1949; March 13, 1949; April 11, 25, 30, 1949; May 6, 7, 11, 12, 17, 1949; September 4, 16, 1949; October 3, 5, 1949. See also del Valle, pp. 294–295.

31. *New York Times,* January 10, 20, 22, 1950.

32. *New York Times,* August 2, 3, 4, 5, 6, 25, 1950; November 16, 1950; *Euzko Deya,* November 15, 22, 1950; *El Socialista,* November 16, 1950; del Valle, pp. 316–317; *New York Times,* November 26, 1950. For information on the suppression of the French and Spanish communists see *Le Figaro,* September 8, 1950; *L' Humanité,* September 8, 1950.

33. Del Valle, pp. 312–315; *New York Times,* June 22, 1951; July 14, 17, 19, 20, 1951; September 8, 1950; October 24, 1950; November 20, 1952; September 27, 1953; *Arriba,* October 2, 1953.

34. *New York Times,* December 15, 1955.
35. Montseny, pp. 233, 245.

13. "THE PRISONS CONSUMED A GENERATION OF FIGHTERS . . ."

1. *Ruta,* July 19, 1947; Borras, p. 274; Sorel, p. 39.
2. Juan M. Molina, *El Movimiento Clandestino en España 1939–1949* (Mexico City: Editores Mexicanos unidos, 1976), pp. 5–7.
3. *Boletín de la Agrupación Militar,* vol. 1, no. 5, July 1945; interview of author with José Mata, Toulouse, April 14, 1974; *New York Times,* February 17, 23, 24, 1946, and March 3, 1946; *Le Républicain* (Perpignan), February 23, 27, 1946; del Valle, pp. 153–155.
4. Emmet John Hughes, *L'Espagne* (Paris: Editions du Temps Present, 1948), quoted by Molina, p. 191; Sorel, p. 10; Molina, p. 191; *Ruta,* vol. 6, no. 216, November 12, 1949; letter from principal commissioner, Perpignan, to regional commissioner, Montpellier, no. 2.158, March 23, 1946, departmental archives, Perpignan; report of Intelligence Division, Office of Chief of Naval Operations, CONFIDENTIAL, no. 127711 April 20, 1945, National Archives, Washington, D.C.; letter from principal commissioner, Perpignan, to regional commissioner, Montpellier, no. 1906, March 14, 1946, from departmental archives, Perpignan; Secret Report, Office of Strategic Services, no. 101759, September 29, 1944, National Archives, Washington, D.C.
5. *A.B.C.,* quoted by Sorel, p. 10; *New York Times,* January 3, July 15, August 14, 1945, and March 5, 28, 1946; report, Office of Strategic Services, SECRET, no. 101759, September 29, 1944, National Archives, Washington, D.C.; report of the Direction Générale, Gouvernement Provisoire de la République Francaise, SECRET, no. 0016480, Algiers, June 29, 1944, National Archives, Washington, D.C.; report, Intelligence Division, Office of Chief of Naval Operations, CONFIDENTIAL, no. 91627, August 23, 1944, National Archives, Washington D.C.; article by C. L. Sulzberger, *New York Times,* February 25, 1946.
6. Tomas Cossias, *La Lucha Contra el Maquis en España* (Madrid: Editorial Nacional, 1956), pp. 21–22, 110, quoted by Sorel, pp. 47–48; Emmet John Hughes, quoted by Molina, p. 191; *Boletín de Información del Gobierno de la República Española,* no. 1, April 14, 1947; *Ruta,* vol. 5, no. 154, August 27, 1948.
7. Fernández; Borras, p. 156; Bertaux, pp. 106–107.
8. Serge Groussard, *Solitude Espagnole* (Paris: Editions Plon, 1948), quoted by Molina, pp. 191–192; Molina, pp. 189–190.
9. Colonel Eulogio Limia Pérez, *Brief General Account of Banditry After the War of Liberation,* July 23, 1957, quoted by Sorel, pp. 46–47.
10. Sorel, pp. 46–47; Molina, pp. 457–461. See also dispatch by Sam Pope Brewer, *New York Times,* August 24, 1947, for reportage on the already evident decline of the clandestine press.
11. Sorel, pp. 38–42.
12. Plenn, pp. 306–313, 214–216; Foltz, pp. 257–258.
13. Based on a series of interviews with Mariano Puzo.

14. Personal interview of author with Pascual Ortiz, January 23, 1978, in Perpignan, the day of Mariano Puzo's funeral.

15. Eric Hobsbawm, *Bandits* (New York: Dell, 1971), pp. 106–107.

EPILOGUE

1. Interview with José Martínez, a young oppositionist who said he had become active in the underground in 1972, April 8, 1974, Perpignan.

2. Interview of author with Mariano Puzo, May 16, 1974.

3. Interview with Miguel Gómez, June 1, 1974.

BIBLIOGRAPHY

Antonio Vilanova, in *Los olvidados* ("The Forgotten Ones," 1969), claimed that the historiography of the French Resistance and liberation had largely ignored the contributions made by Spanish Republicans to eventual victory. He wrote what was at that time the most comprehensive account of Spanish participation in the Maquis movement and noted that his collection of materials was designed to serve the needs of future "disinterested historians" in chronicling the role of the Spanish exiles in World War II. Prior to Vilanova's effort, Spanish contributions to the historiography of the 1939–1945 period were mainly in the form of individual memoirs, which were often written from strongly partisan political points of view.

Since 1969 there has been an upsurge in the number of books written by Spaniards on the subject of their experiences as inmates of German concentration camps and participants in the Allied struggle against fascism. The political flavor persists in many of these works, but there has also been an attempt to organize the mass of raw material into narratives showing the scope and intensity of Spanish involvement with France and the Allies. The most recent effort of this type is Eduardo Pons Prades' *Repúblicanos españoles en la Segunda Guerra Mundial* (1975), a noteworthy attempt to systematize and sift the testimonials of individual Spaniards and to present documentary verification of their roles, in the form of military citations and orders, photographs, statements by French leaders, and other primary sources. The 1976 book of Juan M. Molina, *El movimiento clandestino en España 1939–1949,* is a noteworthy attempt to fill the existing gap of materials dealing with the guerrilla campaign of the Spanish republicans in Spain during and after the Second World War.

However, political bias is still a strong force in the literature. Miguel Angel, for example, in his 1971 book, *Los guerrilleros españoles en Francia 1940–1945,* extols the preeminence of the Communist Party of Spain in organizing cadres in the concentration camps and, later, in forming the national coalition of Unión Nacional Española. His book is replete with communist ideology. Other examples of this type include Alberto E. Fernández, *La España de los maquis* (1971); and José Gros, *Relatos de un guerrillero comunista español* (1972). The anarchist point of view is upheld by José Berruezo, *Contribución a la historia de la C.N.T. de España en el exilio* (1967); and the earlier work by Federica Montseny, *Pasión y muerte de los españoles en Francia* (1951, reprinted in 1969). Both sides are generous in praising the battle valor of political opponents but there is an unmistakable aura of the political in their efforts. Pons Prades and Vilanova attempted to transcend this limitation with some success. But it is important to note that all of the writers agree on the basic facts of Spanish participation in the Resistance and liberation. The personal testimonials of a host of Spaniards have furnished crosschecks on individual accounts and a solid pattern of agreement has emerged on essentials. Although there are differences in recollections concerning dates and numbers of combatants involved there can be no doubt of the authenticity of the war effort itself and the role played by Spanish republican refugees.

French historians are divided on the role of the Spanish republicans in the Resistance and liberation. A number of French writers have spoken in glowing terms of Spanish bravery, comradeship, and unstinting loyalty to the antifascist cause. Pierre Bertaux, *Libération de Toulouse et de sa Région* (1973), devotes considerable space to the Spanish effort and is lavish in his praise of their guerrilla ability. Captain Raymond Dronne, *Le Serment de Kouffra* (1965) and *La Libération de Paris* (1970), speaks with admiration of the Spaniards he commanded in the Second French Armored Division. The members of the Amicale who wrote *L'Insurrection d'Eysses* (1974) were, in their words, awed by the heroism of the Spaniards in the attempted breakout from the prison. Similarly, M. J. Torris, *Narvik* (1946), praised their bravery in the Norwegian campaign. Claude Chombard has many favorable comments on the Spaniards in the *Maquis: A History of the French Resistance Movement* (1976). However, some of the major French works on the Resistance and liberation are more reticent with regard to Spanish republican efforts in these struggles. Robert Aron, *France Reborn: The History of the Liberation*, 1964, speaks of them only in terms of communist threats to General Charles de Gaulle's orderly take-over of power in the south. Paul Dreyfus, *Histoire de la Résistance en Vercors* (1975); Marie Granet, *Ceux de la Résistance* (1964); and Henri Michel, *La Guerre de l'ombre, la Résistance en Europe* (1970), have almost nothing to say about the Spaniards, although they mention the efforts of other foreigners. Other authors follow the same pattern.

Perhaps the tendency to open departmental archives for research will create a new approach to the entire question of French actions involving Spaniards, during both the time of the Third Republic and the Vichy period. I was the first foreign investigator permitted to work in the departmental archives of the Pyrénées-Orientales and the information gathered in this endeavor sheds much corroborative light on Spanish claims concerning the concentration camps and Vichy repression of Spanish resisters. Coupled with newspaper accounts from all points of the political spectrum, it is now possible to detail the life of the Spaniards in the camps, the official suspicion that guided French actions, and the actions taken against the Spanish refugees as potential or actual threats to the Vichy regime and to the German occupying force.

The bibliography is divided into the following categories: Archives; Personal Interviews; Newspapers; Periodical Articles; Documents and Reports; General Background; Memoirs, Accounts, Pamphlets, and Literature.

ARCHIVES

Archives Départementale des Pyrénées-Orientales (Perpignan)
Bibliothèque Nationale (Paris)
Foundation Internationale d'Etudes Historiques et Sociales (formerly in Perpignan, now in Barcelona)
National Archives (Washington, D.C.)

PERSONAL INTERVIEWS

I tape-recorded interviews with a number of Spanish refugees and French people who had been involved with the events of 1939–1955. Following are the names of the most significant of these interviewees. An American who performed conscientious objecter service in the camps for the American Friends Service Committee was also interviewed.

Arquer, Jordi (Perpignan)
Avilés, Encarnación (Perpignan)
Borrillo, Vincente (Toulouse)
Cercos Rodan, José (Perpignan)
Duarte García, Antonio (Toulouse)
Esteban, Eulalio (Perpignan)
Finestres, Francisco (Perpignan)
Germen, Jacqueline (Perpignan)
Gómez, Miguel (Perpignan)
Harvey, Dr. Henry (Littleton, Massachusetts)

Martínez, José (Perpignan)
Mata, José (Toulouse)
Montseny, Federica (Toulouse)
Ortiz, Pascual (Perpignan)
Planes Casals, Jordi (Perpignan)
Puzo, Mariano (Perpignan)
Raluy, Joaquín (Toulouse)
Verdaguer, Pére (Perpignan)

NEWSPAPERS

L'Action Française (Paris)
Adelante (Marseilles)
L'Aube (Paris)
Boletín de Información de la Agrupación Militar de ex-combatientes de la República Española (Toulouse)
Boletín de Información (Soviet embassy, Mexico)
Boletín de Información del Gobierno de la República Española (Paris)
Boletín de la Unión de Intelectuales Españoles (Paris)
Boletín Intercontinental del Movimiento Libertario Español (Toulouse)
Boletín Interior de la C.N.T.
La Dépêche de Toulouse (Toulouse)
L'Epoque (Paris)
España Libre (New York)

L'Espagne Nouvelle (Paris, Nîmes)
Espoir (Toulouse)
Excelsior (Mexico City)
El Federal (Perpignan)
Le Figaro (Paris)
La Garonne (Toulouse)
Gringoire (Paris)
L'Humanité (Paris)
L'Indépéndant (Pau)
L'Indépandant (Perpignan)
Le Matin (Paris)
Le Midi socialiste (Toulouse)
Le Monde (Paris)
New York Herald-Tribune (New York)
New York Times (New York)
Nostra Terra (refugee camp at Le Barcarès)
L'Oeuvre (Paris)

Le Petit Parisien (Paris)
Le Populaire (Paris)
Reconquista de España (Montpellier)
Le Républicain (Perpignan, 1945–
   1955, afterward assumed pre-war

name of *L'Indépendant*)
Ruta (Toulouse)
El Socialista (Toulouse)
The Times (London)
Treball (Perpignan)

PERIODICAL ARTICLES

Allen, Jay. "Hostages of Appeasement," *Survey Graphic,* 28, no. 11 (November 1939):679–82.

Braun, Madaleine. "Spaniards in Exile," *Nation,* 149 (August 5, 1939):158.

Brewer, Sam Pope. "Undercover Press," *New York Times Magazine,* August 24, 1947, p. 37.

Castendyck, F. "Refugee Children in Europe: Spanish Refugees in France," *Social Service Review,* no. 13 (December 1939), pp. 587–92.

Climent, J. B. "España en el exilio," *Cuadernos Americanos,* 126, no. 1 (January-February 1963):98–102.

Cremieux-Brilhac, Jean-Louis. "La bataille des Glières et la 'guerre psychologique,' " *Revue d'histoire de la deuxième guerre mondiale,* no. 99 (July 1975), pp. 45–72.

"Food and Refugees Bring Pressure on Vichy, Madrid," *Nation,* 152 (April 19, 1941):461.

"Food and Refugees," *Nation,* 152 (April 19, 1941):461–62.

"French Concentration Camp," *Nation,* 148 (May 6, 1939):542.

Goubet, Michel. "La Résistance toulousaine, structures, objectifs (printemps-été 1944)," *Revue d'histoire de la deuxième guerre mondiale,* no. 99 (July 1974), pp. 25–43.

Guilloux, Louis. "Refuge in Limbo," *Living Age,* 354 (July 1938):440–45.

———. "The Betrayal of the Refugees," *New Republic,* 98 (February 22, 1939):68–70.

"Save the Spanish Loyalists," *New Republic,* 107 (November 30, 1942):700.

Sheean, Vincent. "Spain: The Aftermath of Defeat," *New Republic,* 100 (September 6, 1939):125–27.

Smith, F. G., Jr. "Spaniards in Exile," *Nation,* 148 (May 13, 1939):556–58.

"Spaniards in Exile," *Current History,* 50 (July 1939):49.

"Spanish Refugees in France," *Commonweal,* 31 (March 15, 1940):443.

Stevens, John. "The Driven People," *New Republic,* 98 (March 15, 1939): 158–59.

"Un Catalan en la Resistencia francesa," *Destino,* July 20, 1974, p. 20.

"The Spanish Refugees," *New Republic,* 99 (June 21, 1939):173–74.

"Victims of Vichy," *The Nation,* 152 (January 11, 1941):32–33.

DOCUMENTS AND REPORTS

Actas de la Diputación Permanenta del Congreso de los Diputados de la República Española, 1945.

Camps Arboix, Joaquín. *Memorandum,* to Raoul Didkowski, prefect of the department of Pyrénées-Orientales.

Congreso de los Diputados. *Extracto oficial de la sesión extraordinaria cele-brada en la ciudad de México, el 17 de agosto de 1945.*
Epistolario Prieto y Negrín, puntos de vista sobre el desarollo y consequencias de la Guerra Civil Española. Paris, 1939.
"Liste des espagnols qui sont passeé au Stalag XI B avant d'aller à Mauthausen." Paris: Amicale Nationale des deportés et familles de disparus de Mauthausen, unpublished.
Peloquin, Général. *Note lue le 23 février 1939 au groupe parlementaire d'amitié franco-espagnole.* Paris, 1939.
Report of the Socialist Parliamentary Delegation on Conditions in the Spanish Refugee Camps. Paris, February 15, 1939.
Rodes, José. *Report on Spanish Refugees.* March 1963.

GENERAL BACKGROUND

Borras, José. *Políticas de los Exilados Españoles 1944–1950.* Paris: Ruedo Ibérico, 1976.
Brenan, Gerald. *The Spanish Labyrinth.* Cambridge: Cambridge University Press, 1967.
Broué, Pierre, and Emile Témime. *The Revolution and the Civil War in Spain.* Translated by Tony White. London: Faber and Faber, 1972.
Cattell, David T. *Soviet Diplomacy and the Spanish Civil War.* Berkeley: University of California Press, 1957.
Fernsworth, Lawrence. *Spain's Struggle for Freedom.* Boston: Beacon Press, 1957.
Fischer, Louis. *Men and Politics: Europe Between the Two World Wars.* 1941. Reprint. New York: Greenwood, 1966.
Foltz, Charles, Jr. *The Masquerade in Spain.* Boston: Houghton Mifflin, 1948.
Gallo, Max. *Histoire de l'Espagne Franquiste* Vol. 2. Paris, 1975.
Gann, Lewis H. *Guerrillas in History.* Stanford: Hoover Institute Press, 1971.
Girard, A., and J. Stoetzel. *Français et Emigrés.* Paris, 1953.
Herr, Richard A. *An Historical Essay on Modern Spain.* Berkeley: University of California Press, 1974.
Jackson, Gabriel. *The Spanish Republic and the Civil War, 1931–1939.* Princeton: Princeton University Press, 1971.
Madariaga, Salvador de. *Spain: A Modern History.* New York: Frederick A. Praeger, 1958.
Pertinax. *The Gravediggers of France.* New York: Fertig, 1942.
Thomas, Hugh. *The Spanish Civil War.* Revised edition. New York: Harper & Row, 1977.

MEMOIRS, ACCOUNTS, PAMPHLETS, AND LITERATURE

Alvarez, Ramón. *Eleuterio Quintanilla, vida y obra del maestro.* Mexico City: Editores Mexicanos Unidos, 1973.
Amicale d'Eysses. *L'Insurrection d'Eysses, 19–23 fevrier 1944.* Paris: Editions Sociales, 1974.
Angel, Miguel. *Los guerrilleros españoles en Francia 1940–1945.* Havana, 1971.

Aron, Robert. *Histoire de l'épuration.* Paris, 1970.

————. *France Reborn: The History of the Liberation.* Translated by Humphrey Hare. New York: Scribner's, 1964.

Aub, Max. *Campo Francés.* Torino, 1965.

Au secours des republicains espagnols. Paris, 1939.

Aziz, Philippe. *Au Service de l'ennemi, la gestapo française en province 1940–1944.* Paris, 1972.

Barea, Arturo. *The Forging of a Rebel.* Translated by Ilsa Barea. New York: Reynal & Hitchcock, 1946.

Baudoin, Madeleine. *Histoire des groupes francs (M.U.R.) des Bouches-du-Rhone.* Paris, 1962.

Baudot, Marcel. *L'Opinion Publique sous l'occupation, l'example d'un département français, 1939–1945.* Paris: Presses Universitaires de France, 1960.

Bazal, Luís. *Ay de los vencidos! Testimonio de la guerra de España, 1936–1939.* Toulouse, 1966.

Berruezo, José. *Contribución a la historia de la C.N.T. de España en el exilio.* Mexico City: Editores Mexicanos Unidos, 1967.

Bertaux, Pierre. *Libération de Toulouse et de sa Région.* Paris: Hachette, 1973.

Blond, Georges. *La Légion Etrangère.* Paris: Stock, 1964.

Blum, Léon. *L'Oeuvre.* Vol. 4, part 1. Paris, 1964.

Brasillach, Robert. *Histoire de la guerre d'Espagne.* Paris, 1939.

Casals, Pablo. *Joys and Sorrows.* As told to Albert E. Kahn. New York: Simon & Schuster, 1970.

————. *The Memoirs of Pablo Casals.* As told to Thomas Dozier. New York, 1959.

Centrale Sanitaire Catholique, Section Belge. *La vérité sur les camps de concentration en France.* Brussels, probably April 1939.

Chombard, Claude. *The Maquis: A History of the French Resistance Movement.* New York: Bobbs-Merrill, 1976.

Comité de solidarité internationale. *Lettre datée du 30 mai 1939 denonçant les traitements infligés aux espagnols réfugiés en France.* Paris, May 30, 1939.

Comité français de coordination pour l'aide aux populations civiles de l'Espagne républicaine. *Asile et travail aux réfugiés espagnols; pour la liquidation des camps de concentration: résolutions de la conférence française d'aide aux réfugiés espagnols.* Paris, June 11, 1939.

Comité international de coordination et d'information pour l'aide à l'Espagne Républicaine. *Temoignages sur Collioure.* Paris, n.d.

Constante, Mariano. *Les Années rouges, de Guernica à Mauthausen.* Vienne: Mercure de France, 1971.

Cookridge, E. H. *Set Europe Ablaze.* New York: Crowell, 1967.

Corredor, J. M. *Conversations with Pablo Casals.* Paris, 1955.

Dansette, Adrien. *Histoire de la Libèration de Paris.* London: Hutchinson, 1956.

De Gaulle, Charles. *The Complete War Memoirs of Charles de Gaulle.* New York: Simon and Schuster, 1972.

Dreifort, John E. *Yvon Delbos at the Quai d'Orsay.* Lawrence, Kansas: University of Kansas Press, 1973.

Dreyfus, Paul. *Histoire de la Résistance en Vercors.* Paris: Arthaud, 1975.

Dronne, Capt. Raymond. *La Libération de Paris.* Paris: Editions Presses de la Cité, 1970.

———. *La Serment de Kouffra.* Paris: Editions du Temps, 1965.

Ennesch, Carmen. *Emigration politiques, d'hier et d'aujourd'hui.* Paris, 1946.

Fagen, Patricia W. *Exiles and Citizens: Spanish Republicans in Mexico.* Austin: University of Texas Press, 1973.

Fernández, Alberto E. *La España de los Maquis.* Mexico City: Ediciones Era, 1971.

Flanner, Janet [Genêt]. *Paris Was Yesterday, 1925–1939.* Edited by Irving Drutman. New York: Viking, 1972.

Garcia (first name unknown). Unpublished memoir of French concentration camps.

Gordon, Ordas Félix. *Mi politica fuera de España.* Mexico City, 1967.

Gouffault, Roger, ed. *Ebensée Kommando de Mauthausen.* Paris: Amicale des déportés et familles de disparus de Mauthausen, n.d.

Granet, Marie. *Le Journal "Defense de la France."* Paris: Presses Universitaires de France, 1961.

———. *Ceux de la Résistance, 1940–1944.* Paris, 1964.

Gros, Jose. *Abriendo camino: Relatos de un guerrillero communista español.* Bucharest: Colleccion Ebro, 1972.

Guiral, Pierre. *Libèration de Marseille.* Paris, 1974.

Hermet, Guy. *Les Espagnoles en France.* Paris: Les Editions ouvrières, 1967.

Hobsbawn, Eric. *Bandits.* New York: Dell, 1971.

Institut Maurice Thorez. *Le Parti Communiste français dans la Résistance.* Paris, 1967.

Izard, Pierre. *La Petite Histoire d'Argelès-sur-mer 1900–1940.* Perpignan: Editions Massana, 1974.

Koestler, Arthur. *Scum of the Earth.* New York: Macmillan, 1968.

Lafitte, Jean. *Ceux qui vivent.* Paris, 1958.

Lévy, Claude. *Les Parias de la Résistance.* Paris, 1970.

Liberovici, Sergio, and Michel L. Staniero. *Cantos de la Nueva Resistencia: Española, 1939–1961.* Montevideo, 1963.

Marra-López, José R. *Narrativa Española fuera de España, 1939–1961.* Madrid: Ediciones Guadarrama, 1963.

Matthews, Herbert L. *A World in Revolution: A Newspaperman's Memoir.* New York: Scribner's, 1971.

Mera, Cipriano. *Guerra, exilio y carcel de un anarco-syndicalista.* Paris, 1976.

Michel, Henri. *Les Mouvements clandestines en Europe.* Paris, 1961.

———. *Les Courants de pensée de la Résistance.* Paris, 1962.

———. *La Guerre de l'ombre, la Résistance en Europe.* Paris, 1970.

Michel, Henri, and Olga Wormser. *Tragédie de la déportation.* Paris, 1970.

Mistral, Silvia. *Exodo: Diario de una refugiada española.* Mexico City: Ediciones Minerva, 1940.

Mitrani, Therèse. *Service d'evasion.* Paris, 1946.

Molina, Juan M. *El movimiento clandestino en España 1939–1949.* Mexico City: Editores Mexicanos Unidos, 1976.

Montseny, Federica. *Pasión y muerte de los españoles refugiados en Francia.* Toulouse: Editions "Espoir," 1969.

Mora, Constancia de la. *In Place of Splendor: The Autobiography of a Spanish Woman.* New York: Harcourt, Brace, 1939.

Olibo, Jean. *Parcours* Perpignan: Editions du Castillet, 1972.

————. *Simples histoires.* Perpignan, 1974.

Orwell, George. *Homage to Catalonia.* New York: Harcourt, Brace & World, 1952.

Palencia, Isabel de. *Smouldering Freedom: The Story of the Spanish Republicans in Exile.* London: Victor Gollancz, 1945.

Paxton, Robert O. *Vichy France: Old Guard and New Order, 1940–1944.* New York: Alfred A. Knopf, 1972.

Payne, Robert, ed. *The Civil War in Spain, 1936–1939.* New York: Capricorn, 1970.

PCF et L'Internationale Communiste. *Face: au pacte Germano-Sovietique et à la drôle de guerre.* Paris, 1974.

Pena, Juan de la. *Arena y Viento.* Barcelona, 1973.

Pétain, Maréchal Philippe. *La France nouvelle: principes de la communauté, et appels et messages 17 mai 1940—17 juin 1941.* Paris: Fasquelle, 1941.

Pietri, François. *La vie de la France sous l'occupation, 1940–1944.* Paris: Plon, 1957.

Pike, David Wingeate. *Vae Victis: Los repúblicanos españoles refugiados en Francia, 1939–1944.* Paris, 1969.

Plenn, Abel. *Wind in the Olive Trees: Spain From the Inside.* New York: Boni & Gaer, 1946.

Pons Prades, Eduardo. *Repúblicanos españoles en la Segunda Guerra Mundial.* Barcelona: Editorial Planeta, 1975.

Puccini, Dario. *Romancero de la resistencia española.* Translated from the Italian by Juan Goytisolo. Mexico City, 1967.

Razola, Manuel, and Mariano Constante, *Triangle Bleu: les républicains espagnols à Mauthausen 1940–1945.* Paris: Gallimard, 1969.

Regler, Gustave. *The Owl of Minerva.* London, 1959.

Roig, Montserrat. *Els Catalans als Camps Nazi.* Barcelona: Edicions 62, 1977.

Rossellon. Argelès-sur-mer, August 31, 1939. Hand-copied periodical of poems, essays, and drawings by Spanish refugee artists living at the Chateau Valmy.

Rubio, Javier. *La emigración española a Francia.* Barcelona: Editorial Ariel, 1974.

St. Martin, Hardie, ed. *Roots and Wings: Poetry From Spain, 1900–1975.* New York: Harper & Row, 1976.

Sierra, Jacques. "La fin de la guerre civile espagnole vue par la presse Toulousaine." Master's thesis. University of Toulouse, 1970.

Simpson, John Hope. *Refugees: A Review of the Situation Since September 1938*. London: Royal Institute of International Affairs, 1939.

Smith, Lois Elwyn. *Mexico and the Spanish Republicans*. Berkeley: University of California Press, 1955.

Sorel, Andrés. *Guerrilla española del siglo XX*. Paris: Collección Ebro, 1970.

Téllez, Antonio. *La guerrilla urbana en España: Sabaté*. Paris: Belibaste, 1972.

———. *La guerrilla urbana en España: Facerías*. Paris: Ruedo Ibérico, 1974.

Tillon, Charles. *Les FTP: la guerrilla en France*. Paris: Editions Julliard, 1962.

Torris, M. J. *Narvik*. Paris: Arthème Fayard, 1946.

Valera, Fernando. *La République Espagnole dans le cadre de la politique internationale*. Mexico City, 1961.

Valle, José Maria del. *Las instituciones de la República Española en exilio*. Paris: Ruedo Ibérico, 1976.

Valley, Emile, and Robert Simon. *Guide de l'ancien camp-de-concentration de Mauthausen*. Paris, n.d.

Vallina, Pedro. *Mis memorias*. Vol. 2. Mexico City: Ediciones Tierra y Libertad, 1971.

Vayo, Julio Alvarez del. *Give Me Combat*. Translated by Donald D. Walsh. Boston: Little, Brown, 1973.

———. *Freedom's Battle*. Translated by Eileen Brooke. Boston: Houghton-Mifflin, 1940.

Vernant, Jacques. *The Refugee in the Post-War World*. London: George Allen & Unwin, 1953.

Vilanova, Antonio. *Los olvidados: Los exilados españoles en la Segunda Guerra Mundial*. Paris, 1969.

Villaceque, F. *Le Département des Pyrénées-Orientales*. St. Germain-en-Laye: Editions M.D.I., 1970.

Wilt, Alan F. *The Atlantic Wall, Hitler's Defenses in the West, 1941–1944*. Ames, Iowa: Iowa State University Press, 1975.

Zugazagoitia, Julian. *Guerra y vicisitudes de los españoles*, vol. 2. Paris: Libreria Española, 1968. First published in Buenos Aires under the title of *Historia de la guerra de España*, 1940.

INDEX